Red was the Blood of Our Forefathers

Episodes from Crow Indian Intertribal Warfare

Red was the Blood of Our Forefathers

Episodes from Crow Indian Intertribal Warfare

Brian L. Keefe

Caxton Press
Caldwell, Idaho
2010

ISBN 978-0-87004-472-4

Library of Congress Cataloging-in-Publication Data

Keefe, Brian.
Red was the blood of our forefathers : episodes from Crow Indian Intertribal warfare / compiled by Brian L. Keefe.
p. cm.
Includes bibliographical references and index.
ISBN 978-0-87004-472-4 (pbk.)
1. Crow Indians--History--Anecdotes. 2. Crow Indians--Wars--Anecdotes. 3. Crow Indians--Social conditions--Anecdotes. I. Title.

E99.C92K44 2010
978.6004'975272--dc22

2009028066

Cover

by Jim D. Nelson.
www.jdnelsonportraits.com

Lithographed and bound in the United States of America

CAXTON PRESS
Caldwell, Idaho
178228

DEDICATION

To my children David and Juliet, Joe Medicine Crow, Winona Plenty Hoops and the Alex Birdinground family, this book is lovingly dedicated.

Table of Contents

ILLUSTRATIONS

FOREWORD

by Joe Medicine Crow.

In August 1992, The "Crow Fair" and celebration was on. There was a huge camp with about 1,000 tepees, tents and trailers everywhere, about 50,000 Indians moving around in parades, dances and activities of all kinds. Drumming and singing went on all day and night.

Going on a foot trail through a dense patch of brush, I discovered an Englishman who had lost his way in the dark and could not distinguish the particular tepee he was staying in from the hundreds of others in that vast camp. He called out to me in an unmistakable London "Cockney" accent, asking if I could give him directions and I replied, "Ho Ho Ho, I smell the blood of an Englishman." He introduced himself as Brian Keefe and after a brief talk together, I asked if he would like to stay with me in our family camp.

After the celebrations were over, I invited him to my ranch at Lodge Grass, and that was the start of a long friendship and of sharing our mutual interest in Crow history. In fact, he had already composed accounts of many Crow battles against the Sioux and Cheyenne and I was amazed that he knew so much, along with the exact details of the more important battles often only related in Crow oral histories. I asked him how he had become so interested in Indians in the first place and he replied that his grandfather had seen the Buffalo Bill Wild West Show when young and had enthralled him with his animated recollections of the performing Indians in that show.

As we started sharing our work, I realized that Brian was very knowledgeable and talented. I started reading his manuscripts and was not only impressed, but amazed how he could write so well. He puts you right in the thick of battle with arrows and bullets whizzing by, war-whoops blaring and horses hooves pounding, along with other battle sounds. But also, he is one who leaves no holds barred, when describing the less pleasant facets of the old-time Indian culture, such as the torture and mutilation of victims and even of themselves during periods of personal grief and despair.

Brian Keefe himself is an attraction, always smiling and conversing in his Cockney accent. People are quickly attracted to him and soon like and enjoy his company. I and other members of my extended family have since adopted him both as grandson and brother and have given him the Indian name, "Spotted Tail Eagle."

Another Englishman named Colin Taylor was also a great writer on the Plains Indian. Unfortunately, though, he died too soon. Now Brian Keefe has arrived, a promising good teller of Indian stories and their history. He is capable and ready to step into Colin Taylor's boots and carry on.

In bringing this introduction to a close, I highly recommend this book and others to follow, which injects life and defines Plains Indian warfare as a dangerous but sporting way, by which young boys and men became good warriors and wise chiefs.

Ah-ho, Ah-ho! Let us now ride into Indian country with Brian Spotted-Tail-Eagle and relive those "Buffalo days" of old.

Joseph Medicine Crow. Ph.D. Lodge Grass, Montana. 2006.

Introduction and Acknowledgments

Sometime around the middle years of the eighteenth century, four widely scattered, Hidatsa-speaking bands came together to create a singular nation by the collective name "Absaroka," meaning, "Children of the Large-Beaked Bird." To other peoples both friendly and hostile they were sometimes known as "Raven men," but more commonly, as "Crows."[1]

Many years earlier while roaming as separate related bands, these peoples had occupied various seats at various times east of the Mississippi River. During the course of their wanderings, they moved slowly west; first into central Minnesota and thence northwest, into the Devil's Lake area of northeast North Dakota. From here one group moved southwest to the Knife River district of the Upper Missouri, and then farther west into what is now the eastern part of Montana. At the same time, another group traveled northwest from the Devil's Lake region and into the southern parts of the Canadian provinces, known today as Saskatchewan and Alberta.[2]

In those days the people were entirely pedestrian and transported their tepees and belongings on the backs of their women and dogs. Generally, they hugged the tree-lined rivers and streams during the course of their meandering and only when horses came among them in quantity, enabling the people to follow the buffalo herds across the vast open Plains, did these same bands become the roving, equestrian hunters as was their condition in more recent historic times.

Crow Country embraced the entire southern half of the state of Montana and the northern half of Wyoming, extending to the Little Missouri River on the east and the headwaters of the Yellowstone on the west. A vast expanse of territory composed of prairie, forest, rivers and mountains, including the high snow-capped peaks of the Bear Tooths; the Crazy Mountain Range; the Big Horns; Wind River Mountains; the Pryors; Absarokas and Grand Tetons.

These lands, rich in game both large and small had long been desired by the Crows, who believed such country had been set aside for them specifically by the Great Spirit *Akbaa-tadia*.[3]

So it came to pass that the Crow people laid claim to the long sought after Big Horn and Yellowstone regions which, henceforth, they regarded as their own. At the base of the highest peak of the Big Horns; known as Cloud Peak to the white man, but what is called by the Crow people, "Extended Mountain," and regarded as the centre of their universe, they planted a number of "Sacred Tobacco Seeds," thereby, establishing the right of the Absaroka to inhabit that country. But they also were obliged to defend it against numerous tribes who coveted those fine hunting grounds. Indeed, *Akbaa-tadia`s* servant Old Man Coyote—say the Crows—once told the Absaroka that by their constant fighting, the people would prove themselves worthy and they alone be regarded as *Awa-kulay*, the "Keepers of the land."

The newly-formed Crow nation then comprised two main divisions, known as the River Crows and Mountain Crows.

The River Band, roaming at will between the Yellowstone and Musselshell rivers of central Montana, at no time exceeded 350 lodges, while their Mountain brethren, claiming the more southern country between the Big Horns and Wind River Mountains below the Yellowstone, could always boast the greater population, comprising at their height of power, circa 1820, about 650 lodges. For this reason the Mountain Crows were sometimes referred to as "The Many Lodge Band." [4]

Like their Hidatsa kinfolk, both Crow divisions adhered to a rigid clan system (i.e. all members of a particular group claiming ancestry from a common forebear), which among the Crows was matrilineal in structure. Perhaps, during the early years of their autonomous bands confederating to create a nation, there had only been eight such clans grouped in pairs, which would have constituted the four original Crow groups mentioned in tribal oral tradition and noted in the Lewis and Clark material. [5] By circa, 1830 at the latest, these clans had expanded to twelve also grouped together in pairs:

[1] Newly-Made-Lodges.
[2] Big-Lodges.

[3] Piegans.
[4] Treacherous-Lodges.

[5] Greasy-Mouths.
[6] Sore [Burned] Lips.

[7] Ties-The-Bundle.
[8] Those-Who-Bring-Home-The-Game.

[9] Streaked-Lodges
[10] Dried-Out-Furs.

[11] Whistling-Waters.
[12] Poor-War-Deeds.[6]

It would appear that a later separatist group from the Hidatsa led by a chief named Bear-With-a-Bad-Heart-Always, constituted an additional clan to raise the total from twelve to thirteen some short time after an outbreak of smallpox between 1780-'82. This being the same group referred to in Hidatsa tradition which is said to have left the parent tribe on the Missouri around that date to take up a nomadic, buffalo-hunting, equestrian existence as a component part of the Absaroka nation. For a number of years following their severance from the Hidatsa, this band retained their Hidatsa identity and only joined the Crows as an integral part of that nation after a significant period had elapsed. Eventually, they were absorbed among one or another Crow clan leaving little trace of their origin. [7]

Each of these paired clans generally roamed separate hunting grounds, remaining apart from other paired groups throughout most of the year. Occasionally, there were brief periods of hostility between one pair of clans and another. When not at loggerheads, all the clans united to form a collective body at least once a year, usually during midsummer, in order to hold religious ceremonies together such as the Sun Dance and the annual Planting of the Sacred Tobacco Seeds. At other times these paired clans or, more properly at this period, "bands," would unite if defensive or offensive action was required to combat mutual foes.

Around 1800 a sizable faction, for the most part composed of Whistling Water clan members, separated from the Mountain Crow and formed a division of its own. Hereafter, this separatist group became known as the Kicked-in-the-Belly band, owing to an unfortunate episode in the past when a Whistling Water clan chief had suffered injury from a horse.[8] As an independent band they originally claimed the southeast portion of Crow territory, between the Little Missouri River on the east and the foothills of the Big Horn Mountains on the west.

Their split from the Mountain Crow was not due to any serious animosity between the two—albeit at a later date the main Whistling Water component was indeed hostile towards one or another Crow clan. The split came because the Kicked-in-the-Bellys preferred a degree of independence, although during the summer months, they often joined with their Mountain Crow cousins to form a united body. In the fall they seperated again to take up residence in their preferred location of winter retreat, usually east of the Big Horns in the lower Powder region.

Throughout most of their subsequent history, the Kicked-in-the-Belly population rarely exceeded 150 lodges and often far less, as band members were constantly moving back and forth between their own breakaway group and those of the Mountain and River Crow. [9] As a rule this separatist group continued to support their nation's ongoing feuds with surrounding tribes. But owing to the Kicked-in-the-Belly`s more eastern location, they were more likely to be engaged in conflicts with the Sioux and Cheyenne. As a result, they probably received more attention from enemy raiders than did their River and Mountain Crow confederates. Certainly, the Kicked-in-the-Belly band was better known to the Sioux and Cheyenne than were others of the Absaroka nation and at a later date, during the mid 1860s, they could be found farther west, then preferring the country about the headwaters of Arrow (now Pryor) Creek, which was thought to be sufficiently distant to afford respite from repeated incursions by Sioux and Cheyenne enemies.

Despite unwelcome attention from the host of hostile groups around them, the Crows as a nation did not adopt a merely defensive stance. They sent out their own war parties against all tribes they regarded as enemies and, as a consequence, the Crow population was apt to suffer accordingly by incurring a greater number of casualties in war, when compared to most other tribes with whom they were in contact.

Prior to the coming of horses onto the Northern Plains, warfare between the various buffalo-hunting tribes seldom resulted in decisive conclusions. Often, when enemy forces met, both sides formed up in opposing lines, each warrior squatting behind a large bull-hide shield which covered most of the body. The respective champions would battle it out in a series of single combats in the no-man's land between the two groups. There might be an occasional exchange of arrow volleys, along with one or two half-hearted charges which were not really intended to make contact. Then, as the light began to fade, the opposing forces would slowly retire from the field and that would be an end to the affair.

At other times, small parties of warriors might trek hundreds of miles on foot in order to reach an enemy camp. They would loiter in hiding until some unsuspecting occupant wandered within their reach. The victim would be killed and scalped if an adult male or carried into captivity if woman or child. Only rarely was an entire village assaulted—and then in a dawn raid while the camp occupants were deep in slumber. The extermination of the foe was not the prime objective, neither was such an idea contemplated.

It was, however, the acquisition of horses in ever increasing number, along with the appearance of guns and metal weapons in Indian hands, which served to accelerate a rise in intertribal warfare. That which previously had been a culture of intermittent feuding became endemic, resulting in a constant cycle of revenge and counter-revenge, deemed necessary to appease the spirits of the dead on one hand and to boost the flagging morale of those who had been dispossessed on the other.

The horse was the one possession that gave the Plains Indian the ability to coexist and compete with his neighbor on an equal footing. And the Red Man, it seemed, could never get enough such animals to satisfy his want.

Whether on the move from one camping site to another; on the hunt or at war, without the horse the Indian could not survive as a nomad on the open plains. A man's wealth was assessed by the number of horses he owned. With horses he bought a wife and hauled his heavy buffalo-hide tepee covers and domestic belongings over the prairie on pole drags, transporting himself and his family as they traversed the grasslands in pursuit of the herds. To increase one's wealth, the raiding of another tribe's stock became the regular past-time for almost every adult male. But if caught by the indignant owners the thieves were invariably killed, which in turn, would necessitate a retaliation raid in order to avenge the loss of fellow tribesmen. At such times, the prize was the scalps of their quarry and the capture of women and children to be adopted as tribal members in order to compensate losses suffered in previous engagements.

Such activity became the means by which any lowly warrior could achieve prestige as the heroic defender of his tribe and, not least, as the fearless nemesis of his people's enemies.

Overnight, war became the main focal point in the social structure and ideology to which the Red Man subscribed. For the wild, unconstrained nomad of the plains, performing upon the field of conflict became the very breath of his nostrils. Warfare was his reason for living; his livelihood and the continuous, unbroken reality of his existence. By harboring such a concept it allowed his tribe to survive in an overpopulated, over-hunted and naturally aggressive environment, while social standing and renown was more easily obtained through one's heroic deeds achieved in battle or on the horse stealing trail.

Indeed, the pursuit of intertribal warfare became an inseparable dimension to that of the Plains Indian's day-to-day existence. One hostile act merely being reciprocated by another, inevitably creating a never-ending cycle of aggression between the tribes and to such degree, that even the original episode which had initiated a feud in the first place was, in most cases, entirely lost to memory. Tribe continued to fight against tribe for successive generations, simply because they supposed they had always done so in the past.

In later years, not even the Old Ones could remember their people's lifestyle as having been any other way. An entire system had since evolved by which a tribal member's war-deeds could be numbered and recognized, thereby, causing one to rise to great heights within the tribe with its attendant authority and respect from one's mentors and peers.

The Crows were no exception. Among the Absaroka, if a man accomplished four specific war deeds, he could rise to the position of chief among his people and was, thereafter, allowed to join the seventeen-member council which as a body, discussed and decided all important issues concerning the united tribe. These four specific war deeds were:

1. Striking a first coup, i.e. being the first to touch an enemy with either the hand or a slender willow-wand commonly known as a "coup-stick."
2. Taking a gun or other weapon from the hands of an enemy.
3. Stealing a tethered horse from the camp of the enemy (usually requiring the thief to cut the halter rope fixed to a picket pin at one end and to the wrist of its sleeping owner at the other).
4. Leading a successful foray against the enemy without losing any party members.[10]

In their military organization the Crows, like most other Plains tribes, had a sophisticated system of warrior societies or clubs, each of which had its own fraternity regalia, dances, ceremonies and taboos. Throughout the first half of the nineteenth century, there existed among the Crows nine such societies:

Stone Hammers.
Ravens.
Foxes (Kit Foxes).
Lump Woods (Knob Sticks).
Half -Shaved Heads.
Little Dogs.
Big Dogs.
Muddy Hands.
Bulls.[11]

These clubs were not age-graded in their make-up as were their counterparts among the Hidatsa and Mandan, although the Stone Hammers were composed mainly of youths between fifteen and twenty years of age, while the Bulls, for the most part, consisted of veteran warriors of forty-five years and over. Membership was usually by invitation, although few were turned away from their society of choice. Each spring one society would be selected by the chief's council to act as camp police throughout that season and ensuing summer, their duties including the control of communal buffalo hunts; arbitrating in both personal and band or clan disputes and generally keeping order within the tribe. The main purpose of these clubs, moreover, was to protect the women, children and old-folk and to defend the camp against its enemies. Many (although not all males of fighting age) belonged to one society or another and members of a particular fraternity considered themselves brothers, no matter what band or clan they were affiliated to.

There was intense rivalry between the different societies as they competed to achieve renown and prestige and so, for a period in time, one society might be predominant while another fell into decline. At a later date, when a decline in members or renown had become profound, certain clubs disbanded altogether, their few remaining members joining another society. Such was the case of the Half-Shaved Heads, which about the year 1835 became obsolete, as also did the Muddy Hands and the Bulls some thirty-five years later. The surviving members of these defunct societies joined the Lump Woods in their stead, while the number of effective warrior societies, overall, was reduced to three, namely, the Foxes, Lump woods and Dogs.[12]

The individual Crow warrior always endeavored to present himself somewhat as a dandy among his peers. His appearance, when wishing to create effect during ceremonial occasions or on the battlefield, was often far superior in the quantity of beads, feathers, paint, ermine tails and artificial hair which he attached about his person. Prominent overall, was the raised clay-adorned forelock above the forehead and dantelanium hair-pipe side pieces in conjunction with a long, matted hair-queue attached to the crown of the head and extending down the back, sometimes reaching the ground by the addition of horse hair and pine-gum decorated with beads or the breast feathers of an eagle. Often the forehead itself was plastered with bright vermilion or red ochre and this, along with the singular hairstyle aforementioned, distinguished the Crow warrior from all others on the Plains.

More important, however, notwithstanding his appearance, ability or talent, each Crow warrior believed that without obtaining mystic power from some supernatural force, he could have no control over his personal destiny. As far as he was concerned, such would then contribute to much distress and bad luck through one's life and, ultimately, guarantee his untimely demise due to some unfavorable circumstance. This power was thought to emanate from the Great Spirit itself, though only made manifest through non-human forms and celestial bodies, including the Sun, Moon and stars, along with natural phenomena of nature, such as thunder and lighting etc. Each of these mystic manifestations were thought to constitute a part of the

Other World which, it was also believed, presented a parallel dimension to that which Mankind, in his more lowly state, was obliged by fate to exist in.

To obtain such power or, more commonly "medicine," it was imperative that the potential recipient actually enter into the realm of the Other World temporarily. This state could only be achieved by undergoing a period of prolonged fasting or some other form of self denial in addition to—in many cases—a more tangible sacrifice, such as self mutilation of the body in order to show sincerity and a serious commitment to one's endeavor. When a state of incognizance had been attained, one could communicate with the Other World in a vision or dream and obtain the benevolence of a particular "Spirit Being." The dreamer also could harness the specific attributes associated with the spirit. The recipient could thereafter not only depend when in time of need, but be blessed with the ability to emulate that being's specialties peculiar to itself. In many cases it gave the recipient the power to either cure sickness, heal wounds, predict forthcoming events, locate missing persons and belongings and bring forth the buffalo and other game when needed. Thus, when a Crow Indian proclaimed that his personal spirit helper was dictating his actions, there was no room for indifference among his peers, who believed in the potency of such medicine; which if ignored would be to the dire detriment of all involved.

Instances in the episodes which follow, where examples of one's personal medicine power loom large, should not be regarded by the reader as historically incorrect or superfluous to the overall text. For such was a very real and overtly important part of the Crow mentality, in relation to their own perspective of reality during the old-time buffalo days, and of their very existence, as compared to the non-Indian view of reality. Certainly, without a Spirit Guardian or Protector, a Crow brave—supposedly—could not achieve success in war and as a consequence, could never rise above that of lowly status within his community lacking due honor and respect. For war was a profound part of his day-to-day existence.

Of the early years of what may be termed The Horse Culture Period, beginning around the date A.D. 1730, the Crows were at war with the Shoshoni, Flathead and Kutenai on the west and with the Blackfoot and Assiniboin to the north. The Crows generally suffered in the contests with these people. As early as circa 1680, while still resident in the South Saskatchewan country northeast of the Yellowstone and Big Horn districts and east of Powder River, the Crows had known the Shoshoni, whose war-bands often appeared from the Southwest searching for isolated camps to raid. Certainly, by the second decade of the eighteenth century, when these Crow groups were wandering the western Buffalo Plains both north and south of the Missouri, they were in regular hostile contact with Shoshoni-speaking peoples, including the Comanche. It was from the Comanche, so tribal oral tradition relates, that the Crows obtained some of their first horses, occasionally through trade but mostly by theft.[13]

At that time the numerous and widely scattered Shoshoni-speaking peoples—the *Nacion du Serpent* or Snakes as the early French and English documents knew them—were mounted and were the terror of all Missouri River tribes, including the Sioux and Cheyenne, then inhabiting the Plains and prairies immediately east and west of that river. For having trading contacts with Pueblo Indian and Spanish settlements to the south, these nomadic Snake war bands, rich in horses and metal weapons, came riding out of the western haze wielding iron axes and fourteen-foot lances tipped with Spanish sword blades. Their bodies and horses were encased in a kind of overlapping leather armor reinforced with a mixture of sand and glue. This rendered both animal and rider virtually impervious to the stone-headed arrows of their enemies. Mercilessly they killed all the men folk they could find; destroyed their victim's lodges and crops and carried off the women and children to be sold in the Spanish slave markets, in exchange for more horses and iron weapons needed to pursue their aggression.

The Missouri River-dwelling Arickara, Mandan and Hidatsa, who were sedentary farmers, fell like grain before the sickle's edge under the pounding hooves of Shoshoni horses. The Crows, then roaming the open country between the mouth of Heart River on the east and the Yellowstone on the west, were fully engaged in defending themselves against Shoshoni marauders, the latter often being aided by Flathead and Kutenai allies. Thus, through necessity, the Crows evolved into a warrior people adhering to a strong military code and organization. No wonder that around the date 1770, the Crows had acquired a significant number of horses, in addition to iron-bladed weapons and a small number of flintlock guns. They supplemented their arsenals through contacts with Hidatsa relatives along the Missouri River. They retaliated in kind against their enemies and even later, when guns came among them in quantity, they beset their foes repeatedly without the least show of mercy.

Indeed, the Crows have a tradition that it was their tribe alone that finally drove the hated Snakes from the Big Horn and Yellowstone country and forced them to seek refuge west of the Rocky Mountains. This was after a great battle had been fought between the two tribes which lasted three days, during which the Crow chief, it is said, caused the sun to stand still, thereby enabling his people to win a great and decisive victory.[14]

Once entrenched in the rich hunting grounds vacated by the Snakes, between the Missouri on the north and the forks of the Platte River in the south, the Crows set up their tepees and claimed hegemony over all that land. It was from this time on that the Crows became a formidable and warlike nation. For the next 100 years they continued to hold their own against each and all the powerful enemies that came against them. Certainly, the Crows were regarded by their neighbors as a belligerent, unquestionably brave and resilient people. The Crows likened themselves to, "A pack of Mountain wolves grouped together in a solid mass—facing outwards—so none could attack before our warriors rushed out and drove the enemy away."[15]

Only by such attributes could the Crows prove themselves at least the equal of the many tribes which surrounded them. Only by such, could they continue to claim sovereignty over the land which, they believed, had been entrusted into their care. Thus, as a united people— the "Driftwood Lodges"[16] —they became strong and affluent by the standards of their day..

Once entrenched firmly in lands promised long ago to their ancestors, the Crows were beset by numerous tribes from both far and near, some of whom, such as the Shoshoni, Kutenai and Flatheads, continued to resist Crow occupation of the country. Other tribes, including the Assiniboin, Gros Ventre and the several Blackfoot-speaking tribes of Blood, Piegan and Siksika to the north, along with Cheyennes to the east, constantly endeavored to increase their pony herds from Crow stock. They also coveted the great tracts of rich hunting grounds, teeming with buffalo, antelope and other game, which comprised a significant part of the Crow Country.

Crow tribal political structures and Indian populations in general, were damaged by a severe smallpox outbreak between the years 1780-'82. The epidemic created in its wake a great upheaval among all peoples residing along the Missouri and roaming the buffalo Plains and prairies. Tribe pushed upon tribe as each took advantage of a weakened neighbor.

Before 1782, the Sioux had been in small number west of the Missouri, prevented from establishing a significant foothold, by the Arickara and Mandan who blocked progress across that river They also were opposed by numerous Plains Apache and Shoshoni-speaking bands—aggressive and fully mounted—who had made travelling the Western Plains a precarious undertaking for any foreign people.

By 1782, however, the country east of the Mississippi had been over-hunted somewhat, so that buffalo and other game became scarce. This increased the pressure between white settlers and displaced East Woodland tribes, particularly between the Dakota Sioux and Chippewa, as they competed against each other for the small amount of game available. This added to the ever-growing incentive for certain tribes to move west across the Missouri. The recent acquisition of horses had given the Sioux, among others, a once undreamed of mobility, whereby, they could follow the herds at their leisure and escape the threat of starvation which, previously, had often encumbered their people during the winter months when buffalo migrated to distant regions.

It was the epidemic of 1780-'82 that dramatically changed the situation. In its aftermath, the Arickara and Mandan with their greatly diminished populations could no longer hold back the tide of migrants from the east, while the Shoshoni and Plains Apache, having also lost heavily in the contagion, retreated to the northwest and southwest respectively and virtually disappeared from the Northern and Central Plains. As a result, the Sioux then swarmed across the Missouri and gradually pushed their way far into the western country.

A large Sioux war-party had gone west as far as the Big Horn Mountains as early as 1726.[17] In 1771, many Crow warriors had been killed by the Yankton.[18] But the Sioux and Crow seldom came into contact owing to the intervening distance between their peoples. But now all at once, it seemed, the Sioux were everywhere; raiding Crow horse herds at will and clashing with parties of Crow buffalo hunters on a regular basis. Indeed, prior to 1800, there is little mention of hostilities with Crows in the numerous Sioux winter-counts. Yet from that date on, these same counts are filled with references to such conflicts and it is evident that an acceleration of intertribal warfare on the Crow front had become a most serious affair for all concerned. [19]

While it is true that peaceful overtures were often made between the warring tribes, prior to the middle years of the nineteenth century, few intertribal pacts actually lasted for any protracted period. Such pacts as were sporadically affected between the Crows and their neighbors were always of a comparatively short duration and existing in a state of chronic warfare was the norm, rather than the exception.

The Crow people were obliged to fight hard and consistently against numerous powerful enemies in order to keep the land which yet they hold—and still can call their own.

Crow traditional history is replete with deeds of the famous warriors and chiefs of their nation and of intertribal warfare. Such stories have been handed down orally through many generations. All persons of Crow blood were once well-versed in the history of their people. In a time now past, when buffalo and deer supplied most all the material needs of those roaming at will across the Northern High Plains, old medicine men and favorite storytellers would recite to avid listeners the legends and heroic deeds of their forebears. And so was instilled into the hearts and minds of the Absaroka a strong sense of national pride, in addition to an acute understanding of their heritage, with a desire to emulate great warriors and other personages who had gone before to the spirit world.

It is a selection of these stories pertaining to what might be termed, The Heroic Age of the Absaroka Nation which are here presented. They have been collected from both oral and archival sources over the course of several summer visits to the Crow reservation in south-eastern Montana. I have spent much time in the company of my good friend Joe Medicine Crow, tribal historian and last of the true chiefs among the Crow tribe, who has personally earned the four specific war deeds entitling him to that position.[20] As a young boy, Joe was told the stories relating to the origin and migrations of his ancestors and of their coming into the Yellowstone and Big Horn country along with stirring episodes of intertribal warfare.

Author's Photo

Joe Medicine Crow and Brian Keefe at Crow Fair, August 1992.

I first met Joe in 1992 when he was seventy-nine years old. We struck up a close friendship which endures to the present day.

Many times, Joe has taken me to remote sites where important battles occurred between the Crows and their tribal enemies. Joe personally told me the stories connected with these sites—stories he heard as they were handed down over the years in the oral history of his people. Joe still can recall the many times, when as a youth, he sat in the company of veteran warriors of the old buffalo days, including his illustrious paternal and maternal grandfathers White Man Runs Him and Medicine Crow 1st, both of whom had been accomplished warriors in their younger days and had personally known "Son of Morning Star," Lt. Colonel George A. Custer. Joe listened attentively as such renowned personages and others, discussed and repeated their accounts of old-time battles, in some of which many of the narrators themselves had been active participants.

Not least among the old-time storytellers of Joe's acquaintance was Plain Feather (b. 1866, d. - 1966).[21] This man had been well-tutored in Crow history by his uncle and mentor Hunts To Die (born 1839),[22] in whose buffalo-hide lodge Plain Feather had lived through his boyhood

Northwestern University Library. by E. S. Curtis

Joe Medicine Crow Collection.

Left, White Man Runs Him, grandfather of Joe Medicine Crow. Right, Plain Feather, informant to Joe Medicine Crow.

and early manhood years. Hunts To Die had been engaged in many fights and in later years, after being invalided from the warpath due to a battle wound, was recognized among the Crows as their tribal historian. As such he was a prime source of information to his young protégé Plain Feather, who in turn, was a good source of information to Joe Medicine Crow.

Alas, many of these stories now exist only in Joe's memory and it is for this reason, that they should be recorded for posterity in the written word.

Included among several other tribal informants of my acquaintance is Winona Plenty Hoops. A grand Crow matriarch four years younger than Joe and one also, who I am honored to regard as a dear friend. Winona is a treasure chest of information. Not only has she graciously allowed me several long interviews over the years, but personally helped perform the requisite ceremony which bestowed upon me the Indian name Spotted Tail Eagle. Among the important information supplied by Winona, she it was who imparted relevant data concerning the woman Among the Willows, who figures prominently throughout one of the stories herein.

Particular thanks are accorded to the late Glen Birdinground of Crow Agency, Montana, a man of exceptional character, integrity and will.

His confinement to a wheelchair in no way prevented his participation in the traditional Crow ceremonies or, of fulfilling to the utmost of his ability his role as tribal judge and, at times, as an independent arbitrator and mediator in settling internal and domestic disputes within the tribe. His memory is held in high esteem by both Indian and White alike and his passing much lamented by all.

Author's photo

Winona Plenty Hoops

Others, who have kindly assisted me when gathering data for the present volume, include:

Alex Bird in Ground. (Crow).
Barney Old Coyote. (Crow).
Bill Tall Bull. (Northern Cheyenne).
James King (Northern Cheyenne).
Wayne Medicine Elk (Southern Cheyenne).
He Owns Her White Horses. (Miniconjou Sioux).
Tom Bull Head. (Hunkpapa Sioux. Fort Yates).
Ron Gaggles. (South Piegan Blackfoot).
Tom Bernardis. (Little Big Horn College. Montana).
Tim McCleary. (Little Big Horn College. Montana).

In addition, warm thanks are extended to Professor John C. Ewers (Arlington, Virginia), Margot Liberty (Sheridan, Wyoming), Scott Burgan (Sheridan, Wyoming), Colin Taylor (Hastings, England), Kim Waters, library director of the Braun research library of the Southwest Museum of Los Angeles, California for locating and copying data from the George Bird Grinnell files. The staff of the Dull Knife College Library and archives, (Northern Cheyenne reservation) Lame Deer. Montana. The staff at Little Big Horn College Library; particularly Magdalene Mountain Horse of the Little Big Horn College Archives, Crow Agency, Montana. The Denver Public Library and Archives, Denver, Colorado. The New York Public Library, New York and, not least, the Smithsonian Institution of Washington D.C for allowing access to their collection of Lakota and Dakota Indian wintercounts.

So it is, that the episodes here related are composite accounts, put together from tribal oral tradition obtained from what Joe and Winona along with other tribe's people imparted to the Author, albeit, presented in my own words to include additional data found in both published and unpublished sources. With this in mind, it must be said that the gist of actual words accredited to certain persons mentioned in the episodes, have also been preserved in the oral accounts and are in no way imaginative. I have, however, used a degree of poetic license in order to present such quotes in a more realistic idiom as, indeed, was then common usage in the vernacular among Indians during the old-time buffalo days.

Author's photo

Glen Birdinground and wife.

Throughout this account, the author has sometimes used the nomenclature "Red Man" and "Red Men" without apology. To those persons ill-informed regarding the true ideology and philosophy to which the Indian subscribed, this will, perhaps, come as a surprise in the modern climate of what is thought to be politically correct. However, the term is not used here in a derogatory sense. Rather, it is merely adhering to the proper idiom as often expressed by Indians themselves. The Indians of old referred to themselves as "Red Men" or "Red People," believing that the Great Spirit created them from their own red earth environment. Hence, they painted themselves and their clothing profusely with red ochre or red-clay pigment, for the color red was and is considered sacred among them and included in conjunction with their concept of creation and regeneration, along with all other things they regard as holy. The term also when employed in this sense, indicates being brave; prepared to shed their blood in defense of their families; their way of life and when forced to protect their homeland from invaders. Thus, it has the additional connotation of "Real Men" or "Real People" and in no way, is meant to be associated with the color of one's skin. Therefore, in order to present a true appreciation of North American Indians in general and as a token of respect, the term "Red Man" is used intermittently throughout.

Having said this, the following selected episodes from the annals of Crow intertribal warfare are illustrative of life when, in a time past, the Red Man roamed free without constraint across the Montana, Dakota and Wyoming Great Plains and are typical examples, describing the military environment in which the Crows and their neighbors, through circumstance, were long obliged to exist.

Notes and Sources

1 The actual species of bird from which the name Apsaroka is derived, is no longer found in the country with which that people are familiar. Neither can one say what its true species may have been. Most likely, the term refers to the cormorant or, perhaps, to the pelican, but today the word has no proper meaning in the Crow dialect. The name does, however, translate from the Hidatsa tongue as `apsi,` meaning `large-beaked` and `roka,` meaning `children.`

2 Information supplied to the Author by Alex Birdinground; August, 1996. Lodge Grass, Montana. See also, Joe Medicine Crow, "From the Heart of the Crow Country," pp.16-20; *The Library of the American Indian*, 1992.

3 Joe Medicine Crow to Author. note pad 1.p.1 Lodge Grass, Montana, August, 1994.

4 Robert H. Lowie, The Crow Indians. p.4. Holt, Rinehart and Winston. 1956.

5 The Lewis and Clark material when referring to Crow bands which, in 1805, constituted the nation as a whole, noted as follows,. . . ..". . ..These people are divided into four bands called by themselves, Ahah-ar-ro-pir-no-pah, Noo-ta, Pa-rees-car and E-hart-sar." The last named, i.e. "Pa-rees-car," represent the explorer's rendition of the Hidatsa form of the Crow name for the "Rich-Prairie-Dogs," which we know from Crow oral tradition, was an earlier and alternative name for the Whistling Water band, while that rendered "E-hart-sar," refers to that band evidently, closely connected to the Hidatsa and is the same group led by the chief "Bear-with-a-bad-heart-always" which left the Hidatsa to join the Crows after the great smallpox epidemic of 1781 / `82. Cf; *History of the Lewis and Clark Expedition*, Edited by Elliot Coues. Dover Publications Inc; New York. [No date] Vol.1.pp.198-192 and Vol. 3. pp. 1154-1155.

6 Lowie, Robert H. *The Crow Indians*, p 216. Holt, Rinehart and Winston, 1956.

7 Curtis, Edward S. *The North American Indian*, Vol. 4. "Crow and Atsina." pp.11-18. Smithsonian Institution, Washington DC. 1907 - 1920.See also, Bowers, Alfred B. *Hidatsa Ceremonial and Social Organization*. pp.23-24. University of Nebraska Press.1956.

8 Joe Medicine Crow to Author, Note pad 1. P.2. August, 1994. [Author`s collection]

9 Edward S. Curtis, *The North American Indian*, Vol. 4, "Crow and Atsina." pp.11 -18. Smithsonian Institution, Washington DC.1907-1920.

10 Edward S. Curtis, loc. cit. p.13. Also, Joe Medicine Crow to Author, Lodge Grass, Montana, note pad 1. P.2. August, 1994.

11 Lowie, Robert H. *The Crow Indians*, p 216. Holt, Rinehart and Winston, 1956.

12 Curtis, Edward S. *The North American Indian*, Vol. 4 "Crow and Atsina." pp.18-20. Smithsonian Institution, Washington DC. 1907 - 1920. Also, Joe Medicine Crow to Author, note pad 1.p.3.August, 1994.

13. Joe Medicine Crow to Author, note pad 1. P.3. August, 1994.

14 Ferris, Warren A. *Life in the Rocky Mountains*, pp.305-306 Denver Old West Publishing Company, 1940.

15 Edward S. Curtis, *The North American Indian*, Vol. 4, "Crow and Atsina." pp.11-18. Smithsonian Institution, Washington D.C.1907-1920.

16 This refers to the coming together of the Crow-speaking peoples, as driftwood comes together to create an entangled [i.e. united] mass along the river bank. Cf; Frery, Rodney. *The World of the Crow Indians*. pp.3-4. University Of Oklahoma press. 1993.

17 Howard, James H. "Yanktonai Ethnohistory and the John K. Bear Winter Count." pp. 28-29. Plains Anthropologist. Memoir no. 11. 1976.

18 Ibid; "John K. Bear winter-count." p. 37. Loc; cit.

19 See, Mallery, Garrick, "Picture writing of the American Indians," Vol. 1 and 2. Tenth Annual Report of the Bureau of American Ethnology, Smithsonian Institution, Washington DC. 1888-`1899. [Various entries beginning around 1789 and continuing late into the nineteenth century].

20 During the Second World War while fighting through France, Joe fought hand to hand with a German soldier and captured his opponent`s gun; led a successful party against a German position during which he ran off a number of horses belonging to a German SS Detachment and, single-handed, captured fifty enemy soldiers. Joe Medicine Crow to Author, Note pad 2. pp.6-7. Lodge Grass 1992. See also; Medicine Crow, Joe. "Counting Coup." pp.107-117. *National Geographic*. Washington D.C. 1996.

21 Bauerle, Phoenicia, [Editor] The Way of the Warrior."pp.21-22. University of Nebraska Press, 2003, pp.21-22

22 Joe Medicine Crow to Author, Lodge Grass, Montana, note pad 1.p.4. 1994. See also, Curtis, Edward S. *The North American Indian*, Vol. 4. "Crow and Atsina" pp.13-20. Smithsonian Institution, Washington D.C. 1907 - 1920.

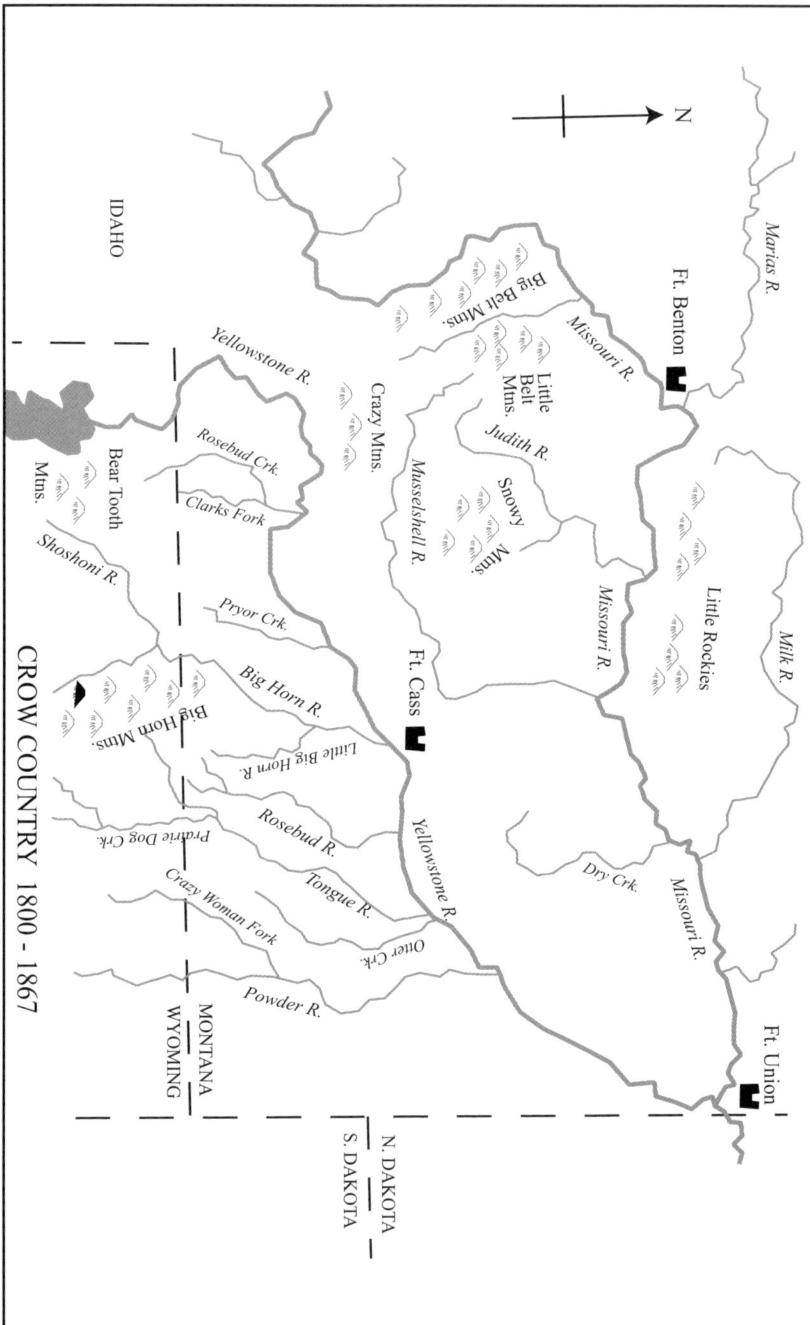
CROW COUNTRY 1800 - 1867
N
IDAHO
MONTANA
WYOMING
N. DAKOTA
S. DAKOTA
Marias R.
Ft. Benton
Missouri R.
Big Belt Mtns.
Little Belt Mtns.
Judith R.
Snowy Mtns.
Little Rockies
Milk R.
Missouri R.
Missouri R.
Dry Crk.
Ft. Union
Yellowstone R.
Crazy Mtns.
Musselshell R.
Ft. Cass
Rosebud Crk.
Clarks Fork
Bear Tooth Mtns.
Shoshoni R.
Pryor Crk.
Big Horn R.
Big Horn Mtns.
Little Big Horn R.
Rosebud R.
Prairie Dog Crk.
Tongue R.
Crazy Woman Fork
Otter Crk.
Yellowstone R.
Powder R.

Chapter One

"Thirty-two in the Hands"

Before the middle years of the second decade of the nineteenth century, warlike incursions undertaken by Crow war parties into Blackfoot territory north of the Missouri, coupled with intermittent raids upon the Nez Perce, Gros Ventre and Assiniboin, had achieved a degree of success, albeit, small scale compared to martial victories of earlier years. But these encounters compensated for a recent spate of attacks on Crow villages by the Sioux and Cheyenne.

The Sioux were not then in any great number farther west than the middle courses of the Cannonball, Grand and Big Cheyenne rivers of North and South Dakota, although their war parties were constantly raiding much farther afield, deep into the heart of Absaroka country. These incursions often were at the instigation of Cheyennes, who already had covetous eyes firmly fixed upon the rich Powder River hunting grounds belonging to the Crow.

The Cheyennes always regarded the Crows as formidable adversaries—brave, resourceful, competent—and often more than a match to contend with when confronted on equal terms. The Crows were well deserving of their reputation and commanded high respect from all their neighbors, both friend and foe. For having driven the Shoshoni and Flatheads from the Yellowstone and Big Horn country half a century earlier, the Crows held undisputed sway over all that territory, even extending their sphere of influence into adjoining areas; north as far as Milk River and beyond; south to the Platte River forks; west to the Rocky Mountains and east as far as the Little Missouri and western fringes of the Black Hills. This period was the "Golden Age," of Crow power in the High Plains. But it was not to last.

By the early 1800s, Blackfoot tribes of Piegan, Siksika and Blood began pushing down from the north, while Cheyenne-speaking bands, aided and abetted by certain tribes of Teton Sioux, encroached from the east. Ultimately, these same hostile pressures obliged the Crows to contract their tribal borders and redefine their territory to that contained by the Powder River on the east; the Judith on the north; south along the lower Yellowstone embracing that river's Tongue, Rosebud and Big Horn tributaries, including the lower valley of Wind River and on the west, as far as the Madison and Pryor rivers and Absaroka Mountains. This area alone became that recognized as Crow Country for the next fifty years.[1]

This is not to say that Crow hunters and war parties did not continue to roam far and wide beyond these borders, although now they did so at their peril; always at risk of being overwhelmed by a larger enemy force.

The eastern borderlands of the old Crow territory along both sides of the Lower Powder (technically still belonging to the Crows), became a kind of no-man's land, wherein could be found war parties from half a dozen tribes; hostile toward each other and all hostile towards the Crow. However, during the first two decades of the nineteenth century, the latter were still a populous and able opponent and although forced to defend themselves on all fronts, they oft-times took the offensive and struck their enemies several heavy blows. Indeed, the year 1819 was long regarded memorable among the Crows, owing to a series of victories gained over war parties belonging to several tribes with whom the Crows were then in conflict. It was a time also when the entire nation was filled with self-confidence, along with a sense of grandeur as to their perceived prowess as a military force on the Northern Plains. Their population by that date had increased twofold since the great smallpox contagion of 1780-'82 and they had reason to consider themselves a match—if not the better—of the many foes around them.[2]

About the year 1815, Paints His Face Red—head chief of the Mountain Crows if not titular head of the entire Crow nation—passed away, although whether in battle or by some other cause, neither the documented data nor tribal oral tradition can say. What we do know is that a man named Long Hair then stepped into the vacant position, perhaps, moreover, due to his exceptional medicine powers, rather than in recognition of his military achievements alone. His inauguration, however, as head chief at that time when about fifty-five years of age, must also include him as a prominent figure in earlier conflicts with his people's enemies. But as paramount chief, he gave up the war trail and put aside the tomahawk and lance, other than defending his camp when attacked or when in transit upon the trail. Instead, he embraced the duties of a civil head chief. His duties were to always look to the benefit of the tribe, as opposed to any personal desire for self aggrandizement and renown. As such, he became beloved and ever-more respected among the Absaroka. His character was often pointed out to aspiring young warriors as a prime example of how a Crow should act and think—always holding the welfare of the people foremost and caring for the young, the old and infirm.[3]

Most white men who knew Long Hair agreed that the chief's most special attribute was his hair, variously recorded as being anywhere between nine and twelve feet long.[4] As far the Crow people were concerned, his singular ability to predict forthcoming events was an even greater attribute. The people held him in awe as a chosen one of *Akbaa-tadia* itself. Such was the foresight of Long Hair, that a number of his predictions were not actually fulfilled until one and even two generations after his death. This phenomenon added to the reverential adulation in which his memory has been held. [5] One pertinent example of his supposed psychic powers occurred, as near as can be calculated, in 1819 and is an event still repeated in the oral traditions of the tribe.

Certainly it seemed by the year 1819, the Crows at last, had achieved ascendency in the endemic warfare of which they were constantly engaged.

Prominent among Crow enemies at this time were the Cheyennes—moreover the latter's less populous Shutaio-speaking bands—which often found themselves on the receiving end in their conflicts with the Crow. But notwithstanding their own inferiority in numbers and certain recent reversals, the Shutaio were determined still to claim the Lower Powder and Tongue River country for themselves. Thus, they continued to engage in persistent warfare with the Crows and seldom did a week pass which did not witness some bloody confrontation between the two. At times, one side or the other would get together a large war party and move deep into their opponent's country, either to exact revenge for some recent defeat or more simply, to antagonize the other in return for some lesser slight upon their honor.

But each victory had its price. This was the case, in 1819, when an unsuccessful horse-stealing raid by a Cheyenne-Shutaio war party led to its destruction by the Mountain Crows under the leadership of Chief Long Hair. Only one of the vanquished party survived and he took news of the slaughter back to his people. The Cheyennes considered the event of such importance that in response, they mounted a punitive expedition against the Crow perpetrators, with the sole intent of inflicting severe damage upon that people's population and their pride.

According to Crow historians, sometime during late summer of 1819, in the Mountain Crow camp, along the west bank of the lower course of Tongue River, Chief Long Hair summoned his chiefs and headmen to his large red and black painted lodge. He said, he wished to tell them something of great importance.

When all were gathered seated cross legged around a central fire, Long Hair took several handfuls of dirt gathered from a mole hill and fashioned a small mound on the ground before him. He then lit his pipe bowl with a burning ember and drew a few puffs. At the same time he mumbled incoherent phrases in a low voice and, at length, after the pipe passed around from left to right and all had inhaled its smoke, Long Hair told the assembly,

> "This day I received a great and powerful vision in which my protectors 'Morning Star' and 'Bear Spirit' appeared and opened my eyes, enabling me to see things which most surely will come to pass. I saw enemies coming towards our camp and white powder smoke bursting from our thunder sticks. Anon, after the smoke had cleared, many lay scalped and bloody around our camp. But they were not the warriors of the Absaroka; they were the bodies of our enemies the 'Striped Arrow People;' Not one remained alive." [6]

All those within the lodge had listened attentively to their chief in reverential silence, but now they murmured to one another as they deliberated upon his words.

After a while, Long Hair held forth his clenched fists with outstretched arms and said, "In these hands I hold the enemy; tell me my chiefs, how many heads (scalps) would you have?"

In response one of the assembled chiefs leaned forward on his haunches and said, "Give us all that you hold."

Long Hair opened his fists and there, exposed for all to see, were eight small bones of a Prairie dog owl; four bones in each palm. "I give you this many," Long Hair said, as he scattered the bones over the dirt mound before him.

The assembled chiefs and headmen again murmured among themselves. They cried *"Ah-ho Ah-ho"* in unison and then another among them said, "Give us more that we may sing our victory songs for many moons to come."

For a while Long Hair sat silent; hands concealed behind his back. Then for a second time he held forth his two clenched fists with outstretched arms and replied, "Again I say, how many heads would you have?"

"Give us all that you hold," was once more the reply,

Long Hair opened his fists, exposing eight more small bones of the Prairie dog owl and these too, he spread on the mole-dirt mound before him.

All those gathered now clapped a hand over their mouth in an expression of wonder, not knowing how or from where the bones had appeared when, but a moment before, they had observed for themselves the chief's empty hands.

Twice more those assembled clamored for the heads of their enemies and twice more, Long Hair repeated his actions, bringing the total times to the sacred number four, so that thirty-two small bones then lay scattered on the dirt mound before him. This, said he, was the number of enemies his Spirit Protectors had promised in his vision. "Thirty-two in the hands."

Long Hair then concluded by saying, "My chiefs be patient ere my vision be fulfilled. Truly, I say unto you it is forthcoming by the time the next moon is born."

The next few days dragged by. But on the fourth morning, scouts came running into the Mountain Crow camp bringing word that a war party of Blood Blackfoot had been sighted not far from the lodges. At once a horde of Crow warriors mounted their war ponies; took up weapons and raced off to confront the foe. The Blackfoot party was defeated with much loss and the triumphant Crows returned to camp waving a number of bloody scalps above their heads, along with human limbs tied to the end of lances and musket barrels. Many of the victorious warriors naturally assumed that this indeed, was the victory earlier predicted by Long Hair—although many scalps less had been taken than "Thirty-two in the hands"—and the great chief merely sat in his lodge, indicating by his lack of enthusiasm that the time was not come for the fulfillment of his prophecy, as the new moon had not yet appeared. [7]

But in truth, the wheels of fate had already been set in motion, turning slowly, to fulfill the prophetic words of Long Hair.

Now some four days earlier in a Cheyenne-Shutaio village, then nestling along the Belle Fourche branch of the Big Cheyenne River north of the Black Hills, the very same day when the Crow chief had been explaining his vision to his headmen in his red and black painted tepee, thirty-two braves assembled in the Soldier Lodge of the Shutaio Crooked Lance Society and made a road to war against the Crows.

In the Soldier Lodge they prepared themselves by singing society songs and chanting incantations to bring them success in their proposed venture. Most of those assembled were Shutaio Crooked Lance members, but, it seems, a few Cheyenne Bow String Society warriors had also been included for good measure. A veteran Shutaio named One-Eyed Antelope was their Pipe Bearer (leader) and it was he who possessed the only gun among them.[8]

Early next morning before the sun was up, the party started on foot in the dim light of dawn toward the west. It was late summer—"The moon when cherries are ripe"—and they expected to find the Crows engaged in their annual religious celebrations, at which time there was sure to be scattered in and around the Crow village thousands of ponies, making it that much easier to steal a large bunch, while at the same time, unsuspecting individuals both male and female, might easily be cut off from the main camp to be either killed or taken captive.

It had seemed as the Crooked Lance party traveled on foot at a leisurely dogtrot, day after day towards its objective, that the powers of the holy men in the Shutaio village who had given blessings and prayers for the party's good fortune, were strong and that the individual guardian totems of each warrior present were also watching over them. For they managed to reach the enemy country without mishap and everything was going according to plan. The entire party was in high spirits and confident of success.[9]

Nevertheless, when at last they crossed the Powder and continued west, moving ever deeper into Crow territory, utmost caution was observed. It would not take many mistakes to be discovered by the Crows. Smaller parties had the advantage of being able to disperse quickly and quietly in the advent of danger and could conceal themselves in the undergrowth that much easier. Also they did not attract so much attention from both man and beast as would thirty or more clod-hopping warriors, bent on horses and scalps. Thus the war party continued to move cautiously through the country, keeping a sharp lookout for enemy sign and at length, upon reaching Tongue River, the Cheyennes found what they were looking for.

The half White—half Cheyenne informant George Bent, stated that the Cheyennes discovered the Crows encamped along the Tongue and while awaiting darkness to fall, whereupon they would attempt to run off a number of the camp's horses, they observed Crow boys driving their animals in close to the lodges. At the same time, Crow warriors were seen mounting their war ponies and appeared to be preparing for a big fight. Many Crows then came out of the village on horseback and began riding up and down the valley where the Cheyennes were hidden. By these actions on the part of the Crows, the Cheyennes guessed that the presence of their own party had been discovered and was about to be attacked. Realizing also that if they remained in the valley they would easily be run down and killed, they all broke cover and raced to the summit of a nearby hill,where they quickly raised a breastwork of stones and prepared to defend themselves.[10]

On the other hand, in an account recorded by the late Northern Cheyenne historian John Stands In Timber, which he put together at a later date than Bent gleaned from the recollections of old Cheyenne and Crow story tellers, it is stated that the Cheyenne party was travelling along the Tongue upstream with scouts out on both flanks. These scouts came in and reported that the Crows must also be on a war trail for they had seen a lot of sign, although they had no idea where exactly the enemy might be. Stands In Timber added that the Crows had, in fact, already discovered the Cheyennes and intended to ambush them at the forks of a tributary of the Tongue now known as Prairie Dog

Author's Photo, 1996

Site of the Crooked Lance massacre on a hill overlooking Prairie Dog Creek. Cheyennes took refuge on the center peak where they were beseiged by Crows.

Creek. Not knowing this, the two Cheyenne scouts went out again, but in a short while one of them returned, reporting once more that he had seen nothing of note. The other scout, however,—a man named Two Bulls—remained ahead of the party but on the east side of the stream (and as it transpired, viewed the whole affair from a concealed position some distance from where his comrades became entrenched). The rest of the Cheyenne party continued on up Prairie Dog Creek to its fork, then traveled along the crest of a low ridge separating the two streams. It was at this point that the party was suddenly attacked by the Crows; quickly surrounded and forced into a desperate fight.[11]

In yet another version obtained by George Bird Grinnell from several Cheyenne and Crow informants, it is asserted that as the Cheyenne party was travelling through the mountains over by Tongue River, with scouts out reconnoitering the area, they suddenly came upon a lone Indian also on foot who immediately turned around and fled, but being hotly pursued by the Cheyennes, was soon overtaken and killed.[12] Joe Medicine Crow added that upon examining their victim, the Cheyennes knew at once he was Crow by the fashion of jewelry and pompadour hairstyle, but whether he had been a scout from the Crow village or had acted as a decoy for a larger force in hiding, is not determined.[13] However, no sooner had his scalp been lifted than a great body of Crow warriors appeared; some on horseback, others on foot and the Cheyennes themselves were forced to flee.[14] All accounts agree that the Cheyenne party had continued travelling slowly between the two forks of the creek, moving along the crest of a ridge which led them to an area of flat land some 300 yards by 200 and it was here, after reaching the flat land, that the concealed body of Crows launched their attack. The Cheyennes took to their heels and on the shale-strewn summit of a nearby hill, overlooking Prairie Dog Creek, they made their stand.

As was typical of these old-time intertribal conflicts, the Crows had paused for a moment before launching their attack and for the Cheyennes; even though momentarily stunned, it was all the time they needed to race away and gain the advantage of higher ground.

Seeing their quarry in flight before them, a large body of Crows charged headlong in pursuit in an effort to cut off the Cheyenne retreat. Their feathered bonnets streamed out behind them in the wind as their half-naked bodies, daubed with red and yellow ochre, strained forward in the saddle in their eagerness to reach the foe. But it was too late. By the time the Crows attempted to charge up the hill, the Cheyennes were well prepared behind crude, but effective breastworks and had dug in, ready for a prolonged and determined contest.

The hill itself was a kind of natural fortress easy to defend. Most of the way around its base was very steep, but at one place it slopped gently from the summit down to the valley floor and here, horses could be ridden up to its crest without difficulty. The Cheyenne defenders entrenched along the top paid particular attention to this slope and the Crows; for all their endeavors, could not gain the height and overrun the position with their cavalry. As the Crow horsemen thundered up the slope, a barrage of well-aimed Cheyenne arrows broke the charge and forced the enemy back down into the valley below.

Had the Crows not hesitated, but immediately charged upon the small Cheyenne force when first seen, they would have taken them by surprise and exterminated them all before they had a chance to flee. As was their usual custom, however, the Crows had reined in their horses in order to allow their enemies the opportunity to witness their savage splendor and to enable the Crows themselves to gloat over the look of surprise and despair on their enemy's faces as the latter comprehended their impending doom. But once behind their breastworks, the Cheyennes could easily repel the Crow onslaughts and each warrior sell his life dearly as befitted a Cut Arm brave.[15]

The failure of their first attack brought the Crows to their senses. They foresaw the folly of continuing a direct assault upon the hill, for other than the loss of many warriors, which such an action would

Photo by Scott Burgan, Sheridan, Wyoming, 2006
Joe Medicine Crow standing at the site where the Cheyenne war party was first discovered by Crows.

undoubtedly incur, it would almost certainly be in vain as long as the Cheyennes remained behind their breastworks and had a plentiful supply of ammunition.

Instead, the Crows surrounded the position and sniped at the defenders from cover with their smoothbore muskets, which the Crows had in abundance, due to a recent trading excursion to their Hidatsa cousins. In this manner they kept the Cheyennes pinned down, preventing their escape and in the meantime, sent runners to the rest of the Crows encamped in the vicinity, with word to come up and assist them.

Chief Long Hair was in the Crow camp at that time. When the couriers came galloping in and proclaimed that Cheyennes were nearby, the chief immediately took sole charge of the situation.

"This is my prophecy about to be fulfilled," he declared and ordered all the fighting men in camp to go out and meet the foe.[16]

Several bands or clans constituted the Mountain Crow division and if they were not then encamped together, they certainly were positioned very near each other and could combine their forces at a moment's notice. Thus, when Long Hair sent runners to inform the rest of the clans what had happened, the entire Mountain Crow population was aroused. War clothes were hastily donned; faces and bodies painted and soon, hundreds of warriors were racing pell mell to the scene of conflict, whooping and yelling like a horde of painted demons. The thought of thirty or more Cut Arm scalps was too much a prize to ignore and following behind the warriors, came the Crow women and children, all eager to watch the fight and witness the annihilation of their mortal foes.

When finally they arrived on the scene, Long Hair held a council of war and spoke to the gathering around him:

> "Now is the time Morning Star and Bear Spirit will fulfill the promise they gave me. Behold, they have given into our hands this day thirty-two of our enemies. Now, I say unto you, before the sun goes down, none of these people will have escaped the scalping knives of the valiant Absaroka." [17]

In response, all those assembled let out a series of wild, horrific war whoops and appeared much excited at the prospect of so certain and easy a victory. Long Hair said,

> "We ourselves have plenty of time. We need not sacrifice our brave young men by engaging in rash actions in order to finish off the enemy too quickly. Let us instead say to our women, return to our camps; take down the lodges and bring them hither and set up our village on this flat land which surrounds the hill where sits the enemy, supposing themselves secure. We will remain in camp at this place until the battle is done and these 'Striped Arrow People' are no more." [18]

Long Hair`s suggestion was met with unanimous approval by all those in council. The tribal crier told the womenfolk to do as their chief had requested. The women returned within an hour, bringing with them travois and packhorses loaded down with tepee covers, lodge poles and all other domestic paraphernalia. Long Hair then directed them to pitch the lodges evenly around the base of the hill, cutting off all avenues of retreat for the besieged Cheyennes. The Cheyennes, meanwhile, viewed these goings on with apprehension from atop their rocky refuge—mingled no doubt with a degree of curiosity—but could only wait and wonder what would happen next.[19]

Once the tepees were erected, the Crows began treating the affair like a festive occasion. Old men beat drums and blew on eagle bone whistles, while the women sang Strong Heart songs in praise of their young sons and husbands to give them courage in the coming fight. Cooking pots were put on boil and many of the non combatants took up favorable positions to get a better view of the impending conflict and satisfy their morbid interest.

Having thus taken time preparing for battle, it was not until midday that the Crows resumed the fight. They let loose a barrage of arrows and musket balls at the defenders from all possible angles and soon, it seemed, almost every surrounding rock and bush concealed a Crow warrior.

Throughout the afternoon the barrage continued. The Cheyennes shot back arrows fired by the Crows to supplement their own dwindling supply of ammunition. Every so often a single musket shot would explode from the gun of One-Eyed Antelope. But the Cheyenne response appeared to have little effect upon the enemy, for as one Crow musket was silenced, there was another to take its place.

Several Cheyennes were wounded; some mortally and their comrades knew that their own demise was imminent. Still, the Crows would not risk another charge and as the day wore on, they also suffered a number of warriors killed and seriously injured owing to the deadly aim of the defenders on the hilltop.

At length the sun began sinking beyond the western horizon and twilight descended over the land. As the light dimimished, so did the firing, until it completely ceased. Crow guards kept watch upon the hill in case the Cheyennes attempted to escape, and through the night, the sound of singing and dancing reverberated over the hills emanating from the valley below. Crow war drums continued to beat monotonously, as the men folk screamed their war cries and the women hurled obscenities at the besieged, who in turn, sang loud their own Strong Heart songs and retorted in defiance that when their brother Cheyennes heard of their deaths, they would send a great force into the Crow country and rub out the entire Absaroka nation.[20]

The next morning, the battle resumed.

Periodically, a lone Crow warrior would brazenly make a dash up the hillside in an endeavor to reach the defenders and count coup. But few ran down again and by midday, the Cheyennes were holding their own and still could not be budged.

It was about this time that a Cheyenne brave in full regalia of scalp shirt, beaded leggings and eagle—feathered bonnet, jumped over the breastworks and ran back and forth outside them inviting the Crows to kill him. He was making a "caw – caw" noise and flapped his arms like a bird in order to ridicule the Crows. The noise was deafening, as every Crow musket spat at him almost simultaneously and a cloud of arrows whistled through the air. By some miracle the lone Cheyenne was not hit and he went back behind the breastworks, to the welcoming cheers of bravado from his comrades. Soon, however, he was again leaping over the breastworks and began to repeat his actions in an expression of contempt for his enemies. Three times he did this brave thing. The third time he was killed by a blanket volley of Crow missiles.[21]

Sketch by Author after a drawing by George Catlin in 1832

Crow Chief He-Who-Jumps-Over- Everyone.

It was soon after the death of this brave Cheyenne that the showers of missiles coming from the breastworks became more sporadic. Eventually, the last Cheyenne arrow was spent. Only One-Eyed Antelope was occasionally shooting with his gun.[22]

A Crow sniper was lodged in a crevice between two rocks close to the Cheyenne position. His deadly aim was causing some havoc within the breastworks and throughout the course of battle, the defenders lost several warriors both dead and seriously wounded to this man. The Cheyennes had now shot away their arrows, but One-Eyed Antelope, their leader, still had a little powder and a few balls with which to return the Crow fire. His companions pointed out the position of the sniper and the next time the Crow exposed himself to view, One-Eyed Antelope fired and blew the sniper's brains out, causing his victim to spring forward and lay head downwards hanging half over the rocks. With cheers of adulation all around him, One-Eyed Antelope reloaded his gun; raised it to the sun and sang a medicine song. He then struck the butt on the ground (moreover to seat the ball rather than an assurance of success) and singling out another of the enemy, he fired again and also killed him outright. Twice more One-Eyed Antelope repeated the procedure and each time he killed a Crow. But after the fourth shot there was silence from within the breastworks, for this was the very last of the Cheyenne's ammunition.[23]

The Crows realized their enemies` predicament and were determined to finish them off before the daylight faded completely. They regrouped and together prepared to make a charge, supposing that only a few defenders were left alive.

Before such could be done, a mournful wail echoed from the hilltop and the Crows knew its meaning. Their opponents were getting ready to die—for they were singing the Crooked Lance death song.[24]

Not desiring to tarry longer, Chief Long Hair raised a solitary war whoop of "Koo-Koo-Hey" and in response, a mass of Crow braves, most of whom were on foot, charged the height from all directions, scrambling up over the rocks and over each other in their eagerness to get at the foe.[25]

A popular Crow medicine man (whose name has been forgotten) wearing a buffalo horned war bonnet and mounted on a fine horse, rode out in front of his warriors and galloping up the slope, was first to reach the Cheyenne position. Bravely he leapt his mount over the stone barricade and landed in the very midst of the defenders. All at once Cheyennes ran up and began flaying about him with their tomahawks and stabbing with their knives. One Cheyenne jumped up on the Crow's horse behind him and tussled for supremacy of the seat and with the aid of his fellows, toppled the rider from the saddle. The Crow medicine man was dead before he touched the ground, but such was the unbridled frenzy of the Cheyennes, that they dragged his body over the rocks and literally, hacked it to pieces.[26]

The next instant the rest of the Crows were on the crest, tearing down the stone breastworks while screaming vengeance for the death of their medicine man.

The remaining Cheyennes bunched together and with knife or tomahawk in hand, prepared for the end. They let out a series of wild, ear-piercing war cries and threw themselves headlong into the mass of Crows around them, stabbing and slashing blindly as they grappled with their enemies in a series of desperate hand-to-hand struggles. But one-by-one the remaining Cheyennes dropped to the ground dead or dying, until all at last lay low.[27]

Two brothers, the sons of an old but highly-respected Shutaio warrior named Red Painted Robe were in this battle, fighting bravely side-by-side and at the end, they too lay together in death on the blood soaked ground, as once they had been together in life.[28]

Northwestern University Library
"The North American Indian," Edward S. Curtis
Bull Goes Hunting, also known as Sees-the-Living-Bull, was a young boy when he witnessed the slaughter of thirty-two Cheyenne warriors in 1819.

The last Cheyenne to be killed, it is said, fought most valiantly. He slew and disabled several Crow warriors before he himself was over powered by sheer weight of numbers. His body was later found nearly at the base of the hill. Apparently, he had broken right through the Crow ranks, but finding no place to run had made his stand and there he stayed, fighting to the end.[29]

The jubilant Crows—including a great number of women and children who had been watching the fight from safe vantage points, wandered over the hillside, dispatching wounded Crooked Lance warriors. They striped the clothing from the bodies and gleefully hacked off the heads and limbs of their victims. The grisly trophies were attached to lances and musket barrels so they could be paraded around the camp during victory celebrations.

A famous Mountain Crow warrior and holy man of a later date named Bull Goes Hunting, also known as Sees the Living Bull, once told Joe Medicine Crow's informant Plain Feather that he—Bull Goes Hunting—was around three or four years old when the fight took place. At that time, after the fighting had finished, an uncle of Bull Goes Hunting took him over the battlefield where the dead and mutilated Crooked Lance warriors lay all around and encouraged his young nephew to touch one or more of the bloodied corpses with his hand in the act of counting coup. Bull Goes Hunting could remember but little of the event, he said, but had been teased about it many times as he grew older, being told that he had been the youngest warrior involved in the fight on that occasion.[30]

All this activity on the hillside had been viewed by the surviving Crooked Lance scout Two Bulls, from a concealed position on a nearby height to the north, not far from the forks of the creek.[31]

Sometime later, after darkness obliged the Crows to retire from the scene, Two Bulls started out on his long and hazardous journey home; with a heavy and vengeful heart.

This lone survivor of the vanquished party must either have lost his bearings or become non cognizant to all around him for a significant length of time, as it is said among the Cheyennes today that it was two moons (months) later, perhaps early November when the first flurries of snow heralding the impending winter began settling on the hilltops, before the occupants of the Shutaio village saw Two Bull's lean and emaciated figure coming from afar and anticipated the sad intelligence he was bringing them. It is said that Two Bulls was still crying over his dead companions; the blooded, mutilated corpses of whom had by then, long been devoured by the wolves of the prairie and birds of the air, so that only their bleaching bones lay as mute testimony to their fate.[32]

After the sad news was received, arms and thighs were gashed; hair cut short or torn out in great hanks from the head. Clothing and tepees were ripped and heart-rendering cries of mourning filled the air. There was hardly a family in the Shutaio camp that did not grieve the loss of a relative.[33]

At once, promises were made among the bereaved kinfolk to mount a grand crusade to avenge the loss of their Crooked Lance tribesmen. But in the meantime, there would be much sorrow within many a Cut Arm lodge throughout the ensuing snows of winter.

During the immediate aftermath of the fight, the Crows had been ecstatic. In total, at least thirty-one Cheyenne scalps dangled from Absaroka belts, albeit that the victors may have taken a heavy toll to obtain them. Years later, Crow participants told the Cheyennes that of the twenty-five casualties they themselves had suffered, most sustained wounds of slight degree and very few had actually been killed outright during the battle. But some Crow informants now say that their true number of dead was really much higher, if those who had been wounded and died later from their injuries are also included.[34]

The Crows had lost a good many warriors both during and following the engagement and thus, the prophecy of their great chief Long Hair may not entirely have been fulfilled. But the victorious chieftain was elevated even higher in his people's esteem, who continued to believe that his personal medicine power—embodied in his extraordinary length of hair—was omnipotent, against which none of their enemies could stand. Had not a victory promised to Long Hair been achieved? And who among the Crows but he, the "chosen one" of *Akbaa-tadia*, possessed such powers?

The Crows were filled with a sense of overconfidence and supposed none could match the prowess of their nation's military might. The bloody Cheyenne scalps were danced and sang over for many moons thereafter, even while "The-Great-North-Giant-Who-Paints-Everything-White" spread its snowy blanket over the land.

It was then said among the Crows that the Great Spirit was smiling upon his children and truly, the Star of the Absaroka shone bright."

NOTES AND SOURCES.

1 Joe Medicine Crow *"Papers. Box 1."* Little Big Horn College Library Archives, Crow Agency, Montana. See also, Curtis, Edward S. *"The North American Indian" Vol. 4 "Crow and Atsina;"* p.13. Smithsonian Institution, Washington DC. 1907 - 20.
2 Bradley, James H. *Contributions to the Historical Society of Montana. Vol. 2* p.50. 1875. See also, Wood, W.R. And Thiessen, T. D. *Early Fur trade on The Northern Plains.* p.206. University of Oklahoma Press. 1985.
3 Joe Medicine Crow to Author, Audio tape recording; Number one. Lodge Grass, Montana, August 1996. [Author's collection].
4 CF; Denig, Edwin, *"Of the Crow Nation"* in *Five Tribes of the Upper Missouri,* University of Oklahoma Press, 1961. pp.193-194 and footnote. See also, Anderson, William M. *The Rocky Mountain Journals of William Marshal Anderson 1834* p.100. University Of Nebraska Press, 1967.
5 Glen Bird-in-Ground [Crow informant] to Author; Crow Agency, Montana, September.1996. Note pad 2. pp.1-3. [Author's collection].
6 Ibid. Crow Agency, Montana, September 1996. Note pad 2. pp.1-3. The term *"Striped Arrow people"* is the recognized interpretation of the Crow name for the Cheyenne, in reference to the latter`s use of turkey or wild sage-hen feathers for their arrow flights.
7 Glen Bird-in-Ground to Author, Crow Agency, Montana, Sep; 1996. Loc. cited. pp.1-3
8 Grinnell, George Bird, *The Fighting Cheyennes* p.26. University of Oklahoma Press, 1956. See also; George Grinnell papers, The *"Cheyenne and Crow Warfare."* pp.1-2.The Southwest Museum, Los Angeles, California. Folder No.494.
9 Joe Medicine Crow to Author. Loc. cit. 1996. Note pad 2. pp.4-5.
10 Hyde, George Edward, *Life of George Bent.* p.23. University of Oklahoma Press, 1967.
11 Stands-in-Timber, John, *Cheyenne Memories,* p.129. Edited by Margot Liberty, University of Oklahoma Press, 1968.
12 Grinnell, George Bird. *The Fighting Cheyennes.* p.25. University of Oklahoma Press. 1956.
13 Joe Medicine Crow to Author, Lodge Grass, Montana, August, 1996.Loc; cited. Note pad 2. pp.4-5.
14 Grinnell, George Bird. *The Fighting Cheyennes.* pp. 25-26. University of Oklahoma Press. 1956.
15 A common appellation sometimes also rendered, *"Cut-Finger"* and applied by some other tribes at a later date to the Cheyenne as a whole, but originally, to the Shutaio alone, owing to the latter`s old-time custom of amputating the right arm of their victims or, of cutting off their enemy's fingers which were then fashioned into a necklace or some other form of personal body adornment.
16 Glen Bird-in-Ground to Author, Crow Agency, Montana, Sep; 1996. Note pad 2. pp.1-3.
17 Ibid. loc. cit. pp.1-3
18 Ibid. loc. cit. pp.1-3.
19 Ibid. loc. cit. pp.1-3
20 Ibid. loc. cit. pp.1-3
21 Ibid. loc. cit. pp.1-3.
22 Grinnell, George Bird. *The Fighting Cheyennes.* pp.25-26. University of Oklahoma Press. 1956.
23 Grinnell, George Bird. *The Fighting Cheyennes.* pp.25-26. University of Oklahoma Press. 1956.
24 Glen Bird-in-Ground to Author, Crow Agency, Montana, Sep; 1996. Loc. cited. pp.1-3
25 Glen Bird-in-Ground to Author, Crow Agency, Montana, Sep; 1996. Loc. cited. pp.1-3
26 Hyde, George Edward. *Life of George Bent.* pp.23-24. University of Oklahoma Press, 1967.
27 Grinnell, George Bird. *The Fighting Cheyennes.* pp. 25-26. University of Oklahoma Press. 1956.
28 Llewellyn and Hoebel. *The Cheyenne Way.* p.3. University of Oklahoma Press. 1968.
29 Stands-in-Timber, John, *Cheyenne Memories,* p.129. Edited by Margot Liberty, University of Oklahoma Press, 1968.
30 Joe Medicine Crow to Author, Lodge Grass, Montana, Sep; 1996. Note pad 2. pp.4-5.
31 Stands-in-Timber, John, *Cheyenne Memories,* Edited by Margot Liberty, University of Oklahoma Press, 1968. p.129.
32 Medicine Elk, Wayne [Southern Cheyenne informant] to Author, Billings, Montana, August, 1994. Note pad 1. p.5.
33 Medicine Elk, Wayne [Southern Cheyenne informant] to Author, Billings, Montana, August, 1994. Note pad 1. p.5.

34 Grinnell, George Bird *The Fighting Cheyennes,* pp. 25-26. University of Oklahoma Press. 1956. See also; George Bird Grinnell papers, Folder No. 494. The Southwest Museum, Los Angeles, California. And, *"Many Crow Captives."* Folder 15. Grinnell papers [Ms.5]

35 Grinnell, George Bird, *The Fighting Cheyennes,* pp. 25-26. Univ. of Okla. Press. 1956.

36 Grinnell, George Bird, *The Fighting Cheyennes,* pp. 25-26. Univ. of Okla. Press. 1956.

37 Millard, Joseph. *The Cheyenne Wars.* pp.34-35. Monarch Books Inc. Derby, Connecticut.1964.

38 George E. Hyde. *Life of George Bent.* University Of Oklahoma Press. pp.23-24. 1967.

39 Grinnell, George Bird, *The Fighting Cheyennes,* pp. 25-26. Univ. of Okla. Press. 1956

40 Joe Medicine Crow to Author, Lodge Grass, Montana, Sep; 1996. Note pad 2. pp.4-5.

41 MacCleary, Tim, to Author. Crow Agency. Montana. August.1998. Note pad 5. p.6. [Author's Collection].

42 Stands-in-Timber, John, *Cheyenne Memories,* p. 129. Edited by Margot Liberty, University of Oklahoma Press, 1968.

Chapter Two

When the 400 Were Stolen
The Revenge of the Cheyennes

As the autumn of 1819 gave way to winter, contrary to the habit of their neighbors, the Crows welcomed the coming snows as a time to step up their raiding of enemy camps. They knew the occupants were likely snowed in and reluctant to move far from lodge fires, either to guard their horses or give pursuit to thieves. In the months following the slaughter of the Crooked Lance Cheyennes, the Crows were filled with confidence. Numerous Crow war parties of various size, sometimes on foot; sometimes on horseback, skirmished with Sioux and Cheyenne enemies to the east and with Blood and Pikunni (Piegan) Blackfoot north of the Missouri River.

Indeed, the Crows gained yet another celebrated victory at this time, when they destroyed a twenty-man war party of horse-stealing Pikunni. These enemies like the Cheyenne Crooked Lance warriors, were discovered before they had even reached the camp they intended to raid. The Crows in overwhelming number lay in ambush and wiped out the Pikunnis.[1]

Suddenly, it seemed, the Crows were gaining victory after victory. Jubilant warriors—faces blackened with a mixture of grease and charcoal as a sign of success—returned home driving stolen horses and carrying plunder such as the weapons and clothing of their victims. They proudly displayed scalps attached to the ends of lances, willow wands and musket barrels, and also captured women and children to be raised as adopted members of the tribe.

Such was the fervor for war during those winter months that Long Hair, the principal Crow chief, often remonstrated his warriors for leaving the women and children unprotected while they pursued their bellicose endeavors. But Long Hair's words seemed to have little effect. For as war parties continued to return victorious, more warriors wished to emulate those deeds. The Cheyenne affair was considered but one success in a spate of Crow victories. There seemed to be little thought of the Cheyennes seeking retribution. Surely, thought the Crows, the Gods and spirit ancestors of the Absaroka were smiling upon their children. Were not the Crows the bravest and fiercest warriors on the Plains? None—not even Long Hair could foresee the great calamity destined to befall his people.

After lengthy periods of celebration within the various Crow camps, for the victories gained the previous autumn and throughout the snows of winter, the "Great North Giant Who Paints Everything White" lifted its icy hand. The sun burst through the clouds changing the sky to azure blue and melted the last snow on the hillsides. Bleak mountains regained their purple serenity and streams and rivers began to swell with the addition of melt waters issuing down from distant heights. Green shoots sprang up from nowhere, it seemed, while tree and bush—only yesterday dull and brittle—became reddish brown and supple. All that was asleep was now awakened and one with ear pressed hard to the ground could hear again the far off rumble of buffalo, moving rapidly, as if beckoned by the hunting instincts of the Northern Nations. Soon, lean, weak horses would be fit and fleet on lush new grass, as spring draped its green mantle across the land.

Meanwhile, far to the east of Crow Country, along timbered streams flowing through the Black Hills, the occupants of the scattered Cheyenne and Shutaio villages began to stir from their customary inertia during the winter season.

Throughout those long, cold months there had been much "Kill Talk" voiced against the Crows. But as the days of spring slowly lengthened into summer, no steps were taken to carry out such threats.

Now it happened that in a certain Shutaio village sited along the north bank of the upper course of the Big Cheyenne, there lived an old man named Red Painted Robe along with his wife who was known as White Buffalo Woman. Their two sons had been killed in the Crooked Lance slaughter the previous year and the hearts of their aging parents weighed heavy with grief. Perhaps far away in the Big Horn country, the Crows were still dancing over their scalps and thus, to show contempt for his people's lethargy in seeking revenge, Red Painted Robe began personally ostracizing himself from tribal society.

Red Painted Robe gave away all his horses and most of his prized possessions, rendering himself a poor man. The chiefs of the warrior societies, however, would allow no one to touch them, for they realized he was trying to tell them something by his actions.

Two Twists, a brave young man of the Crooked Lances—later to become a big tribal chief—went to Red Painted Robe's lodge and challenged his behavior.

"Why do you throw away your horses Grandfather?" he asked.[2]

Red Painted Robe replied, "One throws them away in grief for his two sons, whose bones lie in the enemy country open to the sky and their blood has not been covered."[3]

By this he meant that the spirits of the dead had not yet been compensated by any act of revenge upon the slayers, which should have been the customary response after such an event and was known as "Covering the body."

But still no attempt was made to raise a war party for revenge and the Crows continued to go unpunished.

It was not long after this that Red Painted Robe discarded the rest of his property, including his tepee and actually began shunning the people. He traveled a little distance behind the camp when it was on the move and slept out under the stars at night.

For a second time Two Twists tried to persuade Red Painted Robe to come back into the social life of the camp. He even offered to return all the horses and belongings which the old man had thrown away. But again Red Painted Robe refused. The people became concerned and wondered what they should do to change his mind, for the old man was highly respected within the tribe.

The third time Two Twists spoke to the old man it was for a long time. We are not told in the accounts what words then passed between them, but when Two Twists returned to his own lodge his mind was made up. It would be war! A grand crusade would be organized against the Crows to avenge the two sons of Red Painted Robe. Two Twists made a vow that when the enemy was met, he would be first to open the fight whatever the risks. If the enemy be behind breastworks, then he alone would drive them out.[4]

Two Twists was pledging himself to the role of a suicide warrior, willing to sacrifice his life in order to bring defeat upon the foe. From this time on, Two Twists could take meat from anyone's kettle without fear of rebuttal. He could whip up the laggards when moving camp or on the war trail and was likely to be offered other men's wives as reward for his commitment.

Both Two Twists and Red Painted Robe belonged to the Shutaio-speaking Cheyenne band and the expedition now being planned was, from the outset, a Shutaio initiative. Thus High Backed Wolf, a renowned Shutaio war chief was elected as its leader. It was he who took up the war pipe and organized the whole affair. Throughout the coming weeks, High Backed Wolf carried the war pipe to each of the ten scattered Cheyenne and Shutaio bands, requesting the chiefs to smoke and, thereby, pledge themselves and their warriors to join the proposed crusade.

The head warriors and chiefs of the Hevietanio Cheyenne band were first to be contacted and first to accept the pipe, followed by those of the Omissis and the other eight bands in turn. High Backed Wolf then sought out the camps of several bands of Sioux and a number of Oglala puffed upon the stem. Some Brule Sioux also took it up and perhaps a few Miniconjou from the lower course of the Cheyenne River.

The fact that all Cheyenne and Shutaio band chiefs, along with some of their Sioux Allies, accepted the pipe and a very large number of warriors had pledged to join the venture, now set the whole nation buzzing with excitement. Striking a punitive blow against the Crows suddenly became the topic of prime importance. Indeed, such was the people's enthusiasm, that a man named Sun Getting out Of Bed, the keeper of *Issiwun,* the *"*Sacred Buffalo Hat*"* of the Shutaio, was also offered the pipe, which was the customary way of asking not only for the Hat Keeper's blessings, but that he himself join the proposed expedition and carry the Sacred Hat before the warriors to insure success. Without hesitation, Sun Getting Out Of Bed inhaled the symbolic smoke and so agreed to accompany the grand war party.[5]

During the actual battle, a distinguished warrior would wear the Buffalo Hat and it was he who would be one of the first among the allied host to ride out and meet the foe. At the same time he would not be expected to get too close to danger or act recklessly, lest he was killed or wounded and the sacred headpiece fall into the hands of the enemy. Two Twists asked the keeper if he might wear the Hat when he charged upon the Crows in fulfillment of his vow, but as he had publicly declared his intention to "throw away his life," his request was denied. It was the keeper's wife, the most holy woman among the Shutaio who refused him saying, "You will get the Hat all bloody and that would bring disaster upon our people." [6]

The honor, therefore, was bestowed upon another, a man named Whistling Elk, also a Shutaio, who some informants declare was one of the warriors who led the main allied charge against the Crows on this occasion.

Now among the Cheyennes, a man named Dog-Faced Medicine Man was keeper of that tribe's Sacred Arrow talismans. The Sacred Arrows supposedly had power to cure sickness and bring forth buffalo when needed. Moreover, they were considered a powerful war medicine which, when carried against the foe, were thought to guarantee success. These arrows signified the unity and common interests of the people and were, in effect, the embodiment of the nation representing everything that was Cheyenne both physically and in spirit. When carried in their sacred Kit fox skin bundle before the people, the power emanating from the arrows protected all behind—rendering the people invisible to their enemies. At the same time, their power blinded the enemy, toward whom the points of the arrow shafts would be directed. The Sacred Arrows were the most revered objects among the tribe.[8]

It was probably High Backed Wolf then, who again took the war pipe to the lodge of the Arrow Keeper in the Aorta Cheyenne band camp and offered him the stem. In response, Dog-Faced Medicine Man drew from it the four required puffs and so it was decided, that the nation's Sacred Arrows would also be moved against the Crows.

When the arrows were moved, the whole tribe, including the old men, women and children along with all their dogs and horses, were obliged to join the grand war party and go with the warriors into enemy country. This was to be the war party of war parties—unlike an expedition against the Shoshoni three years earlier when the outcome had proved indecisive. It was decreed by the chiefs that this time, there would be no turning back before the enemy was met and defeated.[9]

The Cheyennes were determined that on this occasion, the Crows would pay dearly for their scalp dances the previous winter.

But revenge was not the only objective. Recent loses by both the Cheyennes and Shutaio on the Crow front, had caused them to reappraise their situation in a more serious light. They came to the conclusion that it was time to achieve their long awaited ambition of wresting the Tongue and Powder River areas from the Crows, so the Cheyennes could take up permanent residence in that territory. The acquisition of these rich but disputed hunting grounds would allow the Cheyennes and Shutaio to expand. At the same time it would protect their independence somewhat, by relieving pressure exerted from the east by the ever increasing Teton Sioux population, which having already crowded into the Lower Cheyenne River district, were spilling over into the Black Hills. Both areas had long been held by Cheyenne-speaking peoples, their right of occupation recognized by all other tribes with whom they were in contact. Any one of a number of setbacks recently suffered by the Cheyennes and Shutaio at Crow hands, merely served to accelerate the advent of a full-scale Cheyenne invasion into Crow Country.

So it was in "the moon when buffalo are fat"—the beginning of June—each of the ten Cheyenne-speaking bands, along with a sizable contingent of Oglala Sioux under the leadership of chiefs. Standing Buffalo, Bull Bear and Old Smoke, assembled their lodges in two large encampments somewhere near the mouth of Cherry Creek. This is not far east from where stands *Novah`voas* (Bear Butte as it is known to the white man), the "Sacred Mountain" and symbolic centre of the Cheyenne Universe.

It was always a big occasion when the entire Cheyenne-speaking nation came together and especially so, when it was known that the powers of the people's most holy palladiums were to be invoked. Thus it was not until after a week or more of nonstop celebration and socializing, that the chiefs and head men decided it was time to take up the more important issues at hand; those of preparing their tribal medicines and themselves for the proposed great venture against the Crows.

Four days were required for the necessary rites pertaining to the Arrows and the Hat to be properly performed, in order to guarantee their full potency. From the moment the ceremonies began until the powers attending both objects had again been ritually harnessed, all revelry in the Cheyenne/Shutaio camps was forbidden. No war parties or hunters were allowed out, lest the spilling of blood by a Cheyenne soiled the Sacred Arrow flights and, in so doing, nullified their protective power.

Even young children were expected to exercise a degree of respectful silence during this four-day period. While the priests were conducting the actual rites of renewal, the adults were encouraged to pray for success in the coming venture. But when at last the Arrow ceremonies were completed, the head men of both the Cheyennes and Sioux instructed their camp heralds to announce the war chiefs` decision; that their entire host would start upon the war trail the following morning.

Accordingly, the very next day a few hours after sunrise, the womenfolk dismantled their lodges; packed the poles and tepee covers along with their domestic belongings on pony drags and a short time later, a long straggling column of people, dogs and horses was travelling the "red road" to war.

High Backed Wolf, the head war chief and real leader of the expedition, was riding in the van and it was he who carried the pipe.

Slowly the winding cavalcade moved west before pausing a while at *Novah `voas,* looming large and invocable, in order that the Cheyenne priests could make offerings to the Sacred Spirit Beings thought to reside at that place. Continuing west, the column skirted the northern edge of the Black Hills before turning northwest and continuing on, headed directly toward the course of the Lower Powder and the country of the Crows.

As it was, their journey over a comparatively short distance compared to the customary extent of tribal wandering, took at least two full weeks to accomplish before the grand host finally entered the country wherein Crow villages might be found. When finally the cavalcade reached a point along the Lower Powder, not far from its junction with the Yellowstone, the Allies set up their base camps—the Cheyennes and Shutaio on the west side of the river; the Sioux on the east side about one mile distant.

In a short while, hundreds of smoke-tanned, buffalo hide tepees had been erected on the open grasslands abutting both banks, each village in the shape of a giant horseshoe, their opening's facing east whence appeared the rising sun. Cooking pots were soon set to boil and the hustle and bustle of camp life commenced.

As twilight fell, the Crooked Lance warrior Two Twists suddenly appeared, mounted astride a fine running horse and bedecked in full regalia of eagle-feathered bonnet, hair fringed war shirt and leggings. He trotted his mount slowly into the centre of the Cheyenne-Shutaio camp circle, then rode around within the inner ring of tepees accompanied by a camp crier, who walking in front leading the warrior's horse, proclaimed aloud to the people in a high-pitched voice:

> "This is the last war trip of Two Twists. . . .From this path he has vowed never to return. He will throw away his life as a sacrifice to his society brothers, who now wait for him in the Spirit Land of our ancestors."[10]

In response to the crier's words, warriors shouted *"Ah ho, Ah ho"* (thank you, thank you), after which the crier continued:

> "Two Twists will give our people a chance to destroy the foe. . . He alone will clear the way for our brave men to charge and make the ground muddy with the blood of our Crow enemies." [11]

And the warriors responded again with shouts of *"Ah ho, Ah ho."*

As the fate of Two Twists continued to be heralded around the camp, the women gathered about him and sang their Strong Heart songs:

"Nothing lives long but the earth and mountains, only the rocks remain forever."[12] Some raised the tremolo in his honor.

Two Twists, in between singing Crooked Lance society songs, spoke to the people:

> "Look at this one who rides among you my brothers. . .Soon he will follow the sons of Red Painted Robe. His friends behold him, he shall not return from this raid."[13]

Many hearts were sad to hear him make his vow, yet at the same time, proud that he was going to bring honor and glory to his tribe. As a consequence, none would interfere or try to dissuade him from the self-destructive path he had chosen.

Late that night, after lodge fires had died down and a myriad of stars shone bright in the heavens, solitary chants and prayers peculiar to the Crooked Lance fraternity emanated from the tepee of Two Twists and wafted over the camp.

Perhaps in a dream or vision on a lonely hilltop, Two Twists had seen a mirror image of himself; scalped and bloody—slain by the Crows. Whether it was to materialize or not, in his Cheyenne mind it was to happen as sure as the grass and leaves would grow again in spring. Thus he had prepared himself to die, but in a way considered honorable among his people; in battle, shunning danger and not looking back.

The next morning, Two Twists and the camp crier both circled the inner ring of lodges for a second time and again the crier informed the people of their champion's chosen fate. As before, the womenfolk sang their Strong Heart songs; raised the tremolo and this time gave him eagle feathers. These were partly a token of respect, but also to imbibe in him the spirit of the eagle, being the fiercest and strongest of birds. The women fixed them to his war bonnet and tied them into his horse's mane and tail as a symbol of his strength.[14]

Come midday, the throb of war drums reverberated within the allied camps and echoed across the surrounding countryside, enjoined with the singing, stomping of feet and wild whooping of the warriors which endured through the ensuing night until the coming dawn. Up and coming warriors, fully armed and garishly painted, but with few or no battle honors to boast of, constantly paraded around the tepees, some on horseback others on foot, proclaiming how brave they would be in the coming fight and of how many heads (scalps) they would take. At the same time, veterans of many a war trail busied themselves in fixing up their war clothes and medicine amulets; straightening arrows and grinding new edges on lance points and battle axes, all in readiness for the great conflict to come.

And while such revelry and other diversions were going on, in a quieter part of the Cheyenne village, gathered under the awnings of a great lodge fashioned from the skins of two large tepees, High Backed Wolf and the headmen of all those present, were holding a council of war and discussing their plan of attack.

The great Allied gathering was now encamped on the very edge of Crow Country, although the precise location of the enemy and their number, the Allies did not know. However, having already dismissed the idea of surprising the Crows, the advantage of striking the initial blow was obvious to all. The first thing the chiefs decided, therefore, was to send out a party of scouts to locate the Crow village, in order to assess its size and find the best route leading to it.

PRELUDE TO DISASTER

Even before the Allies set up their tepees along both banks of the Powder, the Crows, then in camp along the Tongue not far to the west, must have known of their coming. But they could not have known then if their enemies were coming merely to hunt or with hostile intent. The presence of women and children among the Allies would usually have signaled peaceful motives, as very seldom did Indians put their families at risk by including non combatants as part of an invading force. Even so, if the Crows were resolved to stay their ground, then they too should be preparing for a big fight.

It is likely the Crows deemed themselves at least an adequate match to confront the encroaching Allied force, perhaps even superior both in number and in valor. If not, they would have dispersed into the uncompromising interior of their tribal domain where their enemies might not find them. Or they could have positioned themselves in some strategic location for defense where their foes would have less an advantage.

But the Crows did not disperse. Rather they organized their warriors to take the offensive against the invaders.

The village in question belonged to the Mountain Crow, the largest division of the Absaroka nation, comprising at this date about 650 lodges. Only a few days earlier, the whole division had been together holding its annual religious ceremonies. But the great camp since had split into at least three separate bands, each of which had gone off in a different direction to conduct their midsummer hunts. As a consequence, this village on the Tongue—being that nearest the Allies—was reduced to around 200 lodges, which included members from each of the thirteen Crow clans and contained a population of about 1,600 persons, with some 500 males of fighting age.[15]

This was the band led by the Chief Long Hair, who although having been recognized as a fearless and successful warrior in his younger days, now held the position of paramount civil chief of the nation. He was accredited with possessing omnipotent mystic powers, made manifest by his luxuriant growth of hair which trailed on the ground behind him as he walked. Thus, even though around sixty years of age, his people still regarded him as a holy man and shaman of the highest repute in whom they had complete confidence.

Long Hair was a man of much ability with a commanding presence among his peers. Certainly, he was still capable of organizing his followers into a cohesive body during times of defensive or offensive necessity. Not surprisingly then, it was Long Hair who took charge of the situation now that his people were threatened. He wasted no time in taking, what he considered, was appropriate responsive action.

Being aware of the presence of a large enemy force within striking distance of the village, Long Hair called together his subordinate chiefs and head warriors and held his own council of war.

Among this illustrious gathering were included several famous Crow fighting men such as Plays With His Face, High Bull, He-Who-Ties-His-Hair-Before, Wolf's Paunch (Wolf Belly), Sits In The Pine, Mad Bull, Double Face, Wooden Bowl (Big Bowl), Dog That Eats (Eats With Dog), War Eagle Man, The Rain (Big Rain) and an up and coming sub-chief named Alapooish or Sore Belly. Sore Belly was fast earning a reputation as a cunning and fearless war chief possessing a natural ability which, in due time, would cause him to become a great leader among his people.[16]

The council was held in Chief Long Hair's lodge. It was the largest tepee; it is said, ever seen among the Crows. Its upper half was painted red; the lower half adorned with alternating red and white stripes two feet wide, running vertically from a midway point to the ground. Two poles supporting the smoke flaps were also painted red, except for their upper parts touching the smoke flaps themselves and at the foot of each pole, was a small pile of sweet grass. The outside cover of the lodge was scented with beaver bait, while the inside lining was perfumed with some other sweet-smelling plant, its species now forgotten.[17]

Prior to the council's deliberations, Long Hair performed his sacred medicine rites to appease the unseen powers and bestow

Sketch by the Author after a painting from life by George Catlin.
Cheyenne War Chief High-Backed Wolf.

benevolence upon his people. With dirt collected from a mole hill, he made a circle on the ground, after which he placed in the center of the circle a quantity of dried buffalo chips and set them alight. He next took his pipe from a porcupine-quilled, deer skin bag; filled its bowl with a mixture of powdered red willow bark and tobacco and while holding the stem with both hands'the mouthpiece to his lips, moved the bowl in a circular motion over the flames. After mumbling a few incoherent phrases, he lit the bowl with a smoldering buffalo chip and drew several puffs from the stem.[18]

Having completed this procedure, Long Hair told those gathered to send out scouts in a specific direction and at a certain place, which he then described, they would find the enemy camps. His personal medicine helpers Bear Spirit and Morning Star, he said, had told him this and had cast a spell upon the invaders which would prevent them moving away, until that is, the scouts had gathered whatever intelligence they wished to obtain.[19]

This was the first of several peculiar happenings attending the affair. At the same time as the Cheyenne and Sioux chiefs were directing their scouts to go out and locate the whereabouts of the Crows, the Crows were dispatching their scouts to reconnoiter the camps of the Allies.[20]

That same afternoon, ten Crow scouts, their leader wearing the customary wolf skin covering his head and shoulders to signify his office, left the Crow village on the Tongue, and headed east toward the faint sound of beating war drums.

It was just before dusk when these Crow scouts stumbled upon the Cheyenne and Sioux encampments on both sides of the Powder. The size of the Allied force must have taken the scouts back in awe, for here was one of the largest war camps they had ever seen, perhaps

700 lodges; while the surrounding area itself was swarming with both people and horses.

Quickly, the Crows concealed themselves and their ponies in the bed of a dry wash and waited patiently for darkness, when they intended to reconnoiter the camps more closely.

When at last night fell and they thought it safe to move, the scouts rode up out of the wash and trotted their ponies leisurely across an open stretch of land separating the two camps, but on the Cheyenne side of the river.

Unfortunately, a Cheyenne on horseback crossing from one camp to the other suddenly came face to face with the scouts, who were left with no choice but to try and shoot him before he could give the alarm that enemies were about.

In their haste the Crows shot at him with arrows and short-barreled muskets, but their aim was wild and the lone Cheyenne raced back to camp shouting aloud his discovery.

At the time of the encounter with the Crow scouts, many camp occupants were still dancing and singing in anticipation of the great conflict to come and few others had retired for the night. They heard the Crow musket shots and all at once, there was uproar in the camp.

Being in enemy country, most Cheyenne warriors had war ponies picketed close by their lodges, so in the event of danger, they could mount quickly and be ready to defend themselves and their families. Even as their comrade came galloping into their midst, scores of Cheyenne braves were already grabbing weapons; mounting their ponies and minutes later, were on the scene, searching the area for intruders.

For a while the moon was hidden behind the clouds and it was too dark to see anything clearly. But the sound of quirts striking on the backs of ponies indicated to the Cheyennes that they were near their quarry. They rode hard in the direction whence came the whipping sounds and soon overtook two of the enemy, who being on slow horses, were lashing their animals on both flanks in a frantic effort to escape. The Cheyennes soon caught up with these men and promptly killed them both, at which point, the moon suddenly reappeared, shedding its light on the scene and the slain intruders were immediately recognized as Crows.[21]

The Cheyennes were elated. Not only had they drawn first blood from the enemy, but it showed, they thought, that the powers attributed to the Sacred Arrows and the Hat were indeed with them. The two long haired scalps were waved aloft as the warriors galloped back to camp and raced their horses around the inner circle of lodges, whooping loudly. It was a good omen for the expedition's success and as such, it lifted the people's confidence even higher. The whole gathering was now more eager than before to come to grips with the foe, satisfied that their holy palladiums were proving their worth.

The Cheyennes knew, however, that there had been more Crows in the vicinity than the two they had killed. They had not yet sent out their own scouts, but could be certain that when the Crow fugitives got back to their village, they would make it known where the Allied camps were located. High Backed Wolf called all the headmen of the Cheyennes and Shutaio along with those of his Sioux Allies together, for a second council of war.

It was unanimously agreed the Allies should attack the Crow village as soon as possible, before the Crows had time to react to their own scout's report and take evasive action.

Camp criers relayed the chiefs' decision around the lodges and the fighting men began preparing for battle.

It was still a few hours before midnight when the great Allied war party, numbering at least 1,000 warriors—all befeathered and painted and mounted on wiry ponies decorated in a similar manner—started from their two camps along the Powder in search of the Crow village.

The war party headed west in the direction they supposed the fleeing Crow scouts had taken. They hoped to pick up a proper trail at dawn.

Most of the Allied non combatants remained behind in the camps, although a sizable number including women, teenage boys and middle-aged men did follow some distance in the rear, intending to watch the conflict from some nearby vantage point, wherefrom, they could shout encouragement to their warriors. This Allied war party was unusual because of the inclusion of a small number of Shutaio and Cheyenne women who rode alongside the fighting men, determined to join in the fight .[22] For the most part, these were the wives and female relatives of the thirty or more Crooked Lance warriors killed the previous summer. One among them was White Buffalo Woman, the wife of Red Painted Robe. She had publicly vowed to avenge her two sons.

Over one shoulder she carried an enormous gnarled wooden club with which she intended to either kill or maim at least one of her enemies, if she could get close enough to do so. [23]

Meanwhile, the surviving Crow scouts came loping into their village on their exhausted mounts. A small pile of dried buffalo chips was hastily erected in the centre of the camp and the leader of scouts had first to kick over the pile before reporting to the chiefs. Such an act was tantamount to making a vow that what he was about to relate would be the truth. Thus, after complying with custom, the scout leader burst out the news of the ill-fated brush with the Cheyennes. He also described the great size of the Allied camps, along with added intelligence that the number of ponies belonging to the enemy scattered along both banks of the Powder, could be counted in their thousands. The Crow chiefs were alarmed. Like the Cheyennes, they held a council of war. [24]

The Crows could still not have known for sure if the Cheyennes and Sioux had come into the country specifically to fight or to hunt. Nevertheless, so the Crow chiefs reasoned, both the Sioux and Cheyennes were their mortal foes and the chance of enemy raiders sallying forth to harass Crow camps from a base so near was a threat not to be taken lightly.

Chief Long Hair dispatched runners to take word of the Allied presence to the other Crow camps, with an urgent request to organize large war parties and join the warriors of Long Hair's village, whereupon, they could attack the foe together. Then, as an afterthought, thinking that the Allied force would even then be preparing to march against them, Long Hair`s advisers decided not to await the arrival of their kinsmen, but to move the village over to Otter Creek and at the same time, send out their own force without delay to attack the Allied camps before the enemy could start.

All eight Crow warrior societies were eager to be first to get to grips with the foe. Eight separate war bands were formed under their chosen Pipe Holders and these set off in their respective groups, independent of one another, though all travelling in the same general direction. The largest band was the Half–Shaved Heads Society led by War Chief Sore Belly. He, perhaps more than any other, was confident of achieving a great victory over his people's enemies. Long Hair on the other hand, had advised caution and even berated the departing warriors for not leaving behind an adequate force to protect the camp, lest it be attacked while they were away. But his warnings, as usual, fell on deaf ears and the several war bands were soon lost from view in the blackness of the night.[25]

This then was the second of several unusual events. For at the same time as the Cheyennes and Sioux host was striking out in the dark in order to attack the Crow village, the Crow force, now comprising almost all the fighting men of the Mountain Crow division—perhaps some 1,000 warriors—had likewise set off to attack the Allied camps along the Powder.

It was intended that a number of formidable Crow war parties would assault the Allied camps from different directions; if that is, their forces did not succeed in uniting before reaching their objective. Either way, by so doing the Crows might gain the advantage of surprise. Their plan was to kill as many of their enemies as possible, capture a large number of women and children along with the horses and drive the rest of the invaders back across the Powder, expelling them from Crow country once and for all.

In the opposing camps, only women, children and old men, along with one or two of their civil chiefs, were left behind to defend the tepees if the camps themselves were attacked. But, ironically, neither side imagined that their own villages were under immediate threat. Each was certain that their respective war parties could successfully deal with any eventuality.

It is reasonable to suppose that the Crows still deemed themselves superior, as it would have been rare for any Indian war party to deliberately engage an enemy force, especially in an open fight, if it did not think it had the advantage on its side. This was particularly true in the case of intertribal warfare. If the Crows had not thought themselves greater in number, they would have removed their villages from the district as rapidly as possible. They probably would have sought the protection of other Crow bands (such as the River Crows between the Yellowstone and Musselshell to the north) or located themselves in a strong defensive position. During either event, hit-and-run tactics would have been employed to retard their enemy's progress while the Crow camps were in flight, or to disrupt their enemy's organization and thereby, hopefully, prevent a full-scale confrontation in the first place.

The reality was the populations of the various Plains tribes could not stand heavy losses. As a consequence, Indians often acted through expediency, this being what they themselves considered the better part of valor. (Their white American adversaries of a later date, often mistakenly construed such actions on the part of the Indian as a sign of cowardice). This time, however, other than relocating the camp on Otter Creek a short distance from the Tongue, no such evasive action was even contemplated by the Crows, which leads one to suspect that the latter were more than confident of dealing with the current situation successfully.

It was not long after the several Crow war parties had started out from their village, that a young Crow warrior named Red Owl came into the relocated camp. Learning of the departure of the war parties, he at once took up his bow and arrows, mounted his war pony and rode off into the night to catch up with the warriors. He was obliged to ride slowly as he tried to figure out the trail made by his kinsmen, with only a pale moon to give him light.

At this time a young Shutaio named Whistling Elk was out scouting far ahead of the Allied force. This man, although only twenty-one years of age, was already an experienced warrior. He carried a shield painted with a sacred design which he had personally obtained in a vision and this gave him protection not only during daylight hours (as was the case with most other shields) but also at night. Whenever he carried the shield into battle, he always wore a buckskin war shirt and used as his specific weapon, a stone-headed war club with a long elk horn handle. [26]

Whistling Elk saw the lone Crow riding slowly along looking hard at the ground. According to the Cheyenne account, the Crow could not see very well in the dark, but Whistling Elk had the sacred design on his shield to help him.

Once or twice the Crow raised his head and looked around him, but he did not see the Cheyenne who lay quiet, secreted among the bushes along the path the Crow was travelling. For some reason Red Owl dismounted from his horse, probably to inspect the trail more closely and it was then that Whistling Elk charged upon him. Before the Crow could reach for his bow and arrows carried in a quiver slung across his back, the Cheyenne had knocked him twice on the head with his war club. Red Owl fell to the ground and was lying quite still, apparently dead, so Whistling Elk took the Crow's weapons and horse and rode off back to the Allied war party to report what he had done.[27]

When the Allies heard of Whistling Elk`s deed they were in high spirits, thinking that yet another of the enemy had been killed and supposing that the man was likely a scout from the Crow village, they thought their own passage toward it would now go undetected and they might indeed, take it by surprise.

As it transpired, the lone Crow that Whistling Elk had attacked was only stunned. After his assailant rode off, Red Owl soon regained consciousness, whereupon, he headed straight back to the village he had recently left.

Another Crow version of the affair, as told by Little Face to Lieutenant James H. Bradley in 1876, is that Red Owl had been attacked by three Sioux out scouting ahead of the Allied force. They had tried desperately to kill him but bungled the job and Red Owl, by his personal bravery and agility, had managed to get away, although instead of returning directly from whence he came, he caught up with one of the Crow parties (which, according to Little Face, Red Owl was the Pipe Holder) and that he and this group of warriors then returned to the Crow village together. [28]

Whatever the case, the Cheyenne warrior Whistling Elk had neglected to carry out the customary procedure which, among all Indians, would have been to scalp the man, or to inflict some other form of mutilation upon the body, such as cutting the victim's throat as an assurance that he was dead. On this occasion, Red Owl had been spared such attention, a mistake that could have changed the whole outcome of the battle. For even as Red Owl was returning to his village, he could hear the sound of many horses—like the rumbling noise of buffalo on the move—and he knew there must be a very large enemy war party nearby, heading in the same direction he was going. With such intelligence, the Crows could have prepared themselves and their village properly and deployed their own warriors in a favorable position to ambush those of the Allies, while the latter were strung out on the march.[29]

But this was not to be.

It was shortly past midnight when Red Owl came running, almost breathless into the Mountain Crow village on Otter Creek. All the warriors having gone in search of the Allied camps, leaving only the old men, women and children. Red Owl was still bleeding profusely from the head where he had been hit with the Cheyenne's war club. He told the camp occupants that he had been set upon by a number of enemy warriors, who had counted coup upon him and stolen his weapons and his horse. He also told of the many horses he had heard coming towards the village and advised the people to flee at once because they were in imminent danger.

Now it happened that Red Owl had only recently stolen another man's wife and had eloped with her in order to escape the husband's wrath. This was the reason he had been absent from the village when the Crow war parties departed. Because of this, Long Hair and most of the people were not convinced by his story. Knowing of Red Owl's adultery, they agreed among themselves that the man whose wife he had stolen had come across him in the dark and beat him about the head with a pony quirt, as indeed, would not have been uncommon in such instances among the Crows.

Surely, the people said, if the enemy had in truth attacked Red Owl, they would have killed him and taken his scalp. Besides, if there were any Cheyennes or Sioux nearby, then their own Crow war parties would have found them.[30]

The people in the Crow village decided to remain where they were. But just in case there was an element of truth in Red Owl's words, Chief Long Hair commanded that a barricade of logs and brush be placed around the camp. This was duly done, though in a haphazard manner and of a somewhat flimsy nature as a half-hearted precaution against attack.

Red Owl did not bother to argue. Instead, he went immediately to the lodges of his friends and kinfolk who were his clan relatives and told them to quickly get their most prized possessions together and move away as soon as possible, for the whole village was doomed to disaster.

Altogether about fifty families were persuaded to leave the camp. They left their lodges standing, abandoning everything which was too heavy to carry or deemed of little value. They mounted their ponies and leading pack horses behind them, went out into the night with Red Owl to seek a place of safety in the hills.[31]

In the meantime, the Allied war party was making good progress and drawing ever closer to its objective, even though their actual route of travel was slightly off course from the exact location of the Crow village. At the same time, the Crow forces had lost their bearings completely and seemed to be heading away from the Allied camps rather than toward them.

It was now but a few hours before dawn and the third event in a series of peculiarities attending the affair, was about to unfold.

The two great war bands, one composed of several parties of Crows, the other of Allied Cheyennes and Sioux, were travelling in opposite directions and actually passed one another. Only many years later, when the Crows discussed the affair with the Cheyennes and Sioux and compared the routes of their respective groups, did they realize how close they had come to bumping into each other in the dark.

By a stroke of providence on the part of the Allies, the Crow forces missed the Allied camps altogether, although the latter by then may have moved to a different location from where the first body of Crow scouts originally saw them. The Allied war party did find the Crow village, but had some difficulty doing so and the sun was already up before the Crow tepees along Otter Creek were sighted.

This was the same Crow village of Long Hair, the occupants of which, owing to activities in camp the night before, were still curled up on their pallets deep in slumber.

The Cheyennes and Sioux quietly positioned themselves in a long concave line, obscured by a thick growth of timber on the edge of an open space which surrounded the Crow camp. They got ready to conduct the last part of their Sacred Arrow rites, deemed necessary to guarantee full potency before the warriors actually engaged the foe.

Before they could do so, however, there suddenly appeared on the far side of the village, a procession of Crow women and children along with a few old and middle-aged men, coming leisurely towards the tepees: some on horseback, others on foot leading pack horses, but all oblivious to the presence of their enemies. These were, in fact, some of those people who had gone out with Red Owl during the night and now thought it safe to return.

Apparently, Red Owl and his followers had not gone far into the hills when they started quarrelling among themselves. Several complained that it was too cold to stay out and when the sun came up and they could hear no sound of battle, they decided perhaps Red Owl had been lying after all and nothing was going to happen to the village. As a result, about half these people—some twenty-five families—had left their more cautious companions and started back towards the camp.

The Cheyennes and Sioux saw them coming and remaining hidden from view, allowed them to enter the village before making their presence known.

A young Crow girl then about ten years of age, who was taken captive that day by the Cheyennes and later known by the name of White Haired Killer, was a member of this Crow party returning from the hills. She always said that they had no sooner got back to the village and were untying their horses, when the Cheyennes suddenly charged, taking them completely by surprise.

According to another Cheyenne version, the Allies had just arrived on the scene, virtually at the same time as the returning non combatants were approaching the other side of the open ground which surrounded the Crow camp. The sun had been up some short while, but there seemed to be no activity within the camp itself. The Cheyennes also said they had been surprised that no Crow warriors came out to meet them.[32]

Usually, the opposing forces in any large-scale encounter would line up facing each other across a kind of no-man's land between the two. The respective champions would then battle it out in a series of one-on-one contests. Perhaps one side or the other would make a half-hearted charge. This would be the order of conflict until the light began to fade or, until the attacking force considered itself to have made a sufficiently good show and retired from the field. Casualties usually were light, resulting, perhaps, in one or two warriors being killed on each side along with several wounded. The main goal was for the participants to make a satisfactory show of valor.

On this occasion, however, there appeared to be no opposition to the Allied force. Consequently, the Allied host watched and waited in silence, until the last of the returning Crows of Red Owl's people had entered the sleeping village and began unloading the packs from their horses. It was then that the Allies suddenly raised their war cries and in a long colorful line, all at once charged out from the timber and into the open, almost completely surrounding the camp.

The Allied warriors reined up about 100 yards short of the outer perimeter of lodges and thus positioned, in many tight mounted groups, faced the enemy on three sides.

NOTES AND SOURCES.

1 Joe Medicine Crow to Author. Lodge Grass, Montana. August 1996. Note pad 1. pp.4-6.
2 Llewellyn, Karl N. and Hoebel, E. Adamson. *The Cheyenne Way.* pp. 3-6. University of Oklahoma Press, 1967. Also, Bill Tall Bull [Northern Cheyenne informant] to Author, Ashland, Montana. Sep;1994. Note pad 1. pp.7-8.
3 Bill Tall-Bull to Author. September. 1994, Ashland, Montana. Note pad 1. pp.7-8.
4 Llewellyn, Karl N. and Hoebel, E. Adamson, *The Cheyenne Way.* pp.3-6.University of Oklahoma Press, 1967. See also, Bill Tall Bull [Northern Cheyenne informant] to Author, Ashland, Montana, Sep;1994.Note pad 1. pp.7-8.
5 Bill Tall-Bull to Author. September. 1994, Ashland, Montana. Note pad 1. pp.7-8.
6 Llewellyn, Karl N. and Hoebel, E. Adamson, *The Cheyenne Way.* pp.3-6.University of Oklahoma Press, 1967. Also, Bill Tall Bull [Northern Cheyenne informant] to Author, Ashland, Montana, Sep; 1994. Note pad 1. pp. 7-8.
7 Bill Tall-Bull [Northern Cheyenne informant] to Author, Ashland, Montana, Sep; 1994. Note pad 1. pp. 7-8.
8 Bill Tall Bull [Northern Cheyenne informant] to Author, Ashland, Montana, Sep;1994.Note pad 1. pp. 7-8. See also; Hoebel, E. Adamson. *The Cheyenne; Indians of the Great Plains.* pp.7 ff. Holt, Rinehart and Winston Inc. 1960.
9 Bill Tall-Bull [Northern Cheyenne informant] to Author, Ashland, Montana, Sep; 1994. Note pad 1. pp. 7-8.
10 Bill Tall-Bull to Author, "Loc; cit." 1994.Note pad 1. pp.7-8.
11 Bill Tall-Bull [Northern Cheyenne informant] to Author, Ashland, Montana, Sep;1994. Note pad 1. pp. 7-8.
12 Llewellyn, Karl N and Hoebel, E. Adamson. *"The Cheyenne Way."* pp. 3-6. University of Oklahoma Press 1967.
13 Bill Tall-Bull to Author, "Loc; cit." 1994. Note pad 1.pp.7-8.
14 Llewellyn, Karl N and Hoebel, E. Adamson. *"The Cheyenne Way."* pp. 3-6. University of Oklahoma Press 1967.
15 Bradley, James H. *The Bradley Manuscripts.* Book 4. pp.238ff. Montana Historical Society Collections. 1877.
16 Joe Medicine Crow to Author. Lodge Grass, Montana. August. 1994. Note pad 1. pp.6-7. See also; Kappler, Charles.J. *"Indian Laws, Affairs And Treaties." "1825."* pp. 231-236. [Signers of treaty between Crow Indians and the United States in 1825, commonly known as "The Friendship Treaty" or "The Atkinson and O`Fallon Treaty"]. Government Printing Office.Washington DC. [various publications]. See also; Anderson, William Marshall. *"The Rocky Mountain Journals."* pp.99-100. University of Nebraska Press, 1987. Here, Anderson lists the seventeen council chiefs of the Crow nation for the period 1834. Many of those listed would have been Headmen in 1820.
17 Winona Plenty-Hoops to Author. Lodge Grass, Montana, August 1994. Note pad 1. pp.5-6. See also, Joe Medicine-Crow to Author, Lodge Grass, Montana, August, 1996.Note pad 1. pp.6-7.
18 Winona Plenty-Hoops to Author. Lodge Grass, Montana, August 1994. Note pad 1. pp.5-6.
19 Joe Medicine Crow to Author. Lodge Grass, Montana. August. 1994. Note pad 1. pp.6-7.
20 Grinnell, George Bird, *The Fighting Cheyennes,* pp. 25-34. University of Oklahoma Press, 1956. See also; George Bird Grinnell Manuscript Collection (MS. 5). Folder 494 *Early Crow Battles.* Southwest Museum, Los Angeles, California. See also, George Bent letters to George B. Grinnell. June.1905. Letter 26. Southwest Museum, Los Angeles, California.
21 Grinnell, George Bird, *The Fighting Cheyennes,* pp. 25-34. University of Oklahoma Press, 1956. See also; George Bird Grinnell Manuscript Collection (MS. 5). Folder 494 *"Early Crow Battles."* Southwest Museum, Los Angeles, California.
22 Llewellyn, Karl N and Hoebel, E. Adamson. *The Cheyenne Way.* pp. 3-6. University of Oklahoma Press 1967.
23 Llewellyn and Hoebel. 1967. "Loc; cit." pp.3-6.
24 Joe Medicine-Crow to Author. "Loc cit." Note pad 1. pp. 5-6.
25 Grinnell, George Bird, *The Fighting Cheyennes,* pp. 25-34. University of Oklahoma Press, 1956. See also; George Bird Grinnell Manuscript Collection (MS. 5). Folder 494 *"Early Crow Battles."* Southwest Museum, Los Angeles, California.
26 "Ibid."
27 Grinnell, George Bird, *The Fighting Cheyennes,* pp. 25-34. University of Oklahoma Press, 1956. See also; George Bird Grinnell Manuscript Collection (MS. 5). Folder 494 *"Early Crow Battles."*

Southwest Museum, Los Angeles, California.

28 Bradley, James H. *The Bradley Manuscripts. Book four.* pp. 238 ff. Montana Historical Society Collections. 1877.

29 Grinnell, George Bird, *The Fighting Cheyennes,* pp. 25-34. University of Oklahoma Press, 1956. See also; Joe Medicine-Crow to Author. "Loc cit." Note pad 1. pp.5-6.

30 Joe Medicine-Crow to Author. "Loc cit." Note pad 1. pp.5-6.

31 "Ibid." Note pad 1. pp.5-6.

32 Grinnell, George Bird, Manuscript Collection (MS, 5). Folder 491 *"Early Crow Battles."* And; *No. 28. "Cheyenne and Crow Warfare."* Southwest Museum, Los Angeles, California. See also, George Bent to George B. Grinnell. June.1905. Letter 26. Southwest Museum; Braun Library; Grinnell Collection.

Chapter Three

The Destruction of Long Hair's Village

Of the important men among the Allied ranks that day was a Shutiao warrior named Ice. (the grandfather of White Bull born 1834). He belonged to the Contrary Society, whose members were apt to do things backwards and had pledged themselves never to retreat in battle even if it meant certain death. This man was positioned on his war pony a little in front of the Allied line, conspicuous by the stuffed skin of a prairie dog owl tied to his forehead and the red paint of his society order covering his entire body which was naked, but for breech clout and moccasins made from the remnants of old lodge skins. In his left hand Ice held, now stripped of its wolf skin covering, a holy "Thunder Bow Lance;" embodying the spirit power of thunder itself. When the time came for the Allies to charge, it would be he who gave the signal to do so, by passing the lance behind his neck from left hand to the right.[1]

For a while, Ice and a large number among the Allies sat astride their painted ponies as they brandished weapons in the air and sang aloud their war songs. Others beat on bull hide shields with pony quirts and raised a high pitched trill on eagle bone war whistles; in all creating a terrifying din.

This sudden commotion aroused the camp, bringing the occupants running from their lodges, and the sight which met their eyes threw many into a state of panic. Some stood for an instant, gazing at the enemy host around them. Others probably cursed themselves for not heeding the adulterer's words.

The Crow Chief Long Hair assisted by some of the old men, tried to calm the people and restore order within the camp. They did manage to get the people in a defensive frame of mind and the flimsy barricade of logs and brush erected during the night was hastily re-enforced, and the gaps between the tepees filled with camp baggage and anything else the occupants could lay their hands on. All those who could use a weapon now took up positions facing the enemy, ready to defend themselves against the expected onslaught. Mothers with small children in their arms prepared to make their escape, if chance allowed, into the surrounding countryside.

After a while the Sacred Arrow Priest of the Cheyennes, Dog-Faced Medicine Man, dismounted from his steed and stepping out alone in front of a part of the Allied line, stood facing the enemy camp. The Cheyenne and Shutaio warriors arrayed several ranks deep behind him, all at once ceased their chanting and whooping.

Holding the Sacred Arrows wrapped in their kit fox skin in one hand at the end of an outstretched arm, Dog-Faced Medicine Man began humming a sacred song and every now and then, spat juice from a sacred plant he was chewing. He then took one of the holy "Man" or "War" arrows from the bundle and held it horizontally before him, its flint headed point directed at the foe. At the same time he raised his left foot and danced a few steps on one leg. As he danced and sang, he repeatedly stamped his raised foot on the ground and each time he did so, all the onlooking warriors shouted their war cries in unison, while with their own weapons of lances, bows and war clubs, they made threatening gestures and stabbing motions at the enemy in front.

While this was going on, the Cheyenne and Shutaio women positioned among the fighting ranks, along with all those females who had come merely to watch the conflict from a distance, turned their backs to the priest and the Sacred Arrows, for if any female looked upon these, the most holy of tribal talismans, then the power transmitted through them would become nullified and lost.[2]

Twice the Arrow Priest performed his ritual—one time each for the two sacred War Arrows in his care. Then he returned them to their skin bundle. He next tied the bundle to the war lance of a young Cheyenne medicine man, whose duty it would be to carry the talismans against the enemy at the head of the Allied charge.

Now the enemy, having supposedly been blinded by the power of the arrows, would not be able to shoot their missiles straight, while the Cheyennes by the same power, had been rendered invisible and, as a consequence, could not be harmed by the enemy or their weapons.

While this ritual was being performed, a young brave, the same Whistling Elk who had knocked the Crow Red Owl unconscious the night before, donned the Sacred Buffalo Hat of the Shutaio and with attendant ceremony, tied its buckskin thong under his chin to secure it. He would lead the Shutaio wing into battle.

At the same time, other war medicines were being taken from their covers and made ready for use. One of the more important of these among the Cheyennes was a special shield, decorated with a profusion of enemy hair attached to its outer rim and thus, commonly known as the "Scalp Shield." Its more proper name was the "Turner" which describes specifically the attributes of the shield. Its power was closely associated with that of the Sacred Arrows, having the supposed ability to cure sickness and also, to protect the warriors when in battle. But unlike the Arrows which had power to blind the foe, that of the shield actually turned the enemy's missiles away as they sped toward the charging warriors. He who carried this shield into a fight held it in his right hand, holding it by a leather strap affixed to the top of the rim and as he rode toward the enemy, he would swing it in a peculiar fashion, left to right, from one side of his horse to the other, as if fending off invisible missiles on either hand.[3] Some tribal informants declared, that this shield had been given to the Cheyennes at the same time as came the Sacred Arrows among them and by the same person Sweet Medicine, many generations earlier. Certainly, the shield was very old and was carried in nearly every major battle in which the Cheyennes were involved. It still resides among the Northern Cheyennes today and is held in high esteem as a holy talisman, connected to the Arrows and the Hat.

Each of four *Hohk`tsims* or "Wheel Lances" made by a famous Shutaio holy man named Blind Bull, and which were also related to the Sacred Arrows, were having their powers invoked at this time. Their respective owners were holding them aloft, the buckskin mesh of each wheel facing toward the enemy, while prayers were offered up to the respective spirit guardian (thought to be ensnared in the mesh of each wheel] in order to receive the ensnared spirit's favor and protection during the coming conflict.[4]

The Crows, meanwhile, braced themselves behind their makeshift breastworks as they watched these strange maneuvers being conducted by the Allies. They guessed that the latter were making strong medicine against them, while they could make no comparable medicine to counter that of the enemy. They knew they must surely be defeated.

At last, after the preliminaries were completed, High Backed Wolf, the Cheyenne-Shutaio war chief, decided it was time to open the fight.

The young medicine man who now carried the Sacred Arrow bundle tied to his lance, took a position in front of the Cheyenne line, while the wearer of the Sacred Buffalo Hat placed himself at the head of the Shutaio.

After chanting a few war songs and sacred incantations, these two men bearing about their persons the revered tribal palladiums, suddenly raised their war cries together and urging their ponies into a gallop, began riding at oblique angles toward each other from their respective ranks, and as they raced across the open ground their paths crossed diagonally. After which, they circled the Crow camp and passed each other for a second time as they wheeled their ponies around and returned to their own lines, having made a pattern in the shape of a double loop.[5]

On another occasion, when the riders passed each other for the second time, it would have been the moment for the Contrary warrior to give the signal with his Thunder Bow to attack. But this time, as the bearers of the tribal talismans returned at a run to the waiting Allies, Ice, the Contrary, continued to sit motionless upon his steed, still holding the Thunder Bow in his left hand. In this instance, his uncustomary behavior was deliberate in order to allow Two Twists, the Allies` champion, the opportunity to fulfill his vow, which was to ride alone into the enemy camp and clear the way for the Allied warriors who would follow in his wake.

And so as soon as the bearers of the Arrows and the Hat completed their run back to the Allied lines, Two Twists nosed his mount slowly forward to the front of his waiting warriors.

Having gone but a few yards, he reined up, erect in the saddle, in full view of his own people and the Crows. His body was stripped to the waist; his face, arms and chest daubed with bright ochres of red, green and yellow. Two or three eagle feathers with strands of red horsehair flying from their tips were entwined in his raven hair, which, signifying his intention to fight to the death, was left unbraided to fall thick over his shoulders and down to his middle. Hanging from

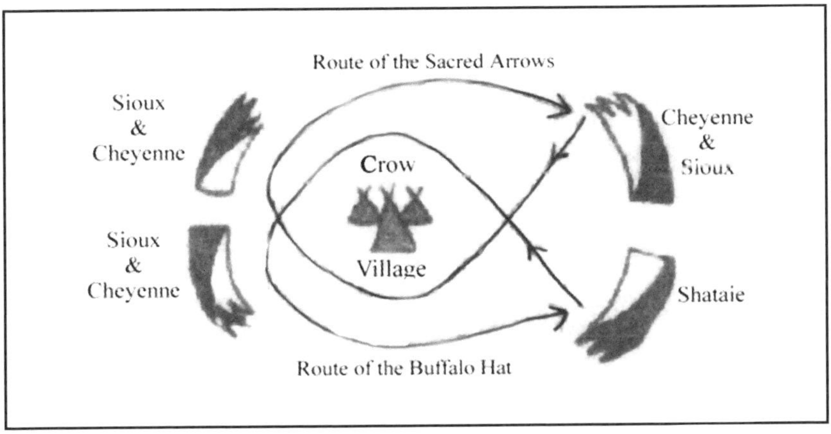

his left arm was his medicine shield, emblazoned with his personal protective totem along with pendent eagle feathers attached to its rim gently fluttering in the breeze. He held his reins in his left hand, while with his right, he gripped the hilt of a Spanish saber, its blade pointing to the ground. A bright red strip of strouding cloth sufficed for a breech clout, while covering his legs was a pair of deer hide leggings, decorated with beads and tufts of human hair in addition to black painted horizontal bars representing his many coups. On his feet he wore a pair of richly beaded moccasins with wolf tails trailing from the heels and these completed his savage attire. His war pony itself looked no less impressive, its face, withers and rump boldly splashed with sacred paint and withal, eagle feathers entwined in its mane and tail, the latter cut short and bobbed up, as was the custom when being ridden into battle.[6]

At length Two Twists raised his eyes to the blue Montana sky, dotted here and there with puffs of cotton-like cloud and sang a song to his dead companions of the Crooked Lance Society. He called to them saying, "Look over your shoulders my brothers, this one is coming behind you." [7]

For a lingering moment silence enveloped the scene, broken only by an occasional neigh from the horses who pawed the ground impatiently, as if eager to gallop into the fray. Then, slowly and deliberately, Two Twists raised his saber above his head. He let out a high pitched war cry, "Hok-A-Hey-Ho-Ho-nee," and kicking his heels into his pony's flanks, he started at a gallop—straight toward the breastworks.

On Two Twists went, his sword flashing in the morning sunlight as he whirled it above his head slicing the air about him. At the same time his moccasined feet drummed hard against his pony's belly, urging every ounce of speed from its flying hooves. The Cheyenne and Shutaio warriors and even their Sioux allies, burst forth a tremendous howl of delight to see their champion thundering forward who, with head raised toward the sky, sang loud his death song so that it rang out clear above the cheers of his people. As he neared the outer ring of tepees, a few Crow arrows and musket balls flew harmlessly past him, and the next instant he had leapt his pony over the breastworks and was in amongst a thick bunch of the enemy, slashing ferociously and blindly with his saber, causing grievous wounds wherever it struck. After slicing off a Crow head with one lustful swipe, he jabbed his mount with the point of the blood-dripping blade and rode back triumphant to where the onlooking Allies waited.[8]

Now the Allies whooped even louder in adulation of his deed, as Two Twists—again erect in the saddle with chest out and head held high—trotted his mount slowly and majestically back and forth along their ranks. His drooping sword in one hand pointing to the ground, his eyes staring ahead as if he himself was oblivious to all, but in truth, reveling in the wild acclaim being heaped upon him. Anon, having allowed his horse to get its second wind, Two Twists turned once more to face the foe, and a moment later was spurring his steed back toward the barricades, himself again yelling and snarling like a wounded cougar. Another great leap and he was over, slashing as before within the camp interior.

At first the Crows—all non combatants—stared in surprise at this lone thunder ball who appeared to want to kill everyone around him. But some among the Crows finally plucked up courage and a large body of old men and teenagers rushed over to assist their kinfolk. Two Twists was pulled from the saddle and dragged under a writhing sea of bodies. The Crows, most of whom did not even have weapons, struck him with sticks, fists and stones.

As the Cheyennes and Shutaio saw their champion go down, the whole countryside reverberated with their screams of anger. Their eyes fell upon Ice, the Contrary,waiting for him to give the signal to attack. Ice quickly passed his sacred Thunder Bow behind him from left hand to the right. A great war cry went up and immediately the

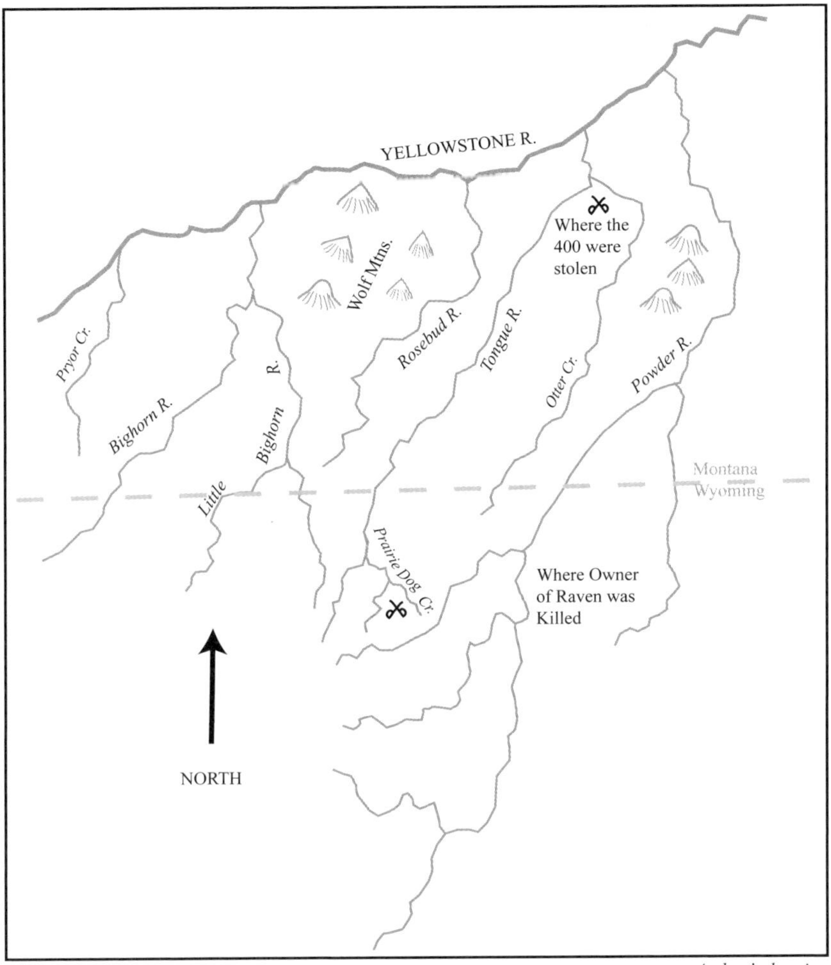

Author's drawing

Map showing approximate sites and surrounding country of the Prairie Dog Creek fight (1819) and the destruction of Long Hair's village (1820).

Allied host, in one great engulfing wave, surged forward, following in the path of Two Twists.

At their head went the Sacred Arrows tied to the lance of the young medicine man and also the Sacred Buffalo Hat of the Shutaio worn by the warrior Whistling Elk. He with the Scalp Shield was also in the van, swinging it too and fro from left to right as he rode, and the few missiles which came from behind the breastworks had little or no effect upon the Allied ranks.

As the charging warriors drew near, they were amazed to see their champion Two Twists bob up, as it were, from under the mass of struggling bodies, his torso, arms and face covered with blood. But he continued to weild his weapon with as much ferocity as ever.

The next moment the Allies had come up, jumping their war ponies over and through all obstacles before them, smashing into the hide lodges and riding down everyone in their path, trampling them under hoof. Breaches appeared in every part of the breastworks and as more and more warriors crowded through them, the gaps grew even wider, until nothing blocked the way.

Racing their ponies around the inner circle of tepees, the Allies bludgeoned their way through huddled groups of Crows, war clubs and arrows flying, their lances dealing death to any male of fighting age and to those who dared show the slightest resistance to their wrath.

The scene within the camp was one of unbridled panic, as the occupants first ran this way then that in desperate attempts to extricate themselves from the trap.

Some of the defenders did manage to mount horses and break through the enemy line, only minutes before the bulk of the attackers came pouring through the breastworks. Others were not so lucky. White Haired Killer, the Crow girl taken captive that day, told her daughter Standing In The Lodge many years later, that just before the Cheyennes and Sioux broke through into the camp, her mother put her and her sister on a horse ready to flee into the hills. White Haired Killer was then about ten years old, but her sister was a lot younger, perhaps only three or four and White Haired Killer was accustomed to looking after her, especially when travelling from one place to another. At such times the younger sister was always tied onto the horse to prevent her falling off. Unfortunately, at this particular time, she did fall off and White Haired Killer was obliged to dismount to pick her up. While in the act of doing so, the Allies came charging through the camp, whooping and yelling, beating on hide shields with their weapons, making a great commotion. White Haired Killer's horse became unmanageable. It reared up on its hind legs then took off, joining the rest of the animals which together, began stampeding around the camp searching for an exit. White Haired Killer was left on her own and on foot, and was taken captive by a Cheyenne warrior even before she had a chance to run.[9]

Author's photo

Sandstone butte "Where they fled around it," during the destruction of Chief Long Hair's village on Otter Creek in 1820. Looking north.

Of those who did manage to get out of the camp before all avenues of escape were cut off, most were women and children, although a few Crow men including the chief Long Hair, were among them.

These men were not cowards, but after defending their ground for a while, they had realized that they alone could not resist the overwhelming onslaught from such a vastly superior force, and as an act of expediency, had joined the stream of fugitives as the latter raced both on foot and on horseback for the safety of some distant hills. The men with Long Hair at their head, fought a desperate rearguard action in order to give the fleeing fugitives a better chance to escape.

A number of Cheyenne and Sioux saw these Crows racing toward the hills, and pulling themselves away from what was going on in the camp, took off in hot pursuit.

Long Hair was lagging behind the fleeing Crows. Seeing that a few of the Allies were drawing close he suddenly reined in his horse, jumped from its back and stood alone facing his attackers who he threatened to shoot with his short-barreled trade gun. His pursuers also reined up, not daring to venture near. Instead, they hovered tentatively around, shouting abuse at the lone Crow and challenging him to come forward and fight. Long Hair stayed his ground and returned the verbal challenges, but after a short while, he vaulted onto his waiting horse and galloped off again, following the path of the fugitives.

The Cheyennes and Sioux resumed the chase and being mounted on war ponies, whereas the Crow chief rode nothing more than a pack horse, the Allies were soon again at his heels and pressing him hard. It was a desperate race that followed, but it was not long before two Sioux warriors caught up, and riding alongside the Long Hair, tried to pull him from the saddle. In the ensuing tussle Long Hair was thrown to the ground. But in an instant, he was again on his feet and braced to defend himself with gun at the ready. His threatening stance and look of determined resolution caused his attackers to draw back, while they awaited their comrades to come up.

Several Crows following in the rear of the fugitives, but ahead of Long Hair, glanced back at that moment. Seeing the danger their chief was in, they turned their horses around, and yelling the Crow war cry at the tops of their voices, 'Koo-Koo-Hey, Koo-Koo-Hey,' raced back to give their assistance. This bunch of Crows composed of old and middle-aged men and armed only with the basic of weapons such as stone headed war clubs and spears, reached their chief just as the rest of the pursuing Allies came into view. Fortunately for Long Hair, his enemies had no chance to finish him off, for the returning Crows quickly surrounded him and by their threatening behavior, indicated to the Cheyennes and Sioux that they were resolved to protect their chief, no matter what the cost.

The number of Allies in this pursuing group was not large, although they evidently had the advantage in age and weaponry. Even so, they decided that on this occasion discretion was the better part of valor and merely hurled a barrage of insults at the Crows, telling them that they were going to take their women captive and describing in minute and lurid detail what sexual treats they had in store for them. They then rode off back the way they had come and allowed the chief and his loyal followers to escape.

The Cheyennes say today that this particular group of Crows was made up of old women and a few very old men. The Cheyennes thought they were not even worthy of killing, certainly, not worth taking as captives. Besides the Cheyenne warriors did not want to miss out on plundering the camp and were eager to get back there before all the worthy captives and horses, along with anything else of

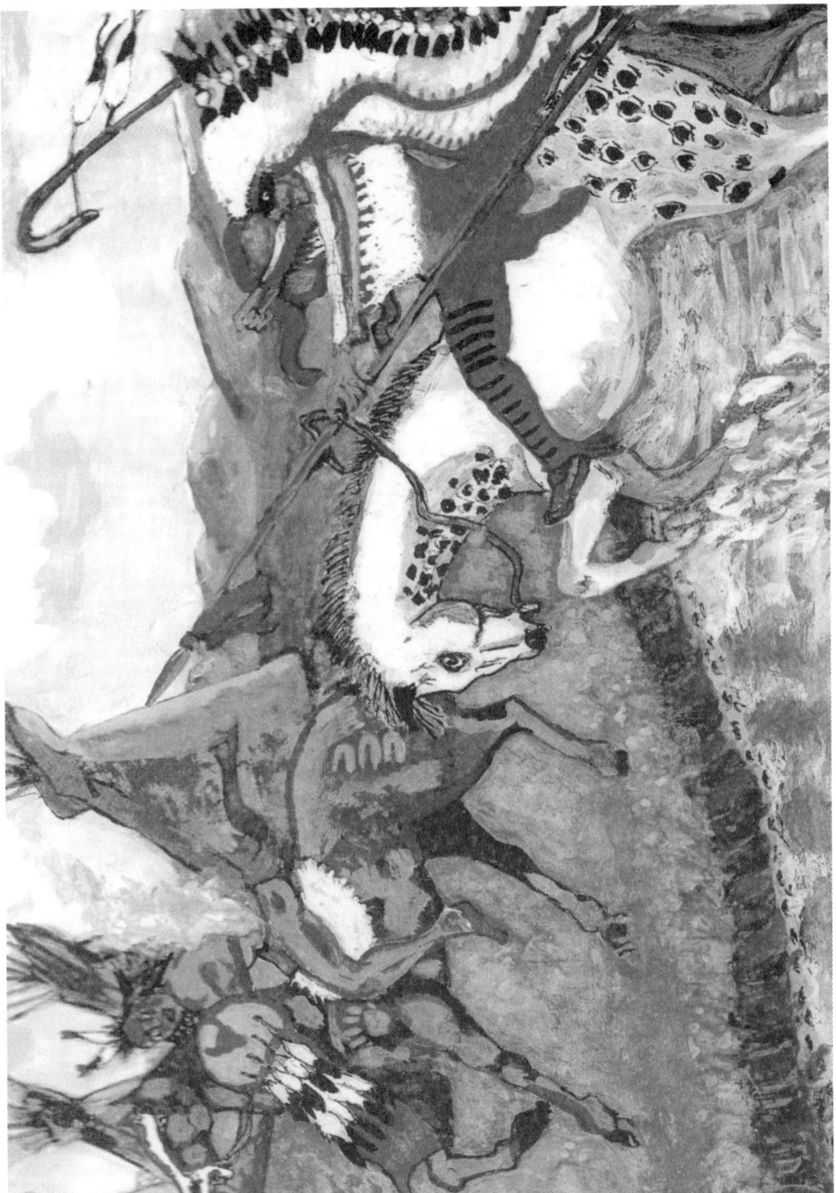

Detail from a larger drawing by the Author

Chief Long Hair confronts the Enemy along Otter Creek, 1820.

value had either been taken or destroyed. This, say the Cheyennes, is why they let these particular Crows escape unmolested.[10]

Another group of Crow fugitives also managed to escape from the camp and were fleeing toward the hills, but in a different direction from Long Hair's group. These people were passing around the foot of a nearby butte when a band of Cheyennes and Sioux got after them, and in the running fight which ensued, the Allies killed them all including the old men, women and even some children. Only one small boy survived the massacre and he ran off on foot in search of the Crow warriors, whose several war parties were still out looking for the Allied camps.

Meanwhile, back in the beleaguered Crow village, the fight was in full swing, and all was now mayhem and confusion. The Allies struck down and scalped all the old and middle-aged men. Dead Crows littered the ground. The victors rounded up the surviving women and children in great bunches. It is said that not a few of the non combatants simply resigned themselves to their fate and offered no resistance. The Allies ushered them this way and that and the Crows obeyed without complaint (which to do so would likely have meant instant death), going along with whomsoever claimed them. Winona Plenty Hoops said that when she was a small girl some very old Crow men, whose mothers and fathers had been young children at the time of the fight, told what they remembered. She recalled how they would emphasize the great number of horses charging around the interior of the camp:

> ". . . .horses, horses, horses," they would say, "bumping into one another, knocking down people and lodges and raising such great clouds of dust, that the defenders found it hard to see before them, while at the same time, they were constantly being showered with stones and clods of earth thrown up by the thousands of flying hooves." [11]

On the Cheyenne side it is said that Bob-Tailed Bull, a famous Cheyenne war chief in later years, rode his pony through the village, striking both left and right with his war lance. He killed and wounded many Crows, and it was he who counted the most coups on the Crow men folk during the battle.

Another Cheyenne named Island (killed at Camp Supply, 1868), who was almost as prolific with his coup stick and charging in among the huddled groups of Crows, counted nearly as many strikes as did Bob-Tailed Bull. But of all the Allied warriors battling in the camp, none was more conspicuous than Ice, the Contrary. Making a cry like the hoot of the prairie dog owl, whose stuffed skin he wore tied to his forehead, he charged on his horse, touching every Crow he could reach with his Thunder Bow. It is remembered that on this day he counted more than 100 coups.[12]

At the same time, High Back Bear, a Shutaio, counted so many coups upon the Crow women and children that no one really knew for sure the proper number.[13]

As for the old man Red Painted Robe, he was always where the fighting was thickest. His hatchet appeared to be everywhere at once. Crying with anger over the death of his two sons, he hacked off a Crow arm in the traditional Shutaio manner and so obtained a grisly trophy with which to dance over in the victory celebrations to come. His wife White Buffalo Woman, skulked around the ruined camp wielding her gigantic wooden club, which she brought down with a terrible vengeance upon Crow heads—both dead or merely wounded—smashing them to pulp. [14]

White Buffalo Woman was only one of a number of Shutaio and Cheyenne women actively engaged in the carnage. They plundered the lodges and destroyed them. They ripped the tepee coverings to shreds with their knives and broke the lodge poles into pieces so they could not be reused. They even smashed the clay cooking pots, such was their hatred of the Crows.[15] And when the majority of fighting was over, the mass of Cheyenne and Shutaio women, who had been watching the unequal contest from a safe distance, ran into the camp wielding knives, clubs and axes. They screamed with savage glee as they pounded and stabbed those of the enemy lying wounded and even those already dead. They stripped the bodies then hacked them to pieces limb-by-limb, some parts of which they paraded around on high, attached to the end of their husband's lance points as grisly trophies of their victory.

While all this was going on, one particularly prominent figure among the Allied warriors, mounted upon a large white mule, paraded around the ruined lodges wearing a strange iron-covered shirt and helmet. Years later Crow survivors recalled that they were much afraid of this man and wondered if he was a human being or a spirit sent to aid their enemies. They remembered he wore a leather shirt covered with small overlapping metal discs and had an iron cap upon his head, creating an imposing spectacle. He sat astride a big Spanish pacing mule, they said, bolt upright in the saddle; truly a sight to behold. In their childish minds they had thought he must have had some kind of wooden frame or brace strapped to his back in order to keep him sitting up so rigid. [16]

In one part of the ruined village, a group of Crows, predominately women and children but including one or two very old men, stood huddled in a bunch, cowering in the midst of the carnage and destruction going on around them. For some unknown reason the Allied warriors left them alone and seemed to take no notice of them. Perhaps, though, they had already been claimed as captives by some Allied warrior or another or were considered too old and decrepit to even be bothered with. [17]

Likewise the Cheyennes did not want the old women, for they were thought to be of little use. They therefore set them free, telling them to go away and find the rest of their people and inform them what the Allies had done.

One very old Crow woman almost totally blind, made her way over to the Cheyenne White Bull's grandmother (who was the wife of Ice, the Contrary) and communicating in the sign language, begged her to give back her granddaughter so as to guide her, for she said her eyes were dead and she would not be able to find the remnants of her people on her own. White Bull's grandmother took pity on her and when a young girl stepped forward from the group of captives in her care, she let the child go with the old woman. All the Crow men, both old and middle aged, were put to death.[20]

The battle over, the Cheyennes and Sioux asked the Crow women why there were hardly any Crow warriors in the village and were told that several big war parties had gone out the night before to attack the Allied camps along the Powder. Apparently, the Allies still did not think their own camps were in immediate danger, probably because they had since been moved from their earlier location. But they quickly packed their plunder on spare horses captured from the village and prepared to leave, lest the Crow war parties return. It was then a little past midday and the triumphant Allies set off for their base camps, driving a great herd of captured ponies before them along with all their Crow prisoners. Most of these latter were on foot and were hurried along, even though forced to carry heavy loads of plunder on their backs.

Northwestern University Library
E. S. Curtis' "The North American Indian"
Crow warrior and chief, Shot In Hand.

The Cheyennes admitted in later years that it had not really been much of a fight, owing to the lack of Crow warriors in the camp and that the whole affair was over in a short time. None of the Allies were actually killed in the battle, for even the suicide warrior Two Twists survived. A number of attackers were wounded, one of whom suffered a serious injury which a few days later proved fatal.

A sizable number of Crows managed to escape into the hills, but the victorious Allies still took a large number of prisoners. George Bent, the half-white half-Cheyenne, asserted that the Cheyennes alone had captured more than 100 of the enemy—all young women and children—and that the Sioux had taken as many captives.[18] Crows say the number of Crow captives and deaths together amounted to around 400. Hence, the event was long remembered among the Crows as "When the four-hundred were stolen."[19]

The Sioux for their part, always remembered the event as "When they fled around it," which refers to that group of Crow fugitives who were chased around a sandstone butte close to Otter Creek and, but for one teenage boy, were massacred by the pursuing Allies.

The Allies left behind them a scene of utter ruin. Not a few of the lodges had been set ablaze and amid the scattered debris of the camp, lay countless mutilated and mangled corpses, some pin cushioned with arrows, while a trail of dead bodies lay scattered along the several routes which groups of Crow fugitives had taken in their efforts to escape.

As late as 1865, George Bent, while roaming the Powder River country with the hostiles, visited the site of the battle and even then, forty-five years after the event, the area, he said, was still littered with broken lodge poles, stone axes, broken pots and arrowheads. [21]

AFTERMATH

According to the Cheyennes, it was just past midday, after the fight in the village was over and the Allies were on their way back to their base camps, that Cheyenne scouts out riding ahead of the column looking for sign of the Crow war parties suddenly came galloping back at great speed and reported that a small band of Crows was coming towards them from the hills.

These people appear to have been yet another group of dissidents belonging to those who had gone out from the Crow camp with Red Owl the previous night, for the party was comprised only of women and children and a few very old men. They were all on horseback and like their predecessors earlier in the day, were leading pack horses loaded down with their personal belongings. Evidently, they too had thought it safe to return, having no idea that the village had already been taken and destroyed.

Quickly a large body of Cheyennes hid themselves among the trees and undergrowth lining both sides of the path the Crows were travelling. When the unsuspecting party came abreast of the hidden warriors, the trap was sprung. Yelling their fearsome war cries, a horde of mounted Cheyenne warriors converged upon the Crows from all sides, taking their quarry completely by surprise. The Crow men were killed outright and the women and children along with their pack ponies, taken captive.

Some of the Crow children taken at this time and who remained hereafter with their captors, marrying into a Cheyenne or Sioux band and raising families of their own, said, "The Cheyennes swept down upon us and drove all our returning ones before them. We had not time to dismount, but were driven forward like a herd of wild horses to the Cheyenne camp." [22]

These captives further confirmed that this event had occurred after the fight in the Crow village had ended.

During all this time the Crow boy who had escaped the beleaguered village and survived the massacre of the fugitives had been following up the trail of one of the Crow war parties which had gone out the night before in search of the Allied camps. When the boy finally caught them up and burst out the news that their own village had been attacked, the warriors became distraught. They cried aloud to the Great Spirit and to their personal totems—begging them to preserve their kinfolk.

The Crow Pipe Holders could not keep the war parties together. Groups of warriors and even individuals, raced off toward the village in an effort to save their people. Thus, the Crow force, which only moments before had been a match for any foe, broke up into two dozen or more separate bands, each warrior heeding only his personal fears and commitment to his loved ones. They completely disregarded the strength of their unity, the one real hope of achieving anything against their enemies. The sub chief Sore Belly did exert all his efforts of persuasion in order to keep the warriors in a cohesive body, but even his own great standing could not deter them from pursuing their individual designs.

Unfortunately, the horses of the Crows were already tired, having been ridden all night in search of the Allied camps and now, racing back toward the village, their animals quickly became exhausted. It was long after the Allied host had left before the Crow warriors began arriving at the scene; a smoldering, corpse-littered ruin. As each of the exhausted groups of warriors came in and beheld the carnage before them, they screamed aloud their grief and swore oaths of vengeance over the bodies of their dead and mutilated kinsfolk.

In the meantime, the great cavalcade of victorious Cheyennes and Sioux continued to snake its winding way across country toward its home camps.

While enroute, a single Crow brave on his way back to the ruined village appeared atop the crest of a hill overlooking the allied column below. He shouted down to the Cheyennes and Sioux and by the use of signs asked if they had harmed his village. Now among the Allies at this time was a young Crow man who had been captured during an earlier attack upon a Crow village, ostensibly in 1801, when Cheyennes and Shutaio in company with Sans Arc, Minniconjou and Brule Sioux, destroyed thirty Crow lodges and took many prisoners. The particular Crow captive—who was known simply as Big Prisoner—had been fully adopted into the Cheyenne tribe and spoke both his captor's tongue and his mother's tongue fluently. Thus, when

Sketch by Author after painting from life by George Catlin in 1832
Crow Indian, Four Wolves

the Crow called from the hill top to the cavalcade returning from the destruction of Long Hair's village, it was Big Prisoner who turned off from the route and conversed with his fellow tribesman. The lone Crow hollered down saying that his own name was Long Jaw and then asked if the Allies had killed the Crow women and children on Otter Creek. Big Prisoner replied that the said women and children had been spared, although most were now captives of the Cheyennes and Sioux. Upon hearing this, the lone Crow turned his pony around and disappeared from the crest and, so the Cheyennes later said, they could hear him crying and lamenting the fate of his people as he rode away. [23]

A little farther on, about fifty Crow warriors returning to the village, came upon the victorious column and from a distance, recognized some of the prisoners being driven along by their captors. The Cheyennes signed to them that they, the Allies, had destroyed the Crow village and taken many prisoners. The Allied force was far too great for this small party of Crows to attack and, therefore, after firing a few arrows and musket balls as a show of defiance, they too hurried on to their village to assess the full extent of damage.[24]

When all the Crow warriors had come in and it was clear that the Allies had left the vicinity, the surviving Crow fugitives who had been lucky enough to have escaped into the hills, came back to the ruins of their camp.

One can imagine the relief among some Crow warriors when they discovered some family members were safe. But for many others there was only heart-rending sorrow, as the men folk searched among the ruins of the camp discovering the dismembered corpses of close relatives or, came to the realization that a missing child, mother or wife had been led off into captivity by their enemies. Hideous screams of anguish filled the air and the blood flowed freely from gashed arms, legs and breasts. Others stabbed their foreheads with knives or sharp stones and pulled the hair from their heads in great hanks, to express their grief.

As the afternoon wore on, it became oppressively hot. The corpses of those slain, both man and beast, lying in heaps and scattered around, quickly became flyblown and bloated. A great stench enveloped the scene and the ghosts of the dead seemed to be everywhere.

The Crow chiefs agreed they should leave as soon as possible. Chief Long Hair gathered the remnants of his people and by nightfall, all had vacated the scene, having left most everything behind. Some were those who endeavored to hastily conceal their dead relatives in secluded spots among the surrounding brush and rocks, although many of the corpses were simply left where they fell to become the prey of the four-leggeds of the prairie and their winged brethren of the air. The world of the Absaroka had been shattered; their once indomitable pride and tribal rationale extinguished. What use to honor the dead when the bonds which had kept the people together were rubbed out? The sacred blood ties of the nation broken; torn asunder and the people themselves dispersed.

With heavy hearts the survivors headed southwest into the Big Horn Mountains, where they could lick their wounds and take stock of the situation.

In reality, the destruction of chief Long Hair's village had been a short fight without decisive consequences. The Crows were still able to hold their own and retain their hunting grounds, while continuing to take offensive action against all their enemies, including the Cheyennes and Sioux.

It would have been a very poor show on the part of the Allies had they not defeated such an inferior force as was trapped in chief Long Hair's Crow village at that time, comprised of old men, children, dogs and women. Had Crow warriors been present in force, the outcome probably would have been very different. Nevertheless, to the Allies way of thinking, they had gained a great victory. None of their own warriors had been killed outright in the battle and only one even seriously injured; they were over laden with booty consisting of captured ponies, camp equipment and women and children captives and, perhaps more importantly, they had inflicted a great humiliation upon the whole Crow nation.

When the victorious Allied column reached its base camps, the women at once took down the lodges and the whole ensemble moved upriver, until they came to a small tributary flowing into the Powder from the east in what is now the northeastern corner of the present day state of Wyoming. It was here, the second night after the battle, that the Allies held a grand victory dance which old Cheyenne veterans of the intertribal war days used to say, was the biggest dance of its kind ever held by their tribe. The celebrations went on for many weeks continuing both night and day. So excited were the participants that the Cheyenne and Shutaio women—noted among all tribes for their chastity and decorum—appeared to go crazy; offering sexual favors to warriors of their choosing. Such an overt expression of promiscuity had not been witnessed among the Cheyennes either before or since and in commemoration of the event, the Allies named the stream along which they were then encamped, "Crazy Woman Creek" by which name it is known today.[25]

Throughout the victory celebrations, Two Twists was the name on everyone's lips. He was the hero of the moment. The fact that he had not pursued his suicide vow to its ultimate end was of little consequence and did not detract from the people's adulation towards him. He had endeavored to carry out his vow to the best of his ability and truly, it had been the fault of the Crows alone that he had not been killed outright in the fight. Thus, there could be no shame because he had inadvertently survived the conflict. He had been a great and respected warrior even before the event, one of the little chiefs of the Shutaio Crooked Lance Society, but now, due to his recent actions, his standing among the tribe was lifted to new heights. (Two years later he would be elected as one of the big tribal chiefs, perhaps to the role of "Sweet-Medicine Chief" itself, the highest warrior rank within the Cheyenne nation).

But with all this, Two Twists was not without humility. Upon his return to camp after the victory at the Crow village, he sent a messenger to Red Painted Robe and the latter's wife and children, requesting them to visit him in his lodge. When his guests arrived, Two Twists personally stripped them of their mourning rags and dressed each in a fine new suit of clothes. To White Buffalo Woman and the children, he gave many presents and to Red Painted Robe himself, he returned all the horses and belongings which the old man had thrown away several moons before.[26]

Red Painted Robe showed his appreciation by taking Two Twists as his adopted son and, from here on, ceased to mourn for his own two beloved sons slain by the Crows. Instead, he joined in the victory celebrations with gusto. Around the central fire he stomped and howled as energetically as any of the younger warriors and screamed with savage delight while waving the severed Crow arm above his head. He struck the onlooking females across their backs and shoulders with the grizzled trophy, sending them running and screaming around the camp. He gave each person who visited his lodge a horse and painted each adult face black with a mixture of charcoal and grease, this being the color of victory.[27]

Meanwhile, scalp dances and victory feasts were held in both Cheyenne and Sioux camps as warriors counted and recounted their many coups, acting out in grim yet graphic pantomime every particular of their deeds. At the same time the womenfolk, particularly those who had actually participated in the fight—now bedecked in their husbands feathered bonnets and hair-fringed war shirts—joined the revelers and shuffled sideways around the dance circle keeping time with the monotonous throbbing of the drums. They raised the tremolo repeatedly and sang praise songs in honor of their men folk, while they paraded aloft scalps, hands, feet and heads taken from the corpses of their unfortunate Crow victims and now attached to the end of long willow wands, lance points and musket barrels.

The captive Crow women—huddled in darkened lodges—wailed their mourning dirges and cried aloud over their slaughtered loved ones whose grizzled remains were being abused before their eyes. The captured children sat together in bunches; bewildered by all that was going on around them. The Cheyennes and Sioux traded off one for the other, haggling over every transaction, as they exchanged a captive for a horse or some other item of plunder obtained from the vanquished village.

At first the Cheyennes and Sioux were united in their victory celebrations, but as so often the case when foreign Indian groups came into close proximity with one another for a prolonged period, congenial relations soon became strained. Inevitably, old tribal rivalries and past grievances both real and imagined came to the fore and in themselves, were usually enough to seriously disrupt any intertribal get together. Whether the open promiscuity of the Cheyenne and Shutaio women gave rise to jealousy among their spouses or, as George Bent asserted, there was a disagreement over the distribution of prisoners, we do not know. But several of the Allied warriors came to blows and the Cheyennes even began fighting among themselves. As the arguments increased, the situation reached the point where warriors on both sides grabbed their weapons and opposed each other in battle array.

Fortunately, the chiefs and headmen of those involved intervened and after much difficult persuasion, managed to calm the situation and prevent a full-scale conflict erupting within the camps. As it was, one or two Cheyenne and Sioux warriors died or were seriously injured during the brief, but heated melee, ironically, by their own tribesmen. Several Crow captives also lost their lives, murdered out of hand in expressions of spite by one side or the other.[28]

At the same time a Sioux warrior, who had suffered serious wounds during the actual attack upon the Crow village, finally succumbed to his injuries and as an act of vengeance, his relatives now set upon one of the female Crow prisoners with their knives; threw her still breathing body onto the camp fire and whooped with delight as she slowly roasted to death.

Now within the bounds of Cheyenne law it was considered a terrible thing to kill a prisoner once he or she had been taken into the captor's lodge. It was deemed as much a crime of homicide as if a Cheyenne had murdered a fellow tribesman and was usually punished as such with the customary term of four years banishment from the tribe. The Sioux, it seems, had no such scruples. This dissension within the Allied camps brought their temporary confederation to an abrupt conclusion.

The next morning, the women of both camps took down their lodges, packed the covers along with their domestic belongings on pony drags and began moving off in different directions. The Sioux contingent headed east toward the headwater district of the Little Missouri, while the Cheyennes and Shutaio moved southeast through the Black Hills and thence to the forks of the Cheyenne River.

And so it was that the grand Allied expedition to punish the Crows finally came to an end. An end of the matter, that is, as far as the Allies were concerned—but not so for the Crows.

Some among the Absaroka blamed chief Long Hair for their great misfortune. Was it not his responsibility, they said, to protect and preserve the people? Why was it that his medicine had failed them? Surely, he must have angered the unseen powers in some way. Others, meanwhile, cursed the young warriors and some even each other for not heeding the great chief's warnings—riding off instead to seek personal acclaim and riches, rather than protecting the camp and its defenseless occupants.[29]

There had been members from all Crow clans in the village lately destroyed and this fact caused additional dissension.

Filled with grief and a temporary lack of tolerance, personal rivalries came to the fore and threatened internal strife. None appeared to listen to the counseling of the chiefs, who tried in vain to calm the situation and allay the people's fears.

The entire Mountain Crow population scattered into numerous, small, individual camps—ignoring even the blood ties of the clan—and dispersed themselves throughout the Big Horn Mountains and beyond. They spent the autumn and winter in seclusion; wallowing in their sorrow. Indeed, the winter was particularly severe, so that not a few of those in mourning actually froze to death in their isolation. Many were those now without mother, wife and children, while the old and decrepit; alone and bereft; with none to give them succor or entice them back into the fold, fended for themselves as best they could—if they could—until such time the people would finally regain their senses and reunite as a tribe.[30]

In the course of time there arose among the Crows the great war chief Alapooish or Sore Belly and he it was, some thirteen years later in 1833, who led his warriors in an elaborate crusade against the Cheyennes, which, although not primarily intended to avenge the disaster attending Long Hair's village, did nonetheless achieve adequate compensation for that event also.[31] This Crow force under Sore Belly lured the enemy into a carefully planned trap with the help of a famous Crow warrior named Plays With His Face and in the ensuing melee, the Crows completely destroyed a Cheyenne village, killed many warriors and took captive a number of women and children.[32] It is a story still prominent in Crow tribal tradition.[33]

For the time being, however, in the immediate aftermath of the destruction of Long Hair's village, the Absaroka nation remained fragmented and irreparably divided. Truly, it would take the persuasions of a great chief to instill again into the people that pride and confidence which had once marked them high above their neighbors, both friend and foe alike. But none could foresee the rise of such a man. Who would eventually heal the great wound which had torn the nation asunder? Surely, thought the Crows, the Gods of the Absaroka had forsaken them. . .The star of their ancestors which once shone bright, was dimmed.

NOTES AND SOURCES.

1 Grinnell, George Bird. *"The Cheyenne Indians."* Vol. 1. pp.79-86. Yale University Press. 1926. See also; George Bent letter to George E. Hyde. Dec; 31st. 1906. Denver Public Library Archives. Colorado.
2 Bill Tall Bull to Author, Ashland, Montana, Sep; 1994.Note pad 1. pp.7-8.
3 Ibid. pp. 7-8.
4 Bill Tall Bull to Author, Ashland, Montana, Sep; 1994. pp. 7-8. See also, Wayne Medicine Elk [Southern Cheyenne informant] to Author, Billings, Montana, August, 1994. Note pad 1. p.5.
5 Bill Tall Bull to Author, Ashland, Montana, Sep; 1994. Note pad 1. pp. 7-8.
6 Bill Tall Bull to Author, Ashland, Montana, Sep; 1994. Note pad 1. pp. 7-8.
7 Bill Tall Bull to Author, Ashland, Montana, Sep; 1994. Note pad 1. pp. 7-8.
8 Llewellyn, Karl N. and Hoebel, E. Adamson. *"The Cheyenne Way."* p.5. University of Oklahoma Press, 1967
9 George Bird Grinnell Manuscript Collection (MS. 5). Folder 494 *"Early Crow Battles."* And *"Many Crow captives"* folder 15. Southwest Museum, Los Angeles, California. See also; Wayne Medicine Elk [Southern Cheyenne informant] to Author, Billings, Montana, August, 1994. Note pad 1. p.5. And; Bill Tall Bull to Author, Ashland, Montana, Sep; 1994.Note pad 1. pp.7-8
10 James H. *"The Bradley Manuscripts."* Montana Historical Society Collections, "Book four." pp. 238ff. 1877. See also; Bill Tall Bull to Author, Ashland, Montana, Sep; 1994. Note pad 1. pp. 7-8.
11 Winona Plenty Hoops, (Crow informant) to Author. Lodge Grass, Montana, August, 1994. Note pad 1. pp. 7-8.
12 George Bird Grinnell Manuscript Collection (MS. 5). Folder 494 *"Early Crow Battles."* Southwest Museum, Los Angeles, California. See also; George Bent letter to George Bird Grinnell. May 26th 1908. Southwest Museum, Los Angeles, California.
13 George Bird Grinnell Manuscript Collection (MS. 5). Folder 494 *"Early Crow Battles."* Southwest Museum, Los Angeles, California. See also; George Bent letter to George Bird Grinnell. May 26th 1908. Southwest Museum, Los Angeles, California.
14 Llewellyn and Hoebel. 1967. "Loc; cit." pp.5-6.
15 James King to Author, Lame Deer, 1994. Note pad I. p. 8. See also, John Stands in Timber *"Papers, 1962."* Dull Knife College Library Archives. Lame Deer, Montana.
16 Winona Plenty Hoops, (Crow informant) to Author. Lodge Grass, Montana, August, 1994. Note pad 1. pp. 7-8. Evidently, a Cheyenne chief named Rising Elk, later known as Dirty Water. At this time he was the proud owner of a "shirt of iron" as it was called, which only a few years before, he had traded from an Arapaho who himself, had acquired it from a Mexican trader from the south. George Bird Grinnell Manuscript Collection (MS. 509). *"Indian Armour – Cheyenne Warfare."* Southwest Museum, Los Angeles, California. Rising Elk was killed during the battle of Sappa Creek between White men and Cheyennes in 1875. C.f. Grinnell, George Bird. *"The Fighting Cheyennes."* pp.368-369. University of Oklahoma Press. 1956.
17 Grinnell, George Bird. *"The Fighting Cheyennes."* pp.368-369. University of Oklahoma Press.1956. See also; Bill Tall Bull to Author, Ashland, Montana, Sep; 1994. Note pad 1. pp. 7-8. And; Wayne Medicine Elk [Southern Cheyenne informant] to Author, Billings, Montana, August, 1994. Note pad 1. pp. 5.
18 George Bent to George B. Grinnell. 1905. (Letter no. 26). Southwest Museum. Los Angeles. California..
19 Grinnell, George Bird, *"The Fighting Cheyennes,"* pp. 25-34. University of Oklahoma Press, 1956. George Bird Grinnell Manuscript Collection (MS. 5). Folder 494 *"Early Crow Battles."* Southwest Museum, Los Angeles, California. See also; Bill Tall Bull to Author, Ashland, Montana, Sep; 1994. Note pad pp.7-8. And; Wayne Medicine Elk [Southern Cheyenne informant] to Author, Billings, Montana, August, 1994. Note pad 1. pp. 5.-6
20 George Bird Grinnell. *"The Fighting Cheyennes,"* pp. 25-34. University of Oklahoma Press, 1956. Also, George Bent letters to George Grinnell. [letter 26] "Loc; cit." 1905.
21 Winona Plenty Hoops to Author. Lodge Grass, Montana, August, 1994. Note pad. pp.7-8.
22 George Bent letters to George Grinnell. [letter 26] "Loc; cit." 1905. See also; George Bird Grinnell. *"The Fighting Cheyennes,"* pp. 25-34. University of Oklahoma Press, 1956.
23 Grinnell, Manuscript Collection (MS. 5). Folder 494 *"Early Crow Battles."* See also; George Bent to George Grinnell. [letter 26] "Loc; cit." 1905. The mention of Big Prisoner is taken from

Margot Liberty`s interview with the Northern Cheyenne historian John Stands in Timber, a transcript copy of which, Margot has very kindly loaned to the present Author with permission to use in this book. Margot Liberty *"papers;" "transcript of interviews with John Stands in Timber."* p.322. 1962.

24 Winona Plenty Hoops to Author. Lodge Grass, Montana, August, 1994. Note pad 1. pp. 7-8.

25 Llewellyn, Karl N. and Hoebel, E. Adamson, *"The Cheyenne Way."* pp.5-6. University of Oklahoma Press, 1967

26 Ibid. pp.5-6.

27 James H. *The Bradley Manuscripts.* Montana Historical Society Collections, "Book four." pp. 238ff. 1877.

28 Joe Medicine Crow to Author. Lodge Grass, Montana. Sep; 1994. Note pad 1. pp. 1-3.

29 Joe Medicine Crow to Author. Lodge Grass, Montana. Sep; 1994. Note pad 1. pp. 1-3.

30 Winona Plenty Hoops to Author. Lodge Grass, Montana, August, 1994. Note pad 1. pp. 7-8.

31 Ibid.

32 Denig, Edwin T, *Five Indian Tribes of the Upper Missouri. "Of the Crow Nation."* pp.165-169. University of Oklahoma Press, 1961. See also; Joe Medicine Crow to Author. Note pad 1. p.6.

Chapter Four

The Brave Crow

As within any social group, serious friction sometimes arises between individual members or rival factions, often creating internal strife and the shedding of kindred blood. The Crows were no exception to the rule.

During the late 1820s, an altercation between rival factions among the "Piegan"(also known as "Treacherous Lodges") Crow clan and that of the "Whistling Waters," escalated to the point that for several years, they regarded each other as mortal enemies and several bloody battles were fought between them. The Whistling Waters generally came off best in these conflicts, but at length, a renowned Whistling Water chief named Little White Bull, became filled with self-recrimination that kindred people were killing each other, when their energies and antagonism would be better directed against the many hostile tribes surrounding them.

In order to atone in some way for what he considered was his responsibility in instigating this inter clan feud in the first place, Little White Bull became determined to "give his body to the wolves" in the next confrontation against one or another of his tribe's hereditary foes.

Before the coming of snow in the latter part of 1829, each of the three autonomous Crow divisions had already moved into their preferred locations of winter retreat. The Kicked-in-the-Bellys had set their tepees along the Big Horn River in the shadow of the mountains of that name, while their Mountain Crow brethren had moved southwest to ensconce themselves adjacent to the lower course of Wind River. The River Crows could be found on the north side of the Yellowstone, in the vicinity of the great sandstone bluff overlooking the present day town of Billings.

At the same time, the Crows' Cheyenne-speaking enemies had also retired to areas where they intended to remain throughout the winter. One band of the latter had chosen the company of its Sioux allies and together, had set their villages about one half-mile apart along the east bank of the Powder near that river's confluence with the Yellowstone. Their smoke-tanned, buffalo hide tepees nestled picturesquely among the trees and brush growing thick along that river's bank.

The Sioux were a combined village of Oglala and Minniconjou, while the Cheyenne consisted predominately of Shutaio band members with a small contingent of Hevitanio. This was before the Shutaio became fully incorporated into the Cheyenne tribal circle and prior to the permanent withdrawal of the Hevitanio from the North Country to the Arkansas, to be nearer William Bent's trading post and the pony herds of their Kiowa and Comanche enemies. Their location near the mouth of the Powder was a favorite wintering ground for the most northern Cheyenne and Shutaio bands, and it was they who enjoyed a more intimate relationship with the Oglala and Minniconjou than did other Cheyenne-speaking groups.

Early in the New Year, a brigade of white trappers arrived at the Sioux and Cheyenne villages. They were led by the famous explorer Jediah Smith and his partner David Jackson. Their number included such notables as Joe Meek, Thomas (Broken Hand) Fitzpatrick and Jim Bridger. They had spent the previous autumn and early part of winter trapping the icy streams in the Wind River district southwest of the Big Horn Mountains and had lost horses, men and equipment to the Crows and Blackfeet in whose war ground they were trespassing. The weather, though, had proved too cold in that region for a prolonged stay and come January, after caching their furs and pelts, Smith and Jackson led their men into the Lower Powder country. Here game was more plentiful during the winter months. The thick growths of brush and timber provided shelter from storms, while the bark and boughs of the abundant Cottonwoods offered forage for their horses and fuel for their fires. Buffalo, in fact, were so numerous in the area at this time, that the trappers were obliged to mount guards to prevent the animals from entering their camp and wrecking it.[1]

It was fortunate for this band of white men that they stumbled upon these friendly Cheyenne and Sioux camps which, by their very presence, would provide protection from marauding hostiles, particularly Arapaho and Gros Ventre—not to mention the Arickara and Blackfeet who were ever the trapper's antagonists. As a consequence, these white men were only too pleased to accept the hospitality of their Indian hosts; to share the warmth of their lodges and the attention of their women. And so it was that Sioux, Cheyenne and white trappers were encamped together this winter. The trapper Joe Meek has left us a graphic description of the occasion:

> ". . . .Throughout the day hunting parties were coming and going. Men were cooking, drying meat, making moccasins, cleaning their arms, wrestling and playing games. Nor was there wanting in the appearance of the camp. . .and that picturesque air imparted by a mingling of the native element, for what with their Indian allies, their native wives and numerous children, the mountaineers camp was a motley assemblage, and the trappers themselves with the affectation of the Indian coxcombry, not the least picturesque individuals. . .the loud resounding stroke of the ax, the sharp report of the rifle, neighing of horses and braying of mules, the Indian war whoop and yell, and all that not unpleasant confusion of sound which accompanies the movement of the creature man."[2.]

No doubt Meek`s biographer added her own literary penchant to his actual words. But the scene described is authentic and what is important, it offers corroboration that white trappers were indeed among the Allies at this time. It might be mentioned in addition to the above description, that the occupants of the combined villages regaled themselves with more than one keg of the white man's "rot gut" whiskey, which of course, was a prerequisite of any trapper's recreational needs.

From their camps along the Powder, both the Cheyennes and Sioux sent out the occasional war party against enemies to the west and north and, according to later Cheyenne testimony, it was because of the unusual severity of weather that they lingered in this area longer than anticipated..[3]

Indeed, the winter of 1829-'30 was particularly severe; to the extent that several tribal calendars identify the year for that reason alone.[4] Excessive inclement weather did not, however, prevent the more determined war party from venturing abroad in its search for horses and scalps and, especially so, when the quarry was likely to be snowed in and virtually immobile. It was an uncomfortable prospect in the depths of mid-season for horse herders to keep constant vigil against thieves, when even members of the particular warrior society delegated as camp guard, would be somewhat lax in their duty, when subzero temperatures and howling blizzards, caused both man and beast to seek shelter from the icy blasts.

The Crows still had plenty of enemies on hand to keep them occupied. If the Cheyennes and Sioux were not enough, the Crows also suffered repeated attacks from their hereditary foe, the Blackfeet. They also were obliged to be on guard against the fickle-minded Shoshoni who, although ostensibly friends and sometimes allies, rarely passed up the opportunity to run off a bunch of Crow horses and, maybe, take a scalp or two if circumstance was in their favor.

It was during the middle part of January, while thick snow still blanketed the land and cutting winds blew from the north, that a large war party of combined Arickara and Sioux (temporarily allied against the common enemy), assaulted the River Crow village on the north bank of the Yellowstone. A sizable number of River Crow fighting men were away from the village, having joined with a party of their Kicked-in-the-Belly cousins to visit the Hidatsa and Kipp`s Trading Post far down the Missouri. Fortunately, Sore Belly, the River Crow chief, had seen to it that there remained an adequate force of warriors in camp to protect the people if attacked. When the Arickara and Sioux charged the village, they were met with a determined resistance. The disaster of 1820 had taught the Crows well. Never again would their villages be left so vulnerable as on that occasion. This time the camp occupants defended themselves courageously and after a prolonged struggle, some of which was hand-to-hand, managed to drive their assailants off.[5]

According to the Mountain Man James P. Beckwourth, who professed to being in this fight defending the camp alongside his adopted Crow brethren, he had three horses shot from under him. He said his faithful battle ax, "was red with the blood of the enemy to the end of the haft; fifteen Siouxs (sic) having fallen beneath it."[6]

The Crows did suffer a number of casualties too, having several warriors killed outright and others seriously wounded, some of whom later died of their injuries.

Sketch by Author from photograph circa 1856.
James P. Beckwourth

It was during this same part of winter that Cheyennes—upon raiding a Crow village—captured a four-year-old boy. Details concerning the episode are lacking, but it might have coincided with the previously mentioned Arickara-Sioux attack. It is highly unlikely that a four-year-old would have been found wandering alone outside the camp perimeter, at a time when enemies were fully expected to be loitering in the immediate vicinity,. It may be assumed, therefore, that in this instance, the Cheyennes had assaulted the Crow village and gained entry before being driven off.[7]

Throughout the early years of this decade, at least one band of Teton Sioux and one or two bands of Cheyenne and Shutaio, tolerated the Arickara to some extent, due in part to a so-called "Friendship Treaty" of 1825 affected between the American government and several Missouri River and Western Plains tribes.[8] Since then, around thirty lodges of Arickara had been allowed by the Sioux and Cheyennes to roam in the vicinity of the North Platte, after they, the Arickara, abandoned their permanent earth and timber villages along the Missouri, owing to recurring troubles with white traders and trappers travelling up and down that river. [9]

We also know that during the initial years of the same decade (1830–1840), certain bands of Cheyenne, Sioux and Arickara were encamped in close proximity to each other in the North Platte district[10] and it is possible—indeed probable—that not only were Cheyennes or Shutaio in friendly contact with Arickaras, but that a number of Cheyennes or

Shutaio were included in the Arickara—Sioux assault upon the Crow village where the Crow youngster was likely captured.

Thus, having constantly to defend themselves and their families against numerous enemy war bands, the Crows felt obliged to retaliate in kind. But more than once during the season did a Crow war party return sad and dejected to its village; a number of bodies draped over the withers of rider-less horses or staggering home on foot, the surviving warriors dragging hide sledges behind them, upon which lay a number of dead and dying comrades.

Some whole parties did not return at all.

Although the Crows were generally deemed by their contemporaries as a nation untutored in the conventional Indian ethics of the Plains (being particularly prone to uncommon sexual practices), they were a hardy and tenacious people, whose warriors were often motivated to acts of extreme unselfish heroism. Neither were they so degenerate as to give up their hunting grounds without a determined show of resistance. Their enemies knew well that the Crows would fight—and fight they did—with a consistency and resolution not always reciprocated by those against them. As late as the mid 1860s, a Lieutenant George Palmer, then garrisoned along the beleaguered Bozeman Trail wrote: "Though lazy and of laxed morals, no other Indians are better fighters than the Crow." [11]

Perhaps Palmer was a little biased in his estimation, having had little if any friendly contact with the wild Cheyennes and Sioux who, at the time of his writing, were at war with all white men, while the Crow were the white man's ally and certainly, the latter`s only native friends in a hostile environment. Nevertheless, such a view is consistent with other firsthand observations on that tribe, both before and after Palmer`s comments. Crow oral tradition recalls a number of instances attesting to their nation's martial capabilities, along with historical anecdotes which exhibit overt courage on the part of individual Crow warriors, if not to say, bordering on the rash and reckless.

Spring came late to the north country in 1830. But at last the ice began to thaw and snow soon disappeared from the lowlands and melted in great blotches on the hill sides. Game herds sauntered leisurely back into the grazing country as the new buds of spring bulged and burst, heralding the continuing life cycle of Mother Nature's world. But forebodings of doom hung heavy over the lodges of the Crows.

Many of their brave young men had not returned from war and the holy men declared, "There was blood upon the moon." Where was their champion, Little White Bull? Perhaps he too was lying stiff and lifeless in the country of his enemies. There was sign that he and his companions had suffered misfortune when pack dogs belonging to the absentees came limping into camp—worn out and bedraggled—the loads missing from their backs.

To the old men in the village with long experience of war, the party's fate was all too obvious, but it would be many weeks before proper details became known to the people and then how the Crow womenfolk would cry and scream aloud for vengeance.

During the middle part of January, the combined force of Kicked-in-the-Belly and River Crows had left their winter camps and traveled some 300 miles east, following the twisting courses of the Yellowstone and Missouri rivers downstream, to visit Joseph Kipp`s Trading Post near the mouth of the Heart River. Here they exchanged buffalo robes and pelts for the white man's trade goods, particularly powder and ball, to see them through to the coming spring. At the same time, they paid an extended visit to their relatives and friends the Hidatsa and Mandan respectively, whose earth lodges stood within close proximity to the fort and to whom the Crows traded about 250 surplus ponies. Usually such excursions lasted no longer than six weeks, although in this case, owing to freezing weather and recurring storms, the month of March —"The Moon when buffalo and horses fill out"—was waxing full and still the Crow trading party was ensconced outside the timber walls of the fort, merely awaiting the skies to clear, before setting out for home.

It was then that a most violent storm blew up in the guise of a howling blizzard, which caused the Crows to seek shelter and sit idly around lodge fires, secure from the raging elements outside. The Crow horses were left to their own devices, spread out over the snow-covered Plain with no herders in attendance. For none would brave the storm until it abated its ferocity.

Meanwhile, a Sioux war party out scouring the countryside for enemies, had earlier spied the Crow horses dotted over the prairie. When at last the storm abated somewhat and, under cover of darkness, the raiders rounded up the scattered herd and drove off 150 head, being all the horses now belonging to the camp after trading their surplus animals to the Hidatsa.

Come morning the Crows discovered their loss and searching around, soon found a broad trail made by the missing animals clearly marked in the snow. Quickly a war party was organized and a short time later, a large group of warriors started out on foot in pursuit of the thieves and the stolen herd.

The pursuing party was eighty strong, including a few Mandan and Hidatsa allies who tagged along for the excitement of the chase. There were only two or three horses among them and instead, they relied upon pack dogs to carry their extra moccasins, dried food and also bundles of hide coverings which they took along as makeshift shelters.

The snow was deep from the previous night's fall, making it difficult for the thieves to move fast, whereas, some of the pursuers wore snowshoes which gave them the advantage in speed and thus, the Crows were confident of catching up with their quarry and retrieving the stolen stock.

At first the trail was easy to follow, but all that day the temperature remained below zero. Again snow began to fall, quickly covering the raider's tracks, while chilling winds blew even harder as the day wore on—tossing loose snow in great billowing clouds which reduced visibility to a few yards. Before long, all the Crows could do was to trudge on laboriously in the direction they supposed the thieves had taken. But day after day they continued their trek through the ever-deepening snow. Even the pack dogs found it difficult to keep up, as every so often they would disappear under drifts of varying depths and had to be dug out by their masters.

At length, wet to the bone, cold and despondent and not knowing if the route they were travelling would eventually lead them to their quarry, the leaders of the party called a halt. The pursuit was proving a futile exercise and if they continued on in such foul weather, they would likely freeze to death in their tracks. Most agreed to give up their quest. Turning around, they began retracing their steps towards Kipp`s Fort.

But there were those among the party who refused to abandon the chase. Taking one pack horse and a few pack dogs with them, they crept silently away from the main body, without the consent of the Pipe Bearers, and set off through the still swirling blizzard, determined to continue searching for the thieves to recapture the stolen herd and, hopefully, obtain a few scalps thrown in for good measure. Among their number was a famed but reckless warrior named Little White Bull and it was he who carried the pipe on this occasion, i.e. led them.

James Beckwourth always rendered this warrior`s name as `Little Grey Bull,` although a proper translation from the Crow language would be "He who is always looking at the albino buffalo." The Crows often referred to him simply as, Little White Buffalo or Little White Bull. He was a member of the Whistling Water Clan of the Kicked-in-the-Belly band and was purported to possess big medicine powers, one of which, supposedly rendered him invulnerable to bullets. Even though a comparatively young man, already he had become a leader of distinction on the warpath and a member of the seventeen-strong chief's council of his nation. As such, he had been one of the signatories to the Friendship Treaty of 1825 between the Absaroka Nation and the American government. He was, indeed, regarded as what the Crows themselves would call, "A Good Man" among his clan and one whom everybody looked up to as an example of virtue and of valor.[12]

Little White Bull walked at the head of his companions, bedecked in a bright red Hudson's Bay blanket coat—commonly called a "capote"—which caused him to stand out in sharp contrast against the whiteness of the snow.[13]

The party comprised twenty-three persons, two of whom were boy servants going along as novices on their first war trip. Their duties would require repairing worn out moccasins of the veteran warriors in the group and performing all other menial tasks, such as collecting firewood, cooking the warrior's meals if needed and gathering brush and dead logs for shelter.

When deeming themselves far enough away from the main body so as not to be overtaken and forced to return with the rest, Little White Bull left a sign on the trail to indicate to any of his people who might wish to know, that they were going into the country of the Cheyenne in search of the spoils of war.[14]

In his memoirs, James Beckwourth implied that he personally knew several of the warriors who made up this second party and further declared, they were, "The Elite;" the "Braves des Braves," of the whole Crow nation at that time.[15]

While in yet another account referring to this same episode, it is reported, ". . .These men scorned to give up on a trail without even a glimpse of the enemy."[16]

It would appear then, that this second group led by Little White Bull, was composed of members belonging to a particular warrior society among the Crows, commonly known as "Big Dogs," whose singular code it was, not to abandon a chase until the enemy was met. Some of their number had sworn never to retreat in the face of danger, even if it meant certain death. These latter wore hide sashes across their chests variously decorated with beads or porcupine quills and were the equivalent of "Dog Ropes," as used by the Cheyennes and some other tribes. Unlike the Cheyennes, however, these Crow "Sash Wearers" were not obliged by society law to stake themselves to the ground and die fighting where they stood, unless a comrade physically whipped them from the field. Although if a fellow member was in need of assistance, then it was the wearer's solemn duty to go to his aid and if circumstance demanded, to sacrifice his own life in defense of his comrade.

The most important man among the Big Dogs was he who wore the Bearskin belt (with paws attached) around his waist. Such a man had pledged to stand his ground whenever his comrades were in retreat and was fully expected to die on the field of combat—and many did just that. If a Bear Belt Wearer came home alive after his comrades had been killed or, in some other way failed to honor his pledge, then he would suffer unbearable disgrace inciting ridicule and accusations of cowardice from the people. On the other hand, the Pipe Bearer or leader of a Big Dog party, even though expected to always take the initiative and be among the first to engage the foe, was not forced by society rules to sacrifice his life rather than retreating from the field; yet, in reality, death was invariably the preferred option. Members of the Big Dog Society were the incorrigible heroes of their tribe and, in all likelihood, made up the bulk of this second Crow war party with Little White Bull at its head. [17]

It was not known among this party where exactly they would find their enemies, although Little White Bull had a good idea regarding the general location where some Cheyenne bands were likely to be encamped in winter quarters. Thus the party was in high spirits; confident that they would catch their enemies huddled in thick buffalo robes waiting for the storm to pass. But the fickle hand of fate was guiding this small party of Crows into a confrontation that would be disastrous to them all.

It was now the latter part of March and still falling snow and biting winds prevailed,

The allied camps of Sioux, Cheyenne and trappers at the mouth of the Powder were yet together, the occupants merely awaiting clear weather before separating into their respective bands to pursue individual objectives.

Whether it had been warriors from these particular Sioux and Cheyenne bands, who had run off the Crow horses outside Kipp`s Fort is not recorded. It is more likely, though, that the raiders had come from some other Sioux band; Yanktonai or Hunkpapa perhaps, whose regular stomping ground was in the Mandan and Hidatsa area and that the occupants of the allied camps along the Powder, were entirely ignorant of the whole affair.

Whatever the case, it was only a matter of time before the small Crow war party led by Little White Bull came lumbering through the snow, heading unwittingly toward these same camps of their mortal foes.

Eventually, however, Little White Bull's party, having endured many days of hard travelling, decided it was time to give up their quest and return home, albeit empty-handed. Unfortunately, their homeward route was now taking them very close to the Lower Powder, where their enemies were actually encamped.

A fierce blizzard was still whipping across the land and the Crows could not distinguish the tepees of their enemies—camouflaged as they were amid the high drifts and snow-covered foliage of the surrounding district. The wind must also have been blowing in the wrong direction or, surely, they would have smelled the smoke from campfires or, at least, caught the sound of neighing horses and the general commotion which likely emanated from the Allied gathering. For in truth, it was the Allies who first discovered the Crows.

According to the Sioux account, it was just as the sun was going down the day before the fight, that the Crow party was sighted by a Sioux herder.[18] While the Cheyennes declare, that some of their own warriors had already started out on a war trail when they spied the Crows from a distance coming towards them. The Cheyenne war party then lay in ambush—they say—and the following morning attacked the Crows and killed them all. [19]

Beckwourth`s memory of the affair seems to concur with the Sioux version, adding that the Crows unwittingly set up their night camp on open scrubland between the Allied villages. The Sioux on one side, the Cheyennes and Shutaio on the other.

All accounts agree, however, that the Crows, under the watchful eyes of their enemies, made camp the night before the battle, completely unaware of the danger they were in.

Another Mountain Man named W. A. Ferris, who was well acquainted with the Crows and although not actually present during the fight but had himself heard the story many times from participants, said that during the night, under cover of a storm, a number of Cheyenne and Sioux warriors secreted themselves near the Crow position and waited patiently for sunrise before launching their attack.[20]

With the coming of dawn the Crows arose from slumber, ate a scant breakfast of dried pemmican and jerky and began reloading their one horse and several pack dogs— ready to resume their homeward journey. Meanwhile the Allied warriors who had endured a cold and sleepless vigil, watched the preparations. When they saw the Crows preparing to leave, they jumped from concealment and attacked.

For an instant the Crows stood frozen in their tracks, bewildered by the sudden appearance of their enemies. Too late they realized their blunder. The next moment the Allies were charging pell mell towards them and the Crows, upon abandoning their pack horse, were in full flight across the snow. But the Crows were completely surrounded. In desperation they made for a nearby hollow which was a stream bed, half-filled with slush and crossed by the trunk of a fallen tree and here, they proposed to make their stand.

Within minutes of the Allies` war cry being raised, a host of Cheyennes and Sioux warriors came tumbling from their lodges, snatching up weapons as they did so and were soon racing over the prairie in the dim light of dawn, each eager to reach the Crows and count the first coup of the battle.

Many of the white trappers, although usually indifferent to intertribal conflicts, lest their involvement jeopardized future dealings with one tribe or the other, were in this instance, only too keen to join in the fray and indulge themselves in the general furor of the occasion. However, as soon as the Crows were secured in their defensive position, the Allies momentarily called off their assault. These were the warriors who had kept vigil through the night and had been first to open the fight.

A Sioux chief then stepped forward and addressed the Crows in their own language supplemented with signs. He told them he was sorry to keep them in suspense, but his warriors were frozen to the bone, having spent a miserable night without fire so as not to give their presence away. They were, he said, compelled to warm themselves before they could proceed. But, the chief concluded, "As soon as we thaw ourselves you will cease to exist, unless you are what your name indicates and fly away or like the prairie dog, you can burrow into the ground." [21]

Accordingly, the Allies lit fires and warmed their limbs, while the poor Crows in turn, merely looked on and shivered with the cold.

According to Joe Medicine Crow's account, as he heard it, Little White Bull now turned to his companions and declared that those among them who wished to make a dash for freedom were at liberty to do so. He, however, had made up his mind to stay and die in this very place and if it be his fate to die alone, then so be it.

Upon hearing these words, his comrades were momentarily silent. But if any among them thought—even fleetingly—of attempting to escape, they said nothing. They regarded each other as brothers, all being of the same warrior fraternity and thus, each was loath to abandon their leader, whatever the dire outcome might be. So it was, that this small band of beleaguered Crows waited in silence and with apprehension for the fight.[22]

By the time the besieging Allies were sufficiently thawed, most of the warriors from the two villages had come up and together, they all at once charged upon the Crows. Those on horseback galloped around the hollow while others on foot, half-naked in spite of the cold, rushed headlong into the attack, brandishing clubs and lances above their heads or shooting arrows as they went. The small party of Crows opened fire with their short-barreled muskets at almost point blank range. They fired as fast as they could reload and the mass of Allies in their reckless excitement went smashing blindly into the hail of leaden balls. Several in their front ranks fell twitching in the snow. The charge broke even before it reached the hollow.

The Allies were forced to withdraw and after counting their wounded in both men and horses, contemplated another strategy

Albeit accidentally, the Crows had chosen a strong position. But their destruction was inevitable considering the numbers set against them. They did nonetheless, manage to keep their enemies at bay and for a while, deter them from making another massed charge.

Indeed, after their initial show of enthusiasm, the Cheyennes and Sioux resorted to sniping from cover and although the Crows returned every shot, the momentum of battle slowed.

Other than the occasional report of a firearm exploding from one side or the other, the contest gave way to the Allies hurling abuse at the Crows and the latter retaliating with their yells of defiance.

Now in the Cheyenne village at this time there was a man named Medicine Water, a Hevitanio band member, fast earning a reputation as an astute and fearless warrior of the Cheyenne Bow String Society. He was also the brother-in-law of Black Lodge, who had owned a famous "iron shirt" with matching helmet before being killed by enemies in the south the previous year. Black Lodge had not been wearing the shirt when killed and after his death, the garment had passed into the hands of Medicine Water, having been given to him by the relatives of its previous owner. Throughout the shirt's history while in Indian hands, it had been worn in many an intertribal conflict and was generally regarded as "big medicine." [23]

Indeed, it was this same iron shirt which had been worn by the Cheyenne Chief Rising Elk ten years earlier during the attack upon Long Hair`s Crow village, when the 400 Crow prisoners had been taken.

Its present owner had not yet worn the shirt in battle, having acquired it only a short time before and because of the untimely death of Black Lodge, he was perhaps a little reluctant to do so until it again proved its worth to show that its medicine was still strong.

Medicine Water was in the Cheyenne camp when the Crow party of Little White Bull had first been discovered, but he had not yet joined the fight. Instead, he sat in his lodge contemplating the situation.

It was at this time that Medicine Water`s brother [whose name has been forgotten], came to him and requested to wear the iron shirt in the fighting then going on around the hollow. He would perform great deeds—he said—and all would see how strong was the power of the shirt. Medicine Water agreed and his brother hastily put it on. The helmet, though, he discarded because of its weight and uneasiness upon the head, restricting free movement—a mistake which would cost him dear.

The iron-clad Cheyenne then mounted his war pony and erect in the saddle, rode out alone into the open space between his people and the enemy. By this time the heavy fighting had ceased and the besiegers were shooting at the Crows from cover. The lone Cheyenne thus arrayed, paraded slowly along the Allied lines—proud and majestic—enabling all present to marvel at his splendor. His sudden appearance occasioned much excitement among his fellow Cheyennes and the Sioux, while, no doubt, drawing forth a few humorous asides from those white trappers in attendance.

After proclaiming aloud his prowess and addressing the enemy with contempt, the iron-clad Cheyenne suddenly let out an ear-splitting war whoop and kicking his pony's flanks with his heels, rode at a gallop straight for the hollow wherein the Crows were crouched.

As their iron-clad nemesis urged his pony forward, a barrage of musket shot burst from the Crow position and the Cheyenne's horse suddenly buckled, keeled over, throwing its rider over its head. Its rider, though, was unscathed. Quickly he regained his feet and so sure of his invulnerability, continued on foot towards the hollow, under the very muzzles of Crow guns.

A great cheer of bravado resounded from the throats of the onlooking Allies. Yet before he had gone a few steps more, a single shot rang out and a well-aimed Crow musket ball struck the Cheyenne in the forehead, killing him outright. His over-weighted body went crashing to the ground, his life's blood staining the whiteness around him.[24]

Seeing him fall, the Cheyennes and Sioux, like a frenzied mob, rushed to the attack in an effort to retrieve the body before the Crows could wreak vengeance upon it. But again the fire from the hollow beat them back and they were forced to leave their champion to the mercy of the foe.

The Crow chief in his bright red blanket coat and carrying only a knife, now leapt from the hollow and rushing over the snow to the prostrate Cheyenne, began stabbing him about the body, screaming oaths of vengeance as he did so. The iron shirt encasing his fallen foe prevented his knife from piercing the flesh and in his continued frenzy, he proceeded to cut off the hands and feet of his victim and to sever the head from its shoulders. The Cheyennes and Sioux howled with anger as they watched their comrade being thus abused and, at the same time, unleashed a shower of missiles at the Crow chief as he calmly went about his grisly work. Try as they might, the Allies failed to bring him down and the Crow remained undaunted as arrows and balls flew thick about him. At length, he rose to his feet and facing the Allies, held aloft the bloodied severed head. He made signs across the field and cried aloud to them in Crow,

"See now Cheyenne dogs, here is your champion. It is this one, 'He that keeps looking at the albino buffalo' who has done this terrible thing." [25]

Next he took hold of the trophy by the braids and swung it around in the air above him, then shook it in the faces of the enemy as he taunted them to, "Come on and fight." [26]

But none of the Allies came forth to meet him.

Finally, after tossing the severed trophy across the snow in an expression of disgust, the lone Crow returned to his companions, having shown that his protective medicine was all-powerful and that he for one, was not afraid of those arrayed against him.

After this, several of the besieged Crows took their turn one by one, of clambering over the bank and standing alone in the no man's land between the hollow and the enemy. They fought with those of the Allies who had courage enough to accept their individual challenges and face them in hand-to-hand combat. More than one Crow was killed and others seriously wounded. But it was Little White Bull himself who prevented their bodies falling into the hands of the foe. As soon as one of his comrades was slain or injured, he would leap over the bank of the hollow and after driving off the victorious attacker, would personally drag the corpse or wounded comrade back to where the remaining Crows were entrenched. It is said in present-day tribal tradition, that Little White Bull even dragged the dead and wounded bodies of his fallen foes into the hollow, whereupon, he and his companions vented their anger and hatred upon them with knives and hatchets, cutting the corpses to pieces and throwing the severed

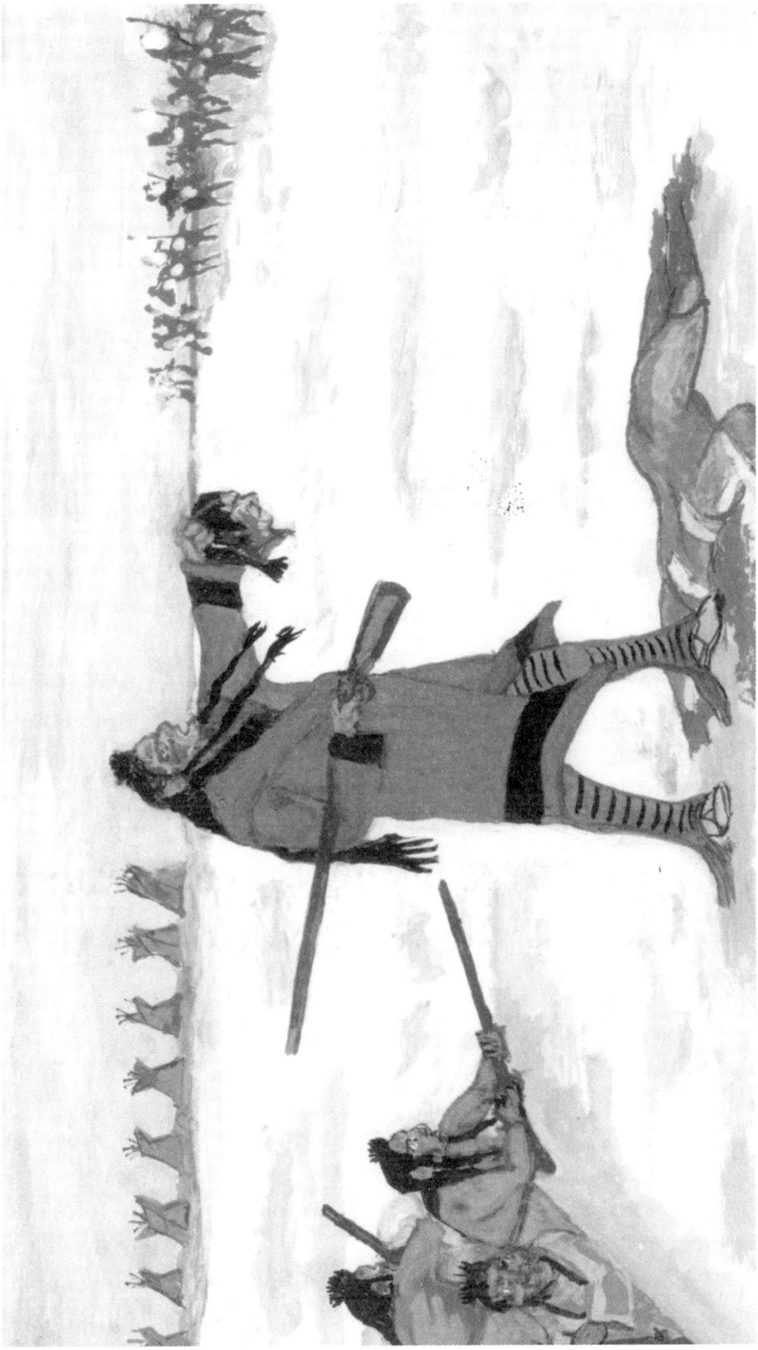

Author's watercolor

Little White Bull defies the enemy.

limbs across the snow toward the enemy who screamed in anger and seethed with an unbridled desire for revenge.[27]

At other times, individual Cheyenne and Sioux warriors charged the Crow position. But each time they were repulsed. Most of these attackers were on foot. They pranced around the hollow in a series of rash and sometimes costly outbursts, dodging from side-to-side, or zigzagging across the field so as to mar their enemies` aim. Meanwhile the rest of the surrounding Allies, continued to pour a steady stream of musket balls and arrows into the Crow position.

These lone assaults, however, proved non-productive and it was not long before such reckless individuals abandoned their attempts and no more did the Allies charge upon the hollow. Again they resorted to sniping from cover, lest they incurred more casualties at the hands of their determined foes. Soon, only the sporadic crack of a musket following a momentary flash and puff of white powder smoke emanating from the muskets on one side and the other, indicated that the conflict was still in progress and it was obvious that the fight had become a stand-off. The Crows could not escape and the Allies could not dislodge them.

Unfortunately for the Crows, every Allied attack left more of their number dead or wounded. Their own aim, though, if we are to accept Beckwourth`s assertion, was not without effect and several Cheyennes and Sioux also lay sprawled in the no-man's land between the two forces.

It is said that three of the defenders resisted manfully. But the others had become so benumbed with cold that they could make but little effort. It is more likely, however, that there was a shortage of ammunition among the Crows—if indeed all of them possessed guns in the first place. It does appear that as the battle progressed, the Crow defense rested almost entirely upon the actions of these three, though opposed by odds of at least fifty to one.

It had been comparatively early in the fight when the Crows slew the iron-clad brother of Medicine Water and as the morning wore on, the firing from the hollow had become more spaced.

The Crows were conserving their ammunition, determined to make every shot count. But still their courage did not falter. Their Death Songs rang out clear above the war whoops and victory chants of their enemies, who continued shooting every time a Crow exposed himself to view and at the same time, shouted threats across the field saying, "We will rub you out and feed your carcasses to our dogs." [28]

Slowly and painfully the hours dragged by. An icy chill was in the air and the blood froze solid in wounds. But when at last the sun reached its highest point in the sky, there came no sound from the hollow.

The Allies supposed that if the Crows were not all dead, then they had expended the last of their ammunition. They ceased their shooting and whooping and a deathly silence enveloped the scene.

After a while the Cheyennes and Sioux slowly stood up from cover, one after the other and quietly surveyed the bloody arena. Dotted around between themselves and the hollow were the dead and wounded—both men and horses—lying stiff and contorted on the frozen ground, some grotesque in their last agonizing throes of death.

By this time the wind had died down, the snow ceased to fall and the battle, it seemed, was over.

Then, suddenly from out of the hollow, like a ghost arising from its slumber, Little White Bull emerged. Cradling his trade musket in the crook of his left arm, he walked slowly yet deliberately toward the Allies who stood motionless before him, wide-eyed with mouths agape. Even the white trappers were amazed at what they saw.

Boldly the lone Crow came on—completely fearless. He was uttering oaths against his antagonists and gesturing in the sign language interspersed with a smattering of broken Sioux, that he had taken so many Sioux and Cheyenne scalps that his lodge was dark with their hair. He had ridden their horses, he boasted, until he was tired of riding. Then, pausing in his tracks, halfway between the Allies and the hollow, he stood motionless—proud and defiant—looking resplendent in his bright red blanket coat; his raised forelock stiffened with yellow clay showing predominant above his red-painted forehead, along with the long matted queue supplanted with beads and pine gum trailing from his crown and down his back, in all presenting an awe-inspiring sight. He beckoned to his enemies to "come close" and give him combat. But they drew back, wondering at his bravery and none would dare go near him.

It is said that Little White Bull also possessed a powerful medicine, which made him bulletproof and no matter how many times his Indian enemies shot at him, their missiles could do no harm. Already that morning the Allies had witnessed his power firsthand and were now in the firm belief that their guns and arrows were useless against him. Without getting close enough to strike with lance or tomahawk, they thought, they would be powerless to bring him down.

A Cheyenne replied in signs across the snow, telling the Crow chief to go home and tell his people what had happened, for he was too brave a man to kill. "You are no good," the Cheyenne said, meaning that he was invulnerable and that their missiles could not kill him. But still the brave Crow refused to leave, He was a man in love with death and again he cried aloud to his enemies and signed to them:

> "This one will not go home. You have slain his warriors and sent them to the land of *Ak-baatat-dia*. . . .Now kill me so that I may go with them. . . .This one does not want to live. . .My heart rejects your offer. . . This one who is called He who keeps looking at the albino buffalo," is waiting. . .Come now if any among you are brave . . .Come close and kill me."[29]

He pointed to the midday sun, standing high in the ashen sky above him .

"This one is like the sun," he said. "You will kill him, but he will not die until Sun itself hangs low in the sky."[30]

The Allies admired Little White Bull's courage. They repeated their offer of freedom. They even promised to supply a horse for his comfort and gave added assurances that no harm would come to him, if he would only vacate the field.

In disgust at the refusal of his enemies to accommodate his wish, the Crow chief gave up his pleading and returned to the hollow which was now filled with frozen corpses. He lay down among his dead companions and again the Allies could hear him calling, begging them to finish him off.

The Cheyennes and Sioux were respectful of Little White Bull`s medicine and realizing that a man who had pledged himself to die was always a dangerous adversary. They exercised extreme caution and continued to keep their distance. When, after a while the lone Crow yet again appeared atop the bloodstained bank and once more advanced towards them, the Allies drew back even farther and still refused to give him combat.

Author's photo

Joe Medicine Crow wears a red "Capote" of the type worn by Little White Bull in the 1830 battle.

Several times throughout the afternoon Little White Bull repeated his actions, advancing boldly towards the enemy—musket cradled in his arms—before returning to the hollow.

The day wore slowly on and all the while the verbal exchanges continued. On the one side the Allies urging him to take his freedom; on the other, the brave Crow hurling insults and abuse at his besiegers and begging them to kill him.

As time passed by, the sun began sinking below the western horizon and the light began to fade.

It was then that the Crow chief emerged from the hollow one last time and again, the Allies called to him saying, "Go away, you are no good." [31]

But as before, Little White Bull just stood there, calm and defiant. He now looked around him as if contemplating his plight, then suddenly, threw down his gun, took his knife from its scabbard and threw that down also and signed again to his enemies:

> "It is a bad thing that you have killed these poor boys. If this one were to go home now he would be grieving the rest of his days. Come my friends kill me, this one is now ready to die!" [32]

Seeing him thus unarmed, a group of Cheyennes and Sioux moved gingerly forward. "He has no weapons," they said to one another. But still they were afraid of his power and none attempted to get close enough to strike the fatal blow. Before long, Little White Bull returned to the hollow and sat down among his dead companions. [33]

Since before midday, after heavy fighting around the hollow had given way to sporadic sniping, most of the white trappers among the Allied host had watched from the sidelines. At length, however, they grew impatient for an end to the affair. If allowed to continue, they thought, then the Allies would eventually leave the field and the Crow chief be allowed to escape unmolested. There were those among the trappers who were less accommodating. According to Beckwourth, one of the trappers had been killed in the fight or, at least seriously wounded and his comrades wanted satisfaction. These men cared little for the so-called medicine of Little White Bull, neither had they any compassion for his plight. Why give him freedom, they reasoned, when he was sure to return with another war party sometime in the future to steal the trapper's horses, if not one or two of their scalps? It was true that although the Crows, ostensibly, professed friendship toward the white man, the Mountain Men knew the Crows were not averse to running off their horses, robbing the odd trapper of his equipment and pelts and even lifting a white man's scalp whenever the fancy took them. The philosophy of the trappers was that an Indian was an Indian no matter to what the tribe—and the fewer of them the better.

It is possible some of the trappers did have compassion for the lone Crow's plight and realizing that the situation was merely prolonging his agony, they were resolved to put him out of his misery.

One of the trappers crept near to the hollow and took up a position where he could just about see the head and shoulders of Little White Bull, who was then sitting on his haunches, resting his elbows on his knees while supporting his chin with his fists. He seemed to be staring hard at the ground, not being bothered to look around him. The trapper took careful aim with his musket, squeezed the trigger and as the weapon barked, the Crow went spinning backwards, his brains splattering out over the slush-filled hollow of death. [34]

Silence enveloped the scene and of the entire Crow party, only the forlorn pack horse, now in the keeping of the enemy, still stood on its feet, breathing the ice-chilled air.

Still, the Allies were reluctant to close in upon the hollow, until they were convinced all resistance had ceased. Finally, several Cheyennes and Sioux crawled forward on their bellies, expecting any moment that Little White Bull would reappear. But when at last they reached the bank, they stood up and looking down from the edge of the hollow, examined their gory work.

There lay the corpse of Little White Bull, amid the frozen contorted bodies of his dead companions. But there was no sign of pain on the Crow chief's face. He looked serene, as if asleep. Perhaps, thought the Allies, he was asleep and was actually bulletproof. They approached him cautiously with raised axes and when near enough, smashed his head to pieces to assure themselves that he was truly dead. Even then, the backside of the Crow chief, it is said, suddenly reared up and the body started turning somersaults head over heels around the hollow. The Cheyennes and Sioux could not stop the carcass moving, although they struck it many blows with their axes and shot arrows into it. At length, the Allies built a fire, threw the chief's body upon it and burned it up until there was nothing left but charred bones and ashes.[35]

The great Crow chief who seemed to defy his foes even in death, was at last with his warrior brothers in the spirit land of his forebears.

To the amazement of the Cheyennes and Sioux, they found huddled in one corner of the hollow hidden among the frozen corpses, the two boy servants of the Crows, shamming death. For the moment the Allies had sated their thirst for blood. They took pity on the boys and took them into captivity with a view to adopting them among their own. The two servants, though, had other ideas. Either fearing torture at the hands of their captors or simply in abhorrence at the prospect of spending the rest of their days among the slayers of their comrades, the youths drew concealed knives and stabbed the guards.[36] Almost immediately they were set upon by their enraged captors and within moments, were hacked to pieces.

The Allies now lost all self-control. They screamed for vengeance and in a frenzy of bloodlust, hauled the Crow bodies from the hollow and butchered the corpses in a truly savage and revolting manner. They tore off the scalps and stripped them of their clothing, then cut off the heads and amputated the frozen limbs before using dogs to drag the mangled corpses to their camps.[37]

The victors danced and sang as they waved their grizzly trophies triumphantly in the air. The Crow heads were raised on poles and paraded among the people, who prodded them with sticks and poked the eyes from the sockets and when the adults had mocked them enough, the children played ball with the skulls, kicking them in and out among the tepees.[38]

The trappers were invited to the revelries as honored guests. Kegs of whiskey were tapped and the white men too, whooped and stomped as energetically as any befeathered Indian. Only a small number of trappers had actually participated in the fight, but of those who did, they had played an important role because they were excellent marksmen. It was, of course, a trapper's musket ball which had snuffed out the life of Little White Bull.

Although few of the Allies had actually been slain outright during the fight, several of warriors died later of wounds. Thus, in contrast to the victory dances and feasting, in more secluded parts of the villages, relatives of the Allies slain, lamented their recently departed kinfolk.

Some wandered aimlessly, wailing monotonous dirges with bone skewers thrust through their bodies, piercing the breast or shoulders and to these, were attached long rawhide thongs, from which depended a dead kinsmen's shield or a buffalo skull, to be dragged laboriously over the rocks, while the mourners themselves bled profusely from numerous self-inflicted wounds.

Such was the price to pay for victory and those who danced and sang in jubilation of deeds performed in the recent affray, made sure they made the most of it. They knew the next time it might be their limbs and scalps being abused and humiliated by the foe.

All agreed the likes of the Crow Chief Little White Bull had not been seen in recent time and even though he was an enemy, the Cheyennes and Sioux could not but marvel at his bravery. The story of his lone stand against such fearful odds was a lesson for all and would be told and retold around lodge fires for many snows to come.

NOTES AND SOURCES.

1 Victor, Mrs. Frances F. *"The River of the West."* pp. 83-84. Hartford, 1870.

2 Ibid. 1870. pp. 83-84.

3 James King. [Northern Cheyenne informant] to Author. Note pad 1. p.8. Lame Deer, Montana. August 1994.

4 Hungry Wolf, Adolph. *"The Blood People."* p. 194. [Bad Head`s winter count]. [1977]. See also; Raczka, Paul M. *"Winter Count."* [Bull Plume] p. 42, Published by; Oldman River Culture Centre, Brocket, Alberta. 1979.

5 Bonner, [T. D.] *"Life and Adventures of James P. Beckwourth."* pp.162-163. [1856] Ross and Haines Co.Ltd. [Reprint] 1956.

6 Ibid. pp.162-163.

7 Joe Medicine Crow to Author. Note pad 2. p.4. Lodge Grass. Montana. 1996.

8 Kappler, Charles.J. *"Indian Laws, Affairs And Treaties." "1825."*pp. 231-236. [Signers of treaty between Crow Indians and the United States in 1825, commonly known as *"The Friendship Treaty"* or *"The Atkinson and O`Fallon Treaty"*]. Government Printing Office.Washington DC. [various publications].

9 The *St. Louis Enquirer*. July 19. 1824.

10 It is inconceivable to suppose that Arickaras should simply take up residence in what was then regarded as Sioux and Cheyenne hunting grounds, without prior consent or knowledge of that area's more aggressive inhabitants who, it might be said, jealously guarded their domain against all uninvited guests. While it is true that the Cheyenne were almost constantly at war with the Arickara at this period, as also were the Sioux, there yet persisted a degree of intermarriage and intertribal trade between them and, on rare occasions, during brief periods of friendship, all three peoples did confederate against mutual enemies, such as the Mandan, Shoshoni or Crow. Cf; Leonard, Zeneas. *"Narrative of Adventures."* pp.94ff. University of Nebraska Press. 1978. Leonard mentions that he and his party of trappers were attacked by Arickaras in the Black Hills near the head of the North Platte [Laramie Mountains?] and also, that the Arickara were then at war with the Crows. See also; Chardron, F.A. *"The Chardron Journal."* pp.80-81. University of Nebraska Press. 1997. Here Chardron states that the Arickara, for several years previous to 1836, had been residing in the Black Hills district, ostensibly, those so named of south-western South Dakota. See also; Hyde, George E. *"The Pawnee Indians."* P.184. University of Oklahoma Press. 1973 where it is stated that the Arickara in several groups, abandoned their Missouri river towns in the summer of 1832. Most went to their Skidi Pawnee relatives near the mouth of the North Platte in Nebraska. However, during their trek, they [the Arickara] stayed sometime in the Black Hills region of South Dakota most likely joining those of their kinfolk already in that area, before moving on and it is evident, that at least thirty Arickara lodges continued to remain in the aforesaid district after the bulk of their people had left..

11 Palmer, George. *" Montana, The magazine of American History."* no.28. [July 1978.] pp. 31-33.

12 Medicine Crow, Joe. Personal interview with Author, Note pad 2. p 4. Lodge Grass. Montana. August.1994.

13 Medicine Crow, Joe. Personal interview with Author, Note pad 2. p.4. Lodge Grass. Montana. August.1994.

14 Bonner, [T. D.] *"Life and Adventures of James P. Beckwourth."* p. 273. [1856] Ross and Haines Co.Ltd. [reprint] 1956.

15 Bonner, T. D. *"Life and Adventures of James P. Beckwourth."* p.273. [1856] Ross and Haines Co. Ltd. [reprint] 1956.

16 Ferris, W. A. *"Life in the Rocky Mountains."* p.307. Denver Old West Publishing Company. 1940.

17 Lowie, Robert H. *"The Crow Indians."* pp. 192-197. Holt, Rinehart and Winston. New York. 1930.

18 Mallery, Garrick. *Picture-Writing of the American Indians.* [i.e. The American Horse Winter count.] Vol. 2. p.553. Dover Publications. New York. Reprint from The Tenth Annual Report of the Bureau of American Ethnology, Smithsonian Institution. Washington DC. 1888-`89.

19 Grinnell, George Bird. *"Papers,"* [1900.] MS.509. Indian Armour. See also the Grinnell papers, MS. 398 *"Story of the iron shirt."* Southwest Museum. Los Angeles. California.

20 Ferris, W. A. *"Life in the Rocky Mountains."* p. 307. Denver Old West Publishing Company. 1940.

21 Ferris, W. A. *"Life in the Rocky Mountains."* p. 307. Denver Old West Publishing Company. 1940. [The details in this and the previous three paragraphs are taken from the Ferris account].

22 Medicine Crow, Joe. Personal interview with Author, Note pad 2. p.4. Lodge Grass. Montana. August.1994.

23 Grinnell, George Bird. *"Papers,"* [1900.] MS.509. Indian Armour. See also the Grinnell papers, MS. 398 *"Story of the iron shirt."* Southwest Museum. Los Angeles. California. See also; Grinnell *"papers."* Folder 5. *"Dog-faced-medicine-man."* P.1. 1905.

24 Grinnell, George Bird. *"Papers,"* [1900.] MS.509. Indian Armour. See also the Grinnell papers, MS. 398 *"Story of the iron shirt."* Southwest Museum. Los Angeles. California. See also; Grinnell *"papers."* Folder 5. *"Dog-faced-medicine-man."* P.1. 1905.

25 James King, [Northern Cheyenne informant.] Interview with Author, August 1994.

26 James King, [Northern Cheyenne informant] Interview with Author, Note pad 1. p.6. Lame Deer. August 1994.

27 Medicine Crow, Joe. Personal interview with Author, Note pad 2. p.4. Lodge Grass. Montana. August.1994.

28 Ferris, W.A. *"Life in the Rocky Mountains."* p. 307. Denver Old West Publishing Company. 1940.

29 Medicine Crow, Joe. Personal interview with Author, Note pad 2. p.4. Lodge Grass. Montana. August.1994.

30 Lowie, Robert H. *"Crow Texts."* p.440. Berkley University of California Press. [1960]. See also; Grinnell, George Bird. *"papers,"* MS. 509. Indian Armour. See also; Grinnell papers, MS. 398 *"Story of the iron shirt."* Southwest Museum. Los Angeles. California.

31 Lowie, Robert H. *"Crow Texts."* p.440. Berkley University of California Press. [1960].

32 James King, [Northern Cheyenne informant] Interview with Author, note pad 1. p.6. Lame Deer. August 1994. See also; Lowie, Robert H. *"Crow Texts."* p.440. Berkley University of California Press. [1960].

33 Lowie, Robert H. *"Crow Texts."* p.440. Berkley University of California Press. [1960].

34 Bonner, T. D. *"Life of Beckwourth."* p.284. [1856.] Ross and Haines Co. Ltd. [reprint] 1956.

35 Lowie, Robert H. *"Crow Texts."* p.440. Berkley University of California Press. [1960].

36 Bonner, [T. D.] *"Life and Adventures of James P. Beckwourth."* p. 284. [1856] Ross and Haines Co.Ltd. [reprint] 1956. Crow informants of Robert H. Lowie early in the twentieth century, when narrating a quasi-historical account of the fight, stated that two of the besieged Crows had actually escaped from the hollow and viewed the whole affair from a nearby hiding place. They, thereafter, carried word of the slaughter back to their own people in the Crow country. Lowie, Robert H. *"Myths and traditions of the Crow Indians."* pp.175-176. University of Nebraska Press. [1993].

37 Ferris, W. A. *"Life in the Rocky Mountains."* p.307. Denver Old West Publishing Company. 1940.

38 Medicine Crow, Joe. Personal interview with Author, Note pad 2. p.4. Lodge Grass. Montana. August.1994.

Chapter Five

Little White Bull is Avenged

The main portion of the party that had pursued the horse thieves returned to the Hidatsa villages west of Kipp`s Fort. They had been back several days when the pack dogs that had been with Little White Bull's party limped into camp. This was the first indication that the latter might have suffered misfortune.[1]

As the weeks passed with no word of the absent warriors, many among the Crows concluded that Little White Bull and his comrades had met with disaster. But there were others who remained optimistic, refusing to accept the signs. Perhaps the party had gone further afield than originally intended.

Was it not only a few years since, that the great River Crow Twines- His-Horse's-Tail returned to his people after a two and half year absence, having undertaken a war trip which led him and his companions into the very heart of the land of *Uuk-a-shee*? ("Lodges made of clay," i.e. Pueblo Indians and Mexicans).[2] It could be that Little White Bull`s party was following in the footsteps of that illustrious predecessor, so the relatives of those missing would allow no mourning rites to proceed until proof of the party's demise was received.

Old men among the Crows—grizzled veterans of many a warpath—were not so naive. They discussed the issue between themselves and speculated upon the manner in which their compatriots might have fallen. As a rule, none would publicly declare their misgivings, for it was considered very bad luck to talk of mishap while a party was still out and unaccounted for. This time, however, their pessimistic murmurings were not subdued. Little White Bull was a highly respected warrior, much loved and admired by his clanfolk and now sorely missed by all.

At length, the trading party got ready to leave the Hidatsas, in order to return to their home camps in the far away Yellowstone Country.

Before they could start, however, the Crows had to buy back some of the ponies they had sold to their hosts. For although a number of horse stealing raids had been conducted against the Hunkpapa, Yankton and the Arickara, the expeditions had not supplied enough animals to transport the Crow party home. Their Hidatsa cousins took full advantage of the situation. The Hidatsa virtually cleaned out the Crows of all the white man`s trade goods they had recently amassed, including guns, powder, ball and an assortment of trinkets and domestic items. It was a despondent, not to mention impoverished Crow group, that finally set out for home.[3]

Once back in the Yellowstone Country, Chief Sore Belly and his headmen convened a council to discuss the possibilities of Little White Bull`s fate. After a period of deliberation, it was decided to send out a group of warriors to search for the missing party and determine if its members be alive or dead.

It was known that Little White Bull had intended to raid the Cheyenne winter camps specifically, and the Crows were fully aware that certain bands often spent the winter months somewhere along the course of the lower Powder or one of its connecting streams. Consequently, it was in that direction in the early part of April that the Crow search party traveled. It was a strong force of around fifty warriors, each of whom was well mounted and armed; several carrying smoothbore trade guns or old muskets with the barrels cut down, so as to be handled more easily from horseback.

As they traveled, the warriors were on the alert, lest they ran foul of one or another roving enemy force which, during this time of year, usually invested the country through which they intended to pass.

In the meantime, owing to a period of severe stormy weather immediately following the Little White Bull slaughter, the Allied camps of Sioux, Cheyenne and trappers at the mouth of the Powder had been prevented from moving—which gave rise to a certain amount of anxiety on the part of the Allies, ere the ghosts of the slain Crow warriors should haunt their killers or, in some other supernatural way, bring calamity upon them. It was not until the beginning of April,

"The Moon when rivers begin to rise," that the bands finally left winter quarters.

The trappers were probably the first to leave, having divided their people into two companies. One headed southwest into the Wind River region to retrieve pelts and furs cached the previous autumn. The other, with Jim Bridger as guide, moved due west to and beyond Rosebud Creek.

Most of the Hevietanio Cheyennes along with their Sioux allies, moved up the Powder, thence across country in a southeasterly direction so as to reach the Laramie branch of the North Fork of the Platte. Here buffalo congregated in large number during spring and early summer and here also, the bulk of the Hevietanio lingered before moving farther south to visit Bent's Trading Post and the pony herds of their Kiowa and Comanche enemies. It seems that the last of the Allied bands to leave the mouth of the Powder was the main Shutaio group, which also moved due west (though independent of the trappers), heading for the rich hunting country along the Tongue, which region they now regarded as their own.

It was only a day or two after the last of the Allied bands left their winter quarters that the Crow search party arrived on the scene.

The Crows rummaged among the abandoned campsites. It was not long before someone stumbled across the scattered remains of their missing kinfolk who had gone with Little White Bull. These were recognized by hair and ear ornaments and personal amulets, still attached to some of the severed heads and mangled limbs left lying amid the debris of the camps.

The Crows were overcome with grief when they realized that the whole party belonging to Little White Bull had been destroyed. As was their custom, the searchers shed copious tears while, at the same time, they swore oaths of vengeance upon the slayers and cried to *Akbaa-tadia* to assist them in seeking revenge.

It was a singular custom among the Crows, whenever they found themselves at an old battle site where a number of their luckless tribesmen had been rubbed out, that the visitors would show their grief and respect by slashing themselves with knives and spilling a certain amount of their own blood, usually over a cairn of stones which the visitors erected for that purpose.[4] But even these Crow warriors, veterans all and hardened by their own experiences in war, were a

Smithsonian Institution

Crow Chief He Who Ties His Hair Before. Author's sketch from a painting from life by George Catlin in 1832.

little surprised to see the extent of mutilations inflicted upon the corpses. They thought that either many of the enemy must have been killed or seriously wounded in the fight or, that some renowned warrior or chief among the victors had been slain, so as to give rise to such an unbridled frenzy of gore.

This party of Crows had only intended to discover the whereabouts of the missing kinsmen and report their findings to Sore Belly in camp along the Yellowstone. But the grisly sight which met their eyes incensed their passions to such extent it was decided to hunt down the culprits and extract some measure of retribution before returning home with news of the disaster.

Several trails led from the abandoned campsites. One of these appeared comparatively fresh and was less broad than the others, indicating that it had been made by a smaller number of people. The Crows followed that track in the hopes of catching their enemies on the move encumbered with pony drags and camp equipment, when they would be at the mercy of the attackers.

The trail proved easy to follow and the searchers had not gone more than six miles upon it before they spotted a small camp of nine lodges, nestling peaceably on the open plain. Surrounding the camp were many loose ponies, milling around seemingly unattended. The people in the camp were unperturbed at the sudden appearance of horsemen only a bow shot away. They apparently supposed the riders to be from their main camp which, it was later learned, was positioned not far distant.

The Crows had no doubt that the trail was evidence enough to assume that the people ahead were not only enemies, but part of those culpable in the actual slaughter of Little White Bull and his comrades.

They realized also that a much larger enemy village was likely to be in the vicinity or, the small number before them would not have placed themselves in such an open and vulnerable position.

The Crows decided to attack the camp head-on without the usual delay, which would have involved their parading in front of the foe, in order to show off their paint and feathers and prancing horses before the battle commenced. The Crows wanted to do as much damage as possible to the camp and its occupants, drive off the ponies and escape the scene before the alarm could be raised to bring reinforcements from other camps in the area.

Without warning, the fifty Crows let out blood-chilling war cries and whipping their mounts into a gallop, charged toward the camp. The warriors beat pony quirts on their hide covered shields and waved blankets above their heads, in an effort to stampede the herd and panic the enemy into precipitous flight.

The startled camp occupants too late realized what was happening. As the Crows came racing toward them, scores of frightened women and children frantically searched for a way of escape. Some of the men bravely stood their ground, facing the charging Crows, and these few were cut down where they stood. The attackers rode in amongst the tepees, wrecking everything in their path. Such was the momentum of the charge, that the defenders had no time to organize a practical defense. Consequently, they were no match against the fury of their attackers. Very soon all resistance was subdued and the whole camp in the hands of the Crows.

While the fight was in progress, two figures were observed standing motionless some distance away on the crest of a small knoll. Apparently they were members of the camp, but having been out hunting, returned too late to assist their beleaguered kinfolk. They had little choice but to watch the destruction of the lodges and the slaughter of their people, powerless to help, lest they sacrificed their own lives with no practical gain. Instead, after a short while, the two observers jumped on their ponies and sped across the plain to raise the alarm among others of their tribesmen and hasten a relief force to the scene.[5]

The Crows had spotted these men on the skyline and saw them race off. They realized the two had a good start and were unlikely to be overtaken before reaching their main village. For this reason, the Crows were reluctant to give chase and allowed them to escape unmolested.[6]

A number of the Crow raiders rounded up the abandoned ponies, while others collected the women and children. Still others, ransacked the ruined tepees, taking weapons, animal skins and an assortment of personal belongings as booty.[7] The dead were scalped and robbed of their clothing and, presumably, mutilated in a similar fashion as had been the bodies of Little White Bull`s party.

Now the victorious Crows were in a vulnerable position. They were deep in hostile country, with perhaps an unknown number of enemy warriors preparing to come against them. It was expedient to remove themselves as quickly as possible into a more favorable area before their own party was surrounded by the full fighting force of the enemy and destroyed.

The Crows hurriedly packed their plunder on the backs of captured ponies and after placing the women and children prisoners astride the more gentle animals in the bunch, set off toward their own country in the north, leaving the ruined camp and a number of grieving widows behind them.

The Crows were not overtaken. They made good their escape without seeing more of the enemy. It was a jubilant party that returned to the Crow village along the Yellowstone. The warriors sang loud their victory songs and waved aloft slender willow wands from the ends of which trailed bloodied enemy topknots. Some warriors shot off captured guns in the air and the Crow women raised the tremolo in their honor. The victors brought with them several female prisoners and a young boy, along with a sizable herd of horses, while captured beaver, otter and other skins could be exchanged at the white man's trading posts for guns and ammunition.

According to the James P. Beckwourth account, if at first any had voiced doubts that the occupants of the camp they had been about to attack were guilty of involvement in the Little White Bull massacre, then their suspicions were fully stifled during the looting of the tepees, at which time weapons and other paraphernalia once belonging to that unfortunate party were found among the abandoned contents. If added proof was needed, sometime later, several of the captured women freely admitted their people's involvement and readily confessed that Little White Bull and his comrades had slain a number of Allied warriors before being killed themselves. [8]

James Beckwourth also stated in his memoirs that he was a member of the Crow search party on this occasion and that during the fight he killed and scalped one of the camp occupants, took his equipment and also captured two children. He said forty-eight of the enemy were slain, while not one of the attacking Crows was injured. [9]

Beckwourth may have been exaggerating. If the camp contained only nine lodges, then by employing the accepted ratio of two males of fighting age per lodge, the bulk of those killed must have been non combatants—women, children and old folk. This, however, is highly unlikely, as a captive woman or child was always considered more valuable a prize than a mere scalp and in no tribe was this more apparent than among the Crows. It would be more feasible to assume that many of the camp occupants ran into the hills before the camp was overrun, which would have been the usual response of non combatants in such circumstances.The Shutaio are most likely to have been the victims on this occasion.

In truth, this Crow victory over some of those responsible for the annihilation of Little White Bull and his party, even though welcomed by the tribe and celebrated accordingly, was but a brief respite in a current spate of misfortune suffered by some smaller Crow parties when engaged against enemy forces. Usually these conflicts took the form of tit-for-tat actions, such as reciprocal raids on their opponent's pony herds or the seeking of revenge for the death of a respected warrior. Such feuding, customarily, reached its height during the spring and summer months. Certainly, during the early part of summer 1830, the Cheyennes were particularly active on the Crow front, taking a number of scalps and stealing horses, without any significant acts of retaliation from the Crows.[13]

Around this date, the Crows possessed more horses per head of population than any other tribe on the Northern Plains. It was estimated by a contemporary observer, that the average number of animals then among them was fifteen horses per lodge, although some tribal members owned in excess of 100.[14] As a consequence, the Crows were almost constantly beset by raiding parties from neighboring tribes and even from more distant peoples who, having heard through the moccasin grapevine of the abundant number of fine ponies in the Crow Country, had made it their vocation in life to redistribute Crow wealth across the Plains. The Crows defended their property with vigor and often retaliated in kind—either to retrieve stolen stock or simply to increase their own herds, if not indeed, merely for the excitement of travelling the warpath which, in reality, was usually far greater an incentive than pure economic necessity alone. The Cheyennes always admitted that it was Crows who stole the greater number of their horses and were one of the tribes against whom the Cheyennes had to fight the hardest.[15]

The Crows could hold their own against their various enemies and, at this date, were slightly superior to the Cheyennes and Shutaio with regard to the number of warriors they could throw into the field. It is also certain that during this particular period (1830 to 1840) the Cheyennes and Shutaio lost as many warriors killed and women and children taken captive at Crow hands, as the Crows did at the hands of the Cheyennes and Shutaio. Generally speaking, it was an equal contest between the two before the late 1850s, by which time the Cheyennes had acquired the full weight of the Teton Sioux to assist them as allies in their hostile endeavors.

During the time in question, however (1830), the Crows had their great war chief Sore Belly among them. He not only brought the tribe many victories, but molded the Crow warriors into a formidable fighting force, respected by all.

THE FIGHT AT ANTELOPE CREEK

The Cheyennes were particularly troublesome on the Crow front during the summer of 1830. Moreover, these were Shutaio bands which hunted the lower Powder country and its tributaries often in close proximity to Crow camps. The Crows laid claim to this same area and were just as intent upon keeping it as the Shutaio were to take it. As a result, Cheyenne and Crow parties were more apt to clash than with war parties from other tribes. A state of near constant feuding existed between the two.

During the early part of this same summer, another Crow party was surprised on the open plains by a Cheyenne/Shutaio war party and completely routed. The survivors reached home badly mauled with several dead and wounded comrades in tow.[16] Once more the Crow women wailed and the whole village responded to their grief. As usual, the relatives of those slain cut finger joints from their hands and stabbed themselves in the head and chest with sharp stones and blunt knives. Then, with blood streaming from self-inflicted wounds, they wiped their bloody hands over the bodies of their menfolk, imploring them to avenge their loss. After several days and nights of watching these exaggerated expressions of grief, the warriors were sufficiently aroused. They harangued the Pipe Holders, requesting them to get up a grand war party which would strike a decisive blow against the "People of the Striped Arrows," as they called the Cheyennes and, thereby, dissuade that people's warriors from counting their coups in Crow Country.

James Beckwourth claims he was asked by the grieving Crows to organize the revenge raid and that he personally planned and directed the resulting expedition.[17] This is unlikely, even though he may have been a participating member of the foray. It is more likely that Crow Chief Sore Belly was in charge on this occasion and that this man not only led the Crow force, but singularly planned the whole affair. Certainly, the ensuing events present a typical example of Sore Belly`s force of mind along with the overall influence he exercised over his warriors.

It was near the end of May, "The moon when horses get fat," that a formidable Crow war party, ostensibly led by Sore Belly, started forth to wreak vengeance on the Cheyennes.

As the warriors rode out of their village, the womenfolk raised the customary tremolo in their honor and sang praise songs to their departing sons and husbands. At the same time, medicine men invoked the powers of the tribe's guardian spirits, beseeching them to aid the warriors in their venture.

It was a large party that started forth, comprising some 150 braves. With them, went a small number of women to cater to the warrior's domestic needs. Each warrior was well armed and mounted on a fine horse, while leading a fast buffalo runner to be used when charging the enemy. A few teenage boys also accompanied the party, to herd the horses at night and attend to various chores at the warrior's request.

For several days the party rode southeast at a leisurely pace, until they came into what was considered Cheyenne Country, then embracing the headwater district of the Little Missouri River.

The Crows exercised extreme caution, being constantly on their guard against surprise attack. The whole party bunched together, keeping away from the skyline or any high point and sent out scouts far to the front and on the flanks to keep a lookout for the foe. They moved ever deeper into the Cheyenne domain and could faintly discern in the distance the lonely eminence of Bear Butte, the "Sacred Mountain" of the "Striped Arrow People," the symbolic centre of the Cheyenne universe.

Continuing on with utmost caution, the Crows altered their direction and came eventually to a small stream, which Beckwourth in his account declares was then named Antelope Creek—a small tributary of the Missouri.[18] At this point the party went into temporary camp. A select body of thirty or more warriors was sent out to search the surrounding countryside for enemy sign and, if possible, to locate the Cheyenne village which chief Sore Belly believed would be in the vicinity.

Now it so happened that each of the ten scattered Cheyenne and Shutaio bands were already moving over the Plains from their respective early summer hunting grounds, heading toward a prearranged rendezvous point somewhere along the south fork of the Platte near the mouth of Crow Creek. Here the whole nation had agreed to congregate along with some of their Sioux allies, in preparation for the crusade against the Pawnees.[19] Consequently, only small groups of stragglers were in the district wherein the Crow scouts were searching, and just such a group was precisely what they found.

It was only a few days later when the Crow scouts returned to their main party, bringing word that they had discovered a small camp of thirty-seven Cheyenne lodges farther downstream along Antelope Creek. The small size of the enemy camp was welcome news and the Crows became excited at the prospect of, at last, being in a position to inflict a crushing blow upon their arch enemies who, in times past, had brought much grief and woe upon the Absaroka nation.

Sore Belly told the scouts to return to the enemy camp and continue watching the foe, but to inform him at once of any further developments. The rest of the party, he said, would follow up the scout's trail, but at its own pace along with the non combatants and their extra horses.

Thus the scouts went out again. But it was not long before some returned to the main party, saying the Cheyennes had now struck their lodges and moved farther downstream. The Cheyennes had pitched their camp at the mouth of a narrow canyon.

Sore Belly sent riders to call in all the scouts but ten, who he ordered to continue observing the enemy position, while he and his leading warriors formulated a plan of attack.

Because of the large number of warriors in the Crow party, Sore Belly decided to pass through the canyon itself and attack the enemy camp head-on from that direction. The Cheyennes, he thought, would then have their backs to the creek and would not be able to use the canyon's narrow defile, either as a means of defense or escape.

Filled with confidence, the Crow war party started off at once. But even before the warriors reached the canyon, the ten scouts came running into them to report that the enemy had moved yet again, still following the course of the creek downstream, but had now set their tepees amid a thick growth of timber bordering the creek bank. By this the scouts believed that the Cheyennes were preparing for a long stay and, evidently, had some inclination of the large enemy force coming against them. At least the Cheyennes must know that enemies were in the area, for they had also secured their best horses among the trees and fortified their position with a barricade of logs and brush. [20]

The Cheyennes indeed, were fully aware of their enemy's presence and had already agreed among themselves, that if they attempted to make a run for it they were sure to be overtaken on the open plain and destroyed, encumbered as they would be with their women and children, a large herd of horses and all their camp equipment.

The Crows must have realized they would be facing a strongly defended position. But they appeared unperturbed and continued in the direction of the Cheyenne village. At length, they came to a prominent hill which the Crow chief and his head warriors ascended in order to reconnoiter the area. From its summit, the Crows looked down upon the enemy camp, while at the same time, gaining a panoramic view of the surrounding country.

The wily Crow chief set his plan into motion. First he sent the non combatants to the rear along with all the common riding horses and ordered the warrior's war ponies to be brought up. The Crows then fixed up their medicine charms, donned war bonnets and feathers and those who owned war shirts put them on. Others regroomed their hair and painted their faces and bodies with protective designs. Then, after mounting their war ponies which were also befeathered and painted, began psyching themselves up for a fight. [21]

Sore Belly`s plan was to divide his force into three groups. One would charge the Cheyenne camp as if intending to stampede the pony herd. Many animals were still grazing freely outside the camp perimeter. They would then feign a retreat and hopefully, draw the Cheyennes out from behind their breastworks and in pursuit. The other two groups of Crows would position themselves behind the brows of two parallel low hills out of sight from the Cheyennes, but on each side of the path the latter would be obliged to take when following the Crows retreating with the captured horses. In short, the first party of Crows, around forty or fifty in number, was to act as a decoy, luring the Cheyenne fighting men away from the camp and into a trap, to be sprung by the main body of Crows concealed behind flanking hills.[22] This was a favorite ruse of the Crows and had proved itself several times in previous years, not least against the Cheyennes.

It was, perhaps, for this reason that the Cheyennes were more than careful not to be caught again in such a way. They were fully alert, although, as yet, ignorant regarding the close proximity of the Crows, as none of their own people had dared go far from the camp once enemies were reported in the vicinity.

It was about midday when the group of Crow decoys came into sight, riding casually toward their objective. Suddenly, two Cheyennes were discovered on foot not far from the village but on the open prairie, and before the two had ran a few yards in their effort to escape, the mounted Crows were upon them. The first of the Crows rode right past them, merely striking each of the two Cheyennes across the head and shoulders in the act of counting coup. But other Crow warriors coming behind, knocked them down with their ponies, killed and scalped them on the spot, then cut them up in the most fiendish manner.

This brief action took place in full view of those in the village and unfortunately for the Crows, the element of surprise was lost. Before they could get any closer to the camp, the Cheyennes were running from their lodges; rounding up their grazing ponies and driving them into the safety of the timber, while the Cheyenne women and children sought refuge behind the barricades, which they now began to reinforce with camp baggage and other domestic paraphernalia. At the same time, the men folk took up defensive positions and faced the fifty mounted Crow warriors across the field.

As a result, the Crows reined in their ponies and hovered tentatively just out of bow shot, while they waited to see what the Cheyennes would do next.

The village occupants could probably have mustered between seventy to eighty fighting men and might easily have put their enemies to flight. But seeing the comparatively small number of Crows arrayed before them, they became convinced that a much larger enemy force must be in the area, merely waiting for them to make the wrong move. The Cheyennes, therefore, did not succumb to the temptation of forsaking their protective breastworks, even though the Crows taunted them, calling them women and threatening to treat them as such when they over ran the camp. But the Cheyennes stood their ground.[23]

The Crows knew a direct assault upon such a well-defended position would inevitably result in much damage being inflicted upon their own ranks, even if the whole Crow force came up to assist them.

Indians, in general, were usually reluctant to storm a timbered position where cavalry could not be used to any great advantage, while a missile of death might issue from an unseen enemy. Even if the assailants outnumbered their opponents, the price of victory would invariably be too high. The Crows also knew that Cheyennes were most determined and fanatical warriors in a fight and when caught in just such a predicament, as they now were, they would unhesitantly sacrifice their own lives in reckless endeavour in order to protect their wives and children.

It should not then be surprising that, on this occasion, the Crows refused to take the initiative and not being able to lure the Cheyennes from their defenses, were content to merely sit astride their ponies in full view of their enemies and shower them with torrents of abuse and insults, while waving the two freshly taken scalps in their faces.

The Cheyennes returned the Crow jibes with fervor, but would not give them the satisfaction of battle, lest, once in the open, they were overwhelmed by the full force of the enemy, which they felt sure was nearby.

The affair was thus a stalemate.[24]

After a few hours of ineffectual baiting, the Crows gave up the field and slowly moved away to join their waiting tribesmen, who were still concealed behind the distant hills.

Despite the stalement, the Crows considered themselves the victors and rightly so to the Indian way of thinking. The Crows had slain two of the enemy; taken their scalps and equipment and also shown themselves the braver (if not the more discretionary) by offering battle, which their enemies, though in superior number as compared to the decoy force, had refused to join. More important to the Indian mind was the fact that the Crows had incurred no loss to themselves. At last, the Crows thought, they had turned the tables on their Cheyenne foes, having earned all the honors themselves and the grieving womenfolk in the Crow village could now wipe away their tears. The Crows were more than satisfied and rode away from the Cheyenne country, their tribal prestige restored.

Meanwhile, the Cheyennes breathed a little easier and offered up prayers of gratitude to their guardian spirits for their people's deliverance.

Some of the more intrepid Cheyennes, however, secretly dogged the retiring Crow column, spying upon its progress in order to satisfy themselves that the enemy had truly given up the fight and was heading out of the country. When the spies returned to their village and reassured the people the Crow were gone, the Cheyenne women hastily dismantled the lodges; packed the covers and domestic belongings on pony drags and very soon, their whole ensemble was on the move, also heading out of the country, but in the opposite direction to the Crows.[25]

Only a few days prior to the above events, a small party of white trappers in the employ of the American Fur Company was moving through the region, following the course of the North Fork of the Platte, enroute to the rich beaver grounds west of the Laramie Mountains. [26]

According to W. A. Ferris, a member of the party, when not far east of the rock formation now known as "Scotts Bluff," the trappers were visited by three Sioux warriors whose village, the Indians said, was close by. The visitors were friendly, being a part of those lately encamped at the mouth of the Powder and, therefore, most likely involved in the actual slaughter of Little White Bull and his comrades. These Sioux warriors warned the trappers that a large war party of

Arapaho and Gros Ventre was in the Black Hills district, waiting to give battle to any group of white men they might happen upon.

Ferris uses the term Black Hills, sometimes rendered Black Mountains, for the range of hills known today as the Laramie Mountains of northeastern Wyoming. He did not mean the more famous hills of that name in the western part of South Dakota which, even as early as 1830, were swarming with Sioux. [27]

The trappers took heed of the warning, but continued travelling west and the following day, May 28, they came within sight of another tepee village. This time they discerned in the distance, a strong party of Red Men mounted on fine war ponies and galloping towards them. At first the white men were alarmed, supposing the riders to be members of the Arapaho—Gros Ventre war party earlier mentioned by the Sioux and, according to the Ferris account, "some horsemen about fifty in number, all armed to the teeth, dashed up in a cloud." [28]

The trappers stood too with loaded muskets at hand, but made no threatening gestures. The Indians, meanwhile, reined up and proudly introduced themselves as Cheyennes, by aspirating their own name of "TsisTsisTsas" and making the sign of the "Cut Arm," by which appellation most other tribes knew them.

This meeting took place—as far as can be ascertained—not far west from the headwater country of the Solomon and Republican rivers in the western part of Nebraska, an area where Pawnees were most likely to be found engaged in their early summer buffalo hunt. Indeed, these Cheyennes, evidently, were part of a larger war party out looking for Pawnee enemies, but they appeared to be most amicable towards the white men. They also corroborated what the Sioux visitors had said the previous day, regarding the presence of Arapaho and Gros Ventre further west and confirmed that the latter were on the warpath against all white men they should meet. [29]

Perhaps some among these Cheyennes knew one or another of the trappers personally, for they remained with them until nightfall, at which time all but one of their number continued on their way.

The Cheyenne village from whence came these fifty warriors was nearby and as the trappers journeyed on the following day, they passed the camp without incident. On June 2, the white men reached the mouth of Laramie Fork, having made a slight detour in order to avoid the mountains and Arapaho and Gros Ventre hostiles. [30]

Still following the twisting course of the North Platte on its south side, on June 13 they came upon a lone tepee left standing by Cheyennes, who only recently had vacated the site.

Inside the tepee the trappers found two raised platforms, on each of which lay the scalped corpse of an adult male. The implements of war and the chase had been carefully laid out beside them, although both bodies, Ferris later remarked ". . ..had been hacked and mangled in a manner truly savage and revolting." [31]

The lone Cheyenne, who had remained behind with the trappers after his companions had ridden off four nights earlier was, evidently at this point, still in company with the trappers, for it must have been he who offered Ferris an explanation concerning the burial tepee at this place.

The bodies were Cheyennes, Ferris was told, killed in a battle with Crows only five days before. Ferris later described the scene:

"Lying upon the ground, a few paces from the teepee, exposed to all the elements, was the body of a dead male child no more than four years old. The poor innocent had been deliberately and horribly maimed and disfigured, evidently by repeated blows from a war club and there was the mark of a deep stab wound in his side." [32]

The white men were told that the child had been a prisoner among the Cheyennes, taken from Crows the previous winter and thus, murdered in retaliation for the deaths of the two Cheyenne warriors now reposing on their funerary scaffolds. Here, so Ferris said, he saw a parallel of Achilles sacrificing at the tomb of Patrocles on the Plains of Troy.[33]

The Cheyenne burial tepee apparently housed the bodies of the two Cheyennes slain by Sore Belly`s Crow party within sight of the Cheyenne village on Antelope Creek. The corpses had been carried to this point on the North Platte where proper funerary rites had been performed in accordance with Cheyenne custom. This was, no doubt, due to the Cheyenne's haste to escape from the district around Antelope Creek, in case roving enemies attacked them again. It would seem also, that as these bodies had warranted so much care and attention from their tribesmen, they may have been chiefs or, certainly, important persons of some kind.

The brutal murder of the Crow infant was contrary to Cheyenne tribal law, which dictated that all prisoners once fed and nurtured in their captor's lodge, be considered adopted members of the tribe and ever after, be accorded the same rights of protection as applicable to the rest of that nation's members. This inexcusable act, however, was not to be the last time Cheyennes committed such a crime. An event in 1833, when eight Crow captives were slaughtered in an act of revenge for eight Cheyenne warriors earlier killed in battle by Crows, being but one other example.[34] In reality, the Crow infant lying beside the burial tepee which Ferris and his companions observed, was the same child who had been captured from the Crows by Cheyennes the previous winter. As it was a Crow captive slaughtered on this occasion, it indicates that the two Cheyennes had themselves been slain by Crows in some very recent engagement.

Here we appear to have an independent source which substantiates Beckwourth`s accounts of two fights, i.e. an attack upon the Crow village in January 1830 where the Crow boy had been captured and also, the Crow-Cheyenne standoff at Antelope Creek, which occurred sometime in late May of the same year.

The name Antelope Creek given by Beckwourth as the site of the May fight, is said by him to have been a tributary of the Missouri. But by this name it cannot be located on any present day map. Perhaps he was referring to that river known today as the "Little Missouri," but which in earlier years, was known by its Indian name of "Antelope Pit River," because numerous antelope drives were once conducted by both Kiowa and Cheyennes in its vicinity. However, this last is not a small creek, but rather a prominent waterway which even from its headwaters, is still some 200 miles or more as the crow flies from the site of the burial tepee visited by Ferris and his companions on the North Platte.

There is another stream, once also called Antelope Creek, but now known as "Loisel`s Creek," which does flow into the Missouri from the west, having its source somewhere in the central part of South Dakota. But as before, its location even from its head, is far too distant from the site of the burial tepee to be deemed feasible as Beckwourth`s stream of that name. One must consider that the time factor between the fight on Antelope Creek, until Ferris and his companions came upon the lone tepee on the North Fork of the Platte, was a period of only five days.

Indians when travelling as a moving village on horseback, rarely exceeded more than twenty miles per day and often considerably less. Even when in rapid flight, forty miles per day would have been regarded as good going, yet the distance from the headwaters of Loisel's Creek to the North Fork of the Platte at a point near the mouth of the Laramie, is some 600 miles as the crow flies and rarely did Indians travel in a straight line. Rather, they meandered along as fresh grass and suitable water dictated.

A more likely location is the stream known today as "Deer Creek" which lies in the very heart of what was then Cheyenne Country abutting the North Platte and where, during the 1850s and early '60s, stood the government Indian agency for the Upper Platte tribes. This creek, which rises in the northwest corner of Wyoming and flows south into the North Fork of the Platte, entering at a point some twenty miles east of the Laramie branch, may have been known alternatively in Beckwourth`s day as "Antelope Creek." The surrounding district during the time in question, was still accessible to the Crows who once had claimed it exclusively for themselves and they knew Cheyenne camps of various size, could be found scattered at random throughout this area during the summer months.

Perhaps, then, Beckwourth was merely in error when he stated that Antelope Creek was a small tributary of the Missouri, when what he probably meant was the North Platte.

The location of present day Deer Creek would fit well with the lapse of time between the conflict in which the two Cheyennes were killed and when the trappers came upon the burial tepee five days later. In all fairness to Beckwourth, though, it must be acknowledged that even as late as Beckwourth`s early days in the Far West, the Platte River was sometimes confused with the Missouri or, and what was more often the case, was regarded as being an extension of it. This misconception had come about during the very early days of French and Spanish exploration, at which time it was thought that the Platte was merely a continuation of the main course of the Missouri; a mistake carried forward by force of habit even into Beckwourth`s time.

It would appear then, that the Cheyenne occupants of the village along Antelope Creek had not, in reality, moved far from the scene of conflict, but were in the process of moving towards a prearranged rendezvous site on the South Fork of the Platte, in order to join the rest of their nation preparing for the grand tribal crusade against the Pawnees. It could only have been an act of providence which prevented the Crow war party from stumbling across the main Cheyenne camp itself, in which case, the tables would doubtless have been turned and not many Crows would have escaped with their scalps.

Whatever the case, the Crows had successfully avenged their champion Little White Bull and his fallen comrades and thus, were free again to raid wherever and to steal the scalps, ponies and women from whomever they pleased.

Notes and Sources

1 Lowie, Robert H. *Mythology of the Crow Indians.* pp.175-176. University of Nebraska Press. 19
2 *"A Dictionary of everyday Crow."* Crow Agency Bilingual Education Program. 1979.
3 Joe Medicine Crow to Author. Note pad 2. p.6. Lodge Grass, Montana. August. 1996.
4 Joe Medicine Crow to Author. Note pad 2. p.6. Lodge Grass, Montana. August. 1996.
5 Bonner, T.D. *Life of James P. Beckwourth."*pp.163-164. Ross and Haines Co. Ltd. 1956.
6 Ibid. p.164.
7 Ibid. p.164.
8 Ibid. p.164.
9 Ibid. p.164.
10 Grinnell, George Bird. *The Fighting Cheyennes.* p.72. University of Oklahoma Press.1956.
11 Joe Medicine Crow to Author. Note pad 2. p.5. Lodge Grass, Montana. August.1996.
12 Ferris, W. A. *Life in the Rocky Mountains.* p.34ff. 1946. Denver Old West Publishing Company. 1940.
13 Bonner, T.D. *Life of James P. Beckwourth.* p.165. Ross and Haines Co. Ltd. 1956.
14 Denig, Edwin. *Five Tribes of the Upper Missouri.* pp144-145. University of Oklahoma Press. 1961.
15 Grinnell, George Bird. *The Fighting Cheyennes.* p.73. University of Oklahoma Press. 1956.
16 Bonner, T.D. *Life of James P. Beckwourth."*pp.168-169. Ross and Haines Co. Ltd. 1956.
17 Ibid. pp.168-169.
18 Ibid. pp.168-169
19.Grinnell, George Bird. *The Fighting Cheyennes.* p.73. University of Oklahoma Press. 1956.
20.Joe Medicine Crow to Author. Note pad 2. p.5. Lodge Grass, Montana. August.1996
21.Joe Medicine Crow to Author. Note pad 2. p.5. Lodge Grass, Montana. August.1996
22.Bonner, T.D. *Life of James P. Beckwourth.* p.169. Ross and Haines Co. Ltd. 1956.
23.Joe Medicine Crow to Author. Note pad 2. p.5. Lodge Grass, Montana. August.1996.
24.Joe Medicine Crow to Author. Note pad 2. p.5. Lodge Grass, Montana. August.1996
25.Joe Medicine Crow to Author. Note pad 2. p.5. Lodge Grass, Montana. August.1996
26.Ferris, W.A. *Life in the Rocky Mountains.* p.34ff. Denver Old West Publishing Company. 1940.
27.Ferris, W.A. *Life in the Rocky Mountains.* p.34ff. Denver Old West Publishing Company. 1940.
28.Ferris, W.A. *Life in the Rocky Mountains.* p.34ff. Denver Old West Publishing Company. 1940.
29.Ferris, W.A. *"Life in the Rocky Mountains."* p.34ff. Denver Old West Publishing Company. 19 40.
30.Ferris, W.A. *Life in the Rocky Mountains.* p.34ff. Denver Old West Publishing Company. 1940.
31.Ferris, W.A. *Life in the Rocky Mountains.* p.34ff. Denver Old West Publishing Company. 1940.
32.Ferris, W.A. *Life in the Rocky Mountains.* p.34ff. Denver Old West Publishing Company.1940.
33.Ferris, W.A. *Life in the Rocky Mountains."*p.34ff. Denver Old West Publishing Company. 1940.
34.Grinnell, George Bird. *The Fighting Cheyennes.* p.31. University of Oklahoma Press. 1956.

Chapter Six

Great Victory Over the Small Robes

One hot afternoon, sitting with Joe Medicine Crow outside his timber-framed house at Lodge Grass, Montana, Joe casually remarked, "You know it Spotted Tail Eagle, we Crows cleaned up on the Blackfoots [sic] many times."

"Yes," I replied, "and sometimes the Blackfoot cleaned up on the Crows."

"This is true," Joe continued, "But did you hear of the time our great chief Twines-His-Horse`s-Tail, destroyed an entire band of Blackfoots and took 160 women and children captive? I don't think the Crow version has ever been written down. I will tell you the story and you can put it in your book."

I was eager to hear the Crow account of that battle and took from my pocket pen and notebook, which I always carried in order to jot down anything I heard of interest when in Joe's company. Indeed, Joe was a mine of information regarding his tribe's history and would often recall obscure anecdotes from his extensive memory which just happened to come to mind.

While I prepared to note down the details of his recital, Joe was lighting a twisted braid of sweet grass and as its perfumed smoke drifted skywards, I could hear him mumbling something in Crow. I knew he was making an apology to the dead for what he was about to relate, as it is still the custom among old-timers on the reservation, not to mention the names or deeds of those who have gone to the spirit world, although exceptions are made if one's intentions are sincere and what is uttered is done "in a good way," as the Crows would say.

The untimely demise of the great River Crow war chief Sore Belly (Alapooish) in 1834, left the Crows despondent and somewhat demoralized. There was none, it was thought, whom the people could turn to as a comparable mentor and protector. The Mountain Crow chief Long Hair was yet alive, but now in his mid-seventies, he was too old for the warpath and recognized more as a holy man, rather than one who could organize the people and instill martial confidence. An indomitable warrior and leader of war parties named Little White Bear, who had been Sore Belly`s right hand man, also was dead, while such men as Spotted Horse and Red Bear, both of whom did later become famous chiefs, were too young at that period to assume overall command.

Not until many years later did the Crows realize that they had among them a war chief worthy of the position, under whose guidance and influence Crow warriors could again prove themselves the formidable adversaries they had previously been of old.

In the aftermath of Sore Belly`s death, the newly-elected paramount chief of the River Crow band was a man named Grizzly Bear. He was also known as Big Bear, Hair On Top, Silver Tip and even Tip of Fur, these last two names being colloquial Crow terms for that animal in reference that when wet, the back fur of the Grizzly is apt to shine like silver in the sun's rays.[1]

This man in his younger days had proved himself an accomplished warrior, but by 1845 he was regarded as a medicine man of high repute and as a civil chief rather than a leader in war. He did achieve some prominence during the winter of 1845-'46 when, under his titular command, Crow warriors wiped out the Oglala White Buffalo Bull and his thirty-seven comrades But as a rule, Grizzly Bear was not one to personally get to grips with the foe. Rather, he directed the strategy of battle from a distance and as a consequence, no longer marked up personal war honors on the field of combat which would have enhanced his reputation. Thus, he has been largely forgotten in Crow oral tradition, notwithstanding that he was elected to the position of "Chief of Chiefs" of the entire Crow nation after the death of the Mountain Crow Chief Long Hair in 1846.

What is specifically remembered of Grizzly Bear, is that he was a close friend and confident of Long Hair and that together, they dabbled in the arts of black magic and sorcery. Stories are still told among the

Edward S. Curtis photo, 1907. Courtesy the Smithsonian Institution

Crow warriors watching for the enemy.

Crows of the power of Grizzly Bear`s medicine. One account relates how he prophesied the coming into camp of a lone enemy. Only a few days later a lone enemy did indeed enter the Crow camp and claim sanctuary in the lodge housing the tribe's "Sacred Tobacco Seeds." It was this same chief Grizzly Bear who also modified the Crow Sun Dance ceremony which, thereafter, became unique compared to the way it was practiced among other Plains tribes, by it being performed among the Crows as a prelude to the tribe seeking vengeance upon its enemies.[2]

As a result of Grizzly Bear not being regarded as a particularly aggressive leader in battle, the role of head war chief of his band was given over to another man, an indomitable warrior named Twines-His-Horse's-Tail. He alone was looked up to by the River Crows as one who would actually lead the warriors into battle and fight alongside them. In records of the day, this man's name was variously rendered as Twists-His-Tail, Rolls His Tail, Rotten Tail and Sore Tail and he has sometimes been confused with the renowned Sore Belly himself, which accounts for several erroneous statements appearing in print regarding both these men. In William Marshall Anderson's contemporary list of Crow chiefs for the period 1834-'35, Twines-His-Horse`s-Tail is called by Anderson, Rotten Tail, with the second name of Yellow Bull, numbered fifteen in rank among the seventeen councilors of the Crow nation.[3] From that date forward, however, as a noted warrior and successful leader of war parties, Twines-His-Horse's-Tail quickly rose to prominence after the death of chief Grizzly Bear. Grizzly Bear's death occurred in mysterious circumstances while on a trip to Washington D.C. in 1851. Government officials selected a Kicked-in-the-Belly chief named Big Robber in his stead. Twines-His-Horse's-Tail—by tribal consent—nonetheless attained the position of paramount chief of both the Mountain and River Crow bands.

It was, in fact, under the warrior leadership of Twines-His-Horse`s-Tail, that his people achieved one of the most celebrated victories in the annals of Crow intertribal warfare.

Born around the beginning of the nineteenth century, Twines-His-Horse`s-Tail had been orphaned at an early age and being very poor, was generally looked down upon by others of his age group. He had two older brothers. The elder was called Large Inside; an abusive, cynical type. The younger, whose name was Eats-Like-A-Wolf, was kind and accommodating. Although poor and thought by many as being unworthy, Twines-His-Horse`s-Tail was raised among the Sore Lip clan and thus, had a number of influential relatives who did manage to instill in him a sense of ambition and pride in his ancestry. As a member of the Sore Lips, he was indirectly related to the late, great Sore Belly.[4]

Twines-His-Horse`s-Tail, it is said, first went to war at an early age. The story current among the Crows is that when Twines-His-

Horse's-Tail was a youth of fourteen or fifteen years, his brother Eats-Like-A-Wolf was engaged in a "Hoop and Arrow" game and had claimed a strike to which his opponent did not agree. Twines-His-Horse's-Tail was standing nearby and was asked by Eats-Like-A-Wolf to give the decision as an independent witness. This he did, giving the point in favor of his brother. The opponent, a man named Ground Bull, was indignant and began insulting Twines-His-Horse's-Tail saying, "Huh, that poor boy knows nothing; He should be asleep somewhere." (meaning he was still a child and should be looked after by the women).[5]

To Twines-His-Horse's-Tail this was a great insult which cut him to the quick. For several days he was sullen and depressed and shunned other people in camp.

He sat alone for a few days on a hill top where today stands the water tower at Crow Agency, while he contemplated his miserable life and what he might do to improve it.

Finally, he abandoned his vigil and told Eats-Like-A-Wolf that he would go on a vision quest and fast at some lonely place, in order to obtain a medicine helper to assist him in achieving a respectful standing within the tribe. This, he knew, was imperative to enable him to be successful when he went to war in search of ponies and scalps, the acquisition of which, would give him wealth and esteem among his people.

At the time of year when cherry leaves are full grown, (spring), Twines-His-Horse's-Tail left the village near the mouth of the Little Big Horn and went out alone into the Wolf Teeth Mountains to seek his vision. He remained out many days, fasting on the top of different high points. But each time to no avail. Eventually, he returned home, despondent as before.

At various times throughout that summer he again went out to fast, still seeking a medicine helper. One of his fasting sites on these occasions was on a hill recognized by the letter "L" affixed to its slope, overlooking the Lodge Grass High School on the present-day Crow reservation.

At last, while fasting on top of Red Rock Hill, called by the Crows "Where the Thunderbird sits" (near the small town of Ranchester, Wyoming), he finally experienced what he had so earnestly been seeking.

In his vision a young maiden appeared and led him inside the hill on which he was fasting. This proved to be the interior of a large lodge and here, Twines-His-Horse's-Tail received his medicine in the form of sacred tobacco seeds. He was also instructed in the rites of a certain ceremony connected with the seeds and was informed that his guardian spirit was the Sun. As a token of this medicine, he was told to carry a small willow hoop meshed with sinew, the same as was used in the "Hoop and Arrow" game.

When Twines-His-Horse's-Tail came down from the hilltop and returned to his people, it was already late summer. The camp had moved farther up river to a site called by the Crows, "Good Bend," where today the Sage Motel stands adjacent to the Little Big Horn, less than a mile south of the monument commemorating Custer`s Last Stand in 1876.

While recuperating in his lodge, Twines-His-Horse's-Tail told his brother Eats-Like-A-Wolf about the vision he had received and the two decided they would go on the warpath as soon as possible, thinking that the "sacred seeds" and the power of Twines-His-Horse`s-Tail's medicine father, the Sun, would give them a successful trip.

In accordance with tribal protocol, they first informed their older brother Large Inside of their intentions, even though they both disliked him and did not really want him along. The older brother at first ridiculed the pair, but then relented and said he would accompany them just in case they had good luck.

That same night the three brothers started out on the war trail on foot and a few hours before sunrise, made their first camp on Ash (now Reno) Creek. It was here that two Crow warriors caught up with them although they had not been invited to join the party. Soon after their arrival, an even larger group of warriors came up and also said they would accompany the three brothers to war.

Whether the elder brother had told others of the venture or, that someone overheard the brother's conversation when planning the trip is not determined. But the party now consisted of around thirty members. The warriors believed Twines-His-Horse`s-Tail had received a very strong medicine to induce him to go to war so soon after returning from his fast. Many in the party, therefore, thought they would return victorious with captured ponies and scalps in abundance.

Reynold Expedition, 1859. Beinecke Library, Yale University

River Crow chiefs Bear's Head, left, and Twines-His-Horse's-Tail.

About midmorning of the second day, the combined party started out. The warriors traveled until sundown, and made camp where the town of Big Horn, Wyoming now stands. The camp was very close to the site "Where Owner of Raven was killed," which refers to the event of 1819 when Long Hair`s Mountain Crows wiped out the thirty or more Cheyenne Crooked Lance warriors on a hill top overlooking Prairie Dog Creek.

While in camp at this place, yet another man joined the party. The new arrival, whose name was He That Glitters, alarmed other members, for he was known to be a jinx; a harbinger of bad luck. He was considered to be very handsome and much sought after by the Crow women both unmarried and married. It is said, that because of his womanizing, a certain Shaman had cast a spell on He That Glitters at the request of a number of cuckolded husbands. Thus, he was doomed to bring catastrophe upon any warriors who allowed him into their company. It was for this reason that he had been prevented from joining war parties. Therefore he could not achieve recognized war deeds (which had to be witnessed by others in order to make them valid). This prevented him from attaining any rank or high standing within the tribe. He That Glitters said he knew Twines-His-Horse`s-Tail had received a very strong medicine and spirit helper while on his vision quest. He said, he needed such powerful medicine in order to break the unlucky spell cast upon him.

If Twines-His-Horse`s-Tail agreed to him accompanying the party, He That Glitters continued, he would not only voluntarily act as the party's scout, but if he succeeded in counting coup, then when they got safely back to their own village, he would give to Twines-His-Horse`s-Tail a fast horse along with all his riding equipment; his own richly decorated costumes and even his buffalo hide lodge including its contents, save his personal medicine bundle.

All these things he promised in reward for Twines-His-Horse`s-Tail sharing the power of his medicine with him. In fact, He That Glitters had previously been known as a brave fighter and a good man, but, unfortunately, he was now `dogged` with bad luck and none would go with him on a war trail. Twines-His-Horse`s-Tail sympathized with his plight, knowing how it felt to be shunned and rejected, and agreed to let him join the party, much to the disdain of the others, including his elder brother Large Inside.

The next day as the group continued its journey, the elder brother of Twines-His-Horse`s-Tail, who had constantly been making cynical remarks concerning the leader's abilities, now said that Twines-His-Horse`s-Tail should make medicine as was the usual practice of a Pipe Holder when this far out on the trail. He told him to get his medicine bundle, but Twines-His-Horse`s-Tail had no such bundle and so the brother hoped to ridicule him again. Twines-His-Horse`s-Tail, however, was not intimidated. Instead, he asked Eats-Like-A-Wolf to bring him an eagle feather along with a buckskin thong; a small bunch of red willow and some other things (now forgotten) and with these items, he fashioned a small willow hoop with a buckskin mesh as used in the "Hoop and Arrow" game.

Twines-His-Horse`s-Tail then told his companions that this was his medicine totem. Again the elder brother scoffed, making more derisive remarks. When He That Glitters bade Twines-His-Horse`s-Tail to perform his ritual and make medicine for the party's success, the brother, Large Inside, laughed aloud saying, "Why, he cannot even make medicine for himself." [6]

A few nights later, Twines-His-Horse`s-Tail performed his medicine ceremony. Afterwards, he told the party that the next day, they would find their Sioux enemies in a small tepee encampment separated from its main body. His medicine, he said, had told him that he, Twines-His-Horse`s-Tail, would count the first coup in the coming fight and also, that he was to have a fine sorrel horse with a single eagle feather tied to its forelock which would be captured from the enemy. He said whoever should capture this horse, must surrender it to him, for his Spirit Helper the Sun had promised it to him alone. In addition, Twines-His-Horse`s-Tail continued, they would capture the Sioux chief's daughter dressed in fine clothes and mounted on a pinto horse.

"She also is mine," he said "and is to be my wife." [7]

He That Glitters reiterated his request that he should count a coup and asked Twines-His-Horse`s-Tail to give him his blessing and paint his face in a sacred manner. Such a request was usually asked only of a respected and successful Shaman and thus, was a great honor bestowed upon Twines-His-Horse`s-Tail.

Early next morning, just as the sun was coming up, Twines-His-Horse`s-Tail went over to where He That Glitters sat; bade him rise to his feet and face the east, whereupon, Twines-His-Horse`s-Tail addressed the Sun saying, "Oh Sun you are this one's Father. . .Look upon this other man before you who is known as He That Glitters. . .He is without power. . . .His luck has been bad. . . ..Today, Oh Sun, take away his affliction; give him a second coup this day." [8]

Having bestowed his blessing upon He That Glitters, Twines-His-Horse`s-Tail prepared himself for battle. He pointed his forefinger at the Sun, then ran it around the edge of his face and behold, a bright red line appeared that represented Sun.

Meanwhile, the rest of the warriors were fixing up their own war paraphernalia and personal protective medicines. When all were ready, they set out together in the direction Twines-His-Horse`s-Tail had said the enemy would be found.

It was not long before a small cluster of white tepees standing at rakish tilts, could clearly be seen in the distance, their brown smoke-tanned tops with thin whispers of smoke curling upwards; standing out in sharp contrast against the blue of the sky.

Twines-His-Horse`s-Tail addressed his medicine father the Sun and referring to his cynical brother Large Inside, he said, "Oh Father, cause this man to suffer this day, but do not let him forfeit his life; give him back to me." (By these words he was requesting that his brother become a better person). [9]

While travelling on, ever closer to the Sioux camp, the Crow party observed an old worn out horse—a stray—grazing along the bank of a small creek. The elder brother of Twines-His-Horse`s-Tail immediately ran over to catch it, hoping to be the first of his comrades to do so, although most of the party were more concerned with taking the better horses to be found among the Sioux lodges.

Twines-His-Horse`s-Tail and the rest of the warriors continued towards their objective. The Sioux had no scouts out and did not know that Crow enemies were nearby until the latter charged the camp and took it by surprise.

A brief skirmish ensued, but it was not long before the Sioux fled, all the men, women and children scattering across the prairie in every direction, searching for a place to hide. Very soon it was over, the victorious Crows standing among the abandoned lodges.

Twines-His-Horse`s-Tail had struck the first coup and He That Glitters the second. Twine-His-Horse`s-Tail had also captured the sorrel horse with an eagle feather tied to its forelock and a young Sioux woman mounted on a pinto horse.

All his predictions had come true, while none of his comrades had been injured in the fray, which showed that the medicine of Twines-His-Horse`s-Tail was strong.

The elder brother Large Inside, had missed most of what had gone on during the attack and was laughed at heartily, when it was learned that all he had to show for the trip was one worn out nag, thought to be worthless, having been abandoned by its owner in the first place.

When at last the successful party returned to its home village, the jubilant warriors held a grand victory dance outside the very tepee of Ground Bull, who previously had jeered at and abused Twines-His-Horse`s-Tail for being poor and unworthy.

At the request of He That Glitters, the dancing warriors sang a derisive song about this man's wife who was known as Buffalo Woman, because He That Glitters—unbeknown to the husband Ground Bull—had earlier had a sexual liaison with her. This, of course, was a great insult to inflict upon the husband and so Twines-His-Horse`s-Tail finally got his revenge.

Now that He That Glitters had thrown off his bad luck, he kept his word to Twines-His-Horse`s-Tail. He took his wife and medicine bundle and moved out of his lodge so that Twines-His-Horse`s-Tail and his new Sioux bride could move in. He also gave him his horse and riding equipment along with his fine clothes as promised.

The once poor orphan boy was now a proven warrior; a holy man of sorts and a lodge owner, along with having a wife, domestic belongings, fine clothes and spare horses to boot.

From here on, Twines-His-Horse`s-Tail often went on the warpath and became known as a successful partisan, so that never did he lack warriors to make up a party.

About the year 1825, he led a group of warriors far south of the Crow Country and was gone two and one-half years. When he and his comrades finally returned to their people, they had many strange and wondrous tales to tell. They had seen cacti as tall and as thick as trees; of strange peoples living in square shaped lodges built on top of one another and fashioned from dried mud bricks. Twines-His-Horse`s-Tail brought back a woman belonging to some hitherto unknown tribe (probably Apache), who he had personally captured when his party destroyed two lodges of people in the desert country of the south. He took the woman as a second wife.[10]

The Swiss artist Rudolph F. Kurz met Twines-His-Horse`s-Tail several times between the years 1850 and 1851. Kurz was then in the employ of the American Fur Company at its Fort Union trading post near the mouth of the Yellowstone. Twines-His-Horse`s-Tail who, by that date, was the leading chief of the River Crows, was always referred to by Kurz as, "Rotten Tail" and was said by Kurz to resemble the European Royal personage of Louis Philippe. The chief's more common mode of dress—according to Kurz—consisted of a white man's style suit of clothes fashioned from a blue blanket along with grey leggings, although he (the chief) wore no shirt, vest, neck cloth or hat. Kurz went on to record that the chief presented the post Factor Edwin Denig, with a "superb military headdress," which the chief personally placed upon Denig`s head and then draped a handsome buffalo robe over the Factor's shoulders. In the opinion of Kurz, when arraigned in such attire, it made the Factor look even more comical than usual.[11]

In time, other than becoming a renowned warrior and head chief of the River Crows, Twines-His-Horse`s-Tail also became recognized as a great medicine man, who could foretell coming events.

Both Joe Medicine Crow and Winona Plenty Hoops were once told by tribal informants of the old buffalo days that at one time, Twines-His-Horse`s-Tail predicted that a certain Crow war party would return after seven days having killed three enemies, one of whom would be lacking a hand. The party did return at the predicted time having killed three Sioux scouts, one of whom was missing a thumb on his right hand. This event actually gave its name to the year in question, being hereafter, known among the Crows as "The winter the thumb less enemy was killed."[12]

On another occasion, Twines-His-Horse`s-Tail told the leader of a war party that he would come back with two Sioux heads and this too, was done as foretold. On a third occasion he correctly prophesied that the same man would go on a war trail, which would take he and his party away from camp for thirteen days and that only one enemy scalp would be taken, while a fourth time, Twines-His-Horse`s-Tail bade the same warrior to bring back three enemy captives and both these events came true as predicted.[13]

At the time of Sore Belly`s death, Twines-His-Horse`s-Tail was in his early thirties and already a Pipe Holder of distinction. Certainly, by 1845, he had risen in popularity to become joint head chief, along with Grizzly Bear, of the entire River Crow band and it was in this year also, that he achieved his greatest victory over his people's enemies.

Throughout the greater part of the nineteenth century apart from one brief interlude of peace, the Crows always regarded the Cheyennes among their most aggressive and consistent opponents. However,

Author's photo

Al Birdinground dressed in Blackfoot costume.

between the years 1841 and 1855, few large-scale conflicts took place between them. This was largely because of an 1840 truce between the Southern Plains tribes, which included Kiowa, Comanche, Kiowa-Apache, Cheyenne and Arapaho. One year later it also embraced certain bands of Teton Sioux.[14] Both the Kiowa and Kiowa-Apache had long been close friends of the Crow, having age-old ties of alliance and intermarriage. This, coupled with the fact that the Arapaho had as many times been at peace with the Crows as they had been at war, ultimately obliged the Cheyennes to reduce their own hostilities on the Crow front, although small, insignificant raids upon each other's pony herds did persist and once in a while a scalp or two was taken. At a later date, the "Horse Creek" or Fitzpatrick Treaty of 1851, which involved Sioux, Cheyenne and Crows along with small contingents from some other Upper Missouri tribes, gave an official stamp to this intertribal truce, which—apart from some minor interruptions—continued to hold good between the majority of Crows, Sioux and Cheyennes until as late as 1855.

This period of abated hostility which began around 1841, enabled the Crows to concentrate upon other foes. The Crow nation found itself engaged in more vigorous offensives against the Gros Ventre and Assiniboin and those several tribes which constituted the Blackfoot confederacy. Against the Gros Ventre and Assiniboin, the Crows could easily hold their own and generally beat them in the contest. But dealing with the Blackfeet—particularly the Blood and Piegan groups—it was a different matter. Constantly Blackfoot war parties from north of the Missouri raided far south in order to attack Crows deep in the latter`s own country and were, at this period, the Crow's most aggressive opponents.

The winter count of Teddy Yellow Fly, a North Blackfoot, for the year 1841 states, "A Crow Indian missing a nose was killed." [15]

During or near 1841, a more important fight took place in which Crows led by Twines-His-Horse`s-Tail, surrounded a Blood-Blackfoot war party and killed a famous warrior known as Berry Child and his twenty-four companions. This was a particularly memorable affair which further enhanced the great River Crow war chief`s reputation.

When the Blood-Blackfoot war party had first started out on foot from its camp in Cypress Hills northeast of Milk River, many more warriors had been included, led by two famous chiefs named Spotted Wolf and Berry Child. However, while enroute south to the Crow country, bad dreams and premonitions of impending disaster plagued some of its members and by the time the party reached the Missouri, the grand host had decided to divide its force. One band under Spotted Wolf returned home while those remaining, comprising only twenty-six warriors including the Pipe Holder Berry Child, continued south to raid the Crows. This smaller Blood party then crossed the Snowy Mountains and reaching the forks of the Musselshell, at last found sign of the enemy—a broad trail leading farther south from an abandoned campsite. Following this trail, the party came to the Yellowstone and another abandoned camp, which telltale signs showed to be only one day old. The enemy was close at hand and the Bloods rested while contemplating their next move. It was at this place, that one of their number was bitten by a rattlesnake and could go no farther. The next morning, after leaving their sick comrade a little food and water, the rest of the party continued its journey, having promised to pick the man up on their return when, hopefully, they would all have stolen Crow horses to ride.

Unfortunately, after these Blood warriors had traveled some distance along a stream called Deer Creek, they were discovered by the Crows, who being on horseback and in much greater number, immediately attacked. The Bloods, after making a brief stand, were obliged to seek cover in a nearby dense patch of cherry bushes. Many of the Bloods were armed with trade guns with adequate amounts of powder and ball about their persons and from here, they managed to keep the Crows at bay by their careful and systematic shooting.

When word of the battle reached the main River Crow camp located nearby, Twines-His-Horse`s-Tail told the occupants to move to the battle site and erect their tepees on flat prairie land encircling the patch of bushes where their enemies were entrenched. The whole River Crow population responded and completely surrounded the foe so that the Bloods had no way of escape. Still, the small Blood party managed to hold its ground all that day and were much relieved when darkness fell and the Crows abandoned the fight `till morning. The tight ring of Crows around their position, however, prevented any Bloods from escaping and come sunrise, the contest was ready to continue. Before the actual fighting commenced, Twines-His-Horse`s-Tail stepped forward from the besieger's lines and addressed the enemy with sign language gestures, saying to the effect, that if the Bloods laid down their weapons, then the Crows would make a pact with them and their two peoples would forever cease hostilities against each other.

"It is useless for you to fight," the Crow chief said, "You are twenty-five brave men but we are three-hundred lodges. Give yourselves up and let us be friends."[16]

The Blood chief Berry Child responded by stepping forward and replying to the Crow chief saying, "It is not the custom of the Blackfeet to surrender and make friends in battle. I have come to war in order to fight and if I must, then also to die. I am here and willing to do so. Here is my body, it waits for you to count coup upon it and here is my scalp. Now who among you will come and take it? I have come to make war, not to make friends." [17]

The Crows thus returned to the offensive and many charges were made, both by foolhardy individuals and large groups of warriors. But they were repulsed by the Bloods and the battle raged on until late that afternoon. By then, however, the last of the defending Bloods had been killed, including Chief Berry Child. Only the man who earlier had been bitten by the snake, survived the war trip and eventually returned safely to his home camp in the Cypress Hills.[18]

The Crows were jubilant over their victory, although not a few of their own warriors had been killed in the two-day engagement and there was much sorrow among the occupants of some lodges in camp. Any loss—especially among the Crows—was a severe blow to the very existence of their nation. In fact, such was the scale of unremitting warfare carried on between the Crows and Blackfeet during this period, that it was obvious to white observers of the day that if allowed to continue unabated, then the Crows would likely be exterminated before another quarter century passed. For the three Blackfoot-speaking tribes combined, far outnumbered the Crows and were always better armed with guns, owing to contacts not only with American traders both along and north of the Missouri, but also with Hudson's Bay Company posts in Canada, so that a regular supply of powder and ball was ever on hand.

ATTACK ON THE SMALL ROBE COLUMN

Prior to the late 1830s, the largest Blackfoot division was that of the Piegan or Pikunni, as they were known to the Crows. This group comprised a number of bands, one of the most powerful of which was that known as the Small Robes, so called either after a chief of that name or, in reference to a singular practice of its womenfolk of wearing a small piece of buffalo hide like a shawl as protection from the sun's scorching rays.[19]

Two prominent chiefs named Rising Head and Lone Walker led the Small Robes. [20] Both were famed fighters and able leaders, well known among all the Blackfoot-speaking tribes and even among their enemies. During the time of their rule, the Small Robes boasted between 200 and 250 lodges and being strong numerically, often roamed the prairies as an independent group.[21] They then claimed as their hunting grounds, both the Three Forks district of west central Montana and the country abutting the Upper Missouri on its south side, which incorporates the northern part of the Judith Basin. This was the most southern limit of what was then regarded as Blackfoot Country.

So formidable were the Small Robes under the leadership of Rising Head and Lone Walker, that their nearest neighbors to the south—the

River Crow—usually refrained from making any concerted attacks upon them, even when the Small Robes pursued their annual habit during the autumn months of conducting hunting trips deep into River Crow lands along the Musselshell. At such times, the Small Robes gathered great quantities of ripe chokecherries and buffalo meat with which they made pemmican to see them through the coming winter.

Small parties of young bucks among both the Small Robes and River Crow persisted in sporadically raiding each other's pony herds. At times, a scalp or two was taken if the opportunity arose. Generally speaking, however, both groups deliberately avoided contact in order to prevent any large scale confrontation.

A number of Joe Medicine Crow`s old informants said a temporary truce was agreed to by the head men of the River Crow and Small Robes, which allowed the tribes to tolerate each other's presence during the short periods when the Small Robes conducted their hunting sojourns in the Crow country.[22] As a result, the Small Robes thought themselves invulnerable. Over the years, they grew more aloof and arrogant. Even other Blackfoot bands came to dislike their attitude and held them in a degree of contempt. While other Blackfoot groups were at war with the Flatheads west of the Rocky Mountains, the Small Robes were friends with those enemies and even traded them guns. This Small Robe relationship with the Flatheads—the enemies of their blood kin—merely served to increase the ostracizing of the Small Robes and actually threatened to engulf the Blackfoot nation in civil war.[23] No wonder that more than one white observer of the period considered the Small Robes a separate tribe merely allied to other Blackfoot groups when, in truth, they were always a sub band of the greater Piegan division.

In 1837, smallpox spread its deadly tentacles among all the Upper Missouri tribes. The Crows did not suffer its ravages so severely as they had in previous years, having built up an immunity since a similar scourge in 1833, but the Blackfeet, especially the Piegan bands, lost heavily. The Small Robes contracted the disease while encamped in the Three Forks area and it ran through their lodges like wild fire. From once having comprised at least 200 families they were, overnight reduced to little more than half that number, while some informants say that their great chief and mentor Lone Walker was likely carried away in the contagion; along with other great warriors and headmen who had made their band the formidable force it had become. Some Small Robe families amalgamated with other Pikunni bands so that the surviving remnant was even further reduced to an estimated eighty lodges. [24]

Unfortunately, as far as the Crows were concerned, this spate of misfortune attending the Piegans did not appear to curtail the arrogance and independent nature of the remaining Small Robes. They continued in their old habits, alliances and attitudes.

The Small Robes still crossed the Missouri River south into the Judith Basin and roamed as far as the Musselshell and beyond during their Autumn hunting expeditions. Only now, these annual southern excursions lasted much longer and were not always confined to one trip during the course of the year. In fact, in the aftermath of the epidemic of 1837, the Small Robes virtually abandoned the Three Forks area as a regular stomping ground, owing to superstitions stemming from the loss of so many of their kinfolk in that country. Instead, they came to prefer the rich buffalo grazing lands abutting both sides of the Musselshell and remained arrogant enough to think they could still roam this latter region at will—notwithstanding their reduced numbers—whenever the fancy took them.[25]

The River Crows, whose rightful country it was, now had little reason to continue tolerating the Small Robes trespassing in their hunting grounds and began to openly show their resentment. Any truce which may once have existed between the Crow and the Small Robes had, at best, been tentative, having come about through reasons of expediency, when the Small Robes had been too strong and aggressive to be confronted on equal terms.

Due to their own small loss in the recent epidemic, while the weight of serious acts of Cheyenne aggression had been somewhat lifted from their shoulders, the whole Apsaroka fighting force could concentrate more fully upon other foes. Feeling themselves as strong if not stronger than the Blackfoot, the River Crows, imparticular, were determined to step up hostilities against all Blackfoot-speaking peoples, including the latter`s Gros Ventre and Sarcee allies and more determinedly against the Small Robes, who might still be found hunting and roaming at will in the Crow domain.

After 1837, the Crows were intermittently at war with the Flatheads. They knew the Small Robes were supplying these enemies with guns and ammunition and affording the Flatheads protection when they came through the mountain passes from the west to kill buffalo and other large game in Crow hunting grounds. Any old agreement which had allowed the Small Robes free and unobstructed access into the northern half of River Crow territory, was now deemed invalid. Chief Grizzly Bear decreed that future trespass by the Small Robes into the Musselshell Country should, from here on, be regarded as an invasion, as indeed would be the case regarding any other foreign encroachment and must be resisted with force and turned back.

It was only a matter of time before a serious class of arms would occur between the River Crows and the Small Robes.

It was in late August 1845, after the breakup of the annual religious gathering of the Crow nation which concluded with the planting ceremony of the Sacred Tobacco Seeds, that the entire River Crow band led by chiefs Grizzly Bear and Twines-His-Horse`s-Tail moved downstream to the mouth of the Yellowstone. They were headed for the Fort Union trading post which stood on the flats overlooking the junction of that river with the Missouri. Here the Crows replenished their supply of guns, powder and ball; knives and metal-bladed tomahawks. They also acquired domestic items including steel awls, glass beads, iron cooking pots and perhaps a few luxuries such as coffee, sugar and molasses. The Crows traded an assortment of furs along with great quantities of buffalo robes and beautifully-tanned deer hides which were much prized by the whites. Crow women were regarded as the finest tanners of hides among all the Upper Missouri tribes.[26]

After two weeks of trading, coupled with horse racing, ceremonial dancing and general revelry, the Crows packed up their lodges and camp equipment on pony drags and set off with their loaded pack animals. They travelled southwest toward the middle course of the Musselshell, where they intended to conduct their autumn hunt.

In those days, the Plains immediately south of the Musselshell were known for the great herds of buffalo which grazed there during the autumn season. There also were a large number of white-tailed deer and antelope. This area was a favorite haunt of the River Crow band, especially at this time of year. Since 1820, after the Chief Sore

Belly moved his people north of the Yellowstone, the area had been regarded by the Crows as their territory.

Several other tribes also hunted the same country during the autumn months, and the Crows were forever on their guard, lest they ran afoul of large enemy war parties. At all times when roaming this region, whether on the move or stationary, the Crow chiefs had scouts out reconnoitering the surrounding area looking for enemy sign. The Crow fighting men were in a constant state of readiness for battle—sleeping with weapons at their side and war ponies tied to the door flaps of their lodges—just in case the foe was nearby and they were obliged to defend themselves and their families or, suddenly called upon to drive foreign interlopers away.

So it was, while encamped somewhere between the north bank of the Yellowstone and the south bank of the Musselshell, that a large war party of River Crows started north, to raid the Assiniboin and Gros Ventres in the Milk River area of the Upper Missouri. This party was led by Chief Twines-His-Horse`s-Tail, who, with his warriors, went on foot, intending to ride home on the Assiniboin and Gros Ventre horses they hoped to steal.

As the party traveled cautiously across the open prairie, its members came across signs which indicated several foreign war parties were also in the region, looking perhaps, for the same Crow camp this party had recently left. Twines-His-Horse`s-Tail was alarmed. The signs clearly showed that the enemy war bands were larger than the River Crow force. It the Crow camp was taken by surprise, a bloody disaster might be the result. Meanwhile, Twines-His-Horse`s-Tail and his party were away on the war trail, seeking personal honors and wealth, instead of protecting their families and loved ones. Twines-His-Horse`s-Tail decided to abort the war trip. The party retraced its steps home in order to alert their people to the potential danger and get ready to defend the camp.

It was because of this—Joe Medicine Crow says—that the occupants of the River Crow camp were on alert, with scouts sent out daily in all directions, particularly to the north, scanning the countryside for enemies.

Several days passed without further excitement in the Crow camp and the people began to relax their vigilance somewhat—many returning their attention to the more mundane activities of camp life.

But one mist-shrouded morning in the early part of October, scouts came galloping into camp, bringing word that they had discovered an entire village of people, moving leisurely in a southern direction across the grasslands of Judith Basin toward a divide which separates that district from the then rich hunting grounds of the south. Evidently, the moving village was heading for the buffalo herds reported to be grazing along the Musselshell on the south side of the divide. It could not, though, be assumed that this was the sole intention of the strangers. There was always the possibility that a host of enemy warriors might sally forth to attack the Crow village or prevent Crow parties from venturing out to hunt. The scouts had recognized these people as their mortal foes, the Blackfeet. It is unclear if they knew they belonged to the Small Robes Pikunni band.[27] Upon hearing the scout's report, the Chief Grizzly Bear called together the important warriors among his people and held a hurried council of war.

Prominent among this illustrious group was War Chief Twines-His-Horse`s-Tail, and such well-known fighting men as Bear`s Head, Double Face (Two Face), Grey Head, Four Rivers and Long Horse.[28]

Some of the Crows were for communicating with the interlopers to ascertain their intentions. But most were eager to attack without warning and drive them from the country.

Twines-His-Horse`s-Tail was most persuasive.

> "These people coming towards us are our Blackfoot enemies. They are the hereditary foes of our people and our blood. Many times past have we held out our hands in friendship and they have grasped them with smiling eyes. . . .but always it is they who are first to break the peace. They have killed our brave men and taken our women and young ones captive when we have been least expecting. . .My chiefs, the earth upon which you tread contains the bones of our Fathers and is impregnated with Apsarooka blood, shed upon it for countless winters by our Blackfoot foes. . . .Truly, it is our blood alone which now gives life to the earth hereabouts. . . . Before us is a chance to right the many wrongs heaped upon us by these Blackfoot dogs and show them that we are Red Men like themselves." [29]

Such emotive words were sufficient for those to think again who had at first resisted the call to arms. All those assembled now clamored unanimously for battle and for striking a heavy blow at the foe. The council's decision was relayed to the people and a great host of warriors began preparing for a fight.

The next morning before noon, about 400 Crow warriors had gathered under the leadership of Twines-His-Horse`s-Tail and another war chief named Bear`s Head. The host travelled north toward Judith Gap not more than seventeen miles distant.

This gap— an accessible pass over the divide—connects Judith Basin on the north with the Musselshell Plains on the south and was known to the Blackfeet as *Itsipohtsi Stuckuyi* meaning, "The place of Mountains on both sides."[30] The Crows knew it as the Little Belt Mountains and as the customary route taken by war and hunting parties when crossing from one side of the divide to the other.

It was obvious to the Crows that the moving Blackfoot village, which was heading south towards the Musselshell, would attempt to cross the divide at the gap. Twines-His-Horse`s-Tail had already decided to secrete his warriors in ambush somewhere near that point and attack upon the enemy column while it was strung out filing over the pass.

After having traveled but a few miles from the Crow camp, Twines-His-Horse`s-Tail halted his warriors; dismounted and began making medicine in order to solicit assistance from his personal Spirit Helper the Sun. First he turned to the east then knelt down and raised his face to the Sun. From a small bundle he took out his buckskin meshed willow hoop trimmed with wolf fur with eagle feathers attached to its rim and held it up before him. Peering into the distance through the centre of the hoop, he sang a sacred song four times with the words, "He who is going, his face I see. Holding a scalp he sees him."[31]

By these words it was meant that the Crow war party would soon meet with the enemy, for the Spirit Helper of Twines-His-Horse`s-Tail had told him where they could be found and also, that in the fight his Crow warriors would take scalps and be victorious. Thus, having reassured the party of its impending victory, Twines-His-Horse`s-Tail remounted his pony and with his companion Pipe Holder Bear`s Head at his side, continued toward the divide, with the great host of Crow warriors following behind.

The Small Robe column, meanwhile, was moving slowly in a southeasterly direction, having previously visited the Fort Lewis trading post on the upper Missouri near the mouth of Milk River. Their first halt since leaving the fort had been in the verdant valley of Arrow Creek. Here the women collected chokecherries with which to make pemmican to help sustain them through the coming winter. The cavalcade then continued on to a stream known as Wolf Creek and thence, to the Judith River, traveling south along the left bank towards the Gap.

The night before the battle, the Small Robes had made camp within sight of the Gap. The next morning (October 9), a few hours after sunrise, they had packed up and continued their march south, unaware they were riding into a trap.

At this point in his recital, Joe Medicine Crow paused a moment and sat with a pensive expression as if he had forgotten something of importance. At length he continued:

> "I am trying to tell the story as it was told to me. We must get the record straight. . .The following summer after the events I am telling, we Crows made a peace with the Pikunni. But, of course, it did not last long. The Pikunni broke it as they always had done in the past. Anyhow, it was during the time of this truce that a band of Pikunni visited the River Crow camp and it was then that we Crows first heard their version of events concerning the fight and why the Small Robes had suffered on that occasion. Old man Plain Feather told me this. He said he had gotten the details from a man named Hunts To Die." [32]

"Was Hunts To Die in the fight at that time?" I asked.

"Yes," replied Joe, "Hunts To Die was a Pikunni, about six years of age when he was taken captive by us Crows when we rubbed out the Small Robes."[33]

Joe then related the circumstances which had led the Small Robe Pikunni into the disastrous confrontation:

> "It had been about the middle of September, I think, that the Small Robes had gone to trade at the newly erected American Fur Company post Fort Lewis on the Missouri. This fort had only become operational a few months earlier and was the

precursor of the more famous Fort Benton which took its place. Fort Lewis was so named in memory of Meriwether Lewis of the Lewis and Clark expedition, but was colloquially known simply as 'The Blackfoot post.' The white man trader in charge at that time was Alexander Culbertson, who later became government agent for the Upper Missouri tribes. At the time the Small Robes arrived at the fort, a band of Blood Blackfoots [sic] was already in attendance and there ensued a period of general revelry and celebration between the two bands. However, this harmonious get together did not endure long before a disagreement of some sort arose between them and when finally the bands concluded their trade and decided to leave, the Bloods moved north and the Small Robe Pikunni south across the Missouri into Judith Basin, in which area they had been accustomed to winter for several years previous.

"According to Plain Feather, the Blackfoots [sic] themselves later admitted that their two bands, the Bloods and Small Robes, had at first agreed to unite and conduct their Autumn hunts together, but this was forgotten when they had their quarrel. If, however, they had remained together—only for a few weeks more—then the Small Robes would not have suffered the disaster which overtook them. For the Crows would likely have finished their hunt and moved from the immediate area before the Small Robes appeared and anyhow, the combined forces of the two Blackfoot bands would have been enough to drive off us Crows. But always in those days, so Plain Feather was told, it was that way with the Small Robes. They could not get along too well with other Blackfoot bands." [34]

"As near as can be calculated it was the early part of October, the time of year we Crows call 'The Moon when leaves have lost their color.'" [35]

It is remembered that the day was unusually hot and sultry for that time of year. The Small Robes were strung out in a long broken column stretching several miles across the prairie, lounging on their ponies, it is said, many half dozing in their saddles.[36] A thousand or more loose ponies wandered both left and right of the straggling column, as young boys acting as herders tried to keep them constantly moving

Author's watercolor, 2006

Crow attack on the Small Robe Pikunni column.

forward instead of stopping to graze. A group of between twenty to thirty scouts was riding up ahead about a mile distant and reaching the top of the divide, they began disappearing over its crest and moving down its southern slope onto the plain below, which stretches south from the foothills towards the Musselshell River.

At the same time, a large number of rank and file warriors were also away from the column, engaged in skinning and cutting meat from buffalo and other large game which they had slaughtered along the way. By midday, the column had actually separated into two bodies between two and three miles apart. The intervening distance was scattered here and there with individual families, moving leisurely along in the noonday heat.

This moving Blackfoot column comprised some eighty families, these being the remnants of the Small Robe band after the effects of smallpox eight years earlier. Their head chief at this time, who probably had attained the position upon the demise or retirement of Lone Walker, was a man whose name has come down to us as Chet-Les-Malakax. This, however, is actually a garbled rendering of a Flathead term, recorded by the Jesuit Missionary Father Nicholas Point when among the aforementioned tribe in March 1844 and who referred to him then as, "The Grand chief of all the Small Robes." [37]

Regrettably, the chief's proper Blackfoot name is not definitely known, although he may have been the same man known as Three Crows, who at the time in question was a renown, if not the head Small Robe chief and who, indeed, was killed in this very battle.

Other warriors of distinction among the Small Robes at this time were Lodge Pole Chief (son of the Piegan chief Lame Bull), Wolf Child (also called, Wolf Son), Rising Head and Little Chief. [38]

Meanwhile, after the body of Pikunni scouts had disappeared over the crest of the divide, the head of the column began its own slow ascent up the same rocky slopes, secure in the belief that the far side had been properly reconnoitered and no danger lay ahead. The Crows must have deliberately waited for the Blackfoot scouts to disappear from view, for it was then that a horde of painted and befeathered Crow warriors, some 400 in number, suddenly appeared astride their war ponies, having been concealed among a thick stand of pine trees off to the right of the column.

Echoing their wild war whoops of "Koo koo hey, Koo koo hey," the Crows waved lances and war clubs in the air, while others fired off guns at random to instill initial terror into the enemy. The charging warriors galloped their ponies down the bottom slopes on the north side of the divide and went smashing headlong into the foe.

Those Small Robe families at the head of the column were taken completely by surprise and were momentarily stunned at the sudden appearance of their mortal foes. But then panic gripped them all.

The women, children and old persons frantically tried to turn their horses around and those who succeeded, before the Crows were upon them, raced back down the slopes and out across the basin the way they had come. As they fled, they shouted at the tops of their voices, "Kahk Tum, Kahk Tum, Isapho, Isapho." (Enemy, Enemy, Crows, Crows.).[39]

There was but a handful of Small Robe warriors, perhaps no more than twenty-five or at the most, thirty, who being a part of those at the head of the column were initially the only Blackfoot fighting men on hand to confront the foe, some of whom by now had already broken off from the main band of charging Crows and were spreading out in small groups in order to pursue those of the Small Robes fleeing across the plain.

These few Blackfoot warriors had no time to don war clothes or feathered bonnets. Most did not carry any other weapon than a knife, lance or tomahawk. Even those who carried guns or bows and arrows could not offer significant resistance.

Unfortunately for the Small Robes, although they had plentiful supplies of ammunition obtained during their recent trading excursion at Fort Lewis, much of it was still being carried on the backs of their pack ponies and most of the warriors had only a limited supply. Of course, within minutes of the Crow charge being launched, the whole front part of the column had been broken up and scattered and consequently, most of the pack animals were either soon in the hands of the Crows or stampeding over the prairie in every direction.

As for the Crows, at least half their number carried some sort of firearm and were fully prepared for a big fight.

At the forefront of the Crows rode Twines-His-Horse`s-Tail, easily identified by his personal war regalia, which consisted of his face and torso being painted with yellow pigment with either a black or red line encircling his face. Around his neck he wore a kind of stole or heavy scarf of rawhide, decorated with eagle down feathers dyed red and a large shell disc at his throat with a single eagle feather attached at its center. This day he carried a long lance with two eagle feathers affixed below the point and with this, he lanced two Small Robe warriors from their horses and counted two first coups in the fight. [40]

The Small Robe scouts, meanwhile, on the far side of the divide, heard the sound of gunfire and realized that the column was under attack. They turned their ponies around and galloped back over the pass. In a desperate effort to check the Crows, they charged into them on the left side of the column. But even this brave and determined show of resistance did not halt the Crows. They continued their pursuit of the fugitives, lancing and killing at random; some warriors taking up women and children across the withers of their mounts, while others herded groups of non combatants in bunches so they could not escape.

Women and children were screaming; horses rearing and galloping around in every direction and a line of broken lodge poles, domestic belongings and all other kinds of paraphernalia littered the route of retreat. What only minutes before had been a peaceful, happy scene of carefree people travelling leisurely over the prairie had turned into one of utter mayhem and confusion.

The reinforcement of twenty-five or more Small Robe scouts could not match the Crows, who continued to weave their horses in and out among the several groups of fleeing Blackfeet—bumping their horses into them and knocking them to the ground, then, depending whether the victim was male or female, taking them up on their ponies as captives or lancing them. They bludgeoned some of the victims to death with clubs and iron hatchets to conserve their own supply of powder and ball. Although the Pikunni scouts fought bravely, they were sorely pressed and outmaneuvered. Their number began to dwindle as they fell to the ground dead or mortally wounded.

Among this band of scouts was one named Hugh Monroe, a white man then living among the Small Robes as a fully fledged tribal member. He survived the battle and in his twilight years, recalled how he was wounded in the left thigh by a Crow missile. At first, he said, he had kept the Crows at bay by keeping up a hot fire upon them with his rifle. But becoming temporarily incapacitated by his wound, he had

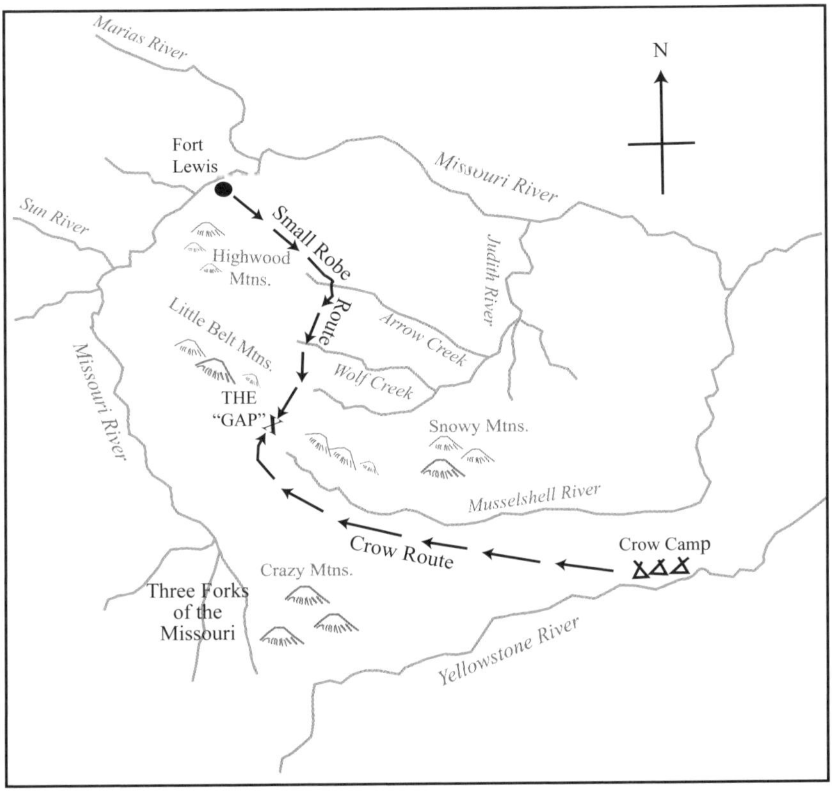

Author's drawing

Map of battle site and surrounding country where Small Robe column was attacked by Crow warriors in 1845.

extricated himself to the rear of the column about two and a half miles distant and thus, his life was saved, due—he supposed—because of a sacred owl-feathered war bonnet he was either wearing or carrying about his person that day. He said only seven of the Small Robe scouts survived the battle.[41]

The Crows later admitted that this handful of Small Robe warriors showed much bravery and for a while, some of their number afoot and on horseback with gun or bow and arrow leveled, made a determined stand. It is said that several female non combatants among the Small Robes took up their dead husband's weapons and turned to face their attackers in an attempt to protect their children, their men and themselves.[42]

Although Twines-His-Horse`s-Tail was the overall leader among the Crows this day, it was his second-in-command, Bear`s Head, who shouted orders to the Crow warriors and determined the strategy as the conflict progressed. Bear`s Head appears to have been the more prominent Crow war chief on the field. His protective medicine power came from the grizzly bear and thus, he could easily be distinguished when in battle and on ceremonial occasions by the profuse use of grizzly bear insignia with which he adorned himself—both about his person and on his accoutrements. He wore moccasins with the claws and hard fore pads of the grizzly bear attached, along with beaded depictions of a bear embroidered upon the upper part of each. In addition, he had painted on both sides of his horse's rump grizzly bear designs, while in contrast, he had emblazoned on his war shield an eagle with out-stretched wings.

Bear's Head was a warrior of exceptional skill and fearlessness and during the battle with the Small Robes, he appeared to be everywhere at once. He stood out prominent among the battling warriors of both sides, owing to a double-tailed eagle feathered bonnet which he wore to great effect, the long tails spewing out behind him as he rode. Many of the Pikunni defenders took careful aim with bows and arrows and trade muskets in an endeavor to bring him down, but all to no avail. Bear`s Head continued to race back and forth along the enemy lines and along the route of the Small Robe`s retreat. Sometimes he could be seen waving a feathered lance above his head and at other times, he was lancing a fleeing foe from the saddle. His fellow Crow warriors watched his every move. They eagerly followed whenever he led them during the different phases of the conflict and responded with alacrity, when he gave the signal to alter tactics. The Crows, under the direction of Bear`s Head, managed to keep up their constant and destructive harassment of the enemy.[43]

Also prominent among the Crows was the warrior Long Horse, then about twenty-five or thirty years of age. Already he was a shirt wearer and a man of proven ability in a hard fight. Ahead of his companions he rode his horse right in amongst the disorganized Small Robe ranks, swinging an iron-bladed tomahawk to his right and left, toppling several enemy warriors from their ponies.[44]

Yet another Crow warrior named Horse Guard; a young man at this time but who, in later years became head chief of the River Crows, was also in this battle. He too, it is said, stood out as a fearless fighter, charging back and forth and in and out among the defending Small Robe warriors. It is not remembered, though, what particular war deeds he earned this day.[45]

Author's collection, photographer unknown

Hugh Monroe, "The White Blackfoot," in old age (about 1897).

Those Small Robes who formed a fairly large group bringing up the rear of the column two or three miles back, had clearly heard the sound of guns firing mixed with the general commotion of battle, and could see the dust clouds thrown up by the hooves of hundreds of stampeding horses. The warriors in this group, which included the Small Robe head chief Three Crows, along with most of that band's other headmen and warriors, were already racing forward to assist their kinfolk as the first groups of refugees reached the rear of the column.

At the same time, those Blackfoot hunters who earlier had been engaged off to each side of the column, skinning or butchering buffalo, also raced back to give their assistance. Soon, there was a great clash of arms as the Crows and the bulk of Small Robe warriors (now some 200 strong) collided. The opposing forces scattered in small groups over the prairie, while they continued to battle each other in a series of individual contests, most of which were hand-to-hand.

Hugh Monroe recalled this phase of the battle through the pen of his biographer James Willard Schultz:

> "Back turned the people, the women and old men madly urging their horses, scattering travois and lodge poles along the way, shrieking for help, calling on the Gods to preserve them. Such fighting men as there were along this part of the line did their utmost to check the rush of the Crows, to cover the retreat of the weak and defenseless. . .The Crows swept all before them for a distance of at least two miles, strewing the

trail with our dead and dying people—men, women, children, even babies." [46]

In another place, the same Schultz, supposedly from the mouth of old Hugh Monroe, described the attacking Crow force:

> "The Crows, in one big, long body, were riding full speed across the stand our men were making, shooting their arrows and few guns as they passed and wheeling out and around for another charge by them. This they had done many times, and so far as I could see, but few of them had fallen. . .the Crows were making another of their wheeling charges. They must have been all of four hundred men, and we there facing them were not two hundred. On they came to pass close on our right, shouting their war cry, their long-tailed bonnets, the fringe of their beautiful clothes, the plumes of their shields all a flutter in the wind. A brave sight they were and fearsome! As they swept past us they shot their arrows, the air was full of them, and we shot at them. Several men on both sides went down, horses were wounded and became unmanageable in their fright, carrying their riders whither they willed. . ." [47]

Fortunately for the remnants of the foremost Pikunni fighters, who had been first to engage the foe and had since been joined by the Pikunni scouts, the timely arrival of these fresh Small Robe warriors did prevent the Crows from completely annihilating their force. They also managed to check the enemy's pursuit of the fugitives.

But the Crows, still outnumbered their opponents and the Small Robe women and children who were not already in the hands of the Crows, sensed that the battle was lost. They fled the scene in an attempt to put distance between themselves and the foe.

There were many brave deeds performed that day, especially by certain warriors among the Small Robes who, without hesitation, sacrificed their own lives in their efforts to halt the Crow assault and save their women and children. One of these last was the head chief Three Crows who, it is said, was killed defending his people in some glorious manner. The Small Robe sub chief Wolf Child suffered the loss of an eye during the fierce fighting going on around the non combatants, but he did manage to survive the conflict and one year later, was elected as the new head chief of the survivors of the Small Robe band.[48]

Some Blackfoot women also joined in the fighting. They mounted ponies and wielding nothing more than sharp pointed digging sticks, stone meat pounders or iron hatchets, brazenly rode alongside their husbands and brothers into the thick of the conflict and fought as ferociously and as valiantly as any male warrior. Many of these brave females, subsequently, were slain alongside their menfolk and even today, they are remembered and revered in Blackfoot oral tradition as "The Manly-hearted women." [49]

Eventually, the opposing forces withdrew from the field of conflict, the Crows riding off a short distance to regroup. The surviving Small Robes bunched themselves together as their warriors got ready to protect the remaining women and children, if the Crows should decide to continue the fight. But after surveying the scene of carnage the Crows were satisfied with what they had achieved. Twines-His-Horse`s-Tail told his assembled, jubilant warriors that they had spilt enough enemy blood for one day,

> " We have earned many war honors," he said, "Many scalps have we taken and many Small Robe women and children are in our hands. We have captured our enemy's ponies and their camp equipment. Let us now vacate the field and leave these poor people to contemplate the mighty Apsarooka." [50]

Having said this, both Twines-His-Horses-Tail and Bear`s Head turned their ponies around and with backs to the enemy, led their warriors slowly away, driving the many Small Robe captives before them like a herd of frightened animals.

After a careful correlation of the various written sources concerning this fight, it can reasonably be estimated that at least 113 Small Robe men, women and children were killed that day. The Hugh Monroe accounts indicate a significant number of Small Robes died later from their wounds.[51] Even a few babies are said to have been slain, but if this was so, say the Crows, then it was by way of accident and not design. The Crows today do not remember their own losses, saying only that the number was remarkably slight. Even Hugh Monroe later admitted that, as far as he knew, only seven Crows were killed in the battle.[52]

Monroe said as a result of this disaster attending the Small Robes, most of the war parties hereafter which left the Pikunni camps, went against the Crows and these were joined in their endeavors by their relatives the Bloods and Blackfoot Proper (Siksika), along with the latter`s allies the Gros Ventre and Sarcee. In the course of two or three years, according to this same source, the Blackfoot-speaking peoples as a collective, killed enough members of the Crow tribe and captured a sufficient number of Crow horses to more than compensate their own loses in the Small Robe massacre.[53]

For the Crows part, although chief Grizzly Bear—being the paramount head of the River Crows—was officially accredited with the victory, the warchiefs Twines-His-Horse`s-Tail and his right hand man Bear`s Head, were regarded by many as being the real leaders. It was Twines-His-Horse`s-Tail, who had shown his people that the power of his "medicine father" and protector the Sun, was omnipotent. From hereon, he was colloquially known as "Rotten Tail" or "Sore Tail," indicating that he had successfully gone to war so many times, that his horse's tail was almost constantly tied up in a bob, as was the Indian custom when riding into battle and which habit caused his pony's rear end to become sore and scabby. [54]

And so it was that the Crow host finally withdrew from the scene of conflict; riding south, as they passed slowly back over the divide known to the Small Robes as "The Place of Mountains on both sides."

Many Crow warriors sang victory songs, while others turned in their saddles and hurled insults at the surviving Small Robes who, in a stupefied state, remained huddled in a bunch, merely watching in silence as the victorious Crows departed.

NOTES AND SOURCES.

1 Joe Medicine Crow to Author. Lodge Grass, Montana. August ,1998. Note pad 3. p.6.
2 Joe Medicine Crow to Author. Lodge Grass, Montana. August ,1998. Note pad 3. p.6.
3 Anderson, William Marshall. *"The Rocky Mountain Journals."* p.232. University of Nebraska Press. 1967.
4 Author`s interview with Crow informant, Winona Plenty Hoops. Lodge Grass, Montana. August 1998. Note pad 3. p.4.
5 Author`s interview with Crow informant, Winona Plenty Hoops. Lodge Grass, Montana. August 1998. Note pad 3. pp.4-5. See also; Lowie, Robert H. *"The Crow Indians."* pp.162-170. Holt, Rinehart and Winston. New York.1956.
6 Medicine Crow, Joe. *"papers"*. Little Big Horn College Archives. Crow Agency. Montana. Box 1. *"Story of Twists-His-Horse`s-Tail"* as told to Joe Medicine Crow by John B.Cummins. Circa. 1960.
7 Interview with Crow informant, Joe Medicine Crow. Lodge Grass, Montana. August 1998. Note pad.3. p.6. See also; Lowie, Robert H. *"The Crow Indians."* pp. 162-170. Holt, Rinehart and Winston. New York.1956. Interview with Crow informant, Joe Medicine Crow. Note pad 3. p.7. Lodge Grass, Montana. August 1998. See also; Lowie, Robert H. *"The Crow Indians."* pp.162-170. Holt, Rinehart and Winston. New York.1956
9 Interview with Crow informant, Joe Medicine Crow. Lodge Grass, Montana. August 1998.
10 Interview with Crow informant, Joe Medicine Crow. Lodge Grass, Montana. August 1998. Note pad 3. p.7. See also; Medicine Crow, Joe *"papers"* Box 1.Little Big Horn College Archives. Crow Agency. Montana. It is further stated in Crow oral tradition that the woman in question wore deer skin boots with the toes turned up, a fashion hitherto unknown to the Crows. Such footwear, however, was peculiar to the desert Apache tribes who, as a consequence, received their sign language appellation of *"Turned-up moccasins."*
11 Hewit, J.N.B. [editor]. *"Journal of Rudolph F. Kurz."* p. 212. Smithsonian Institution, Bureau of American Ethnology. Bulletin. 115. 1937.
12 Interview with Crow informant, Joe Medicine Crow. Note pad 3. p.7. Lodge Grass, Montana. August 1998. See also; Author`s interview with Crow informant, Winona Plenty Hoops. Lodge Grass, Montana. August 1998. Note pad 3. p.4.
13 Interview with Crow informant, Joe Medicine Crow. Lodge Grass, Montana. August 1998. Note pad 3. p.7.
14 Grinnell, George Bird. *The Fighting Cheyennes*. pp.68-69. University of Oklahoma Press.1956.
15 Yellow-Fly, Teddy. *"A Blackfoot Winter-count."* Occasional Papers. Glenbow Archives. No.1. Glenbow-Alberta institute. Calgary, Alberta. MS. 2231.
16 Interview with Crow informant, Joe Medicine Crow. Note pad 3. p.7. Lodge Grass, Montana. August 1998. The presence of the River Crow war-chief Twines-His-Horse`s-Tail was verified by Winona Plenty-Hoops to the Author. Lodge Grass, Montana. August 1998. Note pad 3. p. See also; Grinnell, George Bird. *"The Story Of The Indian."* pp.109-114. New York. 1895.
17 Grinnell, George Bird. *The Story Of The Indian* pp.112-114. New York. 1895
18 Grinnell, George Bird. *The Story Of The Indian,* pp.112-114. New York. 1895
19 Bedford, Denton R. *The Fight At Mountains On Both Sides*. p.14. Indian Historian. Vol.8.No.2. 1974.
20 For a biography of William Jackson, see; Schultz, James Willard. *William Jackson. Indian Scout.* Cambridge, Mass. 1926. William Jackson further mentioned to Schultz that a Piegan Blackfoot chief by the name of Lone-Walker, had been his great grandfather.
21 Ewers, John C. *The Blackfeet, Raiders of the Northwestern Plains.* p.185.ff. University Of Oklahoma Press. 1958. George Catlin in 1832, estimated the Small Robes as comprising 250 lodges and listed them as a separate Blackfoot-speaking tribe when in truth, they were always merely a sub-band of the greater Piegan division Catlin, George. "*The North American Indian."* London. 1841. Reprint Dover Publications.p.52.Vol.1. 1973.
22 Interview with Crow informant, Joe Medicine Crow. Note pad 3. p.7. Lodge Grass, Montana. August 1998.
23 Ewers, John C. *The Blackfeet, Raiders of the Northwestern Plains.* p.185.ff. University Of Oklahoma Press. 1958.
24 Jackson, John C. *The Piikaniii Blackfeet.* pp.130-140. Mountain Press Publishing Company. Missoula, Montana. 2000.
25 Interview with Crow informant, Joe Medicine Crow. Lodge Grass, Montana. August 1998. Note pad 3. p.8.
26 Interview with Crow informant, Joe Medicine Crow. Lodge Grass, Montana. August 1998. Note

pad 3. p. 8.
27 Interview with Crow informant, Joe Medicine Crow. Lodge Grass, Montana. August 1998. Note pad 3. p. 8.
28 Bedford, Denton R. *The Fight At Mountains On Both Sides.* p.14. Indian Historian.Vol.8.No.2. 1974.
29 By this it is meant, *" The Crows are also brave and are prepared to shed their blood in battle."*
30 Interview with Crow informant, Joe Medicine Crow. Lodge Grass, Montana. August 1998. Note pad 3. p.8.
31 Bedford, Denton R. *The Fight At Mountains On Both Sides.* p.17. Indian Historian.Vol.8.No.2. 1974.
32 Interview with Crow informant, Joe Medicine Crow. Lodge Grass, Montana. August 1998. Note pad 3. p.8.
33 Interview with Crow informant, Joe Medicine Crow. Lodge Grass, Montana. August 1998. Note pad 3. p.8.
34 Interview with Crow informant, Joe Medicine Crow. Lodge Grass, Montana. August 1998. Note pad 3. p.8.
35 Interview with Crow informant, Joe Medicine Crow. Lodge Grass, Montana. August 1998. Note pad 3. p.8.
36 Interview with Crow informant, Joe Medicine Crow. Lodge Grass, Montana. August 1998. Note pad 3. p.8.
37 Schultz, James Willard. *My Life As An Indian.* p.101.Houghton Miffin and Company.1907.
38 Ewers, John C. [Editor] *Wilderness Kingdom. The letters and drawings of Father Nicholas Point.* p.185.Holt, Rinehart and Winston. New York.1967.See pages 156, 164,189 and 192 for paintings by Father Point depicting episodes during the fight. See also; Bedford Denton R. *The Fight At Mountains On Both Sides.* p.15. Indian Historian.Vol.8.No.2. 1974. See also; Interview with Crow informant, Joe Medicine Crow. Lodge Grass, Montana. August 1998. Note pad 3. p.8. It might be surmised, however, that as this was merely his Flathead given name, he may well have been the great Lone-Walker himself if, in reality, he had survived the Smallpox epidemic of `37. It is true he would then have been around seventy years of age, although he would still have been held in high esteem as a civil head chief and thus, would have warranted Nicholas Point`s title of "The Grand chief." Schultz mentioned in another place that chief Lone-Walker was still alive during the period 1843-46. *"Blackfeet and Buffalo."* p.317.ff. loc; cit.
39 Schultz, James Willard. *Rising Wolf.* pp. 154-156 Houghton Miffin and Company.1907. More specifically, the Crow attack was launched from a concealed position among the pine trees along the northern foothills of the *"Little Belt Mountains."*
40 Interview with Crow informant, Joe Medicine Crow. Lodge Grass, Montana. August 1998. Note pad 3. p.8.
41 Schultz, James Willard. *My Life As An Indian.* p.102.Houghton Miffin and Company.1907.
42 Bedford, Denton R. *The Fight At Mountains On Both Sides.* p.18. Indian Historian.Vol.8.No.2. 1974.
43. Interview with Crow informant, Joe Medicine Crow. Lodge Grass, Montana. August 1998. Note pad 3. p.8.
44 Interview with Crow informant, Joe Medicine Crow. Lodge Grass, Montana. August 1998. Note pad 3. p.8.
45 Interview with Crow informant, Joe Medicine Crow. Lodge Grass, Montana. August 1998. Note pad 3. p.8.
46 Schultz, James Willard. *My Life As An Indian.* pp.101-102.Houghton Miffin and Company. 1907.
47 Schultz, James Willard. *Rising Wolf.* pp.154-162. Houghton Miffin and Company.1919.
48 Ewers, John C. [Editor] *Wilderness Kingdom. The letters and drawings of Father Nicholas Point.* p.64 for painting of Bear [Wolf] Child Holt, Rinehart and Winston. New York.1967.
49 Bedford, Denton R. *The Fight At Mountains On Both Sides.* p.18. [Chief Bull account] Indian Historian.Vol. 8.No.2. 1974.
50 Interview with Crow informant, Joe Medicine Crow. Lodge Grass, Montana. August 1998. Note pad 3. p.8.
51 Schultz, James Willard. *My Life As An Indian.* pp.101-102 Houghton Miffin and Company. 1907.
52 Schultz, James Willard. *My Life As An Indian.* pp.101-102. Houghton Miffin and Company.1907.
53 Schultz, James Willard. *My Life As An Indian.* pp.101-102. Houghton Miffin and Company.1907.
54 Author`s interview with Crow informant, Winona Plenty Hoops. Lodge Grass, Montana. August 1998. Note pad 3. p.7.

Chapter Seven

Of Pacts and Captives and a Bloody Nose from the Flatheads

The surviving Small Robes feared the Crows might renew the fight. So they were relieved when scouts reported the Crow column was moving south; had crossed the Musselshell and was heading toward the Yellowstone into Crow Country. Only then did the remaining Small Robes return to the scene of slaughter, in order to search for the corpses of kinfolk and salvage what they could from the paraphernalia of wreckage littering the area.

Hugh Monroe recalled that the surviving Small Robes gathered up their dead and buried them in a rocky crevice on the north side of the Little Belt Mountains, covering them with stones and earth as protection against scavenging beasts and foreign war parties. Enemies sometimes would uncover the bodies and abuse them. Other accounts, however, state that the Small Robes carried the remains of their loved ones northeast, across the Judith Basin and deposited them among the crags of the Snowy Mountains, where they were laid to rest with much pomp and ceremony.[1]

The surviving Small Robes abandoned all thoughts of conducting their autumn buffalo hunt. Instead, they moved away from the district, lamenting their terrible fate. Soon afterwards, they broke into several groups, each seeking out one or another Blackfoot-speaking band whose members might offer sympathy for their misfortune and, more importantly, provide food and shelter to see them through the coming winter.

The Small Robe families at the rear of the column, comprising some thirty lodges, had survived, mainly beacause they had not been involved in the actual fighting. On the other hand, of those at the head and middle of the column had been completely routed; all the fighting men and teenage boys slaughtered and the women and children taken into captivity. In total, forty-five lodges were destroyed in this one fight—more than half the Small Robe population. Never again were the Small Robe Pikunni a force to be reckoned with on the Northern Plains.[2]

During their wanderings in the aftermath of the disaster, twenty-three surviving Small Robe lodges returned to Fort Lewis and united with the main Pikunni camp, known as the "Never laugh" band, under Chief Big Lake. Another five lodges amalgamated with the Hard Top-knot Pikunni band of Chief Lone Bull. The following summer, the remaining twelve lodges, now under the leadership of Wolf Child and Lone Wolf, crossed the Rocky Mountains into the Bitterroot Valley of northwestern Montana where they temporarily joined their Flathead allies.[3]

The Crows, meanwhile, returned victorious to their base camp, which had been moved south to a site just north of the Yellowstone about where the town of Billings now stands. The whole River Crow population was ecstatic over their party's astounding success. Twines-His-Horse`s-Tail was elevated even higher in public esteem, while men such as Bear`s Head and Long Horse, who had shown themselves heroes in the fight, were showered with praise songs and honors. Bear`s Head was raised to the position of war chief second only to Twines-His-Horse`s-Tail. Chief Grizzly Bear, however, was still regarded as paramount chief of the River band and not a little of the people's acclaim was bestowed upon him for the great victory. Indeed, now that the entire River Crow population was again gathered together, Grizzly Bear exercised his prerogative by reassuming complete authority as band chief.

The destruction of the Small Robe population in 1845 was of great significance to all the Blackfoot-speaking tribes and their Gros Ventre and Sarsi allies. The event was the main topic of conversation among white trappers and traders on the Northwestern Plains.

Another contemporary reference to the event came from the pens of Jesuit Priests, Father Pierre DeSmet and Father Nicholas Point. Both were then acting as missionaries to the Northwestern tribes. DeSmet received word of the disaster only a few weeks after the event while visiting the Hudson's Bay trading post of Rocky Mountain House on the South Saskatchewan. He reported in a missive sent from that post, dated October 30, 1845:

> "The year 1845 will be a memorable epoch in the sad annals of the Black-Feet nation. . . .The Crows have struck them a mortal blow—fifty families, the entire band of the Petite Robe, were lately massacred, and one hundred and sixty women and children have been led into captivity." [4]

Prior to the great catastrophe, DeSmet was not closely connected with the Small Robes and his information came mainly from his subordinate Nicholas Point—who earlier, had been residing with that tribal group. DeSmet probably also got garbled versions of the affair from both Indians and Whites, then residing among other Pikunni bands. This would explain why in the first instance, DeSmet implies by his terminology, that the name "Petite" (Small) Robe refers to a chief of that name rather than being the band name itself, although in the second instance, DeSmet`s number of lodges destroyed and of captives taken, are in accordance with traditional Crow accounts collected by Joe Medicine Crow. DeSmet does, however, add an interesting postscript to the affair which may or may not be true. DeSmet reported:

> ". . .In the first excitement, numbers of the captives were sacrificed by the Crow squaws to the manes of their husbands, brothers and fathers, or children. . . The survivors were condemned to slavery. . .The smallpox shortly after made its appearance in the conqueror's camp and spread rapidly from lodge to lodge. . .The Blackfeet had suffered from this scourge a few years previous and thousands had fallen victim to it. The Crows therefore interrogated their captives to know by what means they had escaped death. A dark spirit of vengeance seized the latter; they counselled cold baths as the only efficacious remedy to stop the progress of the disease. The sick immediately plunged into the water, and mothers went to the river to bathe their little children. Some plunged into their graves; others gave up their last sigh while endeavouring to reach the shore—and disconsolate mothers returned to their cabins with dead or expiring infants in their arms. Cries of despair succeeded to the shouts of

> victory—desolation and mourning replaced the fanatic, barbarous joy of the Crows. Death visited every tent of the victorious camp." [5]

It was during this same year of 1845 that the Crow Nation did suffer some kind of malady which carried off a good number of their young and very old, including Mountain Crow head chief Long Hair. The contagion seems to have been a virulent strain of measles.[6]

Another reference to the attack on the Small Robe column is found in the writings of Edwin T. Denig who was chief clerk at the Upper Missouri American Fur Company post, Fort Union. Denig first wrote of the affair in 1854 saying, "The Crow Indians a few years since, after killing all the men and boys of 50 lodges of the Blackfeet, took prisoners upward of 200 women and children. . ." [7]

In another account, however, penned by the same Edwin Denig two years later in 1856, he reported,

> "About 12 years ago in a great battle with the Blackfeet in which the Crows killed all the men of 45 lodges of the former, they also took 150 women and children prisoners. These they did not even use harshly, the women were made to work like their own wives—tho` not abused. The children were adopted into their own families, have grown up, and are now [1856] as much Crow as those of their own producing. . ." [8]

After the destruction of the Small Robes there were many Pikunni prisoners in the River Crow camp; certain warriors having in their possession five or six captives each and some others even more.[9]

The large number of prisoners in the long term would have created a disproportionate anomaly among the populace likely to incur dissent, not only in the captor's own lodge, but also among those who did not have a woman of their own. It was for this reason that Chief Grizzly Bear decreed that all the Small Robe captives should be distributed evenly among the River Crow lodges, so that no one family would own more than one captive.[10]

Grizzly Bear's decision preserved harmony. Still such a large number of extra persons to feed and care for continued to pose a strain upon the populace and the initial jubilation which had welcomed the bringing home of so many captives in the first place was short lived.

The Small Robes continued to lament their loss. Many of the surviving men were now without wives, mothers, sisters and daughters and, of course, their youngest children. The entire Pikunni population sympathized with their plight. At length, it was decided among the Pikunni head chiefs that they should hold out the olive branch to the Crows and solicit the return of the captured Small Robe women and children. [11]

Through the intercession of white traders, the truce proposal from the Pikunnis was conveyed to the Crows. At first, the Crows were skeptical of the sincerity of the Pikunni suggestion, but they did agree to desist—for a while at least—from further raiding into Pikunni country. Over a period of time, they even released a number of Small Robe captives as an indication of their tribe's goodwill.[12]

And so it was that a significant number of Small Robe prisoners did not remain long among their captors, but were given their freedom within two or three months of being taken.

Crow tradition today states that in the aftermath of the fight with the Small Robes, an unnamed white man employed by the American Fur Company, who was closely associated with the Crows, did his utmost to persuade the River Crow chiefs to return as many captives as possible to their own people. About fifty Small Robe women were released by their captors, although for what reward or recompense we are not informed. The trader Edwin Denig referred to this same event in his report of 1856, when he wrote,

> ". . .One of our gentlemen now in charge of that nation was with the Crow camp when the battle took place, and for two or three months afterwards, during which time he sought occasions to liberate about 50 women and send them home to their people."[13]

Perhaps this philanthropic white man was none other than Robert Meldrum, who had lived among the Crows since 1827. There were, however, other white men just as closely connected with the tribes. Indeed, Monroe, who was closely associated with the Small Robe Pikunni and other Blackfoot bands, was apt to work for brief periods with several Fur Company posts in the Northern country. He may then have acted in the role as intermediary on the part of the Pikunni, although he was not the man referred to by Denig. Monroe was not

Montana State University Library
Robert Meldrum

with the Crows at the time of the battle, but by his own testimony, was a member of the vanquished Small Robe column itself.

Today the Crows have a story preserved in their oral traditions, albeit a quazi-historical account, of how a temporary truce between themselves and the Pikunni came about. Winona Plenty Hoops, a River Crow and direct descendent of both Sore Belly and Twines-His-Horse's-Tail, gathered information on numerous occasions when, as a young girl, she sat in the company of old veterans of the buffalo days who were friends of her grandfather White Man Runs Him. Many times she had heard them repeat stories which they had heard in their youth.

According to Winona`s version, after the Small Robe women and children had been brought into the Crow camp, Chief Grizzly Bear requested his warriors to each take one of the said women into their lodges and in such a way, the captives (with their accompanying children one assumes), were distributed equally among the River Crow band.[14]

It was not long after this, according to Winona, that a lone Indian was observed on the top of some high point which overlooked the Crow camp. A number of Crows rode out to see what he was doing and when they drew near, they recognized him as Pikunni by his distinctive hair style and manner of dress. Using the sign language, the Crows asked him why he had come to the camp of his enemies and the Pikunni replied in signs that he wished to hold council with their chiefs. Most of the Crows were for killing him right there, but one of their number, who appeared to have much influence over his comrades, was curious and told his companions,

> "This man has traveled a long way. Perhaps he has come here to die or, maybe, he has something important to tell us. He is one and we are many. Therefore, I say unto you, let him speak to our chiefs and maybe some good will come of it." [15]

This same Crow then told the Pikunni that he should enter their village and seek out a big lodge with a medicine pipe affixed above its door flap. He should take down this pipe and carry it inside the lodge and by so doing, he would be safe from harm.

The Crows then returned to their camp and informed Chief Grizzly Bear of all that had been said.

It was sometime later after the sun had set, that the lone Pikunni came down from the hilltop and entered the Crow camp. As instructed, he sought out the tepee so designated and taking the medicine pipe in his hands, entered boldly through the door flap. At the back of the lodge sat chief Grizzly Bear who had been patiently awaiting his arrival. The chief's wife brought food and the Pikunni ate heatedly, after which Grizzly Bear lit a pipe, inhaled a few puffs then passed it to his guest who accepted the offer and smoked.

The Pikunni then told his host that once, long ago, he had lived for a time with the Mountain Crow band and had been happy among them. That is why his own Small Robe people had sent him hither to ask that their captured women and children be returned. In reciprocation, he said, the Pikunnis would give the Crows many presents of horses and guns and a lasting peace would be made between their tribes.

At this point, Grizzly Bear summoned the chiefs and headmen of the River Crows to come to his lodge and hear the words of the Pikunni emissary and when the headmen were assembled, the matter was put to them all and deliberated upon in earnest.

Among the Crows there were already many women who did not have husbands; and also children without proper parents because of the great number of Crow menfolk who had been killed in warfare with tribal enemies. The widows and female orphaned children, even though having been taken into another`s lodge, were considered a burden by those who now looked after them, for they were extra mouths to feed and people to clothe. On the other hand, young boys were always welcome, as they would grow up to become warriors and hunters and help make the tribe strong. But 100 and more extra females, either too young to wed or too old to bear children, were considered of little use.

The Crow chiefs, therefore, unanimously agreed to return those captives who wished to leave and welcomed the prospect of making a lasting peace with their Pikunni enemies, who had proved themselves formidable opponents in the past.

Thus it was decided that next summer, the River Crows and Pikunnis would move their camps to a predesignated place known as "where the Lone tree stands" and there smoke the calumet of peace together. Then all the captive Small Robes who wished to return to their own people would be allowed to do so.

The Pikunni emissary stayed among the Crows for several days. At length, when he was due to leave, he was given two fine ponies and several richly embroidered costumes, in addition to a quantity of tobacco to give to his chiefs as a sign of the Crows` sincere intentions. He was then accompanied by a body of fifty warriors to the south bank of the Musselshell,where the escort left him to continue his own way home.[16]

So it was early the following summer (1846), that the entire Pikunni Blackfoot division and the River Crows came together in two large camps, set about a mile apart on a broad expanse of flat prairie land where stood the "Lone tree." This was then a well-known land mark recognized by several tribes. It stood in the vicinity of the sacred rock known to the Crows as "Where the mountain lion sits," but now known as Pompy`s Pillar, only 100 yards or less from the Yellowstone River, close to Highway 87, not far east of the present-day town of Huntley.

The Pikunnis brought with them many horses along with fine robes and costumes, in addition to a large quantity of guns, which they gave to the Crows in return for relinquishing their captives. There then ensued a week-long period of general revelry and socializing between the two tribes. There were horse races and society dances. As was the custom, warriors from both camps discussed past battles against each other and recounted their many coups.

Both Crows and Pikunnis adopted each other's children and bestowed names upon certain persons among their erstwhile foes in order to honor them. There was even some intermarriage between the tribes and in all, there was friendship and happiness throughout the time of their congregation. But at last, the two tribes divided and in good spirits, the Pikunnis set out for their own country north of the Missouri River. The River Crows broke up into several bands and also went their separate ways.

Author's photo

Pompy's Pillar, "Where the Mountain Lion sits." The Crows and Pukunnis gathered here to make peace and exchange prisoners.

There were, thereafter, very few Pikunni captives left among the Crows.[17]

Present-day Crow memory of the above episode, is compatible in some ways with that of the old Crow woman Pretty Shield, who related her account to Frank Bird Linderman in the early 1930s.[18]

The difference between Pretty Shield`s version, however, with that recalled by Winona Plenty Hoops, is that whereas Pretty Shield referred to the captives as Lacota (Lakota), i.e. Sioux, the present-day Crow version asserts that the story refers to the celebrated victory over the Small Robes in 1845 and not over the Lakota. Pretty Shield, when asked by Frank Linderman to tell a story about a slave (captive) woman, said, "I will tell you about Feather Woman, a Lacota who, with one hundred other Lacota women, was brought to our village by a large war party of Crows." [19]

Pretty Shield went on to recount how the Sioux made a truce with the Crows, in order to get their women and children back and gave the name of the Crow chief involved as Silver Tip, which, as previously noted, was but a variant term for the River Crow head chief more commonly known as Grizzly Bear. What event Pretty Shield had been referring to is not determined in either Crow oral tradition or documented sources. We only know for sure that in 1848, Crows led by chiefs Grizzly Bear and Big Shadow, defeated a war band of combined Miniconjou and Oglala Sioux led by a Minniconjou chief named Red Fish. [20] On that occasion, a small number of women were indeed taken captive by Crows and later returned to their own people, after a more lasting pact had been made between the Crows and Sioux in 1851. (See Chapter 9).

Perhaps Pretty Shield in her account to Linderman, was actually referring to an event on January 1836, when Hidatsas wiped out between forty and fifty lodges of Yanktonai Sioux. It is said that around 100 Yanktonai were killed at that time and at least forty-three women and children taken captive. It is likely that Crows were among the Hidatsa on that occasion, as it was the time of year when the River Crows most often visited their Hidatsa kinfolk. Alternatively, if the Crows had arrived at the Hidatsa town soon after the battle, they may have purchased most of the captives. Either way, the massacre of Yanktonai Sioux at that date, appears to be the only event of such magnitude to have attended any Sioux band between the time of the Crow chief Grizzly Bear`s rule, i.e. between the years 1835 when he became head chief and his death in 1851.[21]

Winona Plenty Hoops said the Crow-Pikunni truce lasted only a short time. After the Pikunni visitors left the Crow camp, some young men among the visitors took the opportunity to steal a few Crow horses, while the Crows themselves responded in the same way. Certainly, before a new moon had waxed full and waned, war parties from both tribes were again raiding each other's camps, stealing horses and sometimes lifting a scalp.

The Small Robe women and children captives who remained in Crow hands became scattered among the thirteen Crow clans which, together, constituted the River, Mountain and Kicked-in-the-Belly bands. Some were taken as wives by Crow men while others became fully accepted as additional members of a family lodge. Despite DeSmet`s derogatory comments about the treatment of the Small Robe captives by the Crows, it is abundantly clear from the trader Edwin Denig and other documentation throughout the whole of the nineteenth century, that foreign persons of captive status among the Crows—generally speaking—quickly settled into their new environment and often chose to remain among their adopted tribe, even after the opportunity arose for them to return to their own people. Denig mentions this fact in his report of 1856 and there are corroboratory statements from various white men who also knew the Crows well.[22]

Another factor was that by the time a captive had the opportunity to return to her native tribe, she already had married into a Crow family and was the mother of several children who she was loath to abandon. Nevertheless, it is a fact that among the Crows, all captives had equal rights and status within the tribe, which was not always the case among most other Plains peoples.

One of the Small Robe Pikunni captives among the Crows was named Sits at the Door, who later became the wife of a Blood Blackfoot chief. With the help of her captor's wife, she made her escape from the Crow camp and walked all the way home from the Yellowstone, north to the Blood country far above the Missouri River. During her long trek, it is said, a wolf aided her in procuring food and supported her when she became weary. Such a story, however, is similar, if indeed not identical to other such tales found among various Plains tribes. It is a common theme that is likely apocryphal.[23]

The writer James Willard Schultz repeated a story told him by the White-Blackfoot Hugh Monroe, which tells of a young man among the Crows called Rock Eater, whose mother had been one of the Small Robe captives taken in 1845. This man returned to his mother's people some twenty-eight years after her capture, merely out of curiosity to determine if his real father and other Blackfoot relatives were still alive.[24]

Bad Head`s Blood Blackfoot winter count for the year 1861 states that a half Piegan-half Crow chief named Medicine Prairie Chicken visited the Bloods in that year. This man had been taken by Crows as a captive when a small boy, most likely during the assault on the Small Robes in 1845.[25]

In the aftermath of the destruction of the Small Robe column and of the Pikunnis holding out the olive branch to the victors, the Blood and Blackfoot proper (Siksika) bands along with their Gros Ventre and Sarcee confederates, continued their hostile forays against the River and Mountain Crow camps whenever they felt the urge to do so. It is hardly surprising that the River Crows were soon once again, fully engaged in reciprocal raids against all Blackfoot-speaking bands and the latter`s allies—including the remnants of the Small Robe Pikunni.

It was not too long, however, before those few people left among the Small Robes got a chance to avenge themselves for the great misfortune which had befallen their people the previous autumn. It was the Flatheads, however, rather than the Small Robe's own Blackfoot-speaking cousins, who helped make this possible.

The Crows knew the Flatheads as formidable and brave fighters who would "drop their robes" as the Indian idiom has it, meaning that their warriors would remain where they were on the field of battle until they were either killed or had won the day.[26] The Flatheads had always been alternatively in a state of war or peace with the Crows, depending upon what the circumstances were at any given time. And it was still customary for the River Crow band to periodically visit Flathead camps to trade horses when it suited the Crows to do so. These periods of peaceful contact between the two, even though usually of brief duration, were apt to occur during the time of mid or late summer, when the whole Flathead tribe joined together and came east across the Rocky Mountains in order to conduct their annual buffalo hunt for meat and hides in Crow Country.

The Flathead country was in the western part of the present day state of Montana in the Bitterroot Valley, near where the town of Missoula now stands, an area which offered good grazing and clear, fresh-running streams overlooked by the Bitterroot Range of the Rocky Mountains. The Flatheads used the Lolo Trail to pass over the mountains, west to east and east to west, on their annual hunting excursions. It had become customary, owing to the small numbers of Flatheads as compared to the Crows, for the chiefs of the former to send a gift of tobacco to the Crow chiefs to show their peaceful intentions and, thereby, obtain permission from the latter to hunt in that tribe's territory. In the past, it had usually been the habit of the Crows to accept the peace offering and then meet with the Flatheads to confirm the truce and agree upon certain conditions regarding the visitor's length of stay and of how many buffalo they should take.

At times the River band of Crows actually joined with the Flatheads, roaming and hunting with them during the latter`s brief sojourn in their country, in part, the Crows say, to protect their guests from the Blackfoot war parties normally in the area at that time of year. But they also wanted to keep an eye on the Flatheads, lest they abuse the privilege granted to them.[27]

Such was the case in late July 1846, following the destruction of the Small Robe column.

The Flatheads, led by their head chief Grizzly Bear Standing (also known as Loyola) and their war chief Plenty Horses (better known in later years as Victor) had, as usual, crossed the Continental Divide from the west by way of the Lolo Trail and entered the rich buffalo country then belonging to the Crows. They had set up their lodges somewhere in the Three Forks district of the Upper Missouri, near the curious rock formation known as Square Buttes and were waiting patiently for the arrival of the River Crows, upon whose eventual presence it would be determined if the two tribes in question be at peace or war.[28]

At times the Crows could show themselves a fickle lot and certainly, it was not unknown for their warriors to act upon whatever whim possessed them at the time.

When at length the Crows did arrive at the prearranged site, they set up their lodges about three miles distant from the Flatheads and that very day, late in the afternoon, a Crow force of about 200 warriors came riding into the Flathead camp with full pomp and ceremony, as befitted such an occasion whenever two tribes came together in peaceable circumstances.

Among the Flatheads at this time were twelve lodges of refugee Small Robe Pikunni, led by the chief named Lone Wolf and also, thirty lodges of Nez Perce who, like the Small Robes, were then considered mortal enemies to the Crows. [29]

The Crows rode into the camp four abreast on gaily decorated ponies with brass hawk bells jingling. Some warriors blew on eagle bone whistles, while others sang society songs and war chants.

At first the Crows were in good humor, but as soon as they noticed the presence of their Small Robe and Nez Perce enemies, their mood suddenly became arrogant and aggressive.

The Crows were better armed than the occupants of the camp and the young Crow men thought themselves far superior in bearing and in valor to what, they supposed, were the more timid and less sophisticated foreign peoples.

The younger men among the Crows began making disparaging remarks toward their hosts; being derisive with regard to the latter`s ability as warriors and generally insulting them in other ways, both in a verbal and physical manner.[30]

The Crow chiefs did try to restrain their young men, but the latter persisted in goading and taunting their hosts, trying to agitate the Flatheads into some hostile act of retaliation. These young Crows even went so far as pointing their guns and other weapons at the more important warriors among the villagers, as if to say they alone could slaughter them all then and there without any risk to themselves. The Flathead warriors became very angry at such a breach of protocol and a deadly confrontation appeared imminent.

The Crow chiefs realized the potentially dangerous situation and with the assistance of the soldier society policing the warriors, began lashing the offending young Crows with their pony quirts and drove them out of the Flathead camp.[31]

For the time being, bloodshed and mayhem had been averted. Soon afterwards, the rest of the Crows departed. But they were in a sullen mood as they returned to their own camp some three miles distant.

That night, the Flathead chiefs and those of their Small Robe and Nez Perce friends discussed the situation. They agreed among themselves that the Crows would likely remain hostile all the while, that is, the Small Robes and Nez Perce remained a part of the camp. But the Flathead chiefs were of one accord and came to a road to protect their guests even if it meant sacrificing their own lives in order to do so.

Thinking now that the Crows would return come morning fully armed and belligerent, the Flathead chiefs and those of their allies, told their respective peoples to prepare themselves for a big fight. The people raised a brush and timber palisade around the camp perimeter and made ready for a prolonged and determined defense.

When dawn broke the following day, a group of young Crows brazenly drove off thirty horses from the Flathead camp, in full view of their owners. It became obvious that the conflict would begin sooner rather than later.

The Flathead warriors, along with those of their Small Robe and Nez Perce allies, mounted their ponies and positioned themselves in a long line in front of the palisade surrounding their lodges.

Denver Public Library Western History Collection
Photographer: Edward Boos
Flathead Chief Grizzly Bear Standing

About mid morning, a great cloud of dust was observed rising in the distance and soon the whole fighting force of Crows appeared, mounted and armed, the morning sun glinting on their musket barrels and lance points; the warriors bedaubed in paint and bedecked in feathers and ermine.

The Flatheads and their allies remained steadfast in line and when the Crows charged and drew close, the defenders let fly a barrage of missiles into the enemy ranks and both musket balls and arrows sent Crow horses and riders crashing to the ground. A young boy among the Allied lines, the son of the Nez Perce chief, was the first to be slain in the contest, killed, it is said, by the Crow chief and by which action, because of the boy's apparently young age, the Allies conjured up all their courage and were determined to have satisfaction from the Crows.

The Crow charge was stopped and the riders, instead of continuing towards the camp, merely veered off to one side and galloped along the line of defenders, back and forth, shooting arrows and guns from under their ponies` necks, while others showed off their riding skills endeavoring to intimidate the foe.

But the defenders were not intimidated. All at once, the Flathead War Chief Plenty Horses, let out his war cry and with scores of fellow warriors at his side, charged forward right into the thick of the Crows and forced the latter to draw back. After a fierce struggle, some of which was hand to hand with tomahawks flying, the Crows rallied and counter charged and in their turn, the Flatheads and their allies were driven back to the palisades. Several more horses went down on both sides and one or two Crows fell to the ground mortally wounded.

Northwestern University Library
"The North American Indian," E.S. Curtis
Crow Medicine Tepee with "Sacred Pipe" on cover.

Yet again the Allies then charged forward and once more the Crows were forced to cede their ground.

At this time there was a young man in the Allied camp who had been sick for many weeks. He was the son of a Flathead chief and, perhaps, he wished to die in some glorious manner fighting the enemies of his people, rather than suffer an ignominious death on his palette which, he thought, would bring neither he nor his family honor. But whatever the reason, he had made up his mind to sacrifice his life in battle. He now mounted a fine horse belonging to his father and when the Flathead warriors and their allies charged out again to harass the Crows, who again were riding around just out of bow shot taunting the allies to come forward, he raced his pony out to the van of his tribesmen and with bow and arrows in hand, soon drew clear of his comrades.

Again the Crows turned to flee but the young Flathead kept after them. He singled out one of the Crows who, he supposed, was a chief of some rank by his attire and riding close behind him, fitted an arrow to his bow ready to shoot. The Crow happened to look around at that moment. He pulled up his horse and faced his pursuer and as the young Flathead released his arrow, the Crow bent low over his pony's neck to avoid the shaft. But to no avail. The arrow struck the Crow under the ribs on his left side and so close was the range, that it buried itself into his torso up to its flights and actually came out above the right shoulder, causing the Crow to fall from his horse, dead.[32]

The rest of the Crows meanwhile, had also paused in their retreat and turned in their saddles in order to watch the outcome of the duel. As their comrade fell to the ground, the Crows released a barrage of musket balls and arrows at the lone Flathead, which caused his horse to fall "perfectly riddled," it is said, while its rider lay unconscious, trapped beneath the weight of his fallen mount.[33] The Crows then rode over to where he lay and thinking their victim dead, merely counted their coups upon him with lance points and musket barrels, then left him where he lay while they carried their dead chief from the field.

By this time the main body of Allies had come up and continuing their charge, they forced the rest of the Crows to withdraw yet again. The Flatheads then dragged the body of their young tribesmen from under the dead horse and carried him back to their lodges. Once in camp the young man quickly regained his senses, whereupon, he was showered with praises by his people and even the older warriors proclaimed their admiration for his deed.

During the many Allied charges and counter charges by the Crows which proved the order of the day, several Flathead women were also caught up in the thick of the fighting.

The Flatheads had among them a renowned female warrior named "Quille," an elderly woman who already had been an active participant on many a warpath with a deserved reputation even her enemies knew well. In this fight with the Crows she was often to be seen in the foremost line of the Allies and at one stage, with only a battle ax in hand, she gave chase to a mounted Crow warrior who was bearing down upon the woman's son whose horse had become exhausted. The Crow, upon seeing this mounted female charging forward, suddenly turned his horse and fled and the woman could not get near enough to strike him. She thus saved the life of her son and when returned to camp after giving up the chase, she declared to all, 'I thought these great talkers (Crows) were men. I was mistaken; it is not worth while even for women to attempt to chase them." [34]

So wrote the Jesuit Priest Father Nicholas Point, who could not, it seems, praise his Flathead neophytes too highly, for they had received and embraced the Christian faith, while the Crows, he declared, were as yet, ". . . .in a savage and heathen state of nature." [35]

The Flatheads particularly, however, were noted among other tribes for the number of women who did actually join their husbands and sons in battle. One other Flathead woman this day was observed walking casually over the battlefield while the fighting raged all around her, gathering up spent arrows as she went, which she then gave to those Flathead warriors whose own supply had become exhausted. But the bravest, it is said, was she who pursued the retreating Crows on horse-

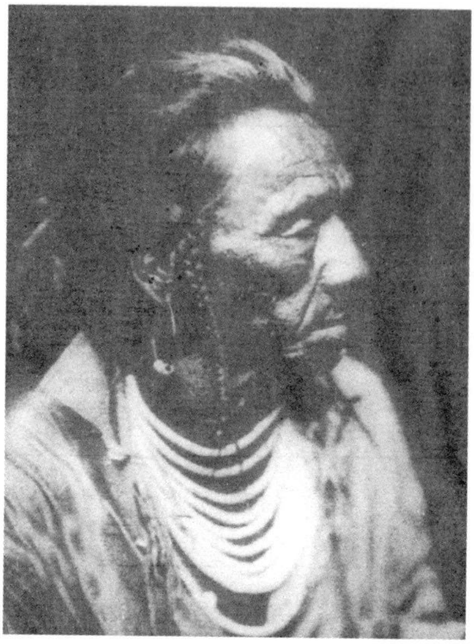

National Anthropological Archives
"An Ancient Crow Warrior."
Circa 1907.

back and had drawn far ahead of her tribesmen. The Crows suddenly wheeled around and the Flathead woman it was who was forced to flee in turn. But to the great surprise of the Crows, as a number of the latter drew close and were about to grab hold of her with outstretched arms, she all at once reined in her horse, turned in the saddle and let fly an arrow from her bow before again racing off at top speed. The Crows were left stupefied by her action and allowed her to escape.[36]

At length, after some nine hours of charge and counter charge, the Crows had enough fighting for one day. They withdrew and left the field to the Allies.

An account of the battle later penned by Father DeSmet from Nicholas Point`s narration, tells us that the last charge was made by the Flatheads led by their War Chief Plenty Horses. The priest also said, "The Crows fled in great disorder, the Flatheads abandoning the pursuit only at sundown, when they had driven the enemy two miles from their camp."[37]

There can be no doubt that victory was with the Flatheads and their allies. The Crows had lost nine warriors dead and fourteen seriously wounded, while on the allies` side, only one Nez Perce had been slain and three allied warriors slightly injured. As a result, the Flatheads and their Small Robe and Nez Perce friends gave thanks to Heaven for their deliverance and the next day, joined together in a grand celebration of their victory. The Small Robes had at last obtained some satisfaction for the slaughter of half their people the previous year. They had acquitted themselves well during the fight as allies to the Flatheads and their warriors accordingly, were honored by the latter, who allowed them to lead the triumphant procession through the camp. The Small Robe chief was then dressed from head to toe in a red costume, signifying the great victory that he and his people as allies to the Flatheads had won.[38]

The Crows dismantled their lodges and vacating the region, moved rapidly back toward the Yellowstone.

Later the next day, when some of Father Point`s Flathead companions passed by the abandoned Crow camp, so DeSmet reported, ". . . .There must have been excessive grief in the camp of the Crows, as they had left dissevered joints of fingers, and numerous stains of blood, caused by the wounds which the parents of the deceased inflict upon themselves on such occasions."[39]

In addition—Father DeSmet continued—while the Crows themselves were preoccupied in bemoaning their losses in the recent battle and grieving in their customary manner, three women captives, still among the Crows since being taken the previous year during the attack upon the Small Robe column, escaped their bondage and made their way to the Flathead camp. Thus, at last, they too were finally reunited with their people

An account from Father Point on the other hand, states that these three women escaped their Crow captors by singing them to sleep with hymns, and one of Father Point's paintings actually portrays this event.[40]

Whatever the case, the Crows later admitted that they themselves had taken a drubbing and as a result, were seething for revenge. But for the moment, any large scale retaliation would have to wait. Instead, they continued moving south and thence southwest as far as the Wind River Mountains. There they joined with their Mountain Crow and Kicked-in-the-Belly brethren and spent the rest of that summer licking their wounds.[41]

NOTES AND SOURCES.

1 Schultz, Willard. *Rising Wolf, Hugh Monroe`s first year on the Plains.* pp.159-162. Houghton Miffin and Company.1919.
2 Denig, Edwin T. *Five Indian Tribes of the Upper Missouri.* Edited by John C. Ewers. i.e. *"Of The Crow Nation."* p.148. University Of Oklahoma Press. 1961.
3 Jackson, John C. *The Piikanii Blackfeet.* pp.130-140. Mountain Press Publishing Company Missoula, Montana. 2000.
4 DeSmet, Pierre J. *Oregon Missions.* p.177. *In Early Western Travels.* Vols 27 and 29. Edited by Rueben Gold Thwaites.
5 DeSmet, Pierre J. *Oregon Missions.* p.177-176. In Thwaites, Reuben Gold. *Early Western Travels.* Vols. 27 and 29. Cleveland. Arthur H. Clark. 1906.
6 DeSmet, Pierre J. *Oregon Missions.* p.177-176. In Thwaites, Reuben Gold. *Early Western Travels.* Vols. 27 and 29. Cleveland. Arthur H. Clark. 1906.
7 Denig, Edwin T. *Annual Report to the Commissioners of Indian Affairs. 1854*, Washington DC.
8 Denig, Edwin T. *Five Indian Tribes of the Upper Missouri.* Edited by John C. Ewers. i.e. *Of The Crow Nation.* p.148. University Of Oklahoma Press. 1961.
9 Prince Maximilian Zu Wied when on the Upper Missouri in 1833, did also mention *"The Little-Robe and his horde"* when designating one of the various Blackfoot-speaking groups. Prince Maximilian Zu Wied. *Travels through the Interior of North America.* London.1843.
10 Interview with Crow informant, Joe Medicine Crow. Lodge Grass, Montana. August.1998. Note pad 3. p.7.
11 Interview with Crow informant, Joe Medicine Crow. Lodge Grass, Montana. August.1998. Note pad 3. p.7.
12 Interview with Crow informant, Joe Medicine Crow. Lodge Grass, Montana. August.1998. Note pad 3. p.7.
13 Denig, Edwin T. *Of the Crow Nation.* pp.551-552. Smithsonian Institution. Washington DC. [ms]. 1854.
14 Interview with Crow informant, Winona Plenty-Hoops. Lodge Grass, Montana. August.1998. Note pad 3. p.9.
15 Interview with Crow informant, Winona Plenty-Hoops. Lodge Grass, Montana. August.1998. Note pad 3. p.9.
16 Interview with Crow informant, Winona Plenty-Hoops. Lodge Grass, Montana. August.1998. Note pad 3. p.9.
17 The place where a "Lone Pine" or "Lone Tree" once stood prominent in an expanse of open prairie, was often utilized by several Plains tribes as a meeting site, whereat, important gatherings would take place and even tribal boundaries were sometimes set by such a marker. Thus, there were several such places on the High Plains, one being near the North Platte River in western Nebraska State; another above the Bow river in Alberta, Canada and, of course, that located near the Yellowstone in the vicinity of Pompy`s Pillar in the southern part of Montana. Interview with Crow informant, Winona Plenty-Hoops.Lodge Grass, Montana. August.1998. Note pad 3. p.9.
18 Linderman, Frank B. *Pretty-Shield.* pp.173-179. University of Nebraska Press. 1972 edition.
19 Linderman, Frank B. *Pretty-Shield.* pp.173-179. University of Nebraska Press. 1972 edition.
20 DeSmet, Pierre J. *Oregon Missions.* p.177-178. Oct; 30th. In *Early Western Travels.* Vols. 27 and 29. Edited by Rueben Gold Thwaites. Cleveland. Arthur H. Clark. 1906.
21 See; Chardon, F.A. *Journal At Fort Clark.* p.52. University of Nebraska Press. 1997; and; *Letter* from David D. Mitchell to W.Faulkner [Indian Agent for the Upper Missouri] 1836.
22 Denig, Edwin T. *Five Indian Tribes Of The Upper Missouri.* Edited by John C. Ewers. i.e. *Of The Crow Nation.* p.148. University Of Oklahoma Press. 1961.
23 McClintock, *The Old North Trail.* pp.473-474. University Of Nebraska Press [reprint] 1992.
24 Schultz, James Willard. *My Life As An Indian.* p.101-102. Houghton Miffin and Company. 1907.
25 Interview of Crow informant Winona Plenty-Hoops with Author, Lodge Grass, Montana. 1998. Note pad 3. p.9. See also; "Bad-Head`s Winter Count." Glenbow Archives. Calgary, Alberta. Canada.
26 Interview with Crow informant, Joe Medicine Crow. Lodge Grass, Montana. August.1998. Note pad 3. p.7.
27 Ewers, John C. [editor]. Denig, Edwin T. *"Five Indian Tribes of the Upper Missouri. [Of the Crow Nation]"* p.147.University of Oklahoma Press. 1961.

28 Ewers, John C. [Editor] *Wilderness Kingdom. The letters and drawings of Father Nicholas Point.* pp.188-195 Holt, Rinehart and Winston. New York.1967.

29 Nicholas Point mentioned a Lone-Wolf as being the big chief of the Small Robes in 1846, and this may have been the same man called Lone-Walker by Monroe, referring, perhaps, to an old `Alpha` wolf which having been ousted from the pack, thus `walks` alone. Ewers, John C. [Editor] *Wilderness Kingdom. The letters and drawings of Father Nicholas Point.* pp.188-195. Holt, Rinehart and Winston. New York.1967.

30 DeSmet, Pierre J. *Oregon Missions.* pp.295-303 In Thwaites, Reuben Gold *Early Western Travels.* Vols. 27 and 29. Cleveland Arthur H. Clark. 1906.

31 Interview of Crow informant Winona Plenty-Hoops with Author, Lodge Grass, Montana. 1998. Note pad 3.p.9.

32 DeSmet, Pierre J. *Oregon Missions.* p.300-301. In Thwaites, Reuben Gold .*Early Western Travels.* Vols. 27 and 29. Cleveland. Arthur H. Clark. 1906.

33 DeSmet, Pierre J. *Oregon Missions.* p.301. In Thwaites, Reuben Gold.*Early Western Travels.* Vols. 27 and 29. Cleveland. Arthur H. Clark. 1906.

34 Ewers, John C. [Editor] *Wilderness Kingdom. The letters and drawings of Father Nicholas Point.* p.192. Holt, Rinehart and Winston. New York.1967. See also; DeSmet, Pierre J. *Oregon Missions.* p.302. In Twaites, Reuben Gold.*Early Western Travels.* Vols. 27 and 29. Cleveland. Arthur H. Clark. 1906.

35 Ewers, John C. [Editor] *Wilderness Kingdom. The letters and drawings of Father Nicholas Point.* p.192. Holt, Rinehart and Winston. New York.1967.

36 Ewers, John C. [Editor] *Wilderness Kingdom. The letters and drawings of Father Nicholas Point.* p.192. Holt, Rinehart and Winston. New York.1967. See also; DeSmet, Pierre J. *Oregon Missions.* p.177-176. In Twaites, Reuben Gold.*Early Western Travels.* Vols. 27 and 29. Cleveland. Arthur H. Clark. 1906.

37 DeSmet, Pierre J. *Oregon Missions.* p.302. In Twaites, Reuben Gold.*Early Western Travels.* Vols. 27 and 29. Cleveland. Arthur H. Clark. 1906.

38 Ewers, John C. [Editor] *Wilderness Kingdom. The letters and drawings of Father Nicholas Point.* p.192. Holt, Rinehart and Winston. New York.1967.

39 DeSmet, Pierre J. *Oregon Missions.* p.302. In Twaites, Reuben Gold.*Early Western Travels.* Vols. 27 and 29. Cleveland. Arthur H. Clark. 1906.

40 Ewers, John C. [Editor] *Wilderness Kingdom. The letters and drawings of Father Nicholas Point.* pp. 164-165. 156-157. Holt, Rinehart and Winston. New York.1967.

41 Interview of Crow informant Winona Plenty-Hoops with Author, Lodge Grass, Montana. 1998. Note pad 3. p.10.

Chapter Eight

Of the Deeds and Time of Big Shadow

The result of a severe cholera epidemic across the Central and Southern Plains during the summer of 1849, followed by outbreaks of smallpox and influenza, was that the spring of 1850 saw potential uprising among many western tribes. Knowing of no other source upon which to lay blame for his people's decimation, the Indian accused the white emigrant for his misfortune, believing that the white man had deliberately transmitted the contagions in an attempt to wipe the Red Man from the face of the Earth and claim the Indian country for himself.

A spate of sporadic raiding of merchant caravans and general harassment of traffic along the emigrant roads ensued and there was talk within the lodges that the tribes should unite their forces and drive all white men from the Plains. The Crows—not having suffered significantly from any malady at this time—still endeavored to show restraint, but even they were growing restless, as unwarranted trespass across their hunting grounds continued unchecked.

The one-time Mountain Man Thomas "Broken Hand" Fitzpatrick, now acting as government agent for the Upper Arkansas and Platte River tribes, was in sympathy for the plight of his Indian wards. As early as 1848, he had submitted a request to Washington D.C. asking that the government make a binding and compassionate treaty with all the western tribes; compensate them for loss of game animals and environment and thereby, prevent a large-scale bloody uprising against white emigrants and settlers alike. At the same time, he suggested that if the various warring tribes could be brought together in order to make lasting pacts between themselves, a just solution might be shared by all.[1]

From book, "Broken Hand"
Thomas Fitzpatrick

As usual, Washington dragged its feet. However, continued reports of Indian harassment along the emigrant trails, coupled with a growing number of claims for government compensation for loss of livestock and destruction to property by Indian raiders, at last made Congress aware of the real potential of an all-out Indian war against the whites. Now those in the corridors of power listened to Fitzpatrick's proposals and, albeit reluctantly, acted upon them.

Early in 1851, Congress finally gave approval for the proposed treaty council to go ahead and appropriated the sum of $100,000 for the holding of meetings and making agreements with, "The wild tribes of the Plains."[2] At once, Fitzpatrick returned to the Indian country and dispatched runners to seek out the various northern tribes in order to summon them to a rendezvous point at Fort Laramie on the North Platte, where the grand treaty gathering would be held.

Among the tribes and delegations which finally assembled, they included members from each of the seven Teton Sioux tribes, both Northern and Southern Cheyennes, Northern and Southern Arapaho, Shoshonis, Hidatsas, Mandans, Arickaras, Assiniboins, Osages and Crows. The Indians made pacts between their respective tribes and also put their marks on the treaty paper itself, thereby agreeing to adhere to such articles as follows:

1. Recognize and admit the right of the United States to form roads and establish military posts in their territory.
2. Solemn obligations to be agreed upon for the maintenance of peace and repairing damages and losses sustained by Whites on the part of the Indians.
3. Indemnity accorded to the Indians for the destruction caused to their hunting grounds, their forests, pasturing, etc., by

travelers from the states who cross their lands. The present of fifty thousand dollars being granted to them on this ground.

4. During fifty coming years, $50,000 to be annually paid in objects and gifts which may prove useful or necessary to the Indian.[3]

Crow territory was redefined as that vast region lying between Powder River on the east north of the Rattlesnake Hills and the Wind River and Absaroka Mountains on the west. The northern boundary was the Musselshell River, although the Dry Creek region where it connects with the Missouri was also awarded as part of the Crow domain.

The commissioners had designated one head chief for each of the tribes in attendance. Among the Crows, Big Shadow, although not the most popular Crow present, was pointed out to the commissioners by interpreter Robert Meldrum, as being the most likely Crow candidate who would accept without fuss the articles presented.

To this man was given the title, "Head chief of all the Crows" and with he alone would the commissioners negotiate.

The appointment, however, was considered a great insult by Crow chiefs Red Bear and Spotted Horse and also by River Crow War Chief Twines-His-Horse`s-Tail, although he was not personally present at the gathering. Rightly, each considered themselves at least the equal, if not actually more eligible than Big Shadow to hold such a position. But none apparently, openly voiced their dissatisfaction at the time and it is likely that the Indians did not fully comprehend the real implications of Big Shadow`s new status in the white man's eyes.[4]

At the close of the council, the paramount Crow Chief Grizzly Bear, along with tribal dignitaries from the Cheyenne, Sioux and Arapaho among others, started forth on the first leg of a trip to Washington D.C., in order to meet with the Great White Father and be over awed by the Capitol`s buildings and all that the white man had to offer. With the Indians at this time went Major Mitchell, Thomas Fitzpatrick and Father DeSmet, along with a number of other white officials of lesser status.

Enroute, the Indian delegates and their white companions came to the small town of Westport on the Missouri, at which point, they embarked on a steamer to take them down river to the sprawling settlement of St. Louis. When stopped at the small town of Brunswick in present-day Chariton County, Missouri—chief Grizzly Bear suddenly had a change of heart regarding going any farther into the unknown. For some unaccountable reason, he went missing from the party and when the steamboat continued its journey, it did so without him. Government documents record only that the Crow chief's body was discovered five or six days later, face down in water and partly eaten by hogs. No additional information now survives, if it ever existed, regarding the cause of death. Today, the true circumstances and details are still open to conjecture. [5]

Thus, upon the demise of Grizzly Bear, it was Big Shadow who government officials regarded as the paramount chief of the Crow Nation, although he remained far from being recognized as such by the majority of Crows. This attitude toward Big Shadow by many of his own people, was not due to a lack of military accomplishments on his part, but rather, because he was thought to hail from lowly stock. For notwithstanding having married into the Brings-Game-Without-Shooting Clan, Big Shadow had been born a member of the "Poor War Deeds," who were descendants of a small refugee Apache-speaking group, adopted into the Mountain Crow as a component part of the "Whistling Water" (Later; Kicked-in-the-Belly) band. Thus, he did not have the ancestry deemed illustrious enough to satisfy the hierarchal element within the united tribe, who could trace their own generic lines through many generations of prominent, full-blood Crow families. [6]

Such was the ambiguity apparent in the ultra democratic culture and ideology to which the Crows subscribed and, it seems, Big Shadow and his reputation has been apt to suffer from such prejudice.

He was, though, a warrior of great presence among his peers; standing some six feet seven inches in his moccasins and hence his name, meaning that he cast an extremely long shadow as he walked.[7]

Conversely, there were those who did recognize Big Shadow for his military deeds and personality alone, not least among his own Kicked-in-the-Belly band. Indeed, they remembered well the great victory eleven years earlier, which he had both prophesied and achieved over Sioux enemies, at a time when Big-Shadow had been but a common Pipe Holder, climbing the proverbial ladder to success and acclaim.

Photograph by Mathew Brady
Father Pierre J. DeSmet

It had happened in late autumn of 1844, that Big Shadow`s brother, Daring White Horse was killed by the Sioux.[8] In response, Big Shadow vowed vengeance upon the killers and pledged to undergo a Sun Dance to propitiate the Great Spirit, in order to be successful in his endeavor.

Come midsummer the following year of 1845, at which time all Crow-speaking clans congregated to hold their annual religious ceremonies, Big Shadow informed the head chief Long Hair that he would perform the Sun dance as promised. Such accordingly was done and for seven days, Big Shadow danced and sang at the pole. On the seventh day, his chest muscles were pierced with bone skewers, to which thongs were attached at one end and to the center post of the Sun Dance Lodge at the other, and there he "swung," pulling against the pole, until the pins were ripped out bodily from his flesh. Fatigue and exhaustion caused Big Shadow to collapse, apparently dead. It took six strong warriors to carry his tortured body in a blanket to his family lodge, and there he remained in an unconscious state for many hours.[9]

That night after regaining consciousness, Big Shadow declared that while in his stupefied state, he had been given a wondrous vision by his personal spirit helper, the Sun. In his vision he had seen the stiff corpses of forty Sioux lying at his feet all scalped and bloody, and such, he said, would come to pass before the grass turned green next spring. He then continued saying, "My Father has given me these enemies in my own time. They will be our Lakota enemies and no other." [10]

The people wondered at his words, albeit not doubting that such a victory would surely come to pass. They thereafter went about their daily routines, merely awaiting the day for the prophecy to be fulfilled.

The months dragged by. Autumn came and went and with it the malady—ostensibly a violent strain of measles which had engulfed the entire Crow nation after the great victory over the Small Robes—also ran its course. But not before it carried off in its wake the renowned chief Long Hair, transporting his spirit to the realm of his ancestors.[11] The death of such a revered personage drew all the Crow bands prematurely together again, this time in order to mourn the great chief's passing. And so it was that by the time the first flurries of snow settled on the hillsides, the Kicked-in-the-Bellys were once more enjoined with their Mountain and River Crow brethren. The bands were still together when, as a united body now under the titular head of the great River Crow chief Grizzly Bear, they moved down the Big Horn River and west of the Mountains of that name to the Stinking (now Shoshoni) River, along the north bank of which, they set up their respective camps a short distance from one another, intending to sit out the winter months.[12]

This area was regarded as Shoshoni country, but during the snows, the latter were usually farther west in their preferred locations of winter retreat in the upper Wind River region, while at this particular date, the Crows were actually at peace with most Shoshoni-speaking bands and it is likely that a number of Shoshonis were actually among the Crows at this time.

About the same time as the Crows were going into winter quarters, the Oyukhpe band of Oglala Sioux led by their famous chief Old Smoke, had moved west of the Black Hills and onto the Laramie Plains in what is now the northcentral part of Wyoming. Here, close to the eastern foothills of the Rocky Mountains, they prepared to spend the winter months, protected somewhat from the swirling blizzards and icy winds of the season.[13] It was from here also that an Oglala war party, comprising thirty-eight warriors led by a young brave named White Buffalo Bull, set out on a war trail heading west, in order to raid Shoshoni camps on the far side of the mountains.

Snow was already deep, so the party went on foot, as horses could not travel easily in such conditions with intermittent blizzards swirling around them, obscuring one's vision to only a few yards in every direction. At length, after several days hard walking, the party went into camp along the banks of a small stream now known as Sage Creek, while they awaited the spate of inclement weather to run its

Northwestern University Library, E. S. Curtis' "The North American Indian"
Crow Indians making an oath to the Sun.

course. They erected a barrier of brush and dead logs around their temporary war camp, as protection against surprise attack and sent out four scouts to inspect the surrounding countryside, lest enemies be near. [14]

These four scouts had not gone far when they espied a party of Crows also on foot, moving disconnectedly along the south side of the Stinking Water. The Crows were small in number, as their main body under chiefs Grizzly Bear and Big Shadow were then on the north side of the river chasing buffalo. But among these Crows on the south side was a prominent veteran leader named Eats With Dog. At this time—especially in such severe weather—they harbored no thoughts of enemies being abroad and had no scouts out reconnoitering the way ahead.[15]

The four Sioux scouts on the other hand, upon sighting the Crows, immediately hid themselves behind a cluster of boulders and when the unsuspecting Crows came near, the scouts opened fire with their short-barrelled muzzleloaders, in doing, killing outright the Crow Pipe Holder Eats With Dog.[16] The rest of the Crows were uninjured but remained where they were, not knowing exactly where their enemies might be hidden and thus, fearful of blundering into them in their own efforts to escape.

Fortunately for this small Crow party, their tribesmen on the north bank heard the sound of gunfire and at once, a great body of warriors led by Big Shadow, crossed the river and galloped their ponies in the direction of the gunshots.[17]

The Sioux scouts, meanwhile, took to their heels and rejoined their comrades on Sage Creek, where they told their leader White Buffalo Bull what they had done. White Buffalo Bull was alarmed. He realized that the scouts had likely stirred up a hornet's nest and soon, an overwhelming body of Crows would most certainly be upon them. In response, he led his followers up a small nearby hill to its summit and after raising a low breastwork of stones and brush, ordered his warriors to sit with weapons ready and prepare to defend themselves against the expected onslaught.

They had not long to wait before the large body of Crows, who had scouts running over the countryside searching for the foe, sighted what they thought was human movement on the hill top and rode over to investigate.

The blizzard had at last ceased its ravages and discerning that a number of Sioux were indeed ensconced on the hilltop, the Crows immediately dismounted and whooping war cries of "Koo Koo Hey, Koo Koo Hey," surrounded the base of the hill. They began shooting arrows and musket balls at the enemy, several of whom were entrenched not more than twenty to thirty yards distant. So close, it is said, that both Crows and Sioux were shouting to each other with words of defiance and hurling epithets of abuse regarding the lack of warrior prowess among their respective opponents.[18]

During the initial exchange of fire, however, it was a Crow who was first to be killed, whereupon his father—in a desperate act of vengeance—charged up the hill alone with only a tomahawk and bull-hide shield for protection. Dodging the Sioux missiles, he managed to reach the breastworks unscathed; leapt over them but died fighting hand to hand in the very midst of the enemy.[19]

A loud cheer resounded from the Crow ranks as they watched their lone tribesman's death. A short while later, another Crow warrior attacked the breastworks alone and head-on, he also intended to commit suicide in a vain-glorious manner and such was the adulation expressed by the onlooking Crows, that two more warriors followed in his wake. Four Crow braves sacrificed their lives in a similar fashion. These actions, though, were hardly conducive to exterminating the enemy and Chief Big Shadow called a halt to any more rash and foolhardy endeavors on the part of his warriors. Instead, he commanded them to creep cautiously up the hillside on all sides, keeping under cover as much as possible and in this way, the Crows managed to reach the summit without further loss to their numbers. When all were in position within close striking distance of the defenders, the Crows in one accord suddenly rose to their feet and charged headlong at the foe.[20]

The surviving Sioux knew their time had come. One among them, ostensibly the Oglala leader White Buffalo Bull—his face painted with white clay pigment—ran blindly into the oncoming Crows and stabbing and slashing with his knife, severely wounded three Crow warriors before he, by sheer weight of numbers, was borne to the ground and killed.[21]

Yet another of the besieged bravely and resolutely stood his ground. This man wore a raven-feathered war bonnet and carried a befeathered buffalo hide shield strapped to his left arm. In his right hand, he gripped the haft of a long-handled war club and there he remained, fending off the many blows directed at him until, he too, was eventually cut down; his body pierced with numerous arrows and musket balls and then hacked to pieces with knives and tomahawks by the vengeful Crows. [22]

After annihilating the enemy, the victorious Crows tied lariats around the necks of the dead Sioux, dragged the bodies down to the base of the hill and laid them in a row. However, the corpse of the

Baptist-Good`s Brule Sioux Winter Count entry for 1845. "Thirty-eight Oglala killed."[29]

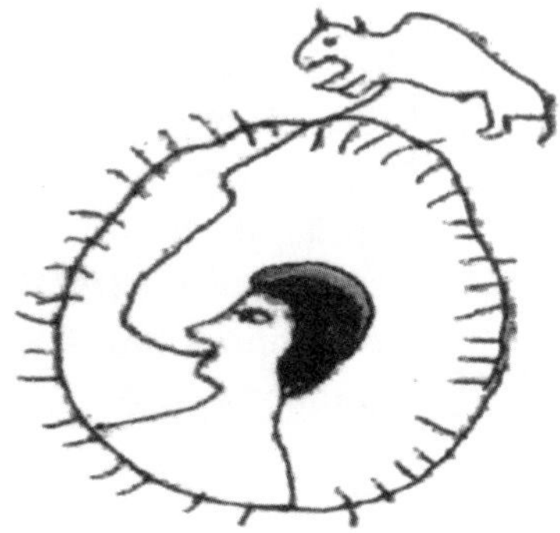

Cloud-Shield`s Oglala Winter Count for 1844/`45. "White-Bull and others killed." [30]

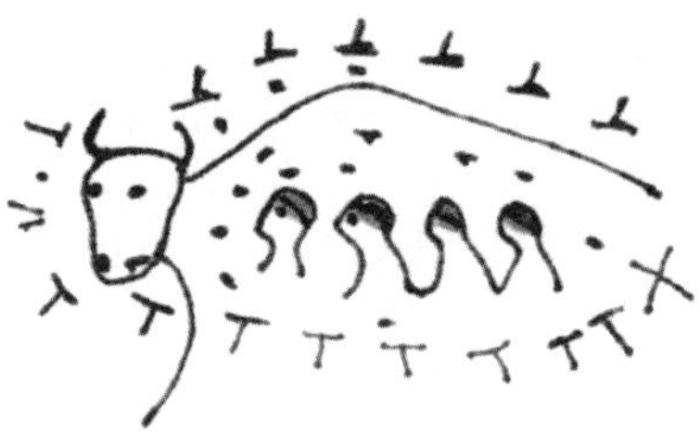

American-Horse`s Oglala Winter Count for 1845/`46. White-Bull killed by Crows and Shoshoni." [31]

Red-Horse-Owner`s Oglala Winter Count for 1845. "White-Buffalo got killed." [32]

Sioux warrior who had stabbed three Crows in the final contest, albeit none seriously enough to forfeit their lives, was laid to one side. His body alone was not abused or mutilated, he being regarded as an exceptionally brave enemy worthy of respect. The rest were scalped and cut to pieces and their severed limbs danced and sang over during the ensuing victory celebrations.[23]

An old Crow who was present at this battle told the Anthropologist Edward Curtis many years later that as the dead Sioux lay there in a long row, scalped and bloody, they reminded him of, ". . .So many bald-headed men." [24]

It is said today in Crow oral tradition, that from the moment the fight around the hill top started, until the last Sioux had fallen, little more than one hour elapsed. The Crows had slain the entire Sioux party—thirty-eight in number—[25] and as they lost no more than four warriors killed, they considered it a great victory, due solely to the prophecy of Big Shadow and the assistance of his personal Medicine Father, the Sun.

Courtesy of; "The Year the Stars Fell. " p.227. University of Nebraska Press. 2007.

The pictogram above is taken from the Brule Sioux "Rosebud" Winter Count [Author unknown] for the year 1847 /`48. The hairstyle designates the man as Crow but wearing a woman`s dress, along with a name glyph representing a Bison hoof attached to the man`s mouth by a line.

From this time on, as head chief of the Fox Warrior Society, Big Shadow became recognized as a successful leader of war parties and in due course, marked up an impressive list of celebrated victories to his credit.

In the meantime, warfare between the Crows and Sioux continued in all its unabated fury and several Sioux winter counts note, that in the year 1847, "A Crow Indian with white testicles was killed." [26]

While for the following year of 1848, almost all the Sioux winter counts note the killing of a Crow Indian hermaphrodite—"They captured a Crow half-man half-woman." [27]

In reality, this Crow man was a transvestite—common among all tribes—named Buffalo Track or something similar, as the name glyph of a hoof print has the connotation of a buffalo`s track or tracks. A particular winter count entry pertaining to Chief Red Cloud`s Oyukhpe Oglala Sioux band, supplies additional data by stating that a woman was among the Crow warriors, but after the fight, when the Sioux took the clothes of their dead enemies as plunder, they discovered that the corpse dressed like a woman, was a man.[28] Most other "counts," however, state that the transvestite had first been taken captive by the

Sioux, who thought they had captured a woman and only later, when found to be a man in female dress, was he killed by his captors.

It was sometime during the following year, that Chief Big Shadow and a war band of Kicked-in-the-Belly warriors achieved yet another important triumph over Sioux enemies, the result of which, due to an episode occurring in its aftermath, inaugurated a prolonged period of peace between Big Shadow`s people and one and another band of Teton Sioux.

It was late summer of 1848. The war pipe had again passed between the Minniconjou, Two Kettle, Hunkpapa and Southern Oglala Sioux bands and a large war party came together to raid the Crows.[33] A significant number of women and children accompanied the expedition, as it was intended to conduct several buffalo hunts in the process. These particular Teton bands claimed the lower courses of the Grand, Cannonball and Cheyenne rivers as their personal hunting grounds, but over-hunting in that region, coupled to a recent drought which deterred the herds from entering the country, had obliged the resident bands to go west into the Powder River area, where buffalo had been reported in abundance.

The grand cavalcade of Sioux, upon reaching the Powder close to its junction with the Yellowstone, set up their tepees in one large circle and the very next morning, most of the warriors started out to hunt. No sign of enemies had been reported and only a handful of fighting men remained behind to protect the old people and the women and children.

Unbeknown to the Sioux, a formidable Crow war party led by the Kicked-in-the-Belly chief Big Shadow, was roaming this same region, looking for interlopers who they would attack and drive from their hunting grounds. The Powder Country was a no man`s land, traversed by numerous foreign tribal bands when both hunting and at war. But the Crows still regarded it as rightly belonging to themselves and resisted any foreign intrusion into the area.

Crow scouts had discovered the Sioux cavalcade, even before the latter`s camps had been set up along the river. Big Shadow's war party had, since that time, been waiting a chance to attack their enemies when the advantage would be on the side of the Crows.

Thus, the very morning after the Sioux warriors departed on their buffalo hunt, the Crow chief declared that this was the opportunity they had been waiting for. They should now assault the unprotected camp, he said, before the bulk of the Sioux returned.[34]

The Crows readied themselves for battle. After allowing the Sioux hunters to go some distance from the camp, 200 of Big Shadow`s warriors led by the chief, charged the undefended tepees and took the occupants by surprise. The Sioux offered little resistance and in a short while, the Crows had scattered the camp occupants; slaughtered between ten and twelve persons regardless of age and sex and, "pursued the survivors with rods and clubs."[35]

This was considered a great insult to the enemy, implying that they were not deemed worth the expenditure of arrows and musket balls.

The Crows after returning to the vanquished camp, plundered the domestic belongings and destroyed the tepee covers. They then rode off at a leisurely pace with at least three women captives and all the camp`s horses in tow.

The Sioux hunters, meanwhile, had not gone too great a distance that they had not caught the sound of battle carried on the wind and fearing the worst, immediately abandoned their hunt and raced back to save their women and children. When at last the host of Sioux warriors arrived, the victorious Crows had already left the scene of carnage. The Sioux survivors—all non combatants who had escaped into the surrounding countryside—came gingerly out from their hiding places and back to the dilapidated camp. They told their returning warriors that the Crows had not been in greater number than the Sioux warriors now present and if they followed the Crows, the Sioux might easily avenge themselves and retrieve their captured kinfolk.[36]

Unfortunately the Sioux ponies were already close to exhaustion, having previously been running buffalo before the hectic race back to camp and all their spare animals had been driven off by the Crows. But the warriors at once started out on foot, determined to catch up with the enemy who, the Sioux believed, would be travelling in a leisurely manner, not thinking a force would follow them up on foot so soon after suffering such a devastating defeat.

But this was not to be. The Crow horses were still in good form and the Crows, not having over exerted themselves during the attack, when they did sight the Sioux in their rear, they merely whipped up their mounts and left their pursuers far behind.[37]

For a while the Sioux warriors continued following the foe, but at length, they realized the futility of their advance and finally gave up the chase. They returned to their ruined camp and after gathering the survivors around them along with whatever was worth salvaging from the wreckage, they left the country and headed east in a ragged and demoralized group.

In the meantime, while en route back to the Crow village, one of the captive Sioux women managed to escape and, eventually reached her people unscathed. The other two captives remained among the Crows. One of these last was the daughter of a well-known Miniconjou Sioux chief named Red Fish.[38] Her younger brother had been killed during the attack on the camp and as the Crows danced and celebrated their victory, they struck this woman around the face with the bloodied scalp of her brother. There were also those among the victors who wished to kill all the captives in revenge for several Crow warriors severely injured during the recent fight. But the Pipe Holder Big Shadow prevented this by giving them as wives to two old Crow veterans, who took them into their respective lodges and fed them, after which—so tribal custom decreed—the captives could not be harmed.

For some time the daughter of the Sioux chief remained among the Crows. But at length, one of the other wives of the old man of the lodge grew jealous of her presence. She told the young captive that she would give her spare moccasins and a parcel of dried meat to sustain her on her journey, for when a convenient opportunity arose, she would allow the captive to escape and return to her own people. Perhaps, though, the Crow woman's new husband heard rumors concerning the plan for hereafter, he directed a companion to sleep by the tepee door to prevent the woman slipping away during the night.

One night, however, the young captive pulled out a number of tent pins at the back of the lodge and while the guard was deep in slumber stretched out across the door way, she crawled out under the lodge cover and hid herself in the underbrush not far from the camp. Next day, the Crow captor sent scouts out on horseback to bring back the missing woman. But they failed to pick up her trail and returned empty handed. After many hours in concealment and long after the

Crows had given up their search, the young woman finally set out alone on her long journey back to her people.[39]

Since his beloved daughter had been taken by the Crows, the father chief Red Fish had been filled with sorrow and self recrimination by her loss. Still consumed with grief, he left his own people and traveled east to Fort Pierre on the Missouri at the mouth of Teton (Bad) River, in order to solicit the aid of white traders in helping to retrieve his daughter from the enemy by their employing intermediaries at the fort`s sister post Fort Union near the mouth of the Yellowstone, and where the Crows went regularly to trade. Red Fish offered eighty fine buffalo robes and a number of his best horses as reward for the trader`s endeavors, but at the same time, he also carried a war pipe to the chiefs of his Hunkpapa and Oglala cousins camped nearby, hoping to persuade them in conducting a great crusade against the Crows,[40] this time to avenge the recent defeat by chief Big Shadow`s people.

Now it happened that the Jesuit Priest, Father Pierre DeSmet, known as "Black Robe" among all the Western tribes, arrived at Fort Pierre the very next day after Red Fish had come in. The still grieving chief at once sought out the Black Robe and told him of his great misfortune. He then earnestly beseeched the priest to speak to the Great Spirit of the white men and intercede on his behalf, so that his daughter be returned to her own people safe and unharmed.

Father DeSmet later reported,

> ". . .in his (Red Fish) visit to me, grasping my hand firmly in his, with tears coursing down his cheeks, and heartbroken with grief, he thus addressed me, while sobs often interrupted his utterance;. . . 'Black Gown, I am a most unhappy father! I have lost my beloved daughter. Pity me, for I have learned that the medicine of the Black Gown (the prayer) is powerful before the great Spirit. . . .Speak to the Master of Life in my favor, and I will preserve hope of seeing my child. . .'" [41]

The Priest went on to report that he duly chastised the old chief for making war on the Crows and directed him to desist in aggression against all his neighbors. Instead, the Priest commanded that Red Fish should embrace the doctrine of the "Master of Life," which DeSmet had now come among his people specifically to impart. The old chief responded by expressing his willingness to do so and, thereafter, departed for his own Minniconjou camp in the west.[42]

The Sioux woman captive, meanwhile, having eluded her captors, had traveled some twenty days since escaping bondage and finally reached an Oglala village close by her own Minniconjou camp in one piece. She was, however, in an emaciated and near-naked condition. After making her presence known to a number of her tribe's people on the outskirts of the Oglala camp, she asked that they send out clothes for her to wear before she returned to the fold. Her mother hurriedly took a bundle of garments to her and then, according to one account, after giving away all her belongings, including her horses, dogs and even her tepee in gratitude for her daughter's return, promptly dropped dead on the spot so overcome was she with ecstasy. The father Red Fish was also ecstatic over his daughter's deliverance. He immediately raised thanks to the white man`s Great Spirit on high and expressed his undying love for his old antagonists, the Crows.[43]

Nine months after returning from her Crow captors, the daughter of Red Fish bore a son conceived during her enforced sojourn among that people and this child, she named simply, "Crow." This was the same man who, at a later date, gave the opening war cry which commenced the subsequent annihilation of Captain Fetterman and his eighty men by Sioux and Cheyennes near Fort Phil Kearney in late December 1866.

Red Fish, in the meantime, had become a changed man and no wonder, that when attending the Horse Creek Treaty meetings some three years later in 1851, he was only too pleased to make peace with the Crows; to embrace his one-time adversary chief Big Shadow and profess his undying loyalty and friendship toward his newly-acquired Crow brothers.

So it was, owing to the capture and release of the daughter of Red Fish, it came about that a prolonged period of peace and harmony was later inaugurated between Big Shadow`s Kicked-in-the-Belly Crow band and those of the western (Upper) Miniconjou and Southern bands of Oglala. But before this, another memorable episode took place, in which a Crow war party from the same band of chief Big Shadow, succeeded in outwitting a superior force of Brule Sioux and was an event to be recounted among several tribes on the Northern and Central Plains for many years to come.

NOTES AND SOURCES.

1 Hafen, Leroy R, and Young, Francis Marion, *Fort Laramie.* p.178. University of Nebraska Press.[Bison reprint]. 1984.

2 Hafen, Leroy R. *Broken Hand.* [The Life of Thomas Fitzpatrick]. p.279. Old West Publishing Company. 1973.

3 DeSmet, Pierre. *Western Missions and Missionaries.* P. 162. Irish University Press. 1972.

4 Medicine Crow, Joe. Several personal interviews with Author. Lodge Grass, Montana. 1994. Note pad 1. P.10.

5 Algier, Keith. *The Crow and The Eagle.* pp.218-220. The Caxton Printers. Ltd. Idaho.1993.

6 Medicine Crow, Joe. Several personal interviews with Author. Lodge Grass, Montana. 1994 .See note book 3. pp.1-4

7 Medicine Crow, Joe. Several personal interviews with Author. Lodge Grass, Montana. 1994 .See note book 3. pp.1-4

8 Curtis, Edward S. *The North American Indian.* Vol.1V. *"Crow and Atsina."* p.80.

9 Medicine Crow, Joe. Several personal interviews with Author. Lodge Grass, Montana. 1994. See note book 3. pp.1-4

10 Curtis, Edward S. *The North American Indian. Vol.1V. "Crow and Atsina."* p.80.

11 Medicine Crow, Joe. Several personal interviews with Author. Lodge Grass, Montana. 1994. See note book 3. pp.1-4

12 Curtis, Edward S. *The North American Indian. Vol.1V. "Crow and Atsina."* p.80.

13 Hyde, George Edward. *Red Cloud`s Folk.* pp. 58-59 University of Oklahoma Press. 1956.

14 Curtis, Edward S. *The North American Indian. Vol.1V. "Crow and Atsina."* p.80

15 Curtis, Edward S. *The North American Indian. Vol.1V. "Crow and Arsina."* p.80 [Eats-With-Dog was one of the Crow signatories to the so-called *"Friendship Treaty"* between the Crows and the American Government in 1825].

16 Curtis, Edward S. *The North American Indian. Vol.1V. "Crow and Atsina."* p.80

17 Medicine Crow, Joe. Several personal interviews with Author. Lodge Grass, Montana. 1994 . See note book 3. pp.1-4

18 Medicine Crow, Joe. Several personal interviews with Author. Lodge Grass, Montana. 1994. See note book 3. pp.1-4

19 Medicine Crow, Joe. Several personal interviews with Author. Lodge Grass, Montana.1994. See note book 3. pp.1-4

20 Medicine Crow, Joe. Several personal interviews with Author. Lodge Grass, Montana. 1994. See note book 3. pp.1-4

21 Medicine Crow, Joe. Several personal interviews with Author. Lodge Grass, Montana. 1994. See note book 3. pp.1-4

22 Medicine Crow, Joe. Several personal interviews with Author. Lodge Grass, Montana. 1994 . See note book 3. pp.1-4

23 Curtis, Edward S. *The North American Indian. Vol.1V. "Crow and Atsina."* p.80

24 Curtis, Edward S. *The North American Indian. Vol.1V. "Crow and Atsina."* p.80

25 Mallery, Garrick. *Picture-Writing of the American Indians* Vol.1. p.322. Dover Publications. New York. Reprint from The Tenth Annual Report of the Bureau of American Ethnology, Smithsonian Institution. Washington DC. 1888-`89.

26 Powers, William. "An Oglala Sioux Winter Count." p.31. [1963 edition of the Magazine "American Indian Tradition."].

27 Powers, William. "An Oglala Sioux Winter Count." p.31. [1963 edition of the Magazine "American Indian Tradition."].

28 Powers, William. "An Oglala Sioux Winter Count." p.31. [1963 edition of the Magazine "American Indian Tradition."].

29 Mallery, Garrick. "Picture-Writing of the American Indians." [Baptist Good`s winter count] Vol.1. p.322. Dover Publications. New York. Reprint from The Tenth Annual Report of the Bureau of American Ethnology, Smithsonian Institution. Washington DC. 1888-`89.

30 *The Year the Stars Fell.* [Edited by Greene, C.S. and Thornton, R.] p.218. Smithsonian Institution. University of Nebraska Press. 2007.

31 *The Year the Stars Fell.* [Edited by Greene, C.S. and Thornton, R.] p.218. Smithsonian Institution. University of Nebraska Press. 2007.

32 Red-Horse-Owner. *Winter count.* Karol, Joseph S. [editor]. p.33. The Booster Publishing Co. Martin, South Dakota. 1969.

33 DeSmet, Pierre. *Western Missions and Missionaries.* pp. 41-43. Irish University Press. 1972.
34 Medicine Crow, Joe. Several personal interviews with Author. Lodge Grass, Montana. 1994. See note book 3. pp.1-4
35 DeSmet, Pierre. *Western Missions and Missionaries.* p. 42. Irish University Press. 1972.
36 Medicine Crow, Joe. Several personal interviews with Author. Lodge Grass, Montana. 1994. See note book 3. pp.1-4
37 Spring, Agnes Wright. *Casper Collins.* p.179. New York Columbia University Press.1937.
38 DeSmet, Pierre. *Western Missions and Missionaries.* Pp. 42-43. Irish University Press. 1972.
39 Spring, Agnes Wright. *Casper Collins.* p.179. New York Columbia University Press. 1937.
40 Spring, Agnes Wright. *Casper Collins.* p.180. New York Columbia University Press. 1937.
41 DeSmet, Pierre. *Western Missions and Missionaries.* pp.42-43. Irish University Press. 1972.
42 DeSmet, Pierre. *Western Missions and Missionaries.* pp.42-43. Irish University Press. 1972.
43 DeSmet, Pierre. *Western Missions and Missionaries.* pp.42-43. Irish University Press. 1972.

Chapter Nine

Escape from Crow Rock and Victory Over the Gros Ventre on Massacre Hill

Near the headwaters of White River, on what is now Bordeaux Creek in the extreme northwest corner of present day Nebraska, there once stood a semi-subterranean, two-room log cabin belonging to a French half-breed trader named James Bordeaux. The surrounding district (now embracing the Rosebud Sioux reservation) was a favorite winter camping ground for the Lower (Southern) Brule bands under their leading chiefs Conquering Bear and Spotted Tail. The trader Bordeaux himself, having married a Brule woman was, consequently, well acquainted with and made welcome among his wife`s people in the capacity of trader, relative and friend.

In late October 1849, a horse stealing party of Crows from Big Shadow`s band and led by a sub chief named White Bear, came in sight of Bordeaux`s place just before dawn and spying the trader`s livestock grazing unattended along the adjacent creek, they ran off the entire herd, which included forty-seven horses and thirty-five mules.[1] The trader and his family managed to flee into the brush while the Crows were preoccupied rounding up the animals, and Bordeaux could only watch as the raiders raced off toward the west and their home camp in the Big Horn country.

When certain that the raiders had left, the trader with his wife and children set out on foot for the Brule camp on Beaver Creek not far to the east. At the camp of his wife`s people, Bordeaux burst out the news of what had happened and requested the Brules to assist him in retrieving the stolen stock. The Brules were only too pleased to offer their services—always being eager for a fight when a few Crow scalps were in the offing—and before midday, a large body of mounted warriors, some 100 strong and each of whom led a fast buffalo runner

Author's photo

James Bordeaux's trading store (renovated) near Chadron, Nebraska.

upon which to charge the enemy, were galloping in hot pursuit of the thieves. A broad trail marked by trampled grass which had not yet started up, coupled with a great dust cloud got up by the fleeing Crows with their captured herd being clearly visible in the distance, indicated the direction their quarry was taking and the Brules had no difficulty following the route.

It was not, however, until late that afternoon that the pursuing Sioux finally came close to the Crows, a few miles east of the present-day town of Chardron. The Crows, realizing that they would not be able to keep hold of the herd in the event of a running fight, immediately divided their force, sending three warriors on ahead with the stolen animals, while the rest turned in their tracks and faced the foe in order to check their advance. Thus, as the stolen herd continued toward the Big Horns, the remaining Crows charged headlong at their pursuers. But the Sioux were in greater number and easily held their ground.

Earlier, the Crows had switched to fresh mounts from among the captured herd and, supposing that the animals the Sioux were riding must be near exhaustion owing to the grueling speed of the chase, they raced their ponies back and forth across the enemy's front, becoming ever more daring in an endeavor to intimidate their pursuers. The Sioux, however, had changed to the fresh buffalo runners they had brought with them in anticipation of just such an event and after two or three charges by both sides, the Crows were forced to give way and

Photo courtesy Nebraska State Historical Society

Crow Rock, near Chardron, Nebraska, where the Crow fought the Sioux in 1849.

soon found themselves hemmed in against the towering wall of a high bluff which formed part of a cluster of high pinnacle-shaped cliffs, abutting the south side of White River.

Now the Crows could neither go forward or back, being entirely surrounded by the superior force of Sioux and only the towering heights offered a glimmer of hope for their preservation. The Crow party thus dismounted and abandoning their ponies, began scrambling up the slippery graveled slope of the butte and over loose boulders which paved the incline to its summit. With one of their pack dogs at their heels, the Crows finally made it to the top which proved to contain a spacious table land, with one or two pine trees sprouting from the rock floor and here they resolved to make their stand. The rest of the way around the butte consisted of a sheer high wall of rock and all the while the Crows securely held their route of ascent, they could easily prevent the Sioux from attacking them in mass.

In the meantime, the Brules sent out scouts to circle the bluffs and examine whether there was any way up or down other than the route the Crows had taken and being assured there was not, they decided to lay siege to the place, knowing it was only a matter of time before those trapped on the summit succumbed from lack of water. Then the height could be scaled in the face of little or no resistance and Crow scalps be obtained with ease. A small number of Sioux did attempt to scale the height, but when only half way up, the besieged Crows began hurling rocks and stones down upon the exposed enemy and the latter were obliged to make a hasty retreat.

At length, darkness covered the land and the Sioux lit bivouac fires while they kept watch on the summit and especially on the slope, lest the Crows attempt to escape in the dark. But as the rear of the butte had previously been examined and deemed too sheer and high a cliff face for the Crows to descend, the Sioux left that part of the butte unguarded.

The lack of guards was fortunate for the Crows. In order to show that they were not yet cowered, they danced and sang throughout the night in defiance of their besiegers. They were not, however, so engrossed in their revelry that they were not formulating a plan to extricate themselves from their predicament.

One Crow, after examining the sheer drop on the unattended side of the butte, suggested that the warriors tie their long rawhide lariats together and attach one end to the trunk of one of the pine trees on the summit, while letting the rest of the rope dangle over the cliff face. This was quickly done, after which, one warrior volunteered to climb down the knotted thong to see if he could reach the ground and whether any of the enemy were guarding that side of the butte. This man told his comrades that if he hollered out, then they would know it was safe to follow, but if they heard no sound, they would know he had been killed and they should not then attempt to leave the summit, as it would mean certain death. The man then slipped over the side and in a moment, was lost from view in the blackness of the night.

It must have been an anxious time, all the while the Crows on the summit waited, with ears strained. How welcome it must have been when they heard him holler that he had safely reached the bottom and all was well.

So it was, while some of the besieging Sioux slept and others kept watch, while still others sang victory songs hoping to unnerve the Crows, the latter—one by one—silently and quickly, shinnied down the hide rope on the far side of the butte. When all had reached the base, they ran across country towards the west, leaving the rope dangling from the cliff top to show their foes how they had outwitted them in this their hour of peril.

There was, however, one Crow warrior who had suffered some kind of injury in the fighting around the base of the butte the previous day and he knew it was a death wound. This man told his companions to leave him on the summit, for he would only hinder the party's escape. At least, he said, he could die an honorable death surrounded by the enemies of his people. Reluctantly the Crows left him to his fate and also the pack dog to keep him company during his lonely vigil.

Smithsonian Institution. Bureau of American Ethnology. Washington DC.

Baptist-Good's Brule Winter Count for 1849/'50 "When we Brought the Crows to a stand." [3]

A Sioux account of the event, related many years later by two old Brule warriors named Cloud Man and Red Leaf who were present on that occasion, stated that the Sioux force remained entrenched around the base of the butte for three days and three nights, before finally venturing to scale the height. When on top, they discovered the corpses of three dead Crows and one live pack dog. The Sioux realized that the fleeing Crows had too much of a head start to be overtaken and therefore, did not attempt to follow.[2] They had for their trouble three Crow scalps and the lone pack dog which they took with them when they returned to their own camp on Beaver Creek. Three enemy scalps were enough for the Sioux to consider the affair a victory and, as such, it was celebrated accordingly.

The Crows, meanwhile, safely reached their Kicked-in-the-Belly home camp of Big Shadow's band without further mishap and where, many days before, their three comrades who had rode on with the stolen herd, had already safely arrived driving the captured animals before them. Thus there was much rejoicing among the Crows when Chief White Bear and his missing warriors finally appeared—but also much grieving for their three comrades who had left their bleaching bones in the Brule country.

It was a miraculous escape for the Crows and a humiliating episode for the Sioux. But in good humor, the story has since been told time and again, not only among the Crows and Sioux, but also among their respective allies, while in addition, throughout the years following, combined parties of Sioux and Crows—albeit, ostensibly at war with each other—several times visited the same cliff top together, in order

Denver Public Library
Western History Collection
Crow Chief White Bear

to inspect the site and discuss with each other their respective versions of the event.

For a long time this collection of pinnacle and tall flat top buttes, situated about two miles northwest of Fort Robinson and some few miles east of the present small town of Crawford, was known among the Sioux as "Where Crows danced" and colloquially by the whites of the area simply as "Dancer`s Hill." Not until the late 1880s was the site officially named "Crow Butte," by which appellation it is still known and is so marked on present-day maps.[4]

While it is true that several other tribes, including the Pawnee and Blackfeet, have similar stories in their oral traditions, which tell of one of their own war parties escaping from the top of a high eminence in a near identical manner, it should not be supposed that the episode above recounted did not, in fact, take place. The Crow version, is well documented. There are official affidavits made by some of those involved, including James Bordeaux, who in 1867 requested compensation for livestock lost.[5] The also are statements from some Crow participants to their agent Major Pease in 1872,[6] which, along with numerous entries in the various Sioux winter counts, authenticate this particular instance involving the Crows and Brule Sioux in 1849.

So it was that the Kicked-in-the-Belly Crow band received further distinction among both its enemies and friends, which only served to enhance the reputation of chief Big Shadow himself. But in truth, Big Shadow's greatest victory was yet to come and involved his warriors and allies rubbing out an entire foreign war party. The event gave the Crow victors the largest number of enemies slain outright in a single contest since the great defeat of the Small Robe Pikunni seven years earlier. It was an event which came about in the following manner.

Fight with the Gros Ventre at Massacre Hill

The Crows and Sioux among others, had congregated at the Fitzpatrick Treaty signing of 1851. They smoked the calumet of peace and, at the same time, agreed to lines of demarcation drawn between Crow hunting grounds and those of their enemies. The Crows did attempt to pursue peaceful relations thereafter and not until they became convinced that other tribes in the agreement were not adhering to their obligations, did the Crows abandon their pacts and renew hostilities. Before this, however, there was a significant reduction in Crow conflicts with the Sioux and Cheyennes and little hostile contact occurred between them during the first few years following the treaty, save the occasional raid for horses upon each other's herds by small groups of young incorrigibles. The peace, overall, held good and in compliance with the treaty agreements made that year of 1851, saw the Crow band of Big Shadow's people paying a friendly visit to the Miniconjou Sioux led by chief Red Fish and his son Lone Horn, then encamped northeast of Horse Creek on the Belle Fourche branch of the Cheyenne River.[7]

In the winter of 1851-'52, these same Kicked-in-the-Belly Crows and Miniconjou Sioux were still together, having now moved west into Crow country itself, with their respective camps standing adjacent to one another along the lower course of the Big Horn River.[8]

Throughout the winter months, congenial revelry and celebrations ensued between the two bands. They conducted communal buffalo hunts. Upon the several occasions when the camps were moved, the bands traveled as one, the Crows in a body leading the way, as was their duty as hosts to defend the people if enemies appeared in front, while the Miniconjou protected the rear, lest the cavalcade be attacked from that quarter. During the course of their congregation, the Crow chief Big Shadow, it is said by Joe Medicine Crow, became great friends with his counterparts chief Red Fish and Lone Horn of the Minniconjou and these three were constantly in each other's company.[9]

One chilly morning just prior to the opening of spring in early 1852, while in camp along the Little Big Horn River, the Miniconjou bade farewell to their hosts and traveled east across the Wolf Teeth Mountains, heading for the Lower Powder on the first leg of their journey into the Belle Fourch Country, where they intended to spend the summer months as had been their habit in previous years.

The Crows, under Big Shadow, initially also went east, but only as far as Rosebud Creek and turning up that stream, set their tepees on that river's east bank midway along its course.

During the same day the Crows set up their Rosebud camp, a war party of sixty Gros Ventres—out after horses and scalps—came across the band and in the darkness of night, drove off seventy-five or more loose ponies which had been hobbled around the perimeter of the camp.

The thieves started toward the northeast and their home country above Milk River north of the international boundary. They would, they thought, be far away by the time the Crows discovered their loss come morning.

When the retreating Gros Ventres reached the lower course of the Tongue, about where the town of Ashland now stands on the eastern edge of the present-day Northern Cheyenne reservation, a blinding snow storm came up and swirling snow and sleet became so dense, it virtually obliterated one's view. Nevertheless, the Gros Ventres continued on, albeit at a much slower pace and unwittingly, their course was turned around to the effect that they were actually travelling southwest, not knowing exactly where they were heading.

Around midmorning the following day, the storm finally died down and regaining visibility, the Gros Ventres discovered to their dismay, that they had been travelling blindly in the opposite direction to that which had been intended. What was more distressing, however, was the fact that they had blundered upon the very same Crow camp straddled along the east bank of Rosebud Creek, from where they had stolen the Crow horses in the first place. The Crows at this time were still running around outside the camp, searching for enemy tracks that might not have been covered during the storm and immediately they spotted the Gros Ventres when the latter halted—momentarily—and gazed in bewilderment at the unwelcome sight before them.[10]

Almost at once, upon sighting the Gros Ventres, the Crow war cry went up from more than 100 throats. Hastily, the warriors of Big Shadow's band grabbed their weapons, mounted war ponies and within minutes were charging towards the foe.

The Gros Ventres immediately abandoned the stolen herd they had been pushing and turned to flee, but the only place where they might gain cover and defend themselves was a rocky butte overlooking the South Fork of Rosebud Creek. Upon reaching this promontory, they urged the ponies they were riding up its slopes and reaching the summit, dismounted and began hastily gathering up loose rocks and large shale which lay scattered around. With this material they built a crudely constructed breastwork, behind which they intended to confront their attackers.

Hardly had the Gros Ventres finished their defenses, when a large body of Crows reached the base of the butte and surrounded the position. Most of the Crows at first held back from actually assaulting the height, knowing how dangerous it would be under a shower of missiles from both guns and bows which were sure to rain down upon them. For the Crows knew only too well that the Gros Ventres always had firearms in abundance, owing to regular trading contacts with Hudson Bay Company posts in the north.[11]

Some few Crows, nonetheless, did recklessly rush the enemy position and several were killed. Only one Crow warrior actually made it to the summit. This man's name was Crazy Head, the alleged half-breed son of the Mountain Man, James Beckwourth.[12] A short while earlier, before the fight proper began, Crazy Head, in an act of bravado, forcibly took away a crooked lance from a fellow Fox Warrior Society member who, as the owner of such a lance, had pledged himself not to retreat in the face of the enemy. Crazy Head declared that he would show the owner of the lance what a brave warrior should do, rather than hesitating to get to grips with the foe. Running in a zigzag manner up the slope, Crazy Head managed to dodge the flying arrows and musket balls fired by the defenders. Upon reaching the low breastworks unscathed, he was at the point of thrusting his coup stick over the breastwork wall, when a Gros Ventre poked his musket through from the other side and fired. Crazy Head received the ball in the abdomen. The wound was not fatal and he succeeded in extricating himself back down the slope and escaping to his own lines, before the marksmanship of the Gros Ventres could finish him off.[13]

After this the Crows showed additional caution and no more of their warriors attempted to scale the height alone.

Northwestern University Library
E. S. Curtis' "North American Indian"
Crow warrior Red Wing

The Gros Ventres on the other hand, now became more confident in their protected refuge. They began shouting abuse and jeering at the Crows. Several Gros Ventres flashed their buttocks and private parts, to show contempt for the timidity of those besieging them.

Meanwhile, Big Shadow and his chiefs were holding a council of war. They had regained most of the ponies stolen the previous night, but, they thought, it would not be good for their reputation across the plains if they refrained from punishing the Gros Ventres, if not actually rubbing them out completely. They realized too that there were around sixty Gros Ventres on the hilltop and the 100 or more of their own Crow braves present, would not be enough to assault the position from all sides to prevent any of the enemy escaping.

It was agreed they should send a message to their friend Red Fish and his Miniconjou band, with a request to assist the Crows in dislodging the enemy from the hilltop, for the Gros Ventres were considered enemies of the Minniconjou also.

A Crow messenger started off at once and after a hard ride, found the Miniconjou camp some several miles east of Rosebud Creek. Here the courier relayed Big Shadow's words to Chief Red Fish who, upon hearing the Crow`s request, replied, "Yes, my warriors are pleased to help their friends the Crows and we will show them how the Minniconjou can fight. . .It is too late in the day to start at once, but first light come morning, I and my warriors will ride out and finish the job you Crows have started." [14]

The Crow messenger then raced back to his people and reported the words of Red Fish. Big Shadow then rode out alone to the base of the butte and shouted aloud to the Gros Ventres in Crow, supplemented with a smattering of Gros Ventres and sign talk gestures. He told them that many more warriors were soon coming to help rub them out and then the Gros Ventres would have all the fighting they could wish for.[15]

The Gros Ventres themselves must have lost heart at these words, but concealing their fears, they again retorted with shouts of defiance and abuse and dared the Crows to do their worst. But, in truth, their leaders knew only too well that their own demise was imminent.[16]

Among the Gros Ventres party were two teenage boys, fourteen or fifteen years of age, out on their first important venture on the "Red road to war." One of these was named No Necklace, but the other boy's name is not remembered.

The Gros Ventres still had a number of horses among them, which they had ridden up the slopes to the summit of the butte. The Gros Ventre chief took pity on the youths because of their age and in an attempt to save their lives, he told each to mount a fast pony and that when twilight fell, they should stampede the remaining ponies down the hillside. In the resulting confusion, while the Crows attempted to capture the loose animals, the two youngsters would have the opportunity to race down the slope on the butte's far side and, hopefully, make their way to their home camp on Milk River. There they could relate the circumstances surrounding those of their comrades obliged to remain on the summit and who's extermination was inevitable.

When the sun sank low and twilight enveloped the land, the two youngsters did as had been suggested and stampeded the loose ponies down the hillside.

Sure enough, the Crows relaxed their vigilance somewhat, as they chased after the loose ponies and the two Gros Ventre boys made their escape in another direction.

A small number of Crows did realize what was happening and gave chase to the two shadowy figures racing across the country. But darkness was rapidly falling and the pursuers soon lost their quarry in the blackness of the night.

One of the boys, No Necklace, jumped from his pony's back and hid in a gully while the Crows continued in the direction they supposed he was travelling. The other Gros Ventre, meanwhile, raced off along a different route, also with a number of Crows hard on his trail. But likewise, he managed to outwit his pursuers and concealed himself in the undergrowth until, finally, the Crows gave up their search and returned to the camp on Rosebud Creek.[17]

As the night slowly passed, the sound of Crow war drums reverberated monotonously around the base of the butte, on top of which the rest of the Gros Ventres were trapped. At the same time, countless bivouac fires indicated to the besieged that the Crows were determined to prevent any more escaping off the summit.

It is likely that few Crows or Gros Ventres actually slept that night, as both waited with grim anticipation for what the morrow would bring.

When dawn eventually broke, the Crows were astir; whooping and singing, while all eyes looked eastward, in expectation of seeing their friends the Miniconjou galloping to the scene of conflict.

The Gros Ventres also scanned the horizon, many with a forlorn hope that the Crow chief had been bluffing and that no help was on its way to "clean them out," as the Indian idiom expressed it.

But Big Shadow had not spoken idle words.

True to his promise, after the sun had been up but a few hours, Red Fish and a horde of Miniconjou were observed riding at breakneck speed towards the butte.

The Gros Ventres, in their elevated position, were first to discern a great dust cloud rising in the distance—moving steadily closer—and they knew they had seen their last sunrise.

When the Sioux did arrive at the scene, the Crows sent up a great tumult in order to both welcome and pay homage to their allies. But the charging Sioux did not rein in their ponies. Instead, they called out to the Crows to stand back and jumping from their mounts while in full gallop, started on foot up the slopes of the rocky height. The Crows in their amazement merely watched, not knowing what was about to happen.[18]

The Sioux advanced upwards toward the Gros Ventre position in two long ranks, one behind the other and as they did so, the rear rank arched their bows and shot volley after volley of arrows so that they fell like rain upon the defenders, thus preventing the latter from exposing themselves in order to fire down on their attackers.[19] The forward Sioux line soon reached the summit unscathed.

A young Miniconjou chief named Makes Room (the Father of Chief Joseph White Bull) ran at the head of his comrades. It was he who was first to reach the breastworks and the first Sioux to count coup by striking one of the defenders with his bow.[20]

At the same time the entire Gros Ventre force—many of who had already exhausted their ammunition—began singing their death songs and drawing their knives and hatchets, they sprinted over the breastworks in a disorganized mass and scampered down the slopes, every man for himself in an effort to escape their entrapped position. They attempted to reach a nearby timber, wherein, they might elude their enemies or, die honorably in hand-to-hand combat.

Crow Chief Red Bear. Sketch by the Author after a drawing from life by George Catlin in 1832. The original is is the Smithsonian Institution.

At this point, the Crows joined the fray and during the Gros Ventres` mad dash down the hillside, a subordinate Crow chief named Repels The Enemy, was unlucky enough to find himself alone between two Gros Ventres. In the desperate situation they were in, these two Gros Ventres grabbed hold of Repels The Enemy and holding him fast, stabbed him to death before they themselves were slain.[21]

The combined Crows and Miniconjou easily outmaneuvered their foes. They cut them down one by one and in small bunches, until almost all had been killed.

Of the sixty Gros Ventres besieged on the hilltop, only six or seven managed to escape the slaughter and finally reached their home country.[22] Among these Gros Ventre survivors were the two teenage boys, who had escaped on horseback the night before the final assault. The morning following their escape, they met up somewhere west of the Crow camp. Together they made their way cautiously to the vicinity of the butte where they had left their hapless companions. They suddenly heard singing followed by a great roar from many throats. This must have been the time—they later supposed—which heralded the final moments of the fight, when the besieged Gros Ventres began singing their death songs and the Crows and Sioux sent up a great hullabaloo, as the former came tumbling amass down the hill side into the arms of the waiting enemy.

It was some time after this, before the two boys came close enough to the butte to see what was going on.[23] By then the fighting was over and the two boys, from a concealed position on a nearby hill, observed a number of people wandering over the slopes of the butte including men, women and children. These latter were collecting trophies from the dead Gros Ventres; the women amputating arms, feet and heads, while the children counted coup on the bodies and collected spent arrows and other items as souvenirs of the bloody event.

For the rest of that day the Gros Ventre youngsters remained hidden and could clearly hear the sound of drums and celebratory songs emanating from the nearby camps, as both Crows and Sioux held scalp dances and reveled in the great victory achieved.

When again darkness fell, the two lone survivors started out for home and many days later, brought word to their people on Milk River, concerning all that had occurred on the butte overlooking the South Fork of Rosebud Creek.[24]

The site of this butte where Crows and their Miniconjou allies wiped out sixty Gros Ventres, has ever since been known colloquially to those residing in its vicinity as "Massacre Hill." [25]

Over the course of time, however, the actual site of this fight has become confused in Cheyenne memories with that of the much earlier conflict on Otter Creek, when chief Long Hair`s Mountain Crow village was destroyed during the great fight of 1820.

According to Northern Cheyenne testimony, it was ten or more years after this Crow-Minniconjou-Gros Ventre fight, that another Gros Ventre party went to visit the site of the battle where so many of their kinfolk had fallen. But while there paying homage to their dead, a large warparty of Cheyennes came upon them and after chasing the Gros Ventres up the same or a nearby butte, wiped out this second party also.[26]

Curiously enough, one of the Gros Ventre survivors of the earlier event, many years later in 1868, actually married a Crow woman and, thereafter, lived among his wife's people for the remainder of his days. In later years he was known as White Shirt, a name dubbed upon him by the local white men with whom he was in contact. His

Joe Medicine Crow renewing peace pact with the Cheyennes, 2008.

Author's photo

given Gros Ventre name was No Necklace. The Crows later told No Necklace that during the night, when he and his young companion had escaped off the butte, they (the Crows) had searched high and low for the fugitives and must several times have passed very close to where they were hiding. But still they could not find them and come dawn, had finally abandoned the search and returned to the battle to be in on the kill when the rest of the Crows and Miniconjou rubbed out the remaining Gros Ventres.[27]

Such then was another great victory accredited to Big Shadow by his followers and even by his enemies the Sioux, who now regarded him as a chief of distinction; to be respected and treated on a par with any great personage among themselves. The Crow-Sioux pact affected the previous year during the Fitzpatrick Treaty at Horse Creek, continued for the time being to hold good, at least, between Big Shadow`s Kicked-in-the-Belly people and the Miniconjou Sioux of Red Fish. But alas, as so many times before, it was a congenial situation destined to fail.

NOTES AND SOURCES.

1.Bordeaux, William J *"Conquering the Mighty Sioux."* pp. 41-45. Sioux Falls, South Dakota. 1929. This information and that following, unless otherwise specified, is taken from Bordeaux`s work.

2.Bordeaux, William J *"Conquering the Mighty Sioux."* pp.41-45. Sioux Falls, South Dakota. 1929.

3.Mallery, Garrick. *"Picture-Writing of the American Indians."* [i.e. The Baptist-Good Winter-count."] Vol.1. p.323. Dover Publications. New York. Reprint from The Tenth Annual Report of the Bureau of American Ethnology, Smithsonian Institution. Washington DC. 1888-`89.

4.Hanson, Charles R. Jr. *"The Battle of Crow Butte."* pp.2-3. The Fur Trade. [magazine] Fall. 1969.

5.Claim No. 619 by James Bordeaux, Records of U.S. Court of Claims. National Archives, Washington DC.

6.Report of 1888-89. Bureau of Ethnology. Washington DC.

7.Bray, Kingsley. *"Lone Horn`s peace."* pp.32ff. "Nebraska History Magazine." LXVI no 1. Spring 1985. See also; Vestal, Stanley. *"New Sources of Indian History."* p.317. University of Oklahoma Press. 1934.

8.Bray, Kingsley. *"Lone Horn`s peace."* pp.32ff. Nebraska History Magazine. LXVI. no 1. Spring 1985. See also; Vestal, Stanley. *"New Sources of Indian History."* p.317. University of Oklahoma Press.1934.

9.Medicine Crow, Joe. Several personal interviews with Author. Lodge Grass, Montana. 1994. See note book 3. pp.1-4

10.Medicine Crow, Joe. Several personal interviews with Author. Lodge Grass, Montana.1994 . See note book 3. pp.1-4

11.Medicine Crow, Joe. Several personal interviews with Author. Lodge Grass, Montana. 1994 through to 2006. See note book 3. pp.1-4

12.Medicine Crow, Joe. Several personal interviews with Author. Lodge Grass, Montana. 1994 through to 2006. See note book 3. pp.1-4

13 Medicine Crow, Joe. Several personal interviews with Author. Lodge Grass, Montana. 1994 through to 2006. See note book 3. pp.1-4

14.Medicine Crow, Joe. Several personal interviews with Author. Lodge Grass, Montana. 1994 through to 2006. See note book 3. pp.1-4

15.Medicine Crow, Joe. Several personal interviews with Author. Lodge Grass, Montana. 1994 through to 2006. See note book 3. pp.1-4

16.Medicine Crow, Joe. Several personal interviews with Author. Lodge Grass, Montana. 1994 through to 2006. See note book 3. pp.1-4

17.Medicine Crow, Joe. Several personal interviews with Author. Lodge Grass, Montana. 1994 through to 2006. See note book 3. pp.1-4

18.Medicine Crow, Joe. Several personal interviews with Author. Lodge Grass, Montana. 1994 through to 2006. See note book 3. pp.1-4

19.Medicine Crow, Joe. Several personal interviews with Author. Lodge Grass, Montana. 1994 through to 2006. See note book 3. pp.1-4

20.Vestal, Stanley. *"New Sources of Indian History."* p.317. University of Oklahoma Press. 1934.

21.Medicine Crow, Joe. Several personal interviews with Author. Lodge Grass, Montana. 1994 through to 2006. See note book 3. pp.1-4

22.Medicine Crow, Joe. Several personal interviews with Author. Lodge Grass, Montana.1994. See note book 3. pp.1-4

23.Stands in Timber, John. Interview with Joe Medicine Crow. 1966. in, *"Joe Medicine Crow papers."* Little Big Horn College Archives. Crow Agency, Montana. See also; Stand-in-Timber, John. *"Little-Coyote`s Story."* Paper in the possession of Dr. Margot Liberty of Sheridan, Wyoming.

24.Stands in Timber, John. Interview with Joe Medicine Crow. 1966. in, *"Joe Medicine Crowpapers."* Little Big Horn College Archives. Crow Agency, Montana. See also; Stand-in-Timber, John. *"Little-Coyote`s Story."* Paper in the possession of Dr. Margot Liberty of Sheridan, Wyoming.

25.Stands in Timber, John. Interview with Joe Medicine Crow. 1966. in, *"Joe Medicine Crow papers."* Little Big Horn College Archives. Crow Agency, Montana. See also; Stand-in-Timber,

John. *"Little-Coyote`s Story."* Paper in the possession of Dr. Margot Liberty of Sheridan, Wyoming.

26.Medicine Crow, Joe. Several personal interviews with Author. Lodge Grass, Montana.1994 through to 2006. See note book 3. pp.1-4

27.Medicine Crow, Joe. Several personal interviews with Author. Lodge Grass, Montana.1994 through to 2006. See note book 3. pp.1-4

Chapter Ten

Rekindling the War Pipe

Following the death of the Crow Chief Grizzly Bear in late 1851, government officials regarded Big Shadow as the nation`s paramount chief, and with he alone would they negotiate when discussing important issues concerning the Mountain, River and Kicked-in-the-Belly Crow bands combined.

Big Shadow, however, had not been first choice of head chief as indicated by the majority of Absaroka, particularly among the Mountain and River Crow groups and, as a result of his lack of authority over the nation as a whole, Big Shadow moved his followers among the Kicked-in-the-Belly people to the North Platte region, where he and his adherents spent most of their time, either stealing, trading or begging from the white man's emigrant trains on their way west to the settlements of Oregon and Utah and the gold fields of California.

How aggressive Big Shadow's people were towards white emigrants during this period, can only be judged by contemporary reports of the day, which include that penned by John H. Holeman, a government representative for the Indian Service, who wrote from Fort Laramie on September 2, 1851:

> "On my route to Utah I passed many trains of emigrants, some for Oregon, some for California, but mostly for Utah. I found many of them in great distress from depredations and robberies committed by the Indians; some were robbed of all their possessions, and even of the clothing on their backs; many had their stock stolen. The Indians who reside about and below Fort Laramie were thought to be the principle aggressors; the Crows especially." [1]

The true situation was likely exaggerated somewhat by Holeman. Much was based upon suspect information from white emigrants who could not distinguish Crow from Sioux or indeed, from any other Plains tribe. Knowing this, the Indians not a few times, were apt to inform those they robbed that they were members of a tribe other than their real one.

As far as we know, no white emigrant actually suffered death at Crow hands, but certainly, Crows were culpable in harassing the emigrants in one way or another. Big Shadow's followers were regarded by most whites with whom they came in contact as being a collection of degenerates; noted for their lack of morals—according to the white man's perception—and neglect of personal cleanliness. By White standards they had a propensity for the arts of begging and theft. The diarist James Chambers summed up this shared opinion of Big Shadow's people when he wrote from Fort Union on March 8, 1856:

> "Crow Indians are a lousy, thieving, beggarly set of rascals. . .got credits and never paid. . .run everywhere through the fort. . .insulted and annoyed everyone. . .The bucks are raping squaws in broad daylight without regard to lookers on, or indeed, they seem to prefer witnesses to the operation. . .Old Rip's thieves and the elderly persons having run their course in these things, have now settled down at begging at which they excel all other tribes. . ." [2]

Big Shadow's people were not so degenerate that they did not continue to retaliate against all whom they considered a threat to their hunting grounds or, to their perceived prestige as warriors. And this they were prepared to show to any who doubted their prowess in such matters or were foolhardy enough to ignore them. But for the present, the Crows held fast to their treaty obligations, by which they had agreed to desist from raiding those old enemies represented at the Horse Creek gathering. In the summer of 1852, the Flying River band of Miniconjou (also known simply as the "Upper" band) under their old chief Red Fish, had again joined the Kicked-in-the-Belly Crows of Big Shadow on the headwaters of the Powder, even though the followers of both chiefs had spent much of their early fighting days battling each other in many a bloody contest.

This time, the Miniconjou brought with them their Hunkpapa associates and together, their two bands camped adjacent to Big Shadow`s Kicked-in-the-Belly Crows; the Hunkpapa, ostensibly, consolidating their pact made at the treaty gathering the previous year and thus, it is evident that the intertribal agreements made at that time were still in vogue one year later. Indeed, the following summer of 1853 saw Crows included among a grand Allied force comprised of Kiowa, Kiowa-Apache, Comanche, Arapaho, Brule Sioux and Cheyennes, which assembled on the headwaters of the Republican River in August that year, as they prepared to launch a crusade against the several Pawnee tribes entrenched along the Lower Loup in eastern Nebraska.[3] It was soon after this allied assemblage, however, that war between the Crows on one side and the Sioux and Northern Cheyenne on the other, again broke out in earnest.

In the meantime, the more eastern Yanktonai Sioux—who had not been a party to the Horse Creek Treaty—had continued in their aggressive attitude towards the Crow. In 1853, four lodges of Crows, comprising thirty-five persons including men, women and children when enroute to visit their Hidatsa relatives, were attacked on the open prairie by a superior force of Yanktonai and exterminated one and all. [4]

Likewise, with regard to the Hunkpapa Sioux, their earlier friendly attitude toward Big Shadow's band the previous year, lasted only as long as their two peoples had been camped together. Soon after, the Hunkpapa again began raiding deep into Crow country. The Hunkpapa excused themselves by declaring that their people always needed horses, which animals they could not raise in their own domain adjacent to the middle Missouri due to a non conducive environment and erratic climate. But, in addition, they had since come to prefer the rich hunting grounds along the Yellowstone and often entered that country without regard to its rightful Crow owners. Such blatant acts of trespass could only result in a renewal of hostilities between the tribes. In 1853, a memorable fight occurred between Hunkpapa interlopers and the then resident River Crow band of chief Twines-His-Horse's-Tail. During this particular event, a brave Crow wearing a peculiar "four-horned" bonnet and carrying a befeathered staff and tomahawk was killed. This man's name is not remembered in present-day Crow oral tradition, although several Lakota Winter Counts recorded the event, which also gave its name to that year in their calendars.

According to Sioux accounts, the fight took place somewhere close to the lower course of the Powder River and the lone Crow warrior referred to had been a very brave man; many times attacking the Sioux force alone. This same Crow then stood his ground in a suicide manner with banner lance in hand and fought off the enemy until he was killed. Such was the effect his brave stand had upon the Hunkpapa, that all those Sioux who had taken part in the fight made copies of the four-horned bonnet which, thereafter, they wore during special occasions when performing a particular dance to commemorate the event.[5]

"The Year The Stars Fell." p.234. Univ. Neb. Press. 2007.

Long-Soldier`s Hunkpapa Winter Count entry for 1853. "A Crow with a four-horned bonnet was killed."

Most other Western Sioux bands, however, including the Miniconjou, Brule, Southern Oglala and Sans Arc, continued to adhere to the pacts of '51 and were actually inclined to distance themselves somewhat from their more belligerent Hunkpapa and Yanktonai cousins.

In 1854, Miniconjou and Brule Sioux warriors wiped out Lieutenant Grattan and his thirty soldiers on the Horse Creek branch of the Laramie, during an altercation over a worn-out cow. The following year, General William S. Harney defeated the offending Sioux on the Bluewater just west of Ash Hollow near the forks of the Platte. Many of the hostiles left the North Platte country and fled northwest into the Yellowstone district west of Powder River, the same area stipulated by treaty as belonging exclusively to the Crow. These migrants once dubbed collectively "Platte River Sioux," hereafter became known simply as "Northern Sioux" and among whom, were included parts of the Oglala, Brule and Miniconjou bands.[6]

In the immediate aftermath of the Grattan affair, a Crow delegation had been made welcome in the Southern Oglala camp of Chief Old Man Afraid of His Horses, at a time the Crows themselves were growing concerned over the influx of white men into the Indian country and of the proposed establishment of military posts in their tribal hunting grounds. Now, following General Harney's offensive, the Sioux sent their own emissaries to the Crows requesting they be allowed into the eastern part of Crow Country and the latter—at least a part of the Mountain Crow and all of Big Shadow's Kicked-in-the-Belly band—initially welcomed the refugees as guests [7]

A report to the government in 1855 stated that around 200 lodges of Crows had recently conducted their autumn buffalo hunt in the company of a band of Miniconjou and that these two peoples remained together throughout the ensuing winter on the headwaters of the Powder.[8] This area, where the Northern Sioux bands could now often be found was, at that date, only occupied as a regular camping and hunting ground by Big Shadow's people. They alone were regarded as being in friendly association with the Miniconjou, rather than the Mountain and River Crows and certainly, without Sioux consent, no Crow would have been allowed free and unobstructed access into the area between the Powder and North Platte. Yet a continuing Crow presence in that same country was mentioned in trader Edwin Denig`s 1856 report that Big Robber's (Big Shadow's) band, " . . .usually make their winter hunt on the head of Powder river, and of late years, take their furs and buffalo robes to the trading houses along the River Platte in the spring, from which they obtain supplies to continue their operations, and move back to winter quarters early in the Fall." [9]

The number of Crow referred to in the above extract, most likely included that small band of forty-four lodges of mixed Cheyennes and Crow of whom Lieutenant James Bradley wrote in 1876, as being members and descendants of chief Long Hair's Mountain Crow village destroyed some fifty-six years earlier, who having been taken captive by the victorious Sioux and Cheyennes, had since married into one or the other of their captor's tribes. By the early 1850s the offspring of these subsequent liaisons, which included Cheyenne, Crow and Sioux, had formed a mixed-blood band or clan of their own and generally remained neutral in the ongoing conflicts between their parent tribes.[10]

In close friendly contact with the mixed Crow, Cheyenne and Sioux band were those of the Flying River band of Miniconjou, the Sans Arc and southern bands of Oglala along with the latter's Northern Cheyenne allies, each of whom dwelt close to the head of the Belle Fourche branch of the Cheyenne River in northeastern Wyoming.

They were much farther south and west than their Northern Oglala, Northern Brule and Hunkpapa brethren east of the lower Powder and about the headwaters of the Grand and Cannonball Rivers. Since the treaty of 1851, the former had continued to practice constraint against the Crows. But hostile clashes still occurred between the latter and the more eastern Hunkpapa and Yanktonai Sioux groups.[11]

By the spring of 1856, however, the number of so-called friendly Sioux groups had increased sufficiently in Crow Country for the latter to become alarmed at the continuation of foreign intrusion into their hunting grounds. The Crows were fully aware that some of these friendly Sioux joined with the Hunkpapa from time-to-time and several hostile clashes had occurred between the Hunkpapas and one and another Crow band. That was the case during the winter of 1855 /'56 when a large force of Hunkpapa again met with Crows on the field of combat and is a story still recounted in Crow oral tradition today.

The Hunkpapa felt obliged through necessity to find more provident hunting grounds to the west, as their own country in both North and South Dakota was fast becoming depopulated of buffalo and other large game, due to a general diminishing and overhunting of the herds. As a consequence, the Hunkpapa chose to spend more time in the company of their Miniconjou and Sans Arc cousins with whom previously they had always been closely associated.

During the tail end of 1855, the Hunkpapa set up their tepees near the mouth of the Yellowstone not far from the Fort Union trading post where they intended to spend the winter months, surrounded by the abundant cottonwoods of that region and close to buffalo, still found in great number in that country. This camping ground was also a convenient base from which to sally forth against neighboring tribes in order to steal horses and, indeed, the Crows, Shoshoni, Flathead and Nez Perce—all of whom within easy travelling distance of the Yellowstone—were rich in such animals and could well afford to relinquish portions of their stock to any party of stealthy thieves.

It was to this purpose that a Hunkpapa horse-stealing party comprised of some 100 warriors, started out in the winter of 1855/'56 from their camp on a small tributary of the Yellowstone between Box Elder Creek and the Powder. The party went on foot and was intent upon raiding the pony herds of a nearby Crow village reported as being in winter quarters somewhere along the lower course of the Tongue. This was, in fact, the Crow village of Big Shadow's people, prior to their taking up permanent winter residence about the headwaters of the Powder.[12]

Among this Sioux group was a popular medicine man or shaman named Sun Dancer. He prophesied that the Hunkpapa party would soon meet the enemy and be successful in their venture. Also included was the later famous Hunkpapa chief and medicine man Sitting Bull, then about twenty-six years old, but already a proven and respected fighter among his band.[13]

After only a few days march, Sioux scouts discovered the Crow village on the Tongue, whereupon, their leader decided they should wait for darkness to fall and then conduct their raid on the Crow pony herd.

Before dawn, after each warrior had mounted what he believed was a fast runner, the raiders drove off a large herd from the village. They were satisfied with their booty and started back at once for their own camp, driving the captured stock before them.

The Crows, however, had plenty of horses left and as soon as they discovered their loss, a sizable war party took up the trail of the thieves, determined to retrieve their horses and chastise the culprits.

It was not long before the Sioux raiders discerned the Crows rapidly following. The Hunkpapa partisan (whose name has been forgotten) directed a number of his party to continue driving the captured ponies forward, while he told the remaining warriors to stand their ground and halt the enemy advance. The determined stance of between seventy and eighty Sioux warriors arrayed in battle order, caused the charging Crows who were in compatible force, to rein in their own mounts and hover tentatively out of bowshot.

The Sioux, likewise, were not eager to start the fight and for a while, the respective parties merely faced each other in a standoff situation and shouted abuse and challenges.

At length, three prominent Crow warriors rode out in front of their line of warriors. One of these three was the Kicked-in-the-Belly Chief, Big Shadow. This day he wore a double-tailed eagle-feathered bonnet, causing him to stand out among his peers, enhanced by his towering six-foot seven-inch frame.

"The Year The Stars Fell." p. 240. University of Neb. Press. 2007.
Long-Soldier`s Hunkpapa Winter Count entry 1856/`57."When the Crow war bonnet was torn."

It was Big Shadow who first let out a wild war yell. Then, with a long lance at the ready, he raced his pony headlong at the foremost line of Sioux. Big Shadow came charging on, seemingly oblivious to the musket balls and arrows flying about him and crashed into the Sioux ranks, counting two first coups upon the enemy before turning his steed around and attempting to ride back to his waiting warriors. Unfortunately, in the act of doing so, a Hunkpapa brave named Loud Bear reached out his arm and managed to grab hold of the flying tail of Big Shadow's bonnet and as the Crow chief galloped on, the headpiece came away from his person. This was considered a great deed performed by Loud Bear, but a great insult to Big Shadow. Even his fellow Crow warriors whooped in derision as their chief came galloping back to their lines and, for all his past glories, never after would Big Shadow be allowed to forget the humiliation he had suffered on this occasion. [14]

After a while, the second of the three Crow warriors made a dash towards the Sioux lines. This man was the indomitable Red Bear, a well-proven and daring war chief with many successful deeds to his credit. At this time, it is said, he was attired in a richly beaded deer hide shirt along with scalp-fringed leggings, while attached to his crown was a single eagle feather fixed in a horizontal position from left to right. As usual, on the right side of his head, he sported a tuft of twisted down feathers of the pelican, for the pelican was his personal protective medicine; representing the messenger of the Morning Star. Upon his face was painted a number of yellow, horizontal, wavy stripes, representing shimmering heat waves. Thus adorned, he was easily recognized even by his enemies who already knew his fame. Red Bear, after riding up close to the Sioux lines, succeeded in killing one named Paints Brown, before retreating back to his people unscathed, as a shower of musket balls and arrows followed in his wake.[15]

And then the third of the three Crow champions (whose name has been forgotten) rode out to confront the Sioux. This man was wearing a red ochre painted war shirt, likewise with ermine tails sewn along its sleeves, thus indicating that he too, was a prominent warrior—or even a chief among his people. Over one shoulder and across his chest were slung two bandoleers, a powder horn attached to one and a bullet, flint and wadding pouch attached to the other. In one hand he held his horse's reins and in the other he carried an old muzzleloader with its barrel cut down so as to be handled more easily from horseback.[16]

Denver Public Library, Westen History Collection

Sioux Chief Sitting Bull

As this third Crow charged forward, the Hunkpapa Sitting Bull rode out to meet him.

Before contact could be made, Sitting Bull jumped from his pony's back and crouching on one knee behind his bull hide shield, raised his smoothbore fusee to his shoulder and took aim at the oncoming Crow. Upon seeing this, the lone Crow also leapt from his horse and with gun grasped in two hands he advanced on foot toward his lone adversary. It was the Crow who fired first and the ball from his piece struck the base of his opponent's shield; entered right through it and ploughed a long furrow through the underside of Sitting Bull`s left foot. The Hunkpapa, however, appeared undaunted and ignoring the pain, he squeezed his trigger. His musket flashed and the charging Crow suddenly leapt into the air and in another instant, lay mortally wounded on the ground. Within seconds, Sitting Bull rose to his feet and hobbled over to his prostrate victim, drew his knife and stabbed his dying adversary in the chest and body. He ripped off the man's scalp, shook it in the faces of the Crows, then returned to his own lines.[17]

Upon witnessing this act, the Crows lost all heart to carry on the fight and giving up thoughts of retrieving their stolen stock, they took up the corpse of their dead comrade, turned their ponies around and slowly vacated the scene, deeming the day a victory for the Sioux.

Jubilantly, the Hunkpapa party jeered at their enemies as the latter disappeared and some even followed the Crows in order to humiliate them further, although this was really only a half-hearted attempt. At length, the whole Hunkpapa force returned to its base camp with the several hundred captured Crow ponies.

This particular fight has ever since been known among the Sioux as "The battle when the war bonnet was torn" and has given its name to the year 1855/'56 in several of the Lakota Winter Counts.[18] The event is also remembered among the Crows, but as "The battle when Chief Big Shadow was stripped," referring to the same occurrence, but in a somewhat derogatory manner regarding the fall from grace of the previously esteemed Kicked-in-the-Belly war chief. [19]

The above indeed, had been a memorable fight, but at this date, the Crows still did not regard the eastern Tetons and Yanktonais a threat to their habitat or to Crow survival in general. As a result, the Crows, more often than not, simply left the Eastern Sioux bands—including the Hunkpapa—alone. Instead, they kept up their close association with the Miniconjou with whom they continued to trade and socialize. But even this amicable relationship was soon to degenerate into yet another bloody war of attrition due to circumstances that could not be controlled.

In the summer of 1856, the Hunkpapa and other Sioux bands (though non-participants in the Grattan affair) received a humiliating berating from General Harney at Fort Pierre on the Missouri. The Miniconjou chief Lone Horn and the great Oglala, Old Man Afraid Of His Horses, paid a visit to the Crows and sat in council with chiefs of both the River and Mountain Crow bands under such notable headmen as Twines His Horses Tail, Two Face, Bear`s Head, Red Bear and Big Shadow. The Sioux chiefs once more attempted to cajole their hosts into allowing the Oglala, Miniconjou and even their Brule and Hunkpapa confederates free range in the Crow Country. But such a request was still too much for the Mountain Crows who, suspecting that any peace with the wild bands of Sioux would only be on a temporary basis—as far as the Sioux were concerned. Once gaining a foothold in the Crow domain, the Sioux were unlikely to let go. The Crows responded to the Oglala request with an emphatic "No!" [20] The Sioux were indignant and departed from the Crows in a sullen mood.

The following summer a grand council was held near Bear Butte in the Black Hills which saw all Teton bands, along with their Northern Cheyenne and Northern Arapaho allies in attendance. The leaders discussed what stance their peoples should take against the ever-encroaching white race. It was also decided that they should move into the Yellowstone and Big Horn country, whether the rightful Crow occupants agreed to their presence or not.[21]

Following the council, even the Flying River band of Miniconjou, now led by chief Lone Horn, confederated with the belligerent Miniconjou and Hunkpapa, under chiefs Lame Deer and Four Horns and it would not be long, before the Minniconjou also were again raiding Crows.

Later that summer, a woman among a visiting party of Crows was shot full of arrows in the Flying River Miniconjou camp. Before winter set in, a Lieutenant K. Warren met with Hunkpapas under their head chief Bear Ribs who told him that the Sioux would not make another peace with the Crows. " [22]

Meanwhile, during this same summer of 1857, the Northern Cheyennes had their own altercation with American troops on the Solomon River in northcentral Kansas and likewise, fled north in favor of the lower Powder and Tongue River districts. Suddenly, the Crows found themselves overwhelmed by another mass of foreign migrants who only recently had been their implacable foes.[23]

Before the year was out and in true Indian fashion, the Crows reacted in the only way they saw fit—by assaulting the interlopers on every possible occasion.

It was in the face of increasing hostility from the Sioux—now joined in a common resolve by their Cheyenne allies—that before the end of 1857, the beleaguered Kicked-in-the-Belly band and with them the more populous Mountain Crow, had abandoned the entire eastern portion of their treaty-stipulated lands as a regular hunting ground. Instead, they spent most of their time far west of the Tongue River where they confederated their forces against the Sioux and Cheyennes, who themselves, continued to press upon them without

Denver Public Library
Crow Chief Four Balls

relent. But still the Crows did not take a merely defensive stance and their war parties persisted in travelling east in order to harass the interlopers, hoping to force them out of the disputed territory by making life too uncomfortable to remain.

In this endeavor, initially, the Crows appear to have had some degree of success, for the report of Indian Agent Major Thomas S. Twiss to the commissioner of Indian affairs late in 1857 stated that the Crows were particularly troublesome by their constant incursions and had forced 200 lodges of Sioux to abandon the country altogether.

Certainly, during the winter of 1857- '58, a party of Crows stole a large herd of horses from a combined Miniconjou and Oglala village then situated along the Belle Fourche branch of the Cheyenne River close to the landmark known today as Devil's Tower [24] and by the spring of 1858, young Crow warriors were again stealing ponies from Sioux and Cheyenne herds on a regular basis; an occupation soon reciprocated by the Sioux and Cheyenne upon the Crows. As a result, a number of tribal members on both sides lost their scalps. The Indian agency of the Upper Platte in a report sent from Deer Creek September 23, 1858 stated:

> "A war party of the Crow tribe stole from the Sioux horses, in January last, on the Cheyenne River; and another war party of the same tribe stole a larger band of horses from the Sioux, in August last, at the Indian Agency. I sent a messenger to the chief of the Crow tribe, and three of the principle men came in and held a "talk" with me, and promised to restore the horses, but have failed to comply with my demands or to fulfil their promises. I feel it incumbent upon me to put a stop to these war parties, if possible, but I am powerless to prevent them, if they refuse to listen to me. Whenever these war parties fall

in with small parties of whites travelling along the Platte, they rob them of some of their property, or force them to give them whatsoever they demand. . ." [25]

According to another report to Washington penned later this same year, on September 23, 1858 by Agent Twiss, the Crows were continuing to make things hot for all Sioux bands they encountered. The truth of the matter, however, was that the Crows were not having it all their own way. But, it seems, government officials in Washington D.C. harboured little, if any real concern as regards Crow welfare and believed the additional statement in the aforementioned report, that the Crows were, ". . .insolent, audacious and lawless." [26.]

Thus, lacking goverment intervention, any earlier consideration that the Crow and Sioux could co-exist peaceably in the same country was thrown to the wind. What originally might have been described as trivial feuding, soon escalated out of control and erupted into yet another full-blown bloody intertribal war.

In 1866, when a Northern Cheyenne chief named Black Horse was asked by Colonel Carrington why his people had driven the Crows from the Yellowstone and still pursued an unrelenting war of conquest and extermination against that tribe, the Cheyenne chief casually remarked,

> "The Sioux helped us. We stole the hunting grounds of the Crows because they were the best. The white man is along the great waters (Missouri and Platte rivers), and we wanted more room. We fight the Crows because they will not take half and give us peace with the other half." [27]

The Crows in 1858, having previously lost heavily to recurring epidemics and constant warfare with numerous tribes, could present a united body of only some 1,000 males of fighting age. As a consequence they were grossly inferior to the fighting element of the western or Teton Sioux, which around this same time comprised some 4,000 warriors, although rarely, if ever, did their combined strength come together at any one time. Indeed, it was only the Northern Oglala, Miniconjou and Northern Brule bands that were in direct and regular contact with Crows during this particular period, thus reducing the effective Sioux fighting force to between 1,500 and 2,000 warriors at most. Were it not that the Crow's old Assiniboin, Atsina and Piegan Blackfoot enemies of the north had three years earlier (1855) [28] agreed to a truce with the Crows, it is likely that the Crows might have compromised with the Sioux and Cheyenne migrants.

Without doubt, the Crows were fully aware of their own precarious position. They could plainly see that their extinction as a tribal entity might be coming unless circumstances changed in their favor. It didn't help that the young Crow warriors continued to raid the pony herds of their Sioux and Cheyenne neighbors.

This same fear that the Crows would soon become extinct was voiced by certain white men well-acquainted with the true state of affairs on the Northern Plains. As early as 1856, the trader Edwin Denig, then chief clerk at Fort Union on the Upper Missouri at the mouth of the Yellowstone, had written to his superiors:

> ". . .Situated as they now are, the Crows cannot exist long as a nation. Without adequate supplies of arms and ammunition, warred against by the Blackfoot on one side and most bands of the Sioux on the other, straying along the Platte trail where they contract rapid and deadly diseases, together with the unnatural customs of destroying their offspring, will soon lead to their extinction. . ." [29]

Captain William F. Raynolds who filed a report to the War Department in 1859, was of the opinion that although the Crows usually held their own in engagements with their enemies, the tribe's natural inferiority in numbers doomed its members to eventual extermination.[30]

Thus the poor Crows, outnumbered and seriously threatened with extinction, were left to fend for themselves, notwithstanding any paper agreement they had signed at the Horse Creek in 1851. Still, they endeavored to survive in the hostile environment surrounding them, even if it meant carrying the war to the very door flaps of their enemies` tepees.

A pertinent example is the disastrous episode commonly known as "The Battle of Rain Hill" which occurred between the Kicked-in-the-Belly Crows and the more eastern Teton Sioux bands including, the Miniconjou, Sans Arc and Hunkpapa. This affair was but one of two dire defeats suffered at the hands of Indian enemies by the Kicked-in-the-Belly people during 1858.

The Battle at Rain Hill occurring prior to the frontier Army taking the field against Sioux and Cheyenne hostiles during the Powder River War of 1865-68, was the first of a number of major conflicts involving Crows during this period. Although other encounters may have had more decisive consequences upon the Crows as a nation, it was because of this affair that the Teton Sioux launched a determined offensive which culminated in a significant portion of Crow country being completely overrun by the invaders.

It is for these reasons that the story of this particular conflict still looms large in Crow oral history and tradition.

It was in late August, 1858, after the conclusion of their annual religious ceremonies, that the Mountain and Kicked-in-the-Belly Crow bands moved their combined villages from the banks of the Big Horn River and relocated about fifty miles west along the upper course of Arrow Creek in the shadow of the Pryor Mountains. There was much excitement among the people, for many young warriors were preparing to go to war.

During the previous year of 1857, two disastrous intertribal engagements had brought much grief upon the lodges of the Kicked-in-the-Belly band. The first of these calamities had occurred when a ten-man Kicked-in-the-Belly horse-stealing party, out against eastern Sioux neighbors, was discovered by the enemy. And after taking refuge atop a bluff since named Captive Butte, near the headwaters of Morreau River, South Dakota, the entire party was wiped out by a superior force of Oglala Sioux. [31]

The second event occurred during late winter the same year on a stream known as Fast Current Creek, which runs near where the present-day town of Red Lodge, Montana now stands. The site is situated in a valley overlooked by the Bear Tooth Mountains. A small Crow camp consisting of thirty lodges, was set upon by a war band of Shoshoni or Bannocks and the entire village "rubbed out." All the camp occupants had either been killed or taken captive, the camp plundered then utterly destroyed. The headman of this camp owned a large red-painted tepee—having perpetuated the design from the original red-striped lodge cover captured from the Small Robe Pikunni in the great battle of 1845—which had given the band its name of The Red Lodge Clan.[32]

In this same Crow camp, there were several prominent Mountain Crow and Kicked-in-the-Belly band members. As a result, the event caused much grief among all the Absaroka clans and many oaths were made to avenge the dastardly act.[33]

Why the Shoshoni reopened their feuding with the Crows at this particular time, is not determined in either contemporary documentation or in the oral histories of the two peoples. However, we do know that a number of Crow warriors had joined against the Shoshoni, as members of both Cheyenne and Sioux war parties during the early period of recent peaceful relations with those tribes. The Shoshoni were fully aware of this fact. In addition, neither the Shoshoni nor their close allies the Shoshoni-speaking Bannocks, had been allowed to sign the Fitzpatrick Treaty paper of 1851. The result was that the Sioux, Cheyenne and even the Crows, did not regard their intertribal pacts as extending to the Shoshoni. On the other hand, it is known that the Shoshoni Chief Washakie had endeavored to uphold the pacts, in spirit at least. This suggests that either a war band of Bannocks or, a renegade group from the Washakie band (which certainly existed at this time), was responsible for wiping out the Red Lodge Crow camp and that Washakie and his followers may have been innocent.

Whatever the case, the Crows were not inclined to differentiate between one group of Shoshoni and another and as far as they were concerned, all Shoshoni-speaking peoples, whether Lemhi, Bannock or Sheep-eater were "fair game."

Both of the above mentioned events, by tribal custom, dictated that retaliatory raids be made by the Crows. In such a way, the Kicked-in-the-Belly's not only allowed themselves to be dragged into yet another period of conflict with the Shoshoni, but at the same time, into a protracted all-out war with the entire Teton Sioux nation.

So it was as a consequence of their recent losses, that certain Crow warriors underwent the ordeal of a Sun Dance. The ceremony, which among the Absaroka, was performed before conducting a punitive expedition against an enemy. By so doing, the warriors who sacrificed their bodies by abstaining from food and drink for four days between sunrise and sunset, then piercing their flesh and "swinging at the pole," hoped to obtain the blessings of *Akbaa-tadia,* whom, they believed, would then aid them to ensure success in their proposed ventures.

Thus, this late summer of 1858, while the Kicked-in-the-Belly and Mountain Crow bands remained united along Arrow Creek, several separate war parties were organized to seek vengeance upon the perpetrators of the earlier attacks. One of these war bands was directed against the Shoshoni and organized by Chief Big Shadow. He declared that he would take a large party to hunt in the Wind River country and take "The Red Road" to avenge his cousins of the Red Lodge destroyed the previous winter. [34]

Meanwhile, two other leading Pipe Holders among the Kicked-in-the-Belly band named Bull Rises Small and Blackbird on the Ground, also carried war pipes around the lodges, proposing a concurrent crusade against the Oglala Sioux, in order to avenge the death of those ten Kicked-in-the-Belly Crows earlier killed at Captive Butte.

NOTES AND SOURCES.

1 Annual report of the Commissioner of Indian Affairs, 1851. Accompanying paper No. 53. p.444 [In; Senate Executive Doc; No 1. 32d Congress, 1st Session.]
2 Chambers, James H.*Original Journals of James Chambers.* Contributions to the Historical Society of Montana. X. [1940]. pp. 100 -149.
3 Grinnell, George Bird. *"The Fighting Cheyennes."* Pp.84-85. University of Oklahoma Press. 1956.
4 Howard, James H. *The John K. Bear Winter Count.* Plains Anthropologist. Memoir 11. 1976. See also; Annual Report to the Commissioner of Indian Affairs. 1853. Accom; paper no. 43. p.358.
5 Mallery, Garrick. *Picture-Writing of the American Indians.* Vol. 2. P.553. Dover Publications. New York. Reprint from the Tenth Annual Report of the Bureau of American Ethnology, Smithsonian Institution. Washington DC. 1888-`89.
6 Hyde, George E. *Red Cloud`s Folk.* Pp. 85-89. University of Nebraska Press. 1937.
7 Annual Report of the Commissioner of Indian Affairs. Washington DC. 1854 and 1855.
8 Ibid.
9 .Edwin T. Denig; "*Of the Crow Nation;*" in *Five Indian tribes of the Upper Missouri,* p.143. Ed. By John C.Ewers, Norman, University of Oklahoma Press, 1961. pp.194 and 195.
10 Bradley, James H. *"manuscript book "F"pp.240-256.* Montana Historical Society Publications. 1879.
11 Kingsly Brey. *"Lone Horn's Peace."* The Nebraska History Magazine. LXVI. No. 1, Spring. 1985. P.32.
12 Interview with Joe Medicine Crow. Lodge Grass, Montana, August, 1994. Note pad 2. P.10.
13 Stanley Vestal. *Sitting Bull. p.* 26. University of Oklahoma Press. 1932.
14 Interview with Joe Medicine Crow. Lodge Grass, Montana, August, 1994. Note pad 2, p.11.
15 Interview with Joe Medicine Crow. Lodge Grass, Montana, August, 1994. Note pad 2. P.11.
16 Stanley Vestal. *Sitting Bull,* P. 29. University of Oklahoma Press. 1932.
17 Stanley Vestal. *Sitting Bull,* P. 30. University of Oklahoma Press. 1932.
18 Howard, James H. *Winter counts as sources of History.* Pp.384-385. Loc; cited.
19Interview with Joe Medicine Crow. Lodge Grass, Montana, August, 1994. Note pad 2. P.11.
20 Kingsly Brey. "Lone Horn's Peace." *The Nebraska History Magazine.* LXV1. No.1. Spring. 1985. p.38. The Oglala Winter-count of Ben-Kindle records for the year 1856,*"The Sioux make peace with the Crows." ["The Portable North American Indian Reader"* The Viking Press Inc., 1973. P.150], while in another `count` also referring to the Oglala, but pertaining to chief Red-Cloud`s band specifically, it is recorded for this same year,. . ."*Crows and Sioux mingle."* [William K. Powers, *"A Winter-Count of the Oglala."* American Indian Tradition. Lincoln, 1967. P.31.]. However, in this last instance it is further said that, *". .after a fierce battle, the two factions decided to quit fighting for the time being."* It would appear that the Indian informant of Powers who imparted this additional information, had merely assumed that a fight had at first occurred, himself not being conversant with the true circumstances regarding the event, in that it actually refers to the friendly visit of the Southern Oglala chief Old-Man-Afraid-Of-His-Horses to a Crow camp in that year.
21 Stanley Vestal. *Sitting Bull.* Pp.91-95. University of Oklahoma Press. 1932. See also; *"Lone-Horn`s Peace."* Kingsly Brey. p. 43. Loc; cit.
22 Report of The Warren Expedition. 1856. Washington DC.
23 Grinnell, George Bird. *The Fighting Cheyennes.* P. 111.ff. University of Oklahoma Press. 1956.
24 Annual Report of the Commissioner of Indian Affairs. Washington DC.
25 Annual Report of the Indian Bureau. Washington DC. 1856. [Indian Agency of the Upper Platte N.T. Deer Creek. Sep 23d. 1858.]
26 Annual Report of the Indian Bureau. Washington DC. 1856. [Indian Agency of the Upper Platte N.T. Deer Creek. Sep 23d. 1858.]
27 Carrington, Margaret. *Apsaroka, Home of the Crows.* Ann Arbor. University of Microfilms International. 1979.
28 Ewers, John C. *The Blackfeet. Raiders of the Northwestern Plains.* Pp.210-225. University of Oklahoma Press. 1958.The peace here referred to between the Piegan Blackfoot, Atsina and Crows, had not really taken effect until 1856, having come about partly in compliance with agreements made in what is known as the *"Stevens` Treaty,"* drawn up in 1855 between the United States Government and the Blackfoot confederacy, but, moreover, because of mutual

loses sustained during a smallpox epidemic which had decimated their respective populations during the winter of 1855 /`56.

29 Denig, Edwin T. *"Report to Washington DC."* 1856.

30 Official Report of the *"Reynold`s Expedition."* Washington DC. [Report on the Exploration of the Yellowstone River.] Government Printing Office. 1859.

31 Howard, James H. *Winter Counts as sources of History.* P. 385. Loc; cited. See also, vestal, Stanley. *Warpath.'*P. . loc; cited.

32.Barney Old Coyote [Crow informant] to Author. August.. 2006. Note pad 3. P. 2. And Joe Medicine Crow to Author. Summer 2006. Several Lakota Winter-Counts confirm the date of this occurrence and in the aforementioned Oglala *`count`* recorded by William Powers [1963 edition of the Magazine *"American Indian Tradition."*], the additional information is given that the fight took place on `Wren Creek` and that the famous Oglala chief Red-Cloud was the Sioux leader at that time. On the other hand, in the *`memo*irs` of the Miniconjou Sioux chief Joseph White-Bull, who narrated his life story to Walter S Campbell [Stanley Vestal], [Vestal, Stanley. *"Warpath. The Story of Chief Joseph White Bull.* "University of Oklahoma Press. 1932.]. He - or indeed his biographer Walter S. Campbell confused this fight of 1857 with that of a later event, in which thirty Crows were rubbed out on top of another butte in a different location during the winter of 1869 /`70.

33 Interview with Joe Medicine Crow. Lodge Grass, Montana, August, 1994. Note pad 2, p.11.

34 Barney Old Coyote [Crow informant] to Author. Summer. Note pad 3. P.2. 2006. And Joe Medicine Crow to Author. Note pad 3. P. 2. Summer 2006.

Chapter Eleven

The Fight at Rain Hill

Big Shadow and a large party, including men, women and children, had already made their departure from Arrow Creek, when a number of warriors remaining in camp accepted the war pipes still being offered by Bull Rises Small and his compatriot in arms, Blackbird on the Ground.

Several famous fighters took hold of the proffered pipes and puffed upon their stems. In all, some seventy warriors—predominantly Kicked-in-the-Belly band members—but including a significant contingent of Mountain Crows—agreed to accompany the proposed expedition against the Sioux to punish the slayers of their kinsmen. Among those who joined this party was a man named Sits-In-the-Middle-of-the-Land, an up and coming Kicked-in-the-Belly sub-chief sometimes alternatively known as Blackfoot and who, at a later date, became head chief of the entire Crow nation including the River, Mountain and Kicked-in-the-Belly bands combined. Also included was Big Otter (alternatively known as Big Forehead) and his brother, Mountain Chief. Both these men were already recognized as great fighters in their own right with many successful forays to their credit. Yet another was Iron Bull, a young man fast earning a reputation as a fearless warrior and potential statesman among his people. This last named had once been the chosen protégé of the veteran Mountain Crow war chief, Red Bear. But, it is said, Iron Bull often ignored tribal protocol. On this occasion, he mounted a fine running horse, harangued the young braves, then led them around the inner circle of lodges while the sun stood high in the sky. Each warrior was dressed in full ceremonial regalia with their wives and sweethearts following behind, singing war songs and raising the tremolo in their honor. Such a thing

The National Archives
Crow Chief Iron Bull and wife, 1873.

should not have been done until the sun sank low on the horizon and was a serious breach of tribal etiquette which, the old men declared, would prove a portent of doom for those about to embark upon the war trail.[1]

The warriors continued to parade around the lodges, chanting special songs which always preceded a raid against the Sioux. A young man who had not yet joined the procession was now moved to do so. Quickly he donned his war attire and was saddling his pony, when an uncle came to him with words of impending disaster, saying, ". . .Son of my brother, from the time of my childhood, never have I known our warriors to sing their war songs in daylight. Truly, I say unto you, something bad will happen to these people." [2.]

This earnest prediction caused the young man to take heed and ponder his uncle's words. In response he took the saddle from his pony and instead, went away and joined a number of friends who together, were watching the procession as it snaked around the camp, stopping first at one lodge then another, while the warriors sang their war songs at the door flaps in order to receive blessings from the occupants within.

Another young man named Iron Eyes was also sitting with those who merely watched the parade. This man's father called No Mane (sometimes erroneously rendered No Neck), who was a renowned chief of the Kicked-in-the-Belly band and a member of the Sore Lip clan, went over to where Iron Eyes was sitting. While striking him across the back and shoulders with his pony quirt, he berated him saying, "My son, when your friends have fear upon their faces and weep within themselves and run this way and that before the enemy, you alone must stay behind and fight. Do not come back, for death comes and you cannot leap over him. Let me cry over a brave man before I grow old." [3]

Having heard these words, Iron Eyes was now obliged to saddle his horse and join the procession as a member of the war party. He had only recently married and perhaps was reluctant to leave his bride so soon after, but to have refused the wishes of his father would have branded him a coward. He would also have been subjected to ridicule from the other young warriors in the party and might even suffer scorn from the womenfolk of his age, including his bride, who only looked with favorable eyes upon those they considered brave and fearless warriors. And so it was that Iron Eyes, in order to banish the recriminations of his father, also prepared himself for war; determined to perform some great—though maybe, reckless deed.

Early next morning before the rest of the camp occupants stirred from their pallets, members of the great war party slipped quietly from the village, straddled along the banks of Arrow Creek and congregated at a prearranged rendezvous a short distance downstream.

At the rendezvous, the two Pipe Holders Bull Rises Small and Blackbird On the Ground, decided upon the route the party should travel to reach their objective, which was of course, the Oglala country east of the Black Hills. It was the Oglalas who had slain ten Crow the year before. But if any other Sioux band or bands were encountered, then the war party would not be averse to attacking them, too.

The warriors were bedecked in feathers and paint and well-armed. Many carried lances and war clubs, in addition to either a short-barreled smooth bore musket with a plentiful supply of powder and ball or a sturdy ash bow with a quiver full of arrows.

They rode horses of various size and color with their favorite war ponies trotting behind, led by twisted buffalo-hair lariats tied around their muzzles. From the saddle bow of each war pony was suspended a bull hide shield, painted with the owner's personal protective medicine design, while tied to many a pommel was a long lance, the iron-bladed tips of which, glinted in the early morning sunlight as the shafts waved high above their ponies` withers. The young Iron Eyes rode a fine bay horse; a split-eared buffalo-runner named "Crop Ears," because the animal actually had unusually short ears. Five women, one the wife of the Pipe Holder Bull Rises Small and another, with a baby boy strapped to a cradle board swinging from her saddlebow, rode with the warriors. There also were three teenage boys, going along as novices on their first war-trip. It would be their duty to watch over the spare horses and other paraphernalia belonging to the party when, eventually, the warriors changed to the backs of their war-ponies ready to engage the foe.[4]

The party traveled several days riding at a leisurely pace, first along Arrow Creek moving downstream as far as its junction with the Yellowstone. Then they moved down that river to the mouth of the Tongue, before turning due east; crossing the Little Missouri and thence heading south toward the headwaters of the Cannonball. They continued south, before finally coming to a halt at the foot of an elongated bluff named White Butte, but then known to several Plains tribes as Rain Hill (also known as "Rainy Butte.") This eminence stands in close proximity to the towns of Bowman, Belfield and New England, all of Slope County in the southeastern part of the present-day state of North Dakota. The hill was—and still is—a well-known landmark in the North Dakota Plains, having received its Indian name owing to the fact that it always seemed to be raining whenever Indians camped in its vicinity.[5]

Here the party made its war camp at the foot of the hill, which would serve as a base of operations during their intended escapade against the Sioux.

According to one account, it had taken the Crow party forty days to reach this point after setting out from their village on Arrow Creek. But if this was so, then we might assume that much time had been spent enroute hunting buffalo and other game or, alternately, that the party had visited their Hidatsa cousins in the earth lodge village then known as "Like a Fishhook." The village was adjacent to Fort Berthold on the south bank of the Missouri near the present-day community of Newtown.

It was late one afternoon when, in their base camp at the foot of Rain Hill, that the leaders of the expedition dispatched a number of scouts to go out on foot and reconnoiter the surrounding countryside looking for sign of the enemy. These men were considered the swiftest runners among the party and, in accordance with custom, each wore upon his head the complete skin of a wolf, the bushy tails of which trailed behind them on the ground, obliterating their tracks.

National Parks Service

White Butte. Know to the Crows as Rain Hill

The following morning not long after sunrise, the scouts returned. As they came in, the camp occupants began hurriedly collecting buffalo chips from the surrounding prairie, which they then placed in a pile in the centre of the camp. The scouts had first to strike this pile with their peeled willow coup sticks before making their report, thereby signifying that what they were about to relate was the truth.

Having followed this procedure, the scouts reported that they had spied smoke from the cooking fires of a big Sioux camp, the lodges of which stood staggered along the course of the Cannonball some distance to the northeast. They had seen many Sioux warriors, they said, engaged in various activities, but were sure that their own presence had not been discovered. It was not learned until later that there were actually at least four separate villages of Sioux, situated in close proximity to one another along the river and that together, they comprised the entire Hunkpapa, Sans Arc, Miniconjou and Two Kettle Teton Sioux bands. [6]

It was also learned later by the Crows, that two of their scouts had in fact been seen observing the Hunkpapa part of the extended camp and for a while, the Sioux had been on the alert lest some of their horses be stolen in the night. The next morning, however, finding none of their horses missing, the Sioux relaxed their vigilance, supposing that the figures seen in the distance had merely been opportunists who posed no real threat to the safety of the camps.

Meanwhile, upon hearing the scout's report, many of the younger Crow warriors began brandishing their weapons in the air and whooping aloud with excitement. Others jumped astride their ponies and started racing around the outer perimeter of the war camp, psyching themselves up for a fight.

The leading Pipe Holder Bull Rises Small was not so jubilant. His face took on a most serious and contemplative aspect and in a low voice, he told those who were not racing around the camp,

> "These are not the Oglala people we are looking for and we are told there are many lodges of our foes with many warriors sitting around each fire; surely this day, by the time the sun goes down, we Crows will be no more." [7]

One of Joe Medicine Crow's old tribal informants was his grandfather, White Man Runs Him. This man always said that there were seven Sioux camps along the river at that time, which may have been the true number, as this was the year following the late summer of 1857, when the Teton Sioux, Northern Cheyenne and Northern Arapaho had held their great tribal council at Bear Butte, in order to determine what stance their people should take in protecting their homelands from White intrusion. The council was convened also to enable the election of a paramount chief, to act as the Allied tribes` spokesman and spiritual leader and which role, incidentally, devolved upon the Hunkpapa chief Sitting Bull, who indeed, was engaged in this same fight around Rain Hill. [8]

The young Crow warriors, nonetheless, were already painting their faces and fixing up medicine charms, so eager were they to get to grips with the foe and it was obvious to the Pipe Holders, that if it was even suggested they abandon the venture and return home, lest their party be overwhelmed, then their words would have no effect upon them. For by now, the majority were determined to strike at least one blow against the enemy—whatever the outcome might be.

And so both Bull Rises Small and Blackbird On The Ground reluctantly decided to make an assault upon the enemy, if only to save face and be able to hold their heads high when and if, they returned safely to their people.

So it was, early next morning, that all the Crow warriors present decked themselves out in their finest war regalia ready for battle.

Author's sketch from an original pen and water color drawing by Swift Dog in Mr. and Mrs. Charles Diker Collection

Hunkpapa Sioux warrior No Two Horns fights a Crow during the 1858 Rain Hill battle.

Mounted on painted and befeathered war ponies, they eagerly set out in the direction where the Sioux camps had been reported. They left the accompanying women and children in camp and herded the pack animals and common horses into a grassy hollow where, it was thought, they would be obscured from view if any wandering party of enemies should pass by.

Joe Medicine Crow obtained his version of the events from another old veteran of the buffalo days named Plain Feather. According to this Crow account:

> "It had been drizzling with rain and a thick fog lay over the land when the Crow warriors first started from Rain Hill. One could hardly see a hand in front of one's face—it was said—and accidentally, the Crows almost ran right into one of the Sioux camps before realizing their mistake. The camp occupants upon discovering their enemies were quick to rally and caused the Crows to make a precipitous retreat." [9]

Unfortunately—so Plain Feather continued—in their haste to get away, the Crows ran into another, even larger Sioux camp a short distance downstream from the first, whereupon, a great swarm of Sioux came running from their lodges, jumped on their ponies and also took up the chase. The combined numbers from the two Sioux villages easily drove the Crows before them, forcing the latter to flee in several separate groups.[10]

According to the Sioux account, it was earlier that same morning when a large party of Hunkpapa Sioux started from their camp on the Cannonball, heading southwest on a hunting expedition. A heavy mist lay over the land and the hunters had actually passed the Crow warriors in the fog without either party being aware of the other's presence. At the same time, those who remained in the Hunkpapa village had begun dismantling their lodges preparatory to moving camp to another site upstream. All the Hunkpapa women and children were in this group along with their hundreds of dogs and spare horses, although there were not more than thirty or forty warriors at most who could defend them in the event of being attacked. These people, nevertheless, had already rolled up their tepee covers and packed camp equipment and personal belongings on pack animals and pole drags. They were merely waiting for the fog to lift a little before starting on their journey.

By mid morning the fog began to thin and as no new sign of strangers had been noted in the vicinity —and none of their horses had been stolen, which certainly would have indicated the presence of enemies nearby—the Sioux at last got ready to move across the prairie. It was then that the Crows arrived on the scene and spied the mass of people and animals spread out in small groups on the open prairie, as the villagers had not yet come together in column formation which would have been their customary mode of travel. The Crows could see that only a small number of warriors were available to accompany the cavalcade, although they could not see much farther as fog still lingered in the distance.

The Crows, it is said by the Sioux, without hesitation charged down from the crest of a nearby hill in three separate groups, the warriors shouting "Koo-Koo-Hey, Koo-Koo-Hey" as they raced their ponies across the prairie floor, trying to split their enemy's number before the latter had time to bunch together and present a defense. One group of charging Crows attempted to cut off those who were herding the spare horses, while another hied after a number of women and children positioned some way off from their kinfolk. Yet another group raced straight toward the Sioux warriors, eager to engage in hand-to-hand combat.

The Sioux later admitted they were taken completely by surprise. They said they also recognized the Crow chief Iron Bull, holding aloft a fur wrapped crooked lance of the Crow Lumpwood Society as he raced ahead of those who sped towards the loose ponies. In one terrifying dash, Iron Bull and those following rounded up a large bunch of animals before any of the Sioux nearby could mount up and make their escape. Women screamed and children ran this way and that, while the few Hunkpapa warriors—most of whom were banded together some distance from the noncombatants—tried to organize themselves in some kind of defensive formation. But the villagers were scattered over a wide area and the small number of Sioux warriors were no match for the Crows. Within minutes of the attack being launched, at least three Sioux—one a small boy—had been cut off from their people and killed. Meanwhile, the rest of the Sioux men folk attempted to defend themselves and their families as best they could, but were in a desperate situation.

Just when it appeared that their whole number would be either captured or killed, a much larger body of Sioux, fresh from one of the camps situated a little way off, but obscured from the Crows by lingering fog, suddenly came charging into the fray and soon it was the Crows who were outnumbered.

This fresh body of fighters were Sans Arc Sioux, who often camped and roamed in close proximity to their Hunkpapa cousins. They just happened to be in the vicinity at the time. The Crows turned to meet this second band of charging enemies, but after a brief though determined struggle, much of which was hand-to-hand, they were forced to give way and take flight across the prairie; racing back the way they had come hotly pursued by a host of Sioux warriors, whose fresh mounts set those the Crows were riding a grueling pace.

Having previously divided their force, the Crows were obliged to flee in three separate groups, while the Sioux, somewhat confused, had likewise to divide their own number into as many groups, in order to give chase to them all.

Iron Bull and others, who had captured a number of ponies when first attacking the stationary villagers, were now obliged to let them go, as they could not drive the animals fast enough not to be overtaken by their pursuers. In the process, Iron Bull received a Sioux lance wound in the right thigh. However, he remained mounted and managed to ride clear of the enemy, although his injury prevented him offering any significant resistance throughout the remainder of the conflict.

During this hectic flight, a lone rider in one of the fleeing Crow groups reined in his pony and in the manner of a suicide warrior, attempted to hold back the charging Sioux in an endeavor to allow his comrades more distance between themselves and the foe. Most of the Sioux pursuing this group also hesitated, not daring to come close to such a potentially dangerous adversary. But one of the more courageous among them, a young Hunkpapa named Swift Hawk, came on. The lone Crow raised his musket and fired, but Swift Hawk bent low over his horse's neck and avoided the shot. He continued racing forward and rode right up to the Crow, counted a first coup upon him with his tomahawk—which also toppled the Crow from his horse—and then killed him. Immediately behind came two more Hunkpapas named Little Elk and Running Antelope, who counted the second and third coups respectively and another, named Chasing Crow took the scalp. The Sioux recalled later that this particular Crow had a large lump or wart on his neck and admitted he had been, "a very brave man." [11.]

Perhaps the rest of the Crows did not witness the death of their comrade, for their retreat had turned into a rout. They raced off in a southwesterly direction toward a stream called Cedar Creek.

At length, close to the present day town of Bowman, west of Cedar Creek in southwestern North Dakota, a bunch of Sioux finally caught up with the fleeing Crows and a series of stands and running fights occurred on the open prairie.

According to Joe Medicine Crow's informant Plain Feather, the two Crow Pipe Holders bringing up the rear, repeatedly called their warriors to turn back and fight. But even they could not hold them as the rest of the Crow party fled with all haste, looking frantically for a place where they could make a stand.

In desperation Bull Rises Small reined in his horse, jumped from the saddle and stood facing the oncoming Sioux, intending to slow the enemy advance and impress upon his comrades how a true warrior should act in the face of danger.

The Sioux remember this man but by the name of Bird Claw Necklace, owing to a specific decoration he wore around his neck. They say this particular Crow fighter had been fleeing behind the rest of his comrades toward the creek, when his horse stepped into a gopher hole and threw him. The Crow managed to regain his feet and stood facing his antagonists with bow in hand. But unfortunately, say the Sioux, he had either already spent the last of his arrows or had lost them from his quiver when being thrown and now had nothing with which to defend himself save his knife. Still, in the heat of the chase, the enemy had no pity for his plight and several Sioux warriors turned off from the general line of pursuit and raced towards him, each eager to strike the first coup upon such a vulnerable foe.

As the Sioux came near on their charging ponies, Bull Rises Small began singing his death song and shed copious tears in an expression of sadness for his impending fate which, he knew, would bring grief and hardship upon his kinfolk and also for the disastrous consequences now looming over his comrades, which he himself as a Pipe Holder, considered was his responsibility alone. Such an overt show of sadness was common practice on the battlefield among all Indians, when they knew death was imminent and was not, as some writers have stated, a sign of cowardice or fear. A Sioux named Sitting Crow rode up alongside this lone Crow and struck him a mortal blow with his lance, thereby counting a first coup. Then came a man named Knocks Them Down (also known as Grindstone) who struck the second coup, Knife Chief (sometimes Knife King) struck the third and the fourth coup went to a man named Two Eagles. These four Sioux whooped in celebration of their deeds, then raced off to rejoin their tribesmen still in pursuit of the main body of Crows, being content for the younger, less-experienced warriors bringing up the rear to scalp the corpse and rob it of its clothes and weapons.[12]

While this was going on, the largest group of fleeing Crows, comprising between forty and forty-five warriors, had become further separated from the rest of their kinsmen and were heading southwest, directly towards Rain Hill from whence they came and where the few

Crow women and children had been left along with the spare Crow horses. It was hoped that if they could reach the hill and change to fresh mounts, then they would be able to draw clear of their pursuers, whose own mounts must soon become jaded owing to the grueling speed of the chase or, if not, then perhaps they could make a stand along the high crest of Rain Hill itself.

Unbeknown to this Crow group, however, racing for the heights, the party of Hunkpapa hunters which had left their village earlier that morning, had also been travelling in a southwesterly direction and had already discovered the Crow war camp and the many grazing ponies secreted in the hollow on the east side of the hill. Having found no opposition, these Sioux had captured the animals and some of the Crow women and children in the vicinity, along with all the paraphernalia of the camp.

One of the Crows captured at this time was the wife of the Pipe Holder Bull Rises Small. This woman was named Among The Willows and was then only twenty-one years old. Many years later she related her version of the affair as regards her capture by the Sioux.

She always said that just as the Crow war party was starting from Rain Hill toward the Sioux villages to the northeast, her husband Bull Rises Small, who earlier had harbored premonitions of disaster, told her that not far to the north was the Hidatsa village.

"They are the same people as us Crows. If things go badly for us with the enemy, then you must mount a fast horse so you will be able to ride through their lines if need be and be able to outrun them to reach the safety of our relatives." [13]

It had been soon after the war party started out to attack the Sioux camps, that the remaining Crow women and boys had taken up positions on top of a knoll rising from the crest of Rain Hill and from where they could see a long way in three directions, although toward the north was broken country which restricted their view. Among the Willows later said that she saw something or someone moving in the distance to the north of the knoll, but the other women had assured her it was only distant clumps of sagebrush waving in the wind and all continued looking toward the eastern horizon, expecting to see their warriors returning victorious from battle.

It was, however, from the north that a lone Sioux warrior, out scouting on foot for deer as a member of the Hunkpapa hunting party, espied the people on the hilltop and also the spare Crow horses milling around in the hollow. He immediately raced away to inform his comrades. This man first crept along a coulee which obscured him from view and it was not until he was some distance away that the Crow women saw him. They assumed he must be one of their own Crow warriors who had gone out hunting earlier that morning and, consequently, had missed joining the war party. Thus, they still did not consider themselves in danger of being attacked.

The lone Sioux soon caught up with his comrades and reported his discovery, whereupon, the entire hunting party changed course and headed for the same hill, intent upon capturing the Crow women and children and, perhaps especially, the herd of spare horses left unattended in the hollow about a mile east of the knoll.

As these Sioux drew near the hill, they rode straight for the horse herd and the Crow women could now clearly see people in that direction. At first some of the women thought the distant riders were members of their own war party who had broken off from the fighting then gone on far to the east and had come back to the foot of the hill in order to exchange tired mounts for fresh animals. Two of the Crow women were not so trusting. Already they had mounted their horses tethered nearby. One of these women rode off, fearing that the men among the pony herd were enemy. Among the Willows was on foot straightening the packs on her pony, when the other woman who had mounted her horse ready to flee, turned in the saddle and called back to Among the Willows urging her to follow. But still Among the Willows remained where she was. Of the two other Crow women and three teenage boys also remaining on the hill top, most insisted that the riders in the distance were their own Crow warriors milling around among the herd, but one of the more discerning women among them said, "Sisters, I am talking through the Pipe stem," (meaning that what she was telling them was the truth) "Those are not our people." [14]

She too then mounted her horse and got ready to ride off. Just then a number of warriors came into view riding along the crest toward the knoll. When still some distance off, one of them gestured in the sign language telling the Crow women and children to stay where they were. The Crows could not make out their costumes clearly and so once again, began to argue among themselves as to whether they were their own people or Sioux.

The two Crow women on horses ready to flee now dismounted and joined the others, who were waiting for the riders to draw close and be recognized. As the strangers came near, one of the women thought she recognized the lance the lead rider was carrying. It looked like a uniquely adorned Crooked lance of the Crow Lumpwood Society which all knew, belonged to Iron Bull and she told her companions as much.

"It must be Iron Bull," they then said to one another and each expressed a sigh of relief thinking they were now safe from harm. [15.]

Suddenly the lead rider began furiously waving his lance and thrusting it repeatedly in the direction of the huddled group on the hill, while at the same time yelling something in a foreign language. Too late the Crows at last realized that those galloping towards them were indeed, their mortal foes, the Sioux.

The Crows on the hill now attempted to jump on their horses, but one of the women was having difficulty doing so, as her horse bucked and reared and became unmanageable. In a short while, many more Sioux had ridden up the slope at the far end of the hill and were racing towards those on the crest. Several of these warriors rode past the woman struggling with her pony, but others drew up alongside and one after the other began striking her about the head and shoulders with their lances, tomahawks and whips in the act of counting coup. She tried desperately to fend off the blows by swinging an ax about her, albeit cutting nothing but air.

The teenage boys, along with two of the remaining women, one of whom was Among the Willows and the other who again had the baby strapped in a cradle board hanging from her saddlebow, did manage to get astride their ponies, speed down the hillside and out across the prairie, heading north away from the Sioux. The Crow boys raced off in one direction and the two women in another. But soon the horses the women were riding began to slow down and when the riders looked back, they saw a number of Sioux coming after them, one behind the other, strung out in a long line, which rose and fell according to the undulating country over which they rode.

Among the Willows was riding a buckskin pony and leading a fine black mare, which was known as a particularly fast runner and in total, these two women had six horses between them. As Among the Willows galloped her steed hard across the rolling grasslands, she jumped from the horse she was riding and onto the black mare in an attempt to out distance her pursuers. Unfortunately, she dropped her pony whip in the process, so that even being on a comparatively fresh mount, she could not get full speed from it. She was kicking the animal repeatedly in the flanks while her companion, riding alongside, was striking it on the rump with her own whip to urge it on. But the Sioux continued to gain ground and when Among the Willows turned in the saddle again to glance at the foe, one of their number—a Sioux chief named Feather Mane—was making signs to the fleeing women, telling them to rein up and they would not be harmed.

It was evident that the women would eventually be caught and knowing this, they did rein in their horses and with apprehension, awaited their pursuers to come up.

This man Feather Mane (also known as Feather on the Head) was the first of the Sioux to reach them. He rode slowly around striking first one of the women with his coup stick and then the other, after which he struck each of the six horses in turn, thereby claiming them as his property. Immediately behind him came three more Sioux, Chief White Buffalo, White Blackbird and another named Cloud Shield, each of whom, likewise, counted their respective coups on both the women and horses. Feather Mane then grasped the arm of Among the Willows, intending to take her up on his own horse as his captive. But another warrior named Looking Elk rode up on the far side of Among the Willows, grabbed hold of her other arm and tried to pull her towards him. There now ensued a tussle between the two Sioux, both of whom pulled in opposite directions, while Among the Willows struggled to retain her seat. This second Sioux became agitated and in spite, made a lunge with his lance at the unarmed woman who, instinctively, raised her hand to fend off the blow and the lance point pierced her forearm.[16.]

In the meantime, her companion—still with the cradle board suspended from her saddlebow—had been struck by two more Sioux named Magpie Eagle and Dry Bones and also suffered a blow to the head, as other Sioux warriors rode up and counted their coups by striking her with clubs and rifle barrels and the blood flowed from her wounds. The third Crow woman who had remained on the hilltop, being unable to mount her horse, was claimed as captive by a Sioux named Water Carrier. The second, who was Among the Willows, was claimed by Looking Elk and the mother of the baby by Long Horns, while the baby itself was claimed by a famous Hunkpapa known as Old Crow. [17.]

Finally, the three women still seated in their saddles, were led back to where the rest of the Sioux were milling around with the captured ponies. In the distance the women could faintly see through the swirling dust, the ghostly shapes of men and horses spread out over the prairie, as fighting went on between the different bunches of Crow warriors and the enemy; the sight of which—so Among the Willows later said—"was like a bad dream." [18.]

Some other Sioux who previously had been fighting the fleeing Crows, reached the place where the women captives were being held. Two or more of their number were very angry. They tried to get close to the women in order to kill them in revenge for Sioux comrades who already had either been killed or severely injured in the chase.

One Sioux managed to fire a shot at the woman who had been unable to mount her horse and had been the first of the Crows to be captured. Luckily, his aim was marred, the ball merely tearing through the woman's dress and creasing her hand. The leading men among the Sioux now held these warriors back from further molesting the captives and advised them to rejoin their comrades who were still fighting and chasing Crow warriors across the prairie.

Three Crow women, one teenage boy and the small child in the cradle board were captured. Some Crow informants say that the rest of the Crow noncombatants including the three teenagers, succeeded in out distancing their pursuers and finally reached the Hidatsa village in the north, and from where, eventually, they made it back to their home camp on the Big Horn. Plain Feather on the other hand, told Joe Medicine Crow that one of these women had hidden one of the boys in a small hollow and placed a blanket over him, after which she covered the blanket with dirt and sage brush in order to disguise it. The woman then rode off and made her escape to the Hidatsa. A little later, a group of Sioux came up having been in pursuit and searching the area, noticed a corner of the blanket sticking out from the ground. They pulled on the blanket and thus discovered the boy concealed beneath and in such a way, at least one of the Crow boys was taken captive. This account from Plain Feather does appear to be the more reliable.[19.]

Author's sketch from an original pen and water color drawing by Swift Dog in Mr. and Mrs. Charles Diker Collection

The Hunkpapa Sioux warrior Swift Dog in pursit of a mounted Crow during the Rain Hill fight of 1858.

Meanwhile, the Hunkpapa hunting party and the San Arcs who had been chasing Crow warriors since the mid morning attack upon the villagers, had joined forces. Now the force included such notable personages as the famous Hunkpapa war chief, Gall, Chief Loud Voiced Elk, Crawler Red Fox, Two Bears and Lame Deer; this last named, later to become a big war chief among the Miniconjou. [20.]

The Hunkpapa chief Sitting Bull was also in this group. He was wearing a long tailed feathered bonnet that day with a single buffalo horn attached to the brow band, denoting his membership of the Strong Heart society, a prestigious warrior fraternity among the Hunkpapa, composed only of those regarded as the bravest within that tribe.

These Sioux chiefs and their warriors now beset the largest of the fleeing Crow groups, chasing them across the prairie and it was in this particular band of Crows that the young Iron Eyes—son of chief No Mane—could be found.

During their flight, both Iron Eyes and Blackbird on the Ground, the second Crow Pipe Holder, had several times hung back from their companions and by threatening to shoot first at one of the enemy and

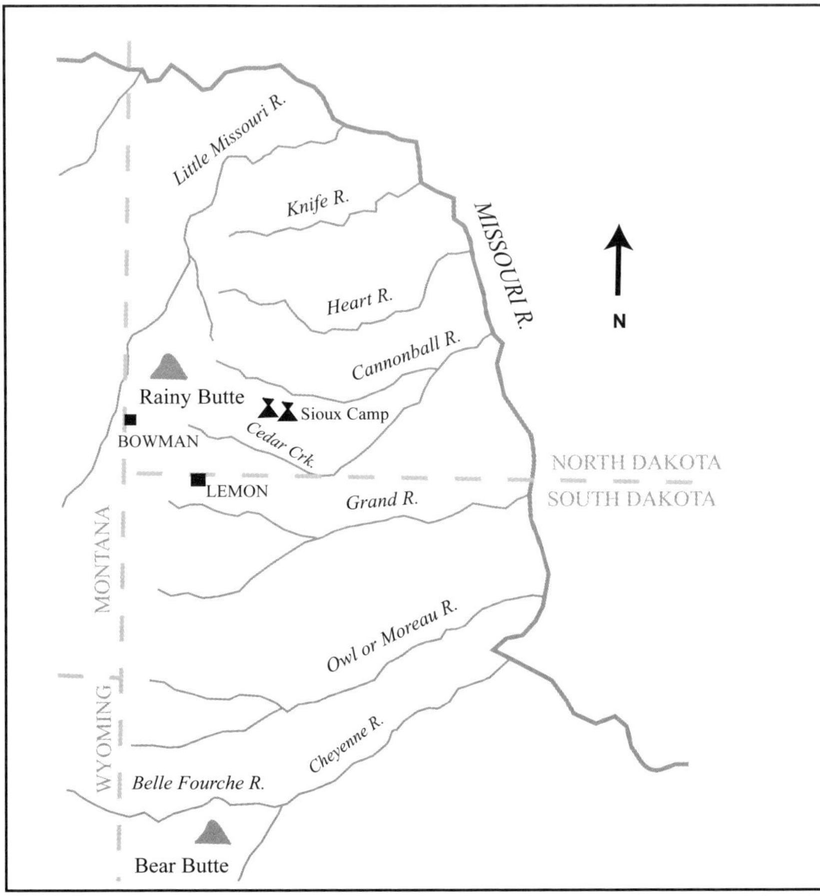

Original drawing by author

Map or Rain Hill battle area and surrounding country.

then another, had held the Sioux at bay, thus allowing the rest of the Crow warriors to widen the gap between themselves and the foe.

After a short while, each of these brave men galloped off to catch up with their comrades, while the Sioux again took up the chase.

Now, with additional numbers of Sioux pursuing them, Black Bird on the Ground dropped back yet again and dismounting from his horse, faced the oncoming foe alone. He jumped around from side to side to confuse his enemy's aim, while every so often he fired a shot from his old trade gun into the Sioux ranks. This time, however, the Sioux managed to get behind him and when suddenly they all charged together, they succeeded in striking him a mortal blow. They then rode their ponies over the brave Crow chief as he lay prostrate on the ground and trampled him under hoof. The Sioux took his horse, weapons and scalp, then stripped his fine attire of ermine and hair-fringed war shirt, hair-fringed leggings and richly beaded moccasins, which they took as trophies of their deed.

The Young Iron Eyes along with other Crows in his group, watched the last stand of their brave leader and now Iron Eyes along with another called Three Thighs, decided to emulate his actions if only to retard their enemies` progress. Most of the Crows in this party thought they were doomed to annihilation. The two lone fighters were probably determined to sacrifice their lives in some spectacular manner, so as to be remembered by their people for many winters to come.

So it was that these two brave Crows reined in their horses. They did not dismount, but remained in the saddle threatening to shoot the foremost Sioux warriors as they came charging towards them. Again the Sioux pulled up their mounts and those who owned guns began shooting at the two Crows who pranced around on their spirited ponies before them. Most of the Sioux shots were wild but one did find its mark and hit Three Thigh`s horse, shattering its hip bone, causing the animal to collapse and throw its rider to the ground. Immediately Iron Eyes took his companion up behind him on his own horse, whereupon, the two raced off to where the rest of their party was waiting, watching the action from a distance out of range from Sioux missiles.

The brave Iron Eyes then returned to his previous position, far in front of his group and along with another warrior named One Boy, who stationed himself a short distance away, again took his stand on horseback facing the oncoming Sioux.

In some way or other, One Boy too was unhorsed and he cried out to Iron Eyes to rescue him. Iron Eyes rode over to where he stood; took him up behind him and in the same manner as before, carried his companion to safety behind the Crow lines. This time though, after Iron Eyes reached his kinsmen and dropped off his comrade, he called to them saying,

> "My friends I have assisted you long enough; my flesh is hot with running—now I will go no further. Tell my father No

Mane, whose words stick in my throat, that his son has died as a brave man should." [21]

Iron Eyes then rode back alone to face the Sioux and for a third time positioned himself in the very path of the enemy, who by now were again charging forward. This time Iron Eyes suddenly jumped from the saddle, slapped his war pony on its rump with the flat of his hand, causing the animal to canter back to the line of watching Crows, then braced himself ready to sell his life dearly in the event. (In another Crow version, after helping One Boy on his horse and sending both horse and rider back to the Crow line, Iron Eyes remained where he was; on foot—facing the foe alone). [22].

Once again most of the Sioux pulled up their horses and hovered just out of range from Iron Eyes, although a number of warriors continued charging towards him. As they drew near they could hear the death song of Iron Eyes ringing out high above their war whoops and the drumming of their horse's hooves. This was the song a Crow warrior sang when he intended to give his body to the wolves.

Such was the bravery of Iron Eyes that both One Boy and Three Thighs, now remounted on spare horses, were stirred by his actions and, while the Sioux were yet some distance away, they rode out to where he stood; likewise dismounted, then sent the horses away. They vowed to spill their blood alongside their brave comrade. Then three more Crows also left their group and joined Iron Eyes and his companions, bringing the total to six Crows resolved to sacrifice their lives for tribal honor. The names of these three are also justifiably remembered among the Crows; they were Mountain Lion, Golden Eagle and Big Forked Horn. [23]

At first, while Iron Eyes had been standing alone, a number of Sioux warriors had continued charging forward shooting from the saddle with guns and arrows as they rode. But now, upon seeing five more of their enemies join Iron Eyes, the Sioux wheeled their ponies around, made a wide arc and raced back to their own people.

The enemy force confronting these few brave men was in overwhelming number, as by now more Sioux warriors had arrived. There were so many Sioux that even though a large number prepared to engage the six Crows, the rest were strong enough to resume the attack upon the main Crow party and force it again to take flight with the Sioux in hot pursuit.

So it was that this group of Crows to which the six brave men belonged, did not witness their comrades' glorious deaths. The Sioux, however, told the Crows later that it was some time before the last of these six was killed and added that Iron Eyes had stood his ground alone, a little way off from his companions. After doing many brave things he had been the first to be cut down, being nearest the Sioux lines. It is said by the Crows that Iron Eyes was surrounded by at least 100 Sioux and was literally "covered up" by his enemies.[24]

Meanwhile, the rest of the Crow party continued fleeing from the Sioux, mile-after-mile over prairie, hill and stream.

Also prominent among the Crow fighters this day was the aspiring sub chief Sits-in-the-Middle-of-the-Land. Standing over six feet two in his moccasins, he was a well-proportioned and muscular man and as usual when engaged in battle, he wore no shirt. Instead, he was stripped to the waist; his torso, arms and shoulders daubed profusely with white and yellow ochre. His hair was long and full-blown and on his head he wore the stuffed skin of a wild goose symbolizing his personal medicine helper. Attached to this headpiece were two long narrow streamers of red strouding trade cloth which trailed out behind him as he rode, while around his neck he wore two wider strouding strips, crossed over his upper chest with the loose ends draped over his shoulders thence hanging down his back to the waist, and decorating this chestpiece were numerous hanks of human hair, representing his many warlike deeds and personal prowess over his enemies. His loud stentorian voice could often be heard above the din of conflict as he galloped his powerful black stallion back and forth across the field, giving encouragement to the embattled Crow warriors.[25]

At length, the sun reached its highest point in the sky and the day became oppressively hot. A number of mounts belonging to both sides were worn out. Many animals had already collapsed from exhaustion due to the heat and grueling speed of the chase and several actually died. As a consequence, every now and then the Crows would pull up their mounts and face their pursuers, who in turn, would also rein up in order to give their horses a breather and during these brief periods of respite, certain warriors on both sides would shout abuse and offer personal challenges to those opposing them across the field.

On one of these occasions, the great Crow warrior and sub chief Big Otter, rode out alone from his line and hurled a challenge at the Sioux for single combat. This man was of a tall well-built stature and had led many successful raids upon his enemies, among whom he was also well-known. He was not, though, particularly liked by his own people, mostly because he was the bullying and arrogant type. According to Joe Medicine Crow, he was usually referred to by others as *Bele-Depic* meaning, "Woman's Labia." Whether this was another of his proper names or, one daubed upon him behind his back, is not definitely determined in the oral accounts.[26.]

It was believed that Big Otter possessed strong medicine power—the spiritual manifestation of the "Bear" —and this, supposedly, made him strong in battle and protected him from being shot with any kind of firearm. It was he also, in the ilk of his great predecessor chief Sore Belly, who always inspected the weapons and mounts of those wishing to accompany him to war. If their accoutrements did not meet his approval, he told the owners to replace them with those of better quality or refused to take them with him. He was a renowned maker of weapons. He would inspect the bows and knives of his followers and break them to show their inferior quality, whereupon, he would then trade them new ones which, conveniently, he invariably had in good supply. As a personal preference Big Otter carried a knife with a large steel blade, acquired in trade from a white trapper some time before. Such a knife was commonly known as a "Green River." It had a broad blade some twelve inches long and could rip a man from crotch to collarbone with one upward stroke. Big Otter wore this knife on his waist belt, but as was the custom of the Crows, it was positioned in front covering his crotch rather than on the right or left hip, so that when grappling hand to hand with an enemy, if the opponent managed to pin his arms, Big Otter could still reach his knife and draw it from the scabbard.

Although Big Otter was generally despised, he was, unquestionably a fearless warrior and considered a welcome addition among his tribesmen whenever they were engaged in a hard fight. Against his people's enemies he was a particularly vicious and cruel adversary; one who revelled in inflicting ultimate pain and humiliation upon his victims and his reputation alone, often deterred the more timid of his foes from facing him on the field of combat.

This day he was mounted on a fine running horse, made prominent by a large white blaze marking on its forehead. Some informants declare that this was the finest horse among all those belonging to the Crows at that time.

At this time Big Otter's party had halted and so had the Sioux group pursuing it. In the distance Big Otter could see dotted over the waving grassland, small bunches of Crows and Sioux, some in flight, some stationary, facing each other in a standoff situation.

Big Otter now waved his musket above his head and shouted across the prairie, calling the scattered Crows to rally round him.

Many Crows saw his signal and managed to ride over and join his group, but still Big Otter would not move from the spot, being determined to allow time for the rest of his scattered tribesmen to reach him. In such a way he did manage to rally most of his warriors and consolidate them again into a single fighting force, although some others were too far away and prevented from reaching him by intervening parties of Sioux.

Meanwhile, those Sioux facing Big Otter's group also called many of their scattered warriors together and soon formed a sizable body, so that both groups of opposing warriors sat their ponies across from each other about one-half-mile apart, waiting to see what the other would do next before deciding whether to fight or flee.

While awaiting the rest of the Crows to join him, Big Otter was still shouting challenges to the Sioux, daring them to send forth their champion to meet him in single combat.

"You are like old women," Big Otter cried, "Come fight me, if any among you are brave." [27]

Now among this particular Sioux group opposing Big Otter, was an old Hunkpapa named Jumping Bull who had been a great warrior in his younger days. He was also the father of Sitting Bull, the great Hunkpapa war chief and holy man later to become so well known around the world. At this time, Sitting Bull was fighting another bunch of Crows in a distant part of the field and so was unaware of what was going on elsewhere.

The rest of the Sioux in Jumping Bull`s party were holding back; hovering about not daring to get to grips with the Crows, who in turn, calmly sat astride their ponies taunting their enemies with verbal threats and obscene gestures. Jumping Bull was shouting at his own warriors trying to induce them to fight, while at the same time, he pointed and gesticulated at the Crows, both to show his contempt for the enemy and to goad them into launching an attack if they dared.

Big Otter took notice of this man. He said to his assembled warriors, "I will see if that person who talks and points is a man." [28.]

Looking resplendent in ermine trimmed war shirt and beaded hair-fringed leggings and moccasins, Big Otter with one companion rode out in front of the Crow line. He began hurling abuse at the hesitant foe while brandishing his short-barrelled powder and ball muzzle-loader above his head and again, called to the Sioux to send out their champion.

The Sioux account records that Jumping Bull had been suffering some time with a raging toothache and only a few days before, had declared to all that he would throw away his life in the next battle with his people's enemies. It was, say the Sioux, because of this that Jumping Bull himself accepted the Crow chief's challenge rather than allowing a younger, more agile warrior the honor, although it seems to be, moreover, that as the Crow challenge had been directed by Big Otter specifically towards Jumping Bull, who alone had been shouting and gesticulating at the Crows, the old man was therefore, obliged to accept the challenge himself lest he incur the disdain of his tribesmen and this especially so, after he had berated his own followers for their timidity. The Crows on the other hand, believed that the Sioux Jumping Bull was also a possessor of *Bear medicine* and thus, like Big Otter, deemed himself invulnerable to their bullets.

Whatever the case, the old Sioux warrior turned in the saddle and cried to his tribesmen, "Leave this man to me." [29]

He jumped down from his horse and fitting an arrow to his bow, started forward on foot to meet his lone adversary.

In response, say the Crows, Big Otter likewise dismounted and after hitting his horse on the rump with the barrel of his musket so that it took off back to the Crow lines, began walking without hesitation toward the oncoming Sioux. Jumping Bull loosed an arrow which actually glanced off the side of Big Otter`s head and flew harmlessly into the air, causing no damage save a slight graze to the skin. Big Otter, meanwhile, aimed his musket and fired but the powder had spilled when he had struck his horse with the barrel and although there was a bright flash in the breech, the gun misfired, causing the ball to roll down the barrel and fall harmlessly to the ground. By then the lone Hunkpapa had loosed off another arrow which again struck the Crow, this time in the shoulder, but caused only a shallow flesh wound which seemed to have little or no effect upon his person.

According to the Sioux version, the Crow's gun had not misfired and the ball struck Jumping Bull in the shoulder, but the old man still came on and actually broke into a run eager to get to grips with his protagonist. The Crow, not having time to reload his piece, now drew his knife and ran to meet him and the two collided with each other in midfield. Hereupon, the Crow chief took hold of Jumping Bull`s deer hide shirt with one hand, while with a savage downward stroke of his knife in the other, struck his opponent a severe blow just above the collarbone. The old Sioux had attempted to pull his own knife from its sheath which was attached to a belt slung over one shoulder. But the belt had slipped around him so that the sheath lay on his back and he was unable to reach it before the Crow's blade struck. The lone Crow, say the Sioux, was a big and powerful man and easily held his victim securely with one hand, while he continued to stab poor Jumping Bull many times in the chest and side. Soon the brave Sioux sank to his knees and the Crow then stabbed him in the top of the head, delivering the blow with such force that the blade actually broke in two, leaving several inches of metal protruding from Jumping Bull`s skull. Too late one of the onlooking Sioux, a man named Many Horses, came galloping over to assist his people's champion. But Jumping Bull by then was already dead; his jubilant killer remounted and trotting slowly away to rejoin his waiting warriors.

The Crow account on the other hand, states that after Big Otter's gun had misfired, he threw it to the ground, drew his knife and ran toward his enemy who already was fixing another arrow to his bowstring. However, before the Sioux could release the shaft, Big Otter grabbed him by the wrist and holding him fast, raised his big Green River knife ready to strike. At this point, say the Crows, Jumping Bull tried to fend off the stroke with his bow and at the same time started to cry as he foresaw his impending doom.[30] Big Otter then released his grip on the old man's wrist and instead, grabbed his adversary by the throat with one hand while with the other, he struck him a terrible blow with his knife which sliced the struggling Sioux from the chest to below the ribs, causing such a gash that when Big Otter propelled the limp body

Smithsonian Institution "Siris" website
Sioux Chief Four Horn's depiction of Sitting Bull's lancing a Crow warrior during the Rain Hill fight.

aside with his knee, the entrails of his victim protruded from the stomach. Still, though, the old Hunkpapa was alive. He sank to his knees and did not immediately keel over, not until Big Otter`s companion who was stationed nearby, finally shot a musket ball into the back of his head and killed him.

The triumphant Big Otter then turned to the onlooking Sioux warriors and cried, "Come on Lakota women, come on and fight." [31]

But none of the Sioux who had witnessed the spectacle were in any mood to accept his challenge. They were sad because Jumping Bull had been held in high esteem both as a warrior and a man of kind yet strong character. They made signs to Big Otter to go away, telling him they would not attempt to follow. Years later the Sioux admitted to the Crows that they were ashamed of themselves for having allowed the old man to die in so ignominious a manner, as they themselves merely watched from a distance, doing nothing to help as he battled for life in such an unequal duel.

The other Crow warrior, say the Sioux, who had been sitting astride his pony only a short distance away, meanwhile trotted his horse over to where Big Otter stood. The Crow war chief mounted up behind him and together they rode slowly back to their waiting comrades. The Crows then rode off at a leisurely trot and when some distance away, the Sioux rode over to where the lifeless form of Jumping Bull lay crumpled and bloody on the ground. Two or three warriors dismounted and attempted to lift the body in order to put it across the withers of a horse and carry it from the field, but as they did so, all of Jumping Bull's insides fell out—spewing over the ground.

While all this had been going on, Sitting Bull, the old man's son, had been fighting in another part of the field. While thus engaged, word was brought him of his father's death and immediately, Sitting Bull raced his pony across the prairie to where the corpse of his father lay. When he came hither and viewed the body's mutilated condition, he also cried many tears while, at the same time, screaming oaths of vengeance upon he that slew him. Sitting Bull now discarded his one-horned single-tailed war bonnet because of the sweltering heat. Instead, he took up a blue-painted bison-hide shield with a blackbird design emblazoned upon its cover; stripped naked but for breech clout and moccasins and tied his long hair in a knot protruding over the forehead. This hair arrangement was a necessary requirement for any warrior carrying this particular shield and was also a fashion of olden days, when his forefathers had ridden into battle determined to perform some desperate deed.[32]

Sitting Bull and a host of warriors then whipped up their ponies and sped after the same bunch of Crows among whom Big Otter was riding. Hearing the renewed war cries of their enemies, the Crows spurred their own mounts into a gallop.

Sitting Bull's horse was a fast runner. As he urged it on it was not long before he caught up with one of the Crows lagging behind his fellows. This Crow was the same man who, as the companion of Big Otter, had actually delivered the coup de grace upon the dying Jumping Bull. Evidently his horse was nearing exhaustion and was about to play out.

As Sitting Bull drew near, he leaned forward in the saddle and lunged with his lance, which pierced the fleeing Crow in the small of the back. The Crow fell from his galloping steed and before he could regain his feet, the Hunkpapa chief had leapt from his own mount and was upon him. With knife drawn, Sitting Bull got astride the Crow and began stabbing him repeatedly in the chest and neck and when supposing him dead, proceeded to cut the limbs from the body in an act of vengeance for the death of his father.[33]

At the same time, the rest of the Sioux were continuing their pursuit of the main body of Crows and the chase went on, it is said, for at least another thirty miles, the Sioux driving the Crows before them in a southwesterly direction. In the process, another Crow was killed. Apparently his horse too had also slackened speed owing to the broiling heat. Suddenly, it pulled up dead in its tracks, completely exhausted—unable to go farther. Its rider was left to the mercy of his foes, who soon came up and surrounded him and their numbers being great, they "covered him up" as the Crows later described it. A Hunkpapa named Pretty Weasel, struck the fatal blow, while two others, named Thunder Hawk and White Bordered Tail, counted the second and third coups respectively.

The next Crow was killed by a man named Shoots Walking and coups were struck upon his body by Gives Goose and Little Tusk. [34.]

Another who lived up to his reputation as a strong and fearless adversary, was the Crow warrior Mountain Chief, the brother of Big Otter and a leading fighter within the Lumpwood Society. This day he was mounted on a fast buffalo runner—a fine grey mare. In previous battles he had been recognized as a loyal and intrepid warrior and usually, he wore on his head the stuffed body of a wild sage hen, this being his personal protective medicine. With total disregard for his own safety, Mountain Chief performed many brave deeds this day, although now he was stripped to the waist and in addition to beaded leggings and moccasins, he wore an eagle-feathered war bonnet, the same which now sits in the museum display of the Smithsonian Institution in Washington D.C. The Sioux took heed of this man, noting how his red and white war paint showed prominent by being applied in great streaks upon his face, arms and torso. Bunches of wolf fur and raven feathers formed a kind of chaplet on his horse's head and with only a bow and arrows with which to defend himself and, albeit, under heavy enemy fire, he oft times raced across the field to where a fellow Crow was in difficulty, having been unhorsed and forced to make a stand on foot in the face of overwhelming odds.

Mountain Chief's awesome appearance instilled fear into the hearts of the Sioux whenever he came charging into the fray, so that the latter were apt to draw back at his approach. He had attached around his horse's neck a large brass hand bell and as he galloped his steed across the grassy plain, the bell rang loud and clear. Those unhorsed Crows likely to be surrounded by the enemy and killed, took great heart when they heard the bell ringing above the human war whoops and drumming of horse's hooves, for they knew they were apt to be snatched from the very jaws of oblivion. Time and again did Mountain Chief charge back towards the foe, taking up an unhorsed comrade on his own mount and riding double, they would gallop off together to the comparative safety of the Crow lines. Mountain Chief performed a number of other brave deeds, the details of which, alas, have since been forgotten, although it is recalled that solely by such acts, more than one of Mountain Chief's comrades-in-arms were saved from what had looked like certain death.[35]

Truly, he was the pride of his Lumpwood Society brothers that day and yet another of the more outstanding heroes of the fight, whose reputation would cause fellow tribesmen to refer to him hereafter as *Baatsey-tsey* meaning, "A Good Man." [36]

But even with such men as Mountain Chief, the Crows continued to be driven across the plain.

As the afternoon wore on, the fleeing Crows became even more strung out in their several little groups and those whose mounts were near exhaustion were lagging ever farther behind. Still, it seemed, a great host of Sioux were in pursuit even though many of their number had dropped far back to the rear—or had simply given up the chase and were already returning home to their respective camps.

There was another among the Crows—a middle-aged man known as Ancient Wolf—who was one of those dropping behind his tribesmen. He was the uncle and mentor to a noted warrior named Strong Falcon—a much younger man—but one already famed as a brave and reckless fighter. At length, realizing that his steed would soon give out, Ancient Wolf called to Strong Falcon who was keeping pace with him, urging him on, "Strong Falcon, when you get home, whose horses will you ride?" [37]

By this he was indicating that his nephew and protégé Strong Falcon who had often cared for his horses and been allowed to ride any of his choice, would be able to have all his uncle's horses for himself, for he, Ancient Wolf, was about to give his body to the enemy.

So saying, Ancient Wolf suddenly reined in his horse, turned it around, dismounted and stood ready with gun in hand facing the oncoming Sioux.

Seeing him thus, Strong Falcon did not hesitate but also reined up, jumped from his own mount and joined his mentor. He too prepared to brave the very jaws of death.

The Sioux, who in this particular pursuing bunch were few in number, soon came up and surrounded the pair and circling around them, shot off arrows and musket balls from under the necks of their ponies as they rode. The two Crows were standing side by side and returned a sporadic but deliberate fire for some time as they endeavored to conserve their ammunition. But at length, they were forced to separate when two or three of the enemy rode directly at them and having forced a gap between the two, the Sioux then concentrated their efforts upon Ancient Wolf who by now, had exhausted his ammunition.

During the ongoing melee, Ancient Wolf was obliged to edge farther away from his companion in order to avoid the flying hooves of the Sioux horses, the riders having singled him out and were badgering him repeatedly. Ancient Wolf swung the butt of his weapon about him, parrying and warding off his assailant's lances and tomahawks but soon, after several more Sioux joined in the fray, he was struck from behind, causing him to fall on his knees, though he remained in an upright position. Almost at this same instant, half a dozen or more Sioux bowstrings twanged and arrow after arrow embedded their iron heads in his torso and limbs. So many, it is said, that although the old Crow was already dead, his body stayed rigid from the waist up; leaning slightly forward but prevented from falling face down by the number of shafts protruding from it—the butt ends touching the ground and keeping the corpse propped up. [38.]

Strong Falcon, meanwhile, was continuing the fight and so ferocious was he this day, that none of the Sioux could get near enough to finish him off. They believed the Crow owned some powerful medicine which would do for them all.

In truth, Strong Falcon was also a possessor of the omnipotent "Bear medicine" which, so most Indians believed, caused its owner to be impervious to iron missiles whether shot from gun or bow and only a hand to hand contest could bring him down.

It is said that Strong Falcon was such a formidable fighter that while in the heat of battle, his face actually took on the aspect of a bear; his teeth fully bared and protruding from his curled back lips, while a frothy white foam bubbled up from his mouth.

Several times the indomitable Strong Falcon lunged at his antagonists, sometimes chasing them across the field. The surrounding Sioux could do him no injury.

While this unequal but strange contest was going on, the bulk of Sioux warriors had drawn far away in their continued pursuit of the rest of the Crows and at length, even those engaged against Strong Falcon said to one another, "We cannot kill this man, his medicine is too strong." [39.]

Already Strong Falcon had seriously wounded a number of his antagonists and this itself was sufficient for the latter to finally abandon their attempts to kill him. They rode off into the distance, some following in the wake of their companions still chasing the main bunch of Crows, others turning around and heading east for their home camps having had enough fighting for one day; and the lone Crow Strong Falcon was left safe and unscathed.

The day, however, was still broiling hot. There was no breeze. Here and there riderless horses stood stationary, both dotted around on the prairie and along the route of the Crow retreat, the animal's necks bent low, having become exhausted and thus abandoned by their owners, if that is, their owners were not already dead.

Soon Strong Falcon could see no more horseback riders neither Crow nor Sioux, they being too far distant and obscured from view by the shimmering heat haze which seemed to envelope the prairie. Only the long looming hulk of Rain Hill now engulfed in shadow, stood out ominous from the rolling prairie floor.

Strong Falcon was afoot and many miles from home.

Seeing abandoned horses scattered over the grassland, he sidled over to one particular animal which appeared slightly less dilapidated than the rest and taking hold of its dragging reins, gently led it away at a slow walk, to a place where both he and horse could rest in the long grass bordering the waters of Cedar Creek. Having found a sheltered spot, Strong Falcon lay down and was soon asleep in the afternoon heat. He had decided to sleep till dark and in the evening, would start out for home which lay many days travel to the west, albeit, through inhospitable country swarming with the mortal enemies of his people.

Meanwhile, far from Strong Falcon`s sight and hearing, the Sioux were yet pursuing the remainder of the still fleeing Crows. The Sioux did manage to count several more coups upon their enemies, but at last, they gave up the chase and slowly retired from the field. They retraced their route of pursuit in order to retrieve a number of dead and injured comrades who had been left in secluded spots along the way. Some others had simply been left where they had fallen, with wads of grass or prairie sage stuffed in wounds to help stem the flow of blood. In the event, several more Sioux warriors also lost their lives, not in the actual battle, but by succumbing to wounds left unattended too long. In later years the Sioux admitted to the Crows that they lost ten men dead that day and many more had suffered wounds of varying degree, some of which injuries affected those unfortunates with severe disability for the rest of their lives. Only three of the slain Sioux were Hunkpapa, which included Sitting Bull's father Jumping Bull, along with the warriors Makes the Enemy and Running Close.[40]

Many Sioux warriors had counted several coups and they had captured three Crow women, a teenage boy and a baby strapped in its cradle board. For these reasons the Sioux considered the affair a great victory over their hereditary enemies. After returning to their home camps along the Cannonball and allowing the customary four days mourning for comrades dead, frenzied scalp and victory dances were held both day and night in each of the Sioux villages for many weeks thereafter. The Hunkpapa warrior earlier known as Burns the Medicine Bundle, received a new name in recognition of deeds he had performed during the fight and hereafter, was famously known as Crow King.[41]

After the Sioux finally abandoned the chase, the Crow survivors came together again in one body. For a while they rested themselves and their jaded mounts, then they too set out for home, but as a morbid, despondent group; bearing between them a number of dead and seriously wounded comrades, as they headed west toward the setting sun sinking beyond the hills, hiding its face from what it had witnessed on the plain around Rain Hill.

At first the remnants of the Crow party walked their ponies as they journeyed towards the Powder River, knowing that by travelling north along that river's course, they would bring themselves to the Yellowstone and thence, continuing southwest, would finally reach their own camps and loved ones they had left behind.

In due time, many among the Sioux would always refer to this fight as, "The Battle of the Long Chase," while some others remembered it simply as "The time Sitting Bull's father was killed." [42] The Crows for their part, remember the event simply as "The fight at Rain Hill" or "The battle at Rainy Butte" [43] and among both peoples, it is yet regarded as an important episode in their respective histories. [44]

NOTES AND SOURCES.

1 Joe Medicine Crow, Interviews with Author. Lodge Grass, Montana. 1994. Note pad 1. Pp. 14 to 16 .
2 Edward S. Curtis. *The North American Indian.* Vol. IV. "Crow and Atsina." P.98. 1905. See also; Joe Medicine Crow, *"papers."* Little Big Horn College Archives. Box 1. "The Death of Iron Eyes". 1967.
3 Edward S. Curtis, Vol. IV. P. 98. Loc, cit. See also; Joe Medicine Crow Interview with Author. Lodge Grass, Montana. 1994. Note pad 1. P. 10.
4 Joe Medicine Crow, Interview with Author. Lodge Grass, Montana. 1994. Note pad 1. P. 10.
5 Vestal., Stanley. *Sitting Bull, Champion of the Sioux.* P. 43. University of Nebraska Press. 1937.
6 Joe Medicine Crow, Interview with Author. Lodge Grass, Montana. 1994. Note pad 1. P. 10.
7 Joe Medicine Crow, Interview with Author. Lodge Grass, Montana. 1994. Note pad 1. P. 11.
8 Vestal., Stanley. *Sitting Bull, Champion of the Sioux.* Pp. 91 to 95. University of Nebraska Press. 1937. See also; Hyde, George E. *Red Clouds Folk.* P.82. University of Oklahoma Press. 1937.
9 Joe Medicine Crow, Interview with Author. Lodge Grass, Montana. 1994. Note pad 1. P. 11.
10 Joe Medicine Crow, Interview with Author. Lodge Grass, Montana. 1994. Note pad 1. P. 12.
11 Vestal., Stanley. *Sitting Bull, Champion of the Sioux.* P 45. University of Nebraska Press. 1937. See also; Joe Medicine Crow, Interview with Author. Lodge Grass, Montana. 1994. Note pad 1. P. 12.
12 Vestal., Stanley. *Sitting Bull, Champion of the Sioux.* P 45. University of Nebraska Press. 1937.
13 Edward S. Curtis. *The North American Indian.* Vol. IV. "Crow and Atsina." P. 101. 1905
14 Edward S. Curtis. *The North American Indian.* Vol. IV. *"Crow and Atsina."* P. 101. 1905
15 Joe Medicine Crow, Interview with Author. Lodge Grass, Montana. 1994. Note pad 1. P. 12.
16 Edward S. Curtis. *The North American Indian* Vol. IV, "Crow and Atsina" P. 102. 1905. See also; Winona Plenty-Hoops to Author. Crow Agency. Summer. 2005. Note pad 3. P. 6.
17 Vestal Stanley. Papers. Walter S. Campbell Collection. Pp. 17-22. Box no. 105. Folder no. 11. University of Nebraska. Archives and Library.
18 Edward S. Curtis. *The North American Indian.* Vol. IV. "Crow and Atsina." P. 102. 1905
19 Originally, there had been five Crow women and three teenage boys who accompanied the war-party of Bull-Rises-Small and Blackbird-on-the-Ground against the Sioux. Three of these women along with one of the boys were taken captive by the Sioux but the remaining two women and two teenage boys, had actually managed to escape on horseback when first the Hunkpapa hunting party was seen among the Crow horse herd on the eastern slope of the hill. These four Crow non-combatants succeeded in outdistancing their pursuers and at length, safely reached their Hidatsa relatives at the latter`s earth-lodge village on the Missouri, far north of Rain Hill at the place where Fort Burford once stood near the present-day community known as Newtown. They stayed among the Hidatsa throughout the rest of that summer and ensuing winter and not until the following spring, did the Hidatsa themselves provide an escort brave enough to hazard the dangerous trip to the Crow country. Thus these particular Crow women and boys were finally returned to their own people. The Crow baby captured in its cradle board during the battle, remained in the care of his Sioux captor Old-Crow until the following summer. At that time, Old-Crow and his Hunkpapa band went on a trading trip to the Hidatsa with whom the Sioux were always alternatively at peace or war but at this time, happened to be at peace. At the Hidatsa town a Crow Indian named Spotted-Horse who was then living among the Hidatsa lodges, succeeded in purchasing the baby from Old-Crow in exchange for many presents. The boy thereafter, remained among the Hidatsa for two years until a number of his Crow relatives, having received word of his whereabouts through the moccasin grapevine, decided to pay a visit to the Hidatsa. Among this party were the same two women who had been escorted back to the Crow camp by Carries-the-Prairie-Chicken and his Sioux companions and one of these women was actually the mother of the young boy now in the care of Spotted-Horse. While at the Hidatsa town the Crow visitors successfully bought the boy from Spotted-Horse for the price of six fine ponies in addition to a large quantity of tanned robes and other goods.The white man trader Henry Boller, then in the employ of the American Fur Company, was in the same village at this time in 1861. He recorded in his *memoirs* how he himself had witnessed the arrival of the Crow party to the Hidatsa and of their making such a purchase from Spotted-Horse. Cf. Robert H. Lowie; p.260 - 261 *Anthropological papers American Museum of Natural History,* vol. XXI. Pp. 260 - 261. also Henry A. Boller, *"Among The Indians,"* p.319, 1867.

20 Vestal., Stanley. *Sitting Bull, Champion of the Sioux.* P 47. University of Nebraska Press. 1937.
21 Joe Medicine Crow, Interview with Author. Lodge Grass, Montana. 1994. Note pad 1. P. 12.
22 Edward S. Curtis. *The North American Indian.* Vol. IV. "Crow and Atsina." P. 99. 1905
23 Joe Medicine Crow, Interview with Author. Lodge Grass, Montana. 1994. Note pad 1. P. 12.
24 Joe Medicine Crow, Interview with Author. Lodge Grass, Montana. 1994. Note pad 1. P. 12.
25 Ibid.
26 Ibid.
27 Ibid.
28 Edward S. Curtis. *The North American Indian.* Vol. IV. "Crow and Atsina." P. 99. 1905
29 Vestal., Stanley. *Sitting Bull, Champion of the Sioux.* P 46. University of Nebraska Press. 1937. See also; Joe Medicine Crow, Interview with Author. Lodge Grass, Montana. 1994. Note pad 1. P. 12.
30 Joe Medicine Crow, Interview with Author. Lodge Grass, Montana. 1994. Note pad 1. P. 12. Again, as with the Sioux statement previously mentioned that the Crow chief Bull-Rises-Small was crying on the field of battle, this Crow suggestion that the Sioux Jumping Bull also shed tears over his impending doom, is likely apocryphal. It would seem that both statements are but tit-for-tat responses by the Crows and Sioux in order to combat derogatory suggestions from each other concerning the courage of their respective champions. See also; Vestal., Stanley. *Sitting Bull, Champion of the Sioux.* P 46-47. University of Nebraska Press. 1937. And ; Edward S. Curtis. *The North American Indian.* Vol. IV. "Crow and Atsina." P. 100. 1905
31 Lowie, Robert H. "Crow Material Culture." P. 260. Anthropological papers; American Museum of Natural History. Vol. XX1. See also; Joe Medicine Crow, Interview with Author. Lodge Grass, Montana. 1994. Note pad 1. P.12.
32 Vestal., Stanley. *Sitting Bull, Champion of the Sioux.* between pp. 266-267. Pictograph no. 6. And p. 317. University of Nebraska Press. 1937.
33 Charles A. Eastman in his book, *Indian heroes and Great Chieftains* p. 108. [1918], mistakenly states – from what he professed was Sioux testimony—that during the hand to hand knife fight between the Crow chief (who Eastman does not name) and the Hunkpapa Jumping Bull, both dealt the other a mortal blow. Jumping Bull, so Eastman said, fell from his saddle and died in a few minutes while his opponent died later from the effects of his wounds.
34 Vestal., Stanley. *Sitting Bull, Champion of the Sioux.* P 47. University of Nebraska Press. 1937.
35 Barney Old Coyote. Crow Indian Informant. Crow Agency. Montana. August. 2004. Note pad 1. P.4.
36 Barney Old Coyote. Crow Indian Informant. Crow Agency. Montana. August. 2004. Note pad 1. P.4. See also; Joe Medicine Crow to Author. Note pad 3. p.5. Joe Medicine Crow asserts that Mountain Chief had been given this bell by the Jesuit Priest, Father DeSmet whom he met at the Fitzpatrick Treaty in 1851. The Priest, Joe added, when previously visiting the Crows, had been in the habit of ringing a hand bell to announce his coming and this bell, being regarded by the Indians as a symbol of the Black Gown's power which emanated from the Great Spirit itself, was much sought after by Mountain Chief, who repeatedly pestered the Priest to present it to him either in trade or as a gift. The chief believed that if he himself possessed such an object, then it could be used as a powerful war-medicine against his people's enemies. Other tribal informants state that the aforesaid chief had merely procured a similar bell from one or another white trader with whom he was in contact, although for the same reason of using it as a war-medicine.
37 Joe Medicine Crow, Interview with Author. Lodge Grass, Montana. 1994. Note pad 1. P. 13.
38 Joe Medicine Crow, Interview with Author. Lodge Grass, Montana. 1994. Note pad 1. P. 13.
39 Edward S. Curtis. *The North American Indian.* Vol. IV. "Crow and Atsina." Pp. 101 and 102. 1905
40 Vestal., Stanley. *Sitting Bull, Champion of the Sioux.* P 47. University of Nebraska Press. 1937.
41 Vestal, Stanley. *New Sources of Indian History.* P. 328. University of Oklahoma Press. 1934.
42 Barney Old-Coyote (Crow informant) to Author. Crow Agency. August 2004. Note pad 1. P. 13. See also; James H.Howard, *Dakota Winter-counts as Sources of History.* pp.385-386, Smithsonian Institution, Bureau of American Ethnology, bulletin. 173. 1960. And Garrick Mallery, "Picture writing of the American Indians." Tenth Annual report of the Bureau of American Ethnology, Smithsonian Institution, 1888-89.
43 Joe Medicine Crow, Interviews with Author. Lodge Grass, Montana. 1994. Note pad 1. P. 14.
44 Of the Sioux accounts [See p. 227. This volume] which refer to the great running battle at Rain Hill, several Teton Sioux winter-counts make reference to it, although there does appear to have been some confusion in the memories of the respective keepers of the counts as to

whether the event actually occurred in 1857,`58, or `59. The High Dog Winter count records for the period 1857/58, "They returned from battle with the Crows, having killed many." Here the pictograph shows a man sporting the customary enemy hairstyle always associated with the Crows and in addition, shows three feathered coup sticks touching the man's head. Swift Dog on the other hand, depicts triumphant Sioux warriors returning from battle, but gives no explanation.[Fig.1.]. Similarly, in the count of His Battle (His Fights), [Fig.2.], also known in later years as Jaw, the caption reads for the same year of 1857/58,"They bring [home] many kills," The pictograph associated with this entry represents the head of a man wearing the same style of enemy hair arrangement as in the High Dog count, but now with the top of the head missing its scalp. The same man is also shown being taken by the hand by a Sioux warrior, which is to indicate to the observer that captives were taken by the Sioux on this occasion. Most probably, this too is a reference to the Rain Hill fight, although it has also been suggested that the event refers to a time the Hunkpapa Sioux had a big fight with Assiniboins in 1857, at which time Sitting Bull the Hunkpapa chief, took a young Assiniboin boy captive who he later adopted as his brother. The captive Assiniboine's name was Plenty Kills which would explain the winter-count caption. He was known among the Sioux themselves as Little-Assiniboin and alternatively as Jumping Bull, a name Sitting Bull himself later bestowed upon him in memory of his own father killed by the Crow chief Big Otter during the battle at Rainy Butte. However, if such was indeed the event intended to be recorded, then the figure portrayed would not be shown missing his scalp which, of course, indicates in Indian symbolism that the person so depicted had been killed. Lone Dog, for his part, depicts the slaying of the Crow woman in the Sioux camp by a Miniconjou brave named White Robe.[Fig.3.]. In yet another winter-count produced by the Yanktonais Sioux Blue Thunder, the death of the Hunkpapa Jumping Bull (Sitting Bull`s father) is inserted as occurring in the year 1858/59 and also mentioned is the fact that the Crows attacked while the Sioux camp was on the move. Conversely, however, the caption then goes on to state, "no one killed that winter." C. F. James H. Howard, "Dakota Winter-counts as Sources of History." pp.385-386, Smithsonian Institution, Bureau of American Ethnology, bulletin 173. 1960. See also; Garrick Mallery, "Picture writing of the American Indians." (various entries between 1857 and 1859). Tenth Annual report of the Bureau of American Ethnology, Smithsonian Institution, 1888-89.

Chapter Twelve

"The Place of Mourning"

Early one morning, five or six days after the debacle at Rain Hill, the remnants of the decimated Crow party reached home. Gone were the Pipe Holders, Bull Rises Small and Blackbird on the Ground. In their stead were the indomitable Big Otter, Mountain Chief and Sits in the Middle of the Land, along with Iron Bull nursing his wounded thigh, leading the survivors on their dilapidated mounts.

The combined populations of both the Mountain and Kicked-in-the-Belly bands were, at that time, still encamped together, although they had since moved from Arrow Creek and their hundreds of clay-whitened, buffalo hide tepees now straddled a southern tributary of the Yellowstone known as Fly Creek, the course of which was then flanked intermittingly by growths of cottonwoods, as it ran through an open stretch of prairie between low ridges on either side.

It was around midday, when a number of village occupants observed a lone figure standing atop one of the aforesaid ridges, some short distance from the camps. The figure was on foot and appeared to be singing a doleful song.

Many villagers stopped what they were doing and stared intently at the strange spectacle, not knowing exactly what or who it might be. At length, a keen-eyed tribesman said that the figure was a man dressed in what appeared to be Crow apparel, whereupon, whispers circulated that perhaps he was a member of one of the parties which had gone out several weeks before, although whether the figure was heralding the return of Big Shadow`s party, which had gone west into Shoshoni country or, that of Bull Rises Small and Blackbird on the Ground which had gone east against the Sioux, no one could deter-

Author's photo

Fly Creek. "The Place of Mourning."

mine. All agreed, however, that something bad must have happened on the war trail. [1] But still the people did not go forth to meet him. Rather, they stood patiently and in silence, waiting to see what would happen next.

They did not wait long before the man on the ridge-top slowly untied the blanket robe from around his waist and holding it by two corners with outstretched arms, raised it chest high before letting it drop to the ground. This action he repeated four times, which was to indicate that a great disaster had occurred and as the people continued to watch, they did so with bated breath.

Many of the spectators at last recognized the lone figure as one who had gone east with Bull Rises Small and Blackbird on the Ground and while they stood watching, the man suddenly ceased his wailing,; rolled up his blanket and grasping one end in his right hand, began striking it on the ground beside him. Those looking on knew only too well what was meant, for each time the robe struck the ground, it represented a tribesman slain, perhaps his body left in the enemy country, to be picked and devoured by wild beasts of the prairie and their winged compatriots of the air. [2]

The villagers watched the figure's every move, while a low keening sound slowly emanated from the throats of the womenfolk, although, as yet, none could have known if any close family members were among those missing. Nevertheless, the fact that Crow tribesmen had been killed, was reason enough to express mutual sadness in a communal manner.

And so it was that the man's robe struck the ground time and again. For many Crows would not be coming home this day.

After striking his rolled-up blanket for the eighteenth time, the lone figure vacated the crest and disappeared from view. At the same time, the villagers in small groups, returned to their respective lodges and soon, not a soul could be seen in the camps.[3]

Still the returning warriors did not come in, but remained ensconced behind a low ridge on one side of the valley. Here they recuperated from their grueling trek and tidied themselves and their war ponies as best they could.

It was many hours later, after the sun dipped behind the western horizon and twilight enveloped the land, that the survivors of the luckless foray—leading their mounts by twisted buffalo hair lariats—walked silently and slowly into camp. Each went directly to his own family lodge where, separately and in their own way, they informed their immediate kinfolk of all that had happened at the place called Rain Hill.

In the darkness of the night, heart-rending laments and pitiful sounds of grieving grew ever louder, as relative after relative reacted to the terrible news of a loved one lost. Soon, it seemed, both camps were filled with sorrow and despair. Mothers and wives gashed their foreheads and bodies with sharpened stones and hacked off a finger joint to show the loss of a husband, brother or son. They screamed and wailed until they were hoarse, while the men folk moaned monotonous dirges or hummed sorrowful lamentations for a brave son or brother, who would not be seen again in the world of the living.

No Mane, the father of brave young Iron Eyes, whose body had been left in the Sioux Country, was besotted with grief and self-recrimination. Alone he sat in his lodge quietly smoking a long-stemmed pipe, waiting in forlorn hope that his beloved son would appear at the tepee door. But as the hours of darkness dragged by and there was no sign of Iron Eyes, No Mane knew within himself that his son must be counted among the dead. At length, he rose to his feet and going to the lodge of one who had returned with the decimated party, No Mane inquired, "How went the fight at Rain Hill?" [4]

This survivor of the fight was none other than Big Otter—the slayer of Sitting Bull`s father. He replied that the expedition had gone very bad for the Crows. Iron Eyes, he said, had been among those who bravely stood their ground and forfeited their lives so that others might live.

"When last I saw your son," Big Otter told No Mane, "he was facing the enemy alone, fighting to give his comrades time to escape. I saw one-hundred Sioux around him and from the mound where I sat my horse, I saw him covered up by the foe." [5]

These words sank deep into No Mane`s heart. He collapsed to the ground as if struck a mortal blow. Upon recovering his senses, he cried aloud his sorrow and made it known how much he regretted the words he had spoken, which, he believed, had induced his son to sacrifice his life in the first place. In accordance with custom he took up his knife and gashed himself many times in the arms and legs, then limped around the lodges lamenting his great misfortune, as the blood flowed profusely from his wounds. He cut his long hair short, dressed himself in worn-out lodge skins and without washing the dried blood from his face and body, spent the coming days and nights bemoaning his loss. During the daylight hours he went out alone among the hills to contemplate his grief and at night, retired to his lodge where he mourned till dawn, crying continually, so that all could hear as he repeated time and again,

> "Iron-Eyes, Iron-Eyes my son, on your bay horse with the short split ears. I will see you no more. I did not know it would be this way. If I had one-hundred sons none would be like Iron-Eyes, my son; my beloved son." [6]

Numerous relatives of those slain also went unto hills overlooking the camps at Fly Creek. They remained out for many weeks both day and night; grieving their loss. Those who stayed among the lodges sympathized with their plight and felt deeply their pangs of abject sorrow. But now they anxiously awaited the return of chief Big Shadow's party, which had gone west into Shoshoni country.

Plain Feather told Joe Medicine Crow that Big Otter survived that dreadful day at Rain Hill (even though the Sioux at first, thought Sitting Bull had killed him during the pursuit across the prairie) and it was Big Otter, among several others in the returning party, who could justifiably boast of earning war deeds that day. However, the most prominent deeds, so the chief's council later agreed, had been performed by Mountain Chief, while rescuing numerous unhorsed comrades and the people bestowed honors upon him accordingly. The majority of survivors cared not to celebrate their deeds. Instead, they skulked around the lodges, constantly moaning, as they contemplated their luckless venture. [7]

Then it happened, only a few days later while the camp occupants were still expressing grief for those lost against the Sioux, that, likewise, after the sun went down, the returning members of Big Shadow's party also filed into camp. These too, without pomp or ceremony which, customarily, would have heralded the return of a successful expedition.

They also brought news of disaster, made apparent by wounded warriors borne home on pole-drags and a number of stiff and lifeless bodies wrapped in blankets, draped over the withers of their horses. One of these blanket-wrapped bundles contained the stiff corpse of the head man of the Kicked-in-the-Belly band; the once towering form of the great chief Big Shadow himself. [8]

The account of what happened to Big Shadow's party and how the head chief met his death, would in time, also pass into tribal folklore as another important episode of heroic conflict in the history of the Absaroka people and is commonly known as "The Battle of Crow-Heart Butte."

Big Shadow's Last Fight

It had been two full moons since Big Shadow and his followers left the combined Mountain and Kicked-in-the-Belly Crow camps then located along Arrow Creek. At that time, Big Shadow's cavalcade, consisting of around sixty lodges with some 370 men, women and children, had traveled southwest across the Big Horn Basin into the valley of the lower course of Wind River, hunting buffalo and antelope and tanning hides as they went.[9] Big Shadow had appeared confident that his band was formidable enough to deter attack from any party of hostiles it may happen to meet, although—as usual among the Crows—scouts were constantly out looking for enemy sign. For it was well-known that Red Cloud's Oglala and certain Northern Cheyenne bands were in the habit of frequenting the same region during this time of year, in order to hunt, cut lodge poles and generally harass any band of enemies that might be encountered by accident or design. On the other hand, Shoshoni and Bannocks might also be abroad conducting their own summer hunts, although it had previously been a matter of indifference to the Crows whether they fought the Shoshoni or not.

However, since the destruction of the Red Lodge camp one winter past, it had been agreed among the Crows, that a Shoshoni presence would no longer be tolerated in a peaceable manner and it has been noted how Big Shadow himself had sworn an oath of vengeance upon all Shoshoni-speaking peoples and was resolved to inflict whatever damage possible upon any and all Shoshonis his band should meet.

Now it happened that this same band of Crows set their tepees along the north bank of Wind River near the present-day town of Kinnear, Wyoming, close to a place now known as "Ford`s Crossing," this being about twenty miles above the town of Riverton and was the point where various war and hunting bands customarily crossed from one side of the river to the other.[10]

At this same time, a large band of Shoshoni under their head chief Washakie, was already encamped not far distant along the south side of the North Fork of Popo Agie Creek, a branch of the Little Wind River close to where the small town of Lander now stands. [11]

Both the Crows and Shoshoni had scouts out reconnoitering the surrounding country and were aware of each other's presence. In earlier years it had been the custom when in close proximity in this area, that a party of emissaries from both tribes would pay a friendly visit to their opposite number in order to make a temporary truce, which would then enable them to hunt the region in peace and depart to their respective tribal territories without fear of being attacked.

The Shoshoni version states emphatically that it was the Shoshoni, initially, who held out the olive branch and while so doing, were treacherously attacked by the Crows, although according to present-day Crow oral tradition, it were they themselves at this time, who first made peaceful overtures to the Shoshoni.

Considering, however, the earlier oath-taking by Big Shadow to exact revenge upon those who destroyed the Red Lodge, the Shoshoni account appears more plausible, while the Crow version—in all likelihood—is used to disguise what actually happened, albeit, staying within the bounds of truth, in so much, that the Crows had pre-planned to lure the unsuspecting Shoshoni into a situation in which the Crows themselves would have the advantage. Such would have been regarded as an ingenious tactic on their part, which was the mentality of all Indians at that date, who always regarded it an accepted facet

Wyoming Chamber of Commerce photograph

Crow Heart Butte

of warfare between the hostile tribes, to employ whatever ruse was deemed necessary to bring defeat upon the foe.

Indeed, a Shoshoni account of the entire episode—narrated in 1890 by a veteran Shoshoni-Flathead warrior later known as Old Man Enos—who actually took part in the fight as a member of chief Washakie`s band—stated that the Crows had sent a message to the Shoshoni camp, suggesting that their two peoples meet and arrange a truce, whereby, they could unite their forces while they continued their hunts and, if need be, confront their mutual Sioux and Cheyenne enemies together if any of the latter's war bands should appear in strength.[12]

According to Joe Medicine Crow`s Crow version of events, when most of the Crow fighting men were away hunting, a large group of Crow women, children and middle-aged men rode over to the Shoshoni camp on what was intended to be a friendly visit. The Shoshonis welcomed them as was the custom whenever erstwhile enemies came in peace and also, in accordance with what was usual on such occasions, the Shoshoni menfolk and those among the Crows, lined up facing each other on their war-ponies and proceeded to go through the motions of a sham battle, with no thoughts of doing actual injury to one another.

Now among the Shoshonis at this time, were a few of their Bannock allies and it were they who, rather than perform the customary mock

Photographer: Rose and Hopkins
Denver Public Library Western History Collection
Washakie, chief of the Shoshoni.

conflict, took the matter more seriously and started a bloodletting fight, with the intent of killing those they still regarded as their virulent foes. The Crows—most of whom were non-combatants with but few fighting men among them—were at the mercy of the Bannocks and in the general furor that followed, not a few Shoshonis also joined in the fray on the side of their allies.

Several Crow men were killed outright while others, including seventeen or eighteen male teenagers were taken captive and the remainder, scattered across the countryside in confusion and terror.

During the melee, the mother of a young Crow girl and boy told her son who later bore the name Rises Up, to mount a fast horse and take word of the attack to the Crow warriors hunting somewhere to the north. This her son did and managed to outdistance his Bannock pursuers. The mother, however, was killed in the fight at the camp and her daughter—then twelve or thirteen years old—was taken captive by Chief Washakie`s son, named Snow Bird.[13]

Washakie probably wasn't present at this time, nor was any other Shoshoni chief with the authority to stop the conflict. But later that day, having been fully appraised of what had happened, the Shoshoni chiefs immediately sent an embassy to the main Crow camp with words of sorrow and regret for what had occurred. The emissaries also carried gifts and promises that they would make reparation to the families of those killed. In addition, they sent back the seventeen or eighteen teenage Crow captives—albeit with their long hair cut short to indicate their being regarded as having no warrior status—as an extra token of Shoshoni goodwill.

In this endeavor, a well-known Shoshoni sub-chief named Little Sun, along with four male companions and one woman—this last accompanying the party to indicate its peaceful mission—rode over to the place at Ford`s Crossing where they expected to meet with the

Crows. As the five Shoshonis came near, there was no sign of hostile intent, but the Crows—after the embassy had ridden boldly into their midst—suddenly expressed their true intentions by promptly slaying five of the embassy, including the chief Little Sun. The lone Shoshoni woman managed to whip up her pony and escape, though hotly pursued by a number of Crow warriors.[14]

In another account, it is stated that only one Shoshoni man and one woman comprised the embassy which went to meet with the Crows, although it is agreed that the woman, after her male companion had been killed, escaped and took word of the treacherous deed to Washakie.[15]

When the Shoshoni chiefs and warriors heard from the woman what had happened to their embassy, they were eager to avenge themselves. But knowing that the Crows were in formidable number, they were hesitant to immediately ride out and confront them. It was then that Chief Washakie took command.

Washakie sent runners to the nearby Bannock camp situated along the Popo Agie, near where the town of Hudson, Wyoming now stands, with a request to the Bannock chief named Taghee, to come and assist his Shoshoni allies against the common enemy. The Bannock chief sent back word that he and his warriors would respond in force, although it would be the next day before they could prepare themselves properly for battle and reach the Shoshoni camp. In the meantime, while awaiting the arrival of the Bannocks, Washakie organized a night raid upon the Crow village, during which, his warriors succeeded in driving off a large number of Crow horses.[16]

On the third day, before noon, the Shoshoni chief led his force out in battle array and positioned his braves in a long line on an open stretch of ground facing that of the Crows, who, by this time, had also arrayed themselves in battle order only a half-mile away with chief Big Shadow at their head.

For a while, neither body of warriors attempted to engage the other in combat. Instead, several of the opposing braves merely raced their ponies to and fro along their opposite lines in the no man's land between the two, drawing forth a few harmless missiles from smoothbore fusils and bows and arrows, so that little if no injury was suffered on either side, save a few bruises or a broken leg or arm caused by being thrown from a stumbling pony. Others rode out in front of their lines and shouted challenges and abuse across the field.

Another account of the battle tells how, during this particular period of confrontation, the Crow chief Big Shadow shouted abuse at the Shoshoni war-chief, calling him, "A squaw and old woman; too afraid to fight." [17]

And as the Shoshoni chief raised his arm ready to signal his warriors to charge, a well-aimed Crow arrow pierced his hand and prevented him giving the command.[18]

When however, the Bannocks eventually arrived on the scene and joined forces with their Shoshoni allies, so they deemed themselves an adequate match for the Crows, Chief Washakie did order a mass charge.

A terrible clash of arms ensued, during which the Shoshoni and Bannocks succeeded in gaining the advantage. They drove the Crows upstream along the river bank and only the setting of the sun caused the Allies to desist and retire for the night.[19]

The Crows also returned to their lodges. As the hours of darkness passed, scouts from the opposing forces kept constant watch on each other's camps, made possible by the glow of lodge fires which lit up the night sky above them.

The Crows appeared to be in no hurry to leave the area, even though the Shoshoni and Bannocks believed they had beaten them by driving them upriver during that day's fighting. On the contrary, the Crows were still full of fight and merely awaiting daybreak when they would renew the contest.

What happened next is somewhat clouded by myth and legend, but without doubt, is an important episode in both Crow and Shoshoni history.

At sunrise the following day, the opposing forces again lined up facing each other on their spirited ponies. Throughout the morning, charges and counter-charges were made. Every time the opposing parties clashed in hand-to-hand combat, several warriors were slain and seriously injured on both sides. But at length, the Crows drove the enemy back, forcing them up a nearby hill known as Black Mountain, close to the heads of Crow Creek and Red Creek. They drove the Shoshonis over the crest and sent them spilling down the other side in disarray.[20]

The battleground now covered a wide area. Warriors were spread out over the hillside and on the plain below on its far side, battling each other in small groups, as countless numbers of loose ponies raced in every direction.

Photographer D. F. Barry
Denver Public Library Western History Collection-
Crow Indian, War Man

At the point when the Shoshoni and Bannocks first topped the crest, while trying to hold back the onrush of Crows, one of their number raced off to the Shoshoni camp, where he told the non-combatants of the village to pack up and move away, as the enemy was getting too close for comfort and might carry the fight to the door flaps of the lodges. The Shoshoni womenfolk, who could see fighting going on along the crest of the hill and down its visible slope, began to cry and wail; some taking out their butcher knives as if preparing to defend themselves if the enemy should get into the camp. Others hid themselves under overhanging ledges along the bank of Crow Creek and were making such a commotion, wailing and bemoaning what they thought would be their fate, it was later said that if the Crows had not been preoccupied in fighting Shoshoni warriors, they would have discovered the women and children under the cut-bank and easily killed them all or taken them captive.[21]

Indeed, it now seemed that the Crows would win the day.

The Shoshoni chief Washakie was charging around on a buckskin-colored horse, while shouting encouragement to his warriors, and instilled new heart into them and together, made a sudden concerted effort to turn the tide. The Shoshoni and Bannocks went crashing into the Crow ranks, driving them back up and over the crest and down the other side from whence they came. They continued chasing the Crows as the latter fled across flat country north of what today is called Tea Pot Butte, which stands about one mile east of a small stream known as Dry Creek.[22]

Despite their earlier success, the Crows were utterly routed and lost thirty warriors killed with many more seriously injured during this part of the fight.[22] It was probably during this phase of battle that the Chief Big Shadow met his death.

There is a story current today in the mythology of the Old West, which tells how Chief Washakie, who wanted to break the stalemate, challenged the Crow chief Big Shadow, saying that they should meet in combat, The members of the losing tribe would leave the region. Chief Big Shadow—so the story continues—accepted the challenge. Big Shadow, was armed with a long lance and bull-hide shield, while his adversary Washakie wielded a long cavalry saber. They charged towards each other on horseback. The Crows, meanwhile, had lined up on one side of the wide stretch of open ground on which the contest was taking place and the Shoshonis and Bannocks on the other. The duel between the two chiefs went back and forth for some time. Finally, by applying his sword with great dexterity, Washakie managed to get the upper hand and eventually, killed his Crow opponent. As the victor, the Shoshoni chief then cut out the heart of his adversary and ate it in order to obtain the spirit of his brave victim.[23]

If there is any truth in such a story, then it would be more likely that one or other of the chiefs in question may well have challenged their opposite number (as was customary among the tribes) and during fight the Crow chief was slain. Another version states only that the Shoshoni chief after cutting out Big Shadow`s heart, stuck it on the iron tip of his lance and later, paraded the grisly trophy among his people during the victory dances which followed. This seems to be the more authentic scenario.[24]

Certainly, this second version is more acceptable, as the Shoshoni informant Old-Man Enos who was actually involved in the battle, coupled with certain statements made by other tribal informants, make no mention of Washakie`s heart-eating episode. They also did not even mention the supposed duel between the chiefs. Big Shadow probably was killed by some other Shoshoni. Another account of the battle does imply that there was another Shoshoni war chief present besides Washakie.[25] It might have been this chief who dueled with Big Shadow. It may have been a Shoshoni chief named Cut Nose or Split Nose, whose seventeen-lodge camp, we know, was at a later date destroyed and its occupants annihilated by a Kicked-in-the-Belly Crow party seeking revenge specifically for Big Shadow`s death.[26]

Whatever the case, the death of their chief threw the Crows into a panic. They abandoned their tepee covers and camp equipment and together, with their women and children fled across the Owl Mountains and back into the Big Horn Basin, with a large number of Shoshoni and Bannocks in pursuit.[27]

Chief Washakie with about 100 Shoshoni and Bannock warriors, continued to chase the fleeing Crows until darkness forced an end to that day's conflict. Throughout the chase, Crow warriors would, every now and then, turn their ponies around and confront their pursuers, who were obliged to rein in their mounts, thus allowing time for the fleeing Crow women and children to put more distance between themselves and the foe. In reality, Washakie's plan was to split the Crow force in two, heading them off in different directions so they would not be able to effectively regroup. The Allies could then destroy the Crow groups piecemeal. To assist Washakie in this design, 100 fresh ponies were sent out from the Shoshoni camp in order to replace those that must have been run to near exhaustion.

A teenage boy who was in the Shoshoni camp at the time, later stated that after pursuing the fleeing Crows and darkness had fallen, about 100 wounded Shoshoni and Bannock warriors were brought into the Shoshoni camp. One poor fellow, the account states, had his nose shot off and one eye shot out. Others were so badly injured that it was obvious that they would not live long. [28]

One prominent Shoshoni war chief (Split Nose?) had gunshot wounds in an arm and leg, although not serious enough to threaten his life. It was this same war-chief who, with a band of fresh warriors, rode out next morning to again give combat to the Crows.

At the same time, a number of Shoshoni and Bannock boys were ordered to go over the battlefield on Black Mountain and across the flat land below in order to scare away the buzzards and coyotes and thereby, prevent them eating the dead and severely injured Shoshoni and Bannock warriors who still lay where they had fallen.[29]

Many Shoshoni and Bannock men and women later wandered over the battlefield and along the route of the Crow retreat. They retrieved the bloodied corpses of their dead kinfolk and scalped every dead Crow they found. Old men too wandered over the field, collecting spent arrows to be used again in future conflicts, along with other items once belonging to the enemy and deemed of some value.

The Shoshonis carried the bodies of their dead kinfolk to a deep washout, where they were laid to rest covered with earth and rocks.[30]

Today on the east side of Dry Creek, there is a large sandstone rock, upon which are etched numerous depictions commemorating this Shoshoni victory over the Crows just north of Tea Pot Butte. As late as 1890, many iron arrow heads, lance points and other artifacts could still be seen littering the ground, while in the side of a collapsed part of a nearby cut-bank, human skulls and bones lay exposed; many showing signs of wounds received in battle. These, one assumes, were the remains of Shoshoni dead, killed during the fierce fighting at that time and laid to rest in the side of the washout.[31]

Not until darkness fell on the fifth day of battle, did most of the Shoshoni and Bannock warriors finally return to their camp. This time, they drove before them a herd of more than 250 captured Crow ponies. In addition, they carried with them countless newly-tanned buffalo robes and bundles of fresh deer hides, blankets, bows, arrows, iron axes and guns, all abandoned by the Crows and taken as well-earned booty by the victors.[32]

The Shoshoni and Bannocks had succeeded in splitting the Crow force. A small party of Crows, comprising twenty-three warriors, became separated from their main body and being closely pressed by a much larger number of enemies, were somehow turned around in their flight and forced south towards Wind River.[33] Surrounded on all sides, this small band of Crows desperately searched for a place to make their stand. They raced their ponies towards a prominent butte not far north of the middle course of the river.

This butte has long been known to Indian peoples familiar with the country. It consists of a high flattop mesa incorporating a few acres with steep sloping sides, offering a strong defensive position. No water is to be found either on top of the butte or around its base and any besieged party on its summit was at a great disadvantage if forced to remain there more than a few days and nights. It stands about thirty miles south of the town of Dubois, Wyoming and is very close to the AYP Highway leading to present-day Yellowstone Park.

Denver Public Library
Western History Collection

Crow warrior Yellow Dog
Also known as Old Coyote.

Ironically, it had been on top of this same butte some eighteen years earlier, that a warband of between forty and fifty Blackfeet had been besieged by a combined force of Crow and Shoshoni, who at that time were at peace with one another.

It had occurred early one morning, that a Blackfoot war party attacked the then combined Crow-Shoshoni camp close to Wind River and in the ensuing mêlée, the Crows and Shoshoni drove the raiders back and obliged them to seek safety on top of the butte. Several times the Crows and Shoshoni charged the height—but to no avail—and the enemy remained firmly entrenched atop their rocky refuge. The Crows and Shoshoni then decided to lay siege and starve their enemies out. They completely surrounded the butte and there they stayed many days and nights, preventing any from escaping off the hill top. On the tenth day of the siege, a small number of Blackfeet came off the butte and went boldly to the Crows and Shoshoni, perhaps in an attempt to make peace, but these men were promptly killed and after this, no more of the Blackfeet attempted to leave the height. For a few days thereafter, the Crows and Shoshoni continued the siege, until on the twelfth day, they finally ascended the slopes and there on the summit, found the remaining Blackfoot warriors lying dead to the last man. Evidently, they had succumbed to a lack of food and water. The Shoshoni account further states that two or three days later, a number of Crow and Shoshoni women climbed the butte in order to inspect the scene where so many of their foes had perished. When these women reached the summit, they discovered a great number of crows, magpies and other winged scavengers, along with coyotes and pack rats devouring the Blackfoot corpses. It was from this fact, so most Indian informants used to say, that ever after, both the Crows and Shoshoni always referred to the rocky height in question, as “Crow Heart Butte.” [34]

Whether this small party of Crow warriors knew the story of the Blackfoot war party once besieged on this same butte, one can only guess. As there was nowhere else in the vicinity where they could make a stand, such knowledge would not have made much difference.

Having taken refuge atop the butte, these twenty-three Crows defended themselves bravely against several attempts by the enemy to scale the height and overrun their position. A small number of Shoshoni and Bannock warriors lost their lives in these attacks. At length, Chief Washakie realized the futility of continuing such assaults. He instructed his warriors to surround the base of the butte and lay siege, until the Crows either succumbed through lack of food and water or, in desperation attempted to break through their enemy’s ranks. The attackers waited several days until there was no sound or sign of movement on the hilltop, then advanced to finish off the Crows.

It is said that the attackers carried all before them, although it seems that little effective resistance was offered by the besieged, due to a scarcity of ammunition among them and the small number of defenders still able to resist. The fight ended quickly. An additional twenty-three bloody Crow scalps in the hands of the victors who, so it was said by the Shoshoni informant Old Man Enos, then cut out the hearts of the dead Crows and ate them, so that the bravery of their enemies might be transferred to themselves.[35] (Perhaps then, this is the actual event which, later, gave rise to the story that Chief Washakie cut out the Crow chief’s heart and ate it).

Throughout the four- to five-day period of fighting, according to one account, forty-nine Shoshonis lost their lives and about 100 injured. This same source also claimed 103 Crows were killed. We can only be certain that fifty-three Crows were killed, although their wounded must have been at least twice or maybe three times that number. [36]

After a few weeks had passed—long enough for the Shoshoni wounded to be fit enough to travel—most of Washakie's people moved camp to Rock Creek and from there, went south to Salt Lake City, ostensibly to trade with the Mormon settlers, but also, in order to seek refuge close to their well-armed white friends. For it was widely believed that the Crows would soon seek vengeance for the great loss and humiliation they had recently suffered in the Wind River country.[37]

The Shoshoni war chief Split Nose and his following remained in the Wind River area, defiant and arrogant in their conviction that they could successfully oppose any enemies they should encounter.

Most Crow prisoners among the Shoshonis were eventually reunited with their own people, although the young sister of the Crow boy Rises Up, who had escaped the initial attack upon the Crow noncombatants, remained among her captors the rest of her days. During her first three years of captivity, she lived in the lodge of the Shoshoni warrior Snow Bird (son of Chief Washakie). She was then known by the Shoshoni name *Ah-ah-why-per-sie,* meaning simply, "Crow Maiden" and was the title she bore ever after. However, when in 1861, her captor Snow Bird was killed fighting the Sioux and Cheyenne, Washakie himself took her into his own lodge, as was the custom, in order that she continue to be fed and cared for within the tribe and later, after she had reached full womanhood, the old chief took her as his second wife and she bore him three sons.[38]

Many years later, after intertribal warfare ceased and the Indians were confined to their respective reservations, a party of Crows paid a friendly visit to their old Shoshoni enemies. During their sojourn in the Shoshoni camp, a middle-aged Crow woman thought she recognized Washakie`s young wife as once having been her childhood friend. When the Crow woman asked her if this was so, *Ah-ah-why-per-sie* broke down in tears and replied,

> "Yes, I am that person. For a long time I yearned to see my family and friends, but now I have children of my own and can never leave them to go back and live among my own people." [39]

She then asked if her brother was still alive and was told that his name was now Rises Up and that he too had a wife and children. One of Rises Up's sons later became the wise and respected tribal councillor of the Absaroka and government Senator Robert Yellow Tail, who was the father of the author's friend, Winona Plenty Hoops.

Thus, the Crow captive who became the Shoshoni chief's wife was Robert Yellow Tail's aunt and since those days, these two illustrious families among both the Crows and Shoshoni have always considered themselves related.

Such then are the circumstances surrounding the demise of the famous head chief Big Shadow and of the humiliating defeat suffered by his luckless band at the hands of their Shoshoni enemies.

And so it was that the arrival of this second defeated party into the camps then strung out along Fly Creek, coupled with details attending its misfortune, could not have come at a more inopportune time. The general atmosphere of sorrow already engulfing the Crow lodges due to losses sustained during the debacle around Rain Hill, now reached new heights as additional losses incurred in the Shoshoni country were made known to the people. The piteous wailing and abject grief expressed by Crow womenfolk caused despondency and despair to permeate every lodge. Not one family among the whole Kicked-in-the-Belly band, it seemed, had not suffered the recent death of a kinsman.

From that day forward, the site where then stood the combined Mountain and Kicked-in-the-Belly camps, has ever since been known among the Crows as "The Place of Mourning" or, more simply, *Anmaal-apammu`ua,* meaning "Where They Wailed." [40]

NOTES AND SOURCES.

1 Joe Medicine Crow, Interview with Author. Lodge Grass, Montana. 1994. Note pad 1. P.12.
2 Ibid.*Loc; cit.*
3 Ibid. *Loc; cit.*
4 Joe Medicine Crow, Interview with Author. Lodge Grass, Montana. 1994. Note pad 1. P.12. See also; Edward S. Curtis. *The North American Indian. Vol. IV.* "Crow and Atsina." Pp. 99-100. 1905
5 Joe Medicine Crow, Interview with Author. Lodge Grass, Montana. 1994. Note pad 1. P.12. See also; Edward S. Curtis. *The North American Indian. Vol. IV.* "Crow and Atsina." Pp. 99-100. 190
6 Edward S. Curtis. *The North American Indian. Vol. IV.* "Crow and Atsina." Pp. 99-100. 1905
7 Joe Medicine Crow, Interview with Author. Lodge Grass, Montana. 1994. Note pad 1. P.13.
8 Joe Medicine Crow, Interview with Author. Lodge Grass, Montana. 1994. Note pad `1. P.13.
9 Joe Medicine Crow, Interview with Author. Lodge Grass, Montana. 1994. Note pad 1. P.13.
10 Crabb, Edward L. Letter to Hebard, Grace R. *papers.* May 26, 1927. "Old Enos account of the battle at Crow Heart Butte." Hebard collection. Accession 400,008 – *Washakie manuscript* - Box no. 58. Folder 18. University of Wyoming.
11 Hebard, Grace R. *"papers." "Old Enos account." Loc; cit.*
12 Hebard, Grace R. *"papers." "Old Enos account." Loc; cit.*
13 Hebard, Grace R. *"papers." "Old Enos account." Loc; cit.*
14 Crabb, Edward L. Letter to Hebard, Grace R. *papers.* May 26, 1927. "Old Enos account of the battle at Crow Heart Butte." Hebard collection. Accession 400,008 – *Washakie manuscript* - Box no. 58. Folder 18. University of Wyoming.
15 Trenholm, Virginia C. *The Shoshonis.* P. 173. University of Oklahoma Press. 1964.
16 Joe Medicine Crow, Interview with Author. Lodge Grass, Montana. 1994. Note pad 1. P.13.
17 Trenholm, Virginia C. *The Shoshonis.* P. 173. University of Oklahoma Press. 1964. See also; Joe Medicine Crow, Interview with Author. Lodge Grass, Montana. 1994. Note pad 1. P.13.
18 Trenholm, Virginia C. *The Shoshoni,s* P. 173. University of Oklahoma Press. 1964.
19 Wilson, Elijah Nicholas. *The White Indian Boy.* Pp. 93-94. [edited by Howard R. Driggs]. Paragon Press. Salt Lake. Utah.1991.
20 Wilson, Elijah Nicholas. *The White Indian Boy.* P. 92. [edited by Howard R. Driggs]. Paragon Press. Salt Lake. Utah. 1991.
21 Crabb, Edward L. Letter to Hebard, Grace R. *papers.* May 26, 1927. "Old Enos account of the battle at Crow Heart Butte." Hebard collection. Accession 400,008 – *Washakie manuscript* - Box no. 58. Folder 18. University of Wyoming.
22 Hebard, Grace R. *"papers." "Old Enos account."* Loc; cit.
23 Trenholm, Virginia C. *The Shoshonis.* P. 173. University of Oklahoma Press. 1964.
24 Trenholm, Virginia C. *The Shoshonis.* Pp.173-174 University of Oklahoma Press. 1964. See also; Compton, J. E. *"letter to Grace Hebard."* January 28th. 1927. Hebard collection. Accession 400,008 – *Washakie manuscript* - Box no. 58. Folder 18. University of Wyoming.
25 Wilson, Elijah Nicholas. *The White Indian Boy.* P. 92. [edited by Howard R. Driggs]. Paragon Press. Salt Lake. Utah. 1991.
26 Joe Medicine Crow, Interview with Author. Lodge Grass, Montana. 1994. Note pad 1. P.13.
27 Hebard, Grace R. *papers. "Old Enos account."* Loc; cit. See also; Wilson, Elijah Nicholas. *The White Indian Boy.* Pp. 93-94.[edited by Howard R. Driggs]. Paragon Press. Salt Lake. Utah. 1991. In 1858, the then Agent for the Upper Missouri tribes, William Redford, told the Commissioner of Indian Affairs, Charles E. Mix, ". . . The Crows are at war with the Sioux and Big Robber (sic; Big Shadow) and thirty braves have been killed." Here, Agent Redford was merely alluding to the fact that the earlier period of peace between the Crows and certain bands of Sioux had been broken. It would appear, therefore, that the Commissioner himself had assumed, from Redford`s comment, that chief Big-Shadow had been killed by Sioux, rather than at the hands of the Shoshoni. That this was the case regarding the Commissioner's official report, Agent Twiss, when making his own report regarding the Upper Platte Indians late that same year of `58, made mention of a recent Crow - Sioux fight, but did not report the death of Big Shadow. Thus, most probably, Agent Twiss was alluding to the Fight at Rain Hill and, perhaps, was unaware at the time of Big Shadow`s demise. An event he would undoubtedly have referred to and been fully aware of, if the Sioux had then been involved.

28 Wilson, Elijah Nicholas. *The White Indian Boy.* Pp. 93-94.[edited by Howard R. Driggs]. Paragon Press. Salt Lake. Utah. 1991.
29 Wilson, Elijah Nicholas. *The White Indian Boy.* Pp. 93-94.[edited by Howard R. Driggs]. Paragon Press. Salt Lake. Utah. 1991.
30 Wilson, Elijah Nicholas. *The White Indian Boy.* P.95. [edited by Howard R. Driggs]. Paragon Press. Salt Lake. Utah. 1991.
31 Edward L. Crabb, Letter to Grace R. Hebard 1926. Hebard Collection. Accession no.400,008. *"Washaki manuscript."* Box 58. Folder 18. University of Wyoming.
32 Wilson, Elijah Nicholas. *The White Indian Boy.* P.95. [edited by Howard R. Driggs]. Paragon Press. Salt Lake. Utah. 1991.
33 Compton, J. E. *"letter to Grace Hebard."* January 28, 1927. Hebard collection. Accession 400,008 – *Washakie manuscript* - Box no. 58. Folder 18. University of Wyoming.
34 Compton, J. E. *"letter to Grace Hebard."* January 28, 1927. Hebard collection. Accession 400,008. – *Washakie manuscript* - Box no. 58. Folder 18. University of Wyoming.
35 Crabb, Edward L. Letter to Hebard, Grace R. *papers.* May 26, 1927. *"Old Enos account of the battle at Crow Heart Butte."* Hebard collection. Accession 400,008 – *Washakie manuscript* - Box no. 58. Folder 18. University of Wyoming.
36 Wilson, Elijah Nicholas. *The White Indian Boy.* Pp. 95-96.[edited by Howard R. Driggs]. Paragon Press. Salt Lake. Utah. 1991.
37 Wilson, Elijah Nicholas. *The White Indian Boy.* P.96. [edited by HowarR.Driggs]. Paragon Press. Salt Lake. Utah.1991.
38 Joe Medicine Crow, Interview with Author. Lodge Grass, Montana. 1994. Note pad 1. P.13.
39 Joe Medicine Crow, Interview with Author. Lodge Grass, Montana. 1994. Note pad 1. P.13.
40 MacCleary, Tim. *Crow Place Names.* Little Big Horn College. Crow Agency. Montana. A copy of which is in the possession of Joe Medicine Crow. Lodge Grass. Montana.

Chapter Thirteen

Return of the Rain Hill Captives

In the aftermath of chief Big Shadow`s death, the Kicked-in-the-Belly band came under the leadership of First-Feather-on-the-Tail, a renowned Mountain Crow war chief, who was visiting the Kicked-in-the-Bellys when the survivors of the Rain Hill fight and those of the Shoshoni expedition returned to camp. The Kicked-in-the-Belly`s themselves had encouraged him to assume the role as leader of their band—albeit a temporary position—until a proper selection could be made.[1]

When the Mountain Crows and Kicked-in-the-Bellys went their separate ways, after vacating the camping grounds along Fly Creek, First-Feather-on-the-Tail led the Kicked-in-the-Bellys south to the Little Big Horn. Along that river's east bank, they again set up their tepees just across from where today, stands the Custer monument about one mile south of present Crow Agency.[2]

It was while in camp at this location, that the Crows found some solace to help ease the sorrow of their recent losses. For it was here that the warrior Strong Falcon—long given up for dead by his tribesmen after the fight around Rain Hill—finally came limping into camp; bedraggled and exhausted, but miraculously, he had survived the ordeal of his long lonely journey.

He told his people that the horse he had ridden when he left Cedar Creek had given out the following morning. He had been obliged to continue his hazardous journey on foot. He had stumbled over the rugged terrain, constantly dodging enemy war parties which seemed to be crisscrossing the country in every direction, forcing him to hide during the day and travel only at night. Having no weapons with which to hunt and his moccasins long since worn out, he had suffered acutely from extreme hunger and lacerated feet, while his clothes became so ragged and torn, they had given no protection against the cold and chilly nights.

Such was his emaciated appearance, that when first he entered his home camp he had frightened the occupants somewhat, who initially thought him a ghost returned from the spirit land of the dead. However, great was the people's joy when they realized it was Strong Falcon in living form. They then thanked *Akbaa-tadia* for his safe return.[3]

It was only a few days after this that one of the Crow women taken captive by the Sioux at Rain Hill, also returned to her own people, safe and sound.

The Crow woman was the same Among the Willows who was now the widow of Bull Rises Small and one of three women taken prisoner at Rain Hill. This woman survived well into the twentieth century and often related her story. The mother of Winona Plenty Hoops knew her personally and during Winona`s younger years, she heard her mother relate the experiences of Among The Willows many times.

According to Among the Willow`s account, it was late afternoon after breaking off hostilities during the battle around the butte, that a large band of Sioux participants galloped into their home camps along the Cannonball, whooping and hollering and singing victory songs. They waved Crow scalps and captured weapons in the air. Into the Sans Arc camp rode Among the Willows along with a second female captive and teenage boy. The third Crow woman was taken to the camp of the Hunkpapa in the keeping of the Sioux warrior Old Crow, who proudly displayed the Crow baby still strapped in its cradle board, but now swinging from the horn of Old Crow`s saddlebow.[4]

Among the Willows always said that when the captives entered the Sans Arc camp, they noticed many horses milling around which had been taken from the Crows during the fighting that day. Some of these animals had arrows sticking in various parts of their bodies and many had their heads hanging low; almost touching the ground, having been run so hard that they were completely exhausted.

Once among the Sans Arcs, Among the Willows and her companion were placed in a large lodge. Hanging from a tripod was a calf-skin bundle. This bundle contained the Sacred Buffalo Calf Pipe of the Lakota; a most important holy object revered by all Teton Sioux bands. The two captives were in the lodge of the Sacred Pipe's keeper, a highly respected man who as a sign of office, had his hair tied in a bun over his forehead.

Soon after this, an old Sioux woman carrying a small child entered the lodge. This was probably the keeper's wife, for it soon became evident to Among the Willows that this woman was also regarded as a holy person of high standing. Among the Willows said the woman was kind. She took the sacred bundle from its tripod, passed it over the bodies of the two captives then placed it in the hands of Among the Willows, telling her to hold it close to her breast and it would keep her safe. A little later a man entered, who the Crow women recognized as a Sioux warrior named Kills Them. His sister several years past had married a Crow man and her brother, Kills Them, had visited her from time-to-time in the Crow country. This man sat beside the Crow women and when yet another warrior entered the lodge, Kills Them said to him, "These two women are sad and frightened. We should help them get back to their own people." [5]

Smithsonian Institutuin "Sirir" Website

Crow chiefs in 1873. From left: Long Horse, Sits-in-the-Middle-of-the-Land, White Calf.

The visitor replied that the warriors who had captured the women had already claimed them as their wives. They and their relatives were like mad bulls, he said, and would prove too strong to oppose. He said he personally would have nothing to do with the women and left the tepee as abruptly as he had entered.

Another man then came in and after hearing the proposal from Kills Them of freeing the captives, he turned to the women and said, "The River Crows once spared my life so in return, I will do what I can to get you home." [6]

The following night Among the Willows found herself in the lodge of Looking Elk, who had succeeded in taking her captive after his altercation with Feather Mane. It was then that a brother of Chief Sitting Bull came over from the adjacent Hunkpapa camp and entering the lodge of Looking Elk, declared his intention to kill Among the Willows in revenge for the death of his father Jumping Bull. Fortunately, Looking Elk and his adherents prevented him doing so, for it was their responsibility to protect their prisoner as if she was one of their own, once she had been taken into her captor's lodge and given food. The visitor at first was in an ugly mood but after receiving many presents to help compensate the loss of his father, he was persuaded to leave without carrying out his threat.

In the meantime, Sitting Bull was wandering around the Hunkpapa camp lamenting the death of his father. His hair was uncombed and sprinkled with dirt and ashes, and dirt and ashes were on his face and hands. He was clothed in rags and went barefoot so that all would know his extent of grief by the humiliation he was inflicting upon himself. Others among the Hunkpapa were moved by Sitting Bull`s plight. They told him they would kill the Crow captives and thereby ease his sorrow.

"No," cried Sitting Bull, "These Crow women have also lost husbands, brothers and sons. This one`s father Jumping Bull was a warrior and a glorious death in battle was his reward. See no harm befalls these women for it is my wish and it is this one, Sitting Bull, who speaks." [7]

Sitting Bull was a man with much influence among his people. His relatives and friends respected his wishes and the women captives were left alone.

Meanwhile, Among the Willow`s Crow companion was taken to the Hunkpapa camp where she joined the other Crow female already there. Among the Willows remained in the Sans Arc camp, but was now given over to her captor's uncle as a bed companion for the night. The next day, however, Looking Elk, her captor, took her back, which angered the uncle and this man threatened to kill Among the Willows in order to spite his nephew.

Among the Willows took fright. She ran from the lodge and went instead to that of Yellow Tooth, another Sans Arc who she knew. He also had visited among her Crow people several times in the past. She begged him to protect her from harm and Yellow Tooth agreed.

When a short time later Looking Elk`s uncle in the company of some belligerent companions came after her, Yellow Tooth kept his word and protected her saying, "If any of you wish harm to this woman then first kill me, for this woman is my guest and has eaten in my lodge." [8]

Yellow Tooth was a brave and renowned fighter. His words alone were enough to cower his uninvited visitors, who in response, turned around and left the lodge immediately and Among the Willows was saved from near certain death a second time.

About three or four days later, after those Sioux who had lost relatives in the Rain Hill fight had performed their mourning rituals, a grand victory celebration was held which went on both day and night for several weeks. The Sioux warriors sang, danced and feasted and recounted their many coups gained in the recent fray. All the while the Crow captives in their continued sadness and despair, were obliged to listen to a monotonous refrain taken up by the Sioux women who repeatedly sang, "Crows cry, Crows cry." [9] (They were referring to the number of widows and other grieving relatives which their great victory over the Crows had created.)

It was during this time of celebration that the corpse of Sitting Bull`s father, along with those of other Sioux warriors slain in the fight, were buried among rocks overlooking the north bank of the south fork of Cedar Creek, a place not far from present-day Lemon, on the North Dakota-South Dakota stateline.[10]

Among the Willows said a few weeks later, the several bands of Sioux dismantled their lodges and together, moved southwest to the vicinity of Bear Butte, which eminence stands just northeast of the Black Hills of South Dakota. Here they joined the Northern Cheyennes and other Sioux bands which congregated in order to hold their Sun dances together.

Among the Willows remembered well, Winona Plenty Hoops said, how sad and lonely she had felt during that time of the Sun dances and, especially so, when a Sioux warrior cut one of the long braids from her head which he first tied to a Crow scalp taken in the fight around Rain Hill, then attached both hanks to the centre pole of the Sun dance lodge itself. But not all the Sioux proved so callous. Among the Willows was seated within the big Sun-dance arbor when the same Sioux warrior, whose life had once been spared by the River Crows,

Northwestern University Library
E. S. Curtis, "The North American Indian."
Crow Warrior, Two Whistles

came and stood beside her and began praying to the sun with the words, "Oh Grandfather Sun who sees all things. Let this woman go home to her people." [11]

Other warriors then came over to where Among the Willows was sitting and uttered various things which the Crow woman could not properly understand, so she knew not what was said. It was, however, after the Sun dances had finished, that the Sioux women in Yellow Tooth`s lodge began making extra moccasins for Among the Willows and one moonlit night after giving her the moccasins along with a bundle of dried meat, they instructed her in which direction to travel and bade her go home to her own people. That very night, Among the Willows set out alone on her homeward journey.

She traveled in a west-northwest direction from the Sun Dance camp, crossing the Little Missouri, Powder and Tongue rivers and continued due west, until after four days and four nights of hard walking, she finally reached the Little Big Horn River. Here she located her home camp of the Kicked-in-the-Belly band.

Dotted around on the rolling bench land overlooking the Crow camp, Among the Willows could see little brush shelters, in which were living those relatives still in mourning for kinsmen lost at Rain Hill and those slain with Big Shadow`s party by the Shoshoni. The people saw her from a long way off—ragged and weary as she stumbled towards them—and many camp occupants ran along the river bank to welcome her home. The Kicked-in-the-Belly sub-chief Sits-In-The-Middle-Of-The-Land also came out to meet her. As he walked, he began cutting his arms and legs with his knife, as a token of thanks to *Akbaa-tadia* for returning Among the Willows to her people and when he came near, he threw his arms around her and hugged her while all the Crows rejoiced at her deliverance back into the bosom of the tribe.

Owing to the ordeal of Among The Willows as a captive of the Sioux and that, previously, she had several times accompanied her late husband Bull Rises Small to war, she was accorded the status of "Woman Warrior," of whom there had been but few among the Crows in past times. Hereafter, during parades through the camp, Among The Willows was allowed the honor of wearing an eagle-feathered bonnet and of joining in the victory dances as a participating warrior. It appears also from Crow oral tradition that only a short time after her return, she remarried to become the wife of Big Otter, little knowing that this man too would soon meet his own demise at the hands of tribal enemies. [12]

Of the two other Crow women captives and the teenage boy, they remained for the time being among the Sioux. For the most part the women were not treated harshly, although the teenage boy did not survive the ordeal.

It is said that in one of the Sioux camps there lived a half-Piegan half-Crow man named Carries the Prairie Chicken. He was married to a Sioux woman and had lived among his wife's people for a number of years. Perhaps, as my informant Joe Medicine Crow suggested, the teenage Crow captive had said bad words to this man; accusing him of being a traitor to his own people and Carries the Prairie Chicken, in a fit of rage, promptly counted coup on the boy then killed him. But whatever the reason, even the Sioux themselves regarded this act with disdain for once a captive had been taken into the captor's lodge and fed, it was the owner's obligation to protect the captive as if he or she was one of his own. As a rule, if the slayer had been Sioux then he might have suffered a term of banishment from the tribe, but in this case, as the slayer was actually a Crow and his victim also Crow, no such punishment was invoked. [13]

The affair blew over, although it was soon evident that by his deed, Carries the Prairie Chicken had lost much of the respect he may have previously enjoyed among his wife's people. It was probably for this reason that Carries the Prairie Chicken decided to visit the Crows, perhaps with the intention of rejoining his own people and starting a new life and family.

Somehow, Carries the Prairie Chicken managed to convince a number of Hunkpapa associates that it was in their tribe's interest to patch up their broken peace with the Crows and, he said, what better way to show the Crows their sincerity and commitment, than by returning the captives as a show of goodwill. Whether Sitting Bull had a part to play in this matter is not recorded, although he obviously was aware of all that was going on and, it may be assumed by his earlier show of sympathy towards the captive women, that at least he was not adverse to the idea.

The Hunkpapa chiefs, after deciding their course of action in compliance to the suggestion from Carries the Prairie Chicken, instructed three Hunkpapa warriors named Long Horn, Swift Bull and Wide Skirt to trade a number of fine horses to the Sioux husbands of the captives and, in such a way, managed to buy the women from them. [14]

It was these same three Sioux warriors who agreed to accompany the said women in order to offer the latter`s kinfolk the pipe of peace. And thus, about the beginning of autumn the three Sioux emissaries led by Carries the Prairie Chicken, along with the two Crow women and a number of pack-ponies laden with presents, started out for Crow country far to the west.

After many days travelling, the party at length found the Kicked-in-the-Belly camp still sited along the Little Big Horn, but now relocated farther upstream near the mouth of Reno Creek.

The Crows came out to meet them and showing signs of friendship, welcomed the visitors to their camp, as was Indian custom whenever strangers—be they erstwhile foes—came in peace. The Crows thanked the Sioux delegates for returning the captives and held a grand feast in honor of their guests and in celebration for their lost women coming home.

One of the returned women told her people that their escort, Carries the Prairie Chicken, had counted coup on the teenage boy taken captive at Rain Hill and then killed him in the Sioux camp. A Sioux chief, she said, had whipped Carries the Prairie Chicken and would have killed him, had not other Sioux warriors intervened. Upon hearing this the Crows became very angry. Some warriors decided that they themselves would kill Carries the Prairie Chicken, for he was not originally of their blood, but had been taken captive from the Small

Robe Pikunni when young. The Crow chiefs, however, prevented any such action. Chief Sits-in-the-Middle-of-the-Land took charge of the aggressive situation. He addressed the surrounding Crows saying, "This man has come to us in peace. He is a guest in our camp and is under the same protection as are his Sioux companions." [15]

Denver Public Library
Western History Department
Crow warrior, Two Leggings.

This action on the part of the Crow chief sufficed to calm the belligerent warriors and they desisted from their design. At length, Carries the Prairie Chicken and his three Sioux companions were allowed to leave the camp and return home safely.

The Crows treated the Sioux emissaries well and with due respect as befitted those who came in friendship. More importantly, however, the Kicked-in-the-Belly chiefs and headmen had also agreed that their band and Hunkpapa Sioux should meet together at a pre-designated place before the year was out and forge a pact between their peoples. The Crows had then given their Sioux guests many presents which included clothing, buffalo robes and horses and bade them a safe journey home, but no such gifts or kind words were bestowed upon Carries the Prairie Chicken.

The Three Sioux delegates departed in good spirits, while it is said that the Kicked-in-the-Bellys neither saw nor heard of Carries the Prairie Chicken again.[16]

REGAINING THE ASCENDENCY AND THE REHABILITATION OF NO MANE

So it was near the end of the year, but before the snows arrived, that the Kicked-in-the-Belly Crows and Hunkpapa Sioux, once again set their camps adjacent to one another, this time along the banks of the Little Big Horn, and smoked the calumet of peace.

Long-Soldier`s Hunkpapa Winter Count entry for the year, 1858 / `59. "After peace was made, Crows still wanted to fight."

Smithsonian Institution. Museum of the American Indian. Washington DC.

For several weeks the two camps remained together as Crow and Sioux feasted, danced and sang. They traded with and visited each other, while adopting and bestowing names upon each other's children. A Miniconjou Sioux named Fast Horse, who had spent much time among the Crows since the pact between the latter and his Miniconjou people due to the Fitzpatrick Treaty of 1851, acted as go-between among the gathered bands. He also married a Crow woman and remained with his wife's people among the River Crow band.

A number of times before, according to Crow oral tradition, the Crows and one or another band of Sioux had come together in such a way. But, unfortunately, this particular period of mutual amicability, as was the case with most other pacts between their peoples, did not last longer than the return of the Hunkpapa to their own country along the Grand and Cannonball rivers. Almost immediately, both Crows and Hunkpapa resumed raiding each other's pony herds and tribal members were again regularly killed on both sides. Late in this same year of 1858, the River Crows were subjected to a concerted attack by a combined allied force of Sioux, Northern Cheyennes and Arapaho. The attackers were defeated and driven off with much loss and before the year was out, Hunkpapas killed the River Crow Chief Yellow Calf. Over the course of the ensuing months, other Crow chiefs including Three Crows and First-Feather-on-The-Tail were also to lose their lives in fights with the Sioux.[17] Anon, even War Chief Big Otter—who had proved himself prominent in countless conflicts with his people's enemies—was destined to meet his death when engaged against yet another grand war party of Teton Sioux.

Big Otter had risen somewhat in esteem among his people, owing to his exploits on the field of conflict during the fight around Rain Hill and, from then on, never had he lacked warriors enough to accompany him on the war trail. His people's recent misfortunes, it seemed, had in no way diminished his personal enthusiasm for war, neither had his heart changed its desire to inflict whatever form of pain, humiliation and misery, which he could devise upon his enemies.

One memorable episode occurred during the winter of 1858-1859, after the Kicked-in-the-Bellys had again separated from their Mountain Crow brethren and were encamped somewhere close to the eastern foothills of the Big Horn Mountains. A party of stealthy thieves came one night to the Crow camp and escaped with a number of horses, including several mounts belonging to Chief Big Otter.

Northwestern University Library
E. S. Curtis, "The North American Indian"
Crow Warrior, Bird-on-the-Ground.

The next morning, even though snow lay thick on the ground and a swirling blizzard was starting up, Big Otter, upon discovering that his favorite horses were among those missing, got together a few friends and without further delay started out after the thieves who, by telltale moccasin prints left in the snow, proved to be a small band of Pikunni Blackfoot. Big Otter's party consisted only of four warriors including himself, but they soon picked up the raider's trail and did not hesitate to follow it up.

The thieves had been unable to make good progress owing to the depth of snow and inclement weather. The very next day, their Crow pursuers after ascending the summit of a high hill from where they could survey the surrounding countryside, espied one of the Pikunnis on foot leading his horse which, evidently, had become exhausted during its enforced trek. The lone Pikunni had thus dropped behind and was now separated from the rest of his party.

The Crows were mounted on comparatively fresh horses. They edged their ponies down the hillside towards the man on foot. They knew they had him at their mercy.

Upon seeing enemies riding towards him, the lone Pikunni took fright. He carried a pistol and as the leading Crow, who happened to be Big Otter, came near, he fired twice but both shots were wild. They missed the man and instead, hit Big Otter`s horse, causing the animal to stumble to the ground throwing Big Otter from the saddle as it did so. The Pikunni then shot again as Big Otter raised up from his fallen mount. But even these shots missed their mark and the Crow chief came on, lumbering through the snow towards his adversary without regard for personal safety. Twice more the Pikunni shot at Big Otter, emptying his gun in the process but without success, whereupon, he discarded the weapon and stood braced with knife in hand, ready to meet his oncoming attacker. Undaunted, Big Otter continued forward, avoiding the man's vicious swipes with his knife. Big Otter grasped his enemy by the arm; spun him around repeatedly, before suddenly letting go so the Pikunni fell down disorientated as he lay immobile at Big Otter`s feet. Big Otter was a tall and powerfully-built man. He placed one foot on his enemy's left arm and taking hold of the man's right arm, cut it off at the shoulder with his large Green River blade. He then cut off the left arm while the man was still conscious, after which he slashed the Pikunni`s throat, then severed his victim's head completely from the body.[18]

We are not told if the Crows succeeded in retrieving all the stolen horses, but the return of Big Otter's party the following day, with him holding aloft the severed head and leading one at least of the missing ponies, while two of his companions each carried a severed arm, and the third waved the Pikunni scalp attached to the end of his musket barrel, caused much excitement in the Kicked-in-the-Belly camp.

Thus the Crows danced and sang over the Blackfoot scalp and limbs that Big Otter and his companions brought in. Then, early in the new year, during a fight with the Sioux, a Crow party rubbed out the Miniconjou chief Big Crow. Big Shadow and his fallen comrades were finally avenged when another Crow war party led by Red Bear and Spotted Horse, slew the Shoshoni chief Split Nose—the likely killer of Big Shadow—and as a result, destroyed seventeen lodges of that people and most of the occupants thereof save a dozen Shoshoni children who were taken captive by the Crows. This event too, is well-remembered in Crow oral tradition. [19]

Following these successes, most Crow who had been lamenting kinsmen lost at Rain Hill and those killed with Big Shadow and his followers, ceased their wailings and washed the dried blood and ashes from their faces and bodies. Enemies had been killed, which to the Crow way of thinking, compensated for their own sadness when they thought of all the ills which had befallen them the previous year.

Northwestern University Library
E. S. Curtis, "The North American Indian"
Crow Warrior, Old Dog.

In truth, the Crows knew the loss of fellow tribesmen was an unavoidable consequence of their warrior culture; indeed, of their very existence as a nation, surrounded as they were by a host of inveterate enemies whose sole intention, it seemed, was to obliterate the Absaroka people from the earth. It was not long, therefore, before the reality of everyday life brought those grieving to their senses and only the craving for revenge again permeated their minds.

But No Mane was not yet satisfied.

Few of those enemies killed had been Sioux and thus, No Mane and his spouse continued to bemoan the loss of their son Iron Eyes, whose bones still lay on the plain around Rain Hill. Together, his grieving parents continued to sit out among the hills or on the open prairie away from their people. No Mane`s hair was still cut short and unkempt, while both his and his wife's clothing, consisting of worn-out pieces of old lodge skins, became extremely torn and dirty. It is said that as No Mane sat motionless lamenting his loss, magpies flew down from the sky and perched on his shoulders, pecking at his tattered clothing. At the same time pack rats gnawed and chewed at his robe and leggings, while No Mane seemed oblivious to all around him.[20]

The seasons rolled by. Winter came again and went, as did the ensueing spring and the hot days of summer burst forth warming the land and the hearts of the people. Yet still No Mane and his spouse went on with their grieving as they persisted in their lonely vigils away from all comforts of the camp.

For two full years after the debacle around Rain Hill, No Mane continued to grieve. But then the mighty Big Otter fell too, although the Crows won an astounding victory, taking twenty enemy scalps in the process.

It happened in mid summer of 1860—probably in response to the Crows' killing of the Minniconjou chief Big Crow earlier in the year—that a large war party of Sioux comprising several hundred braves, came against the Crows. The Kicked-in-the-Belly and Mountain bands were again encamped together along Fly Creek, and a fierce battle ensued. An Oglala warrior, born in 1832 named His Fights (also known as Jaw), mentioned the affair when an old man to the Anthropologist / Photographer Edward S. Curtis who, subsequently, wrote from His-Fights` own words:

> "When a young man, He, (His-Fights) again went against the Apsaroka. When the enemy was sighted, Whiteman's Fire, the medicine man, donned his headdress of buffalo horns and eagle feathers, and while the chief held forward the war-pipe he prayed, each of the warriors extending his own pipe toward the enemy. Then the medicine man rode towards the war pipe, which now lay on the ground, dismounted, and sat in front of it, while His Fights raised it and gave it to Whiteman's Fire, saying, 'Brother-in-law, go and tell the warriors what you have seen.' A bit of pulverized buffalo-chip was placed on top of the tobacco in the pipe and fire applied, after which the medicine man smoked. Then he pointed with his thumbs and thrust one hand after the other in the direction of the enemy, exclaiming, 'She! She!'—indicating that his heart was hot against them (the Crows). 'I see a hundred horses coming toward us. We will kill the Raven Men and one of them will be dressed like a chief.' They (the Sioux) then charged, and succeeded in running off about eight hundred horses. The Apsaroka rushed out, and two boys and three men, one of the latter wearing a shirt covered

> with weasel skins, were killed. It was afterward learned that he was Big Otter. In the retreat twenty Sioux were killed and about half the horses lost. . ." [21]

Thus the career of Big Otter finally came to an end. He, who for many a year had been both feared and respected, even by his enemies. The Sioux had known this man well and in the Oglala winter count of Iron-Crow, the year 1859 /`60 is recorded as, "Winter when the Knife carrier was killed." [22] This was the name by which the once indomitable Big Otter had been colloquially known among the Sioux, owing to his deadly use of his large knife. [23]

Among the Crows as a fighter, Big Otter was sorely missed, but as a person, his demise did not really amount to much. The fight, despite the Crow losses, was celebrated for the great victory it was, being regarded as just compensation for the many Crow deaths incurred over the previous two years at Sioux hands. It was also thought sufficient a victory to wipe out the humiliation which, as a nation, the Crows deemed they had suffered to prowess and prestige, by all that had taken place that dreadful day when, in the all-engulfing shadow of Rain Hill, their warriors had been driven from the field with much slaughter.

At last, it seemed, the Crows were in the ascendency again, as they continued to battle against the numerous enemy tribes around them. In this they showed resolute determination and performed exceptional deeds of valor, which often marked them high above their adversaries. Indeed, many important trials of strength incurring both victory and defeat, were to be the lot of the valiant Absaroka before intertribal war-days came to an end.

For the time being, however, the triumph in mid-summer of 1860, made evident by twenty Oglala scalps tied to Crow willow wands, along with numerous guns and richly ornamented clothing taken from the vanquished foe, the old man No Mane was satisfied at last, that the beloved Iron Eyes had been fully avenged. [24] Both No-Mane and his wife now put an end to their grieving—and indulged themselves again in the social life of the camp.

NOTES AND SOURCES.

1 Joe Medicine Crow, Interviews with Author. Lodge Grass, Montana. 1994. Note pad 1. Pp.14-15.
2 Joe Medicine Crow, Interviews with Author. Lodge Grass, Montana. 1994. Note pad 1. Pp.14-15.
3 Joe Medicine Crow, Interviews with Author. Lodge Grass, Montana. 1994. Note pad 1. Pp.14-15.
4 Vestal., Stanley. *Sitting Bull* p. 48. University of Nebraska Press. 1937.
5 Winona Plenty-Hoops to Author. 1998. Note pad 3. P.7. See also; Edward S. Curtis. *The North American Indian.* Vol. IV. "Crow and Atsina." Pp. 96ff. 1905.
6 Winona Plenty Hoops to Author. 1998. Note pad 3. P.7. See also; Edward S. Curtis. *The North American Indian.* Vol. IV. "Crow and Atsina." Pp. 96ff. 1905.
7 Vestal., Stanley. *Sitting Bull* p. 48. University of Nebraska Press. 1937. See also; Joe Medicine Crow, Interviews with Author. Lodge Grass, Montana. 1994. Note pad1. Pp.14-15.
8 Winona Plenty Hoops to Author. 1998. Note pad 3. P.7. See also; Edward S. Curtis. *The North American Indian.* Vol. IV. "Crow and Atsina." Pp. 96ff. 1905. Here Curtis (from Among-the-Willow`s testimony) gives this Sioux man`s name as, Yellow-Buffalo-Tooth.
9 Winona Plenty Hoops to Author. 1998. Note pad 3. P.7. See also; Vestal, Stanley. *Sitting Bull* Pp. 47-48. University of Nebraska Press. 1937.
10 Vestal., Stanley. *Sitting Bull* p. 48. University of Nebraska Press. 1937.
11.Winona Plenty Hoops to Author. 1998. Note pad 3. P.7. See also; Edward S. Curtis. *The North American Indian.* Vol. IV. "Crow and Atsina." Pp. 96ff. 1905.
12 Winona Plenty Hoops to Author. 1998. Note pad 3. P.8.
13 Winona Plenty Hoops to Author. 1998. Note pad 3. P.8.
14 Vestal., Stanley. *Sitting Bull* pp. 48-49. University of Nebraska Press. 1937.
15 Winona Plenty Hoops to Author. 1998. Note pad 3. P.8.
16 Joe Medicine Crow, Interviews with Author. Lodge Grass, Montana. 1994. Note pad 1. Pp.14-15.
17 Edward S. Curtis. *The North American Indian,* Vol. IV. "Crow and Atsina." 1905. See also; James H. Howard, *Dakota Winter-counts as sources of History* pp.385-386, [various entries.]Smithsonian Institution, Bureau of American Ethnology, bulletin *173.* 1960. And; Garrick Mallery, "Picture writing of the American Indians." (various entries.)Tenth Annual report of the Bureau of American Ethnology, Smithsonian Institution, 1888-89.
18 Lowie, Robert H. "Material Culture of the Crows." P. 261. Anthropological papers. American Museum of natural history. 1922.
19 Joe Medicine Crow, Interviews with Author. Lodge Grass, Montana. 1994. Note pad 1. Pp.14-15. See also; Bauerle, Phoenicia. (Editor). *The Way of the Warrior, the Saga of Red Bear.* Pp. 39-75. University of Nebraska Press. 2003
20 Edward S. Curtis. *The North American Indian.* Vol. IV. "Crow and Atsina." Pp. 90ff. 1905
21 Edward S. Curtis. *The North American Indian.* Vol. V. "Sioux." P. 186. 1905
22 Walker, James R. *Lakota Society,* P. 143. University of Nebraska Press. 1982.
23 Winona Plenty-Hoops to Author. 1998. Note pad 3. P.8. See also; Joe Medicine Crow, Interviews with Author. Lodge Grass, Montana. 1994. Note pad 1. Pp.14-15. and; Edward S. Curtis. *The North American Indian.* Vol. IV. "Crow and Atsina." Pp. 90.ff. 1905

Northwestern University Library, Edward S. Curtis photograph, "The North American Indian"

"Crow Chiefs"

Selective Bibliography

Unpublished Sources

Bent, George, "Letters to George Hyde", 1905-1915. (Letter no. 26). Denver Public Library, Denver. Colorado.

Crabb, Jack, "Letters to Grace Hebard", Hebard Collection.

Denig, Edwin T., "Report to Washington D.C.1856", Government Printing Office, Washington DC.

Fitzpatrick, Thomas, "Letters", Government Printing office, Washington, D.C.

Grinnell, George Bird, Manuscript Collection (MS. 5)."Folder 494 "Early Crow Battles", Southwest Museum, Los Angeles

Hebard, Grace R, "Papers; [Old Enos Account.]."

Keefe, Brian L, "Letters sent and received, notebooks and audio tapes of interviews with tribal informants among the Crow, Piegan Blackfoot, Hunkpapa Sioux, Minniconjou Sioux, Kiowa, Shoshoni, Northern and Southern Cheyenne. 1967 through to 2006." [in Author's possession].

McCleary, Tim, "Crow Place names and their meanings", Copy in the Joe Medicine Crow Collection. Lodge Grass, Montana.

Medicine Crow, Joseph, "Papers", Boxes 1, 2 and 3. Little Big Horn College Archives, Crow Agency, Montana.

Michelson, Truman, "Papers and Field Notes", Smithsonian Institution, Washington, D.C.

Missouri Republican [newspaper], St. Louis, September 26 to November 30, 1851.

"Report of the Commissioner of Indian Affairs", Washington, D.C., 1851.

"Report of the Indian Bureau", Government Printing Office, Washington, D.C., 1856.

"The Warren Expedition" Government Printing Office, Washington, D.C., 1856.

"The Reynold`s Expedition", Government Printing Office, Washington, D.C., 1859.

Stands In Timber, John, "Papers", Dull Knife College Library and Archives. Lame Deer, Montana.

Vestal, Stanley, "Papers", University of Oklahoma Library and Archives, Norman, Oklahoma.

Yellow Fly, Teddy. "Winter Count" [Blackfoot], Glenbow Museum Archives, Calgary, Alberta, Canada.

Published Sources

Algier, Keith, *The Crow and The Eagle,* The Caxton Printers. Ltd., Caldwell, Idaho,1993.

Anderson, William M, *The Rocky Mountain Journals of William Marshal Anderson. 1834,* University of Nebraska Press, 1967.

Audubon, John James, *Journals,* Vol. 2., New York.

Barbour, Barton H., *Fort Union,* University of Oklahoma Press, 2001.

Bauerle, Phoenicia [Editor], *The Way of the Warrior,* University of Nebraska Press. 2003

Bedford, Denton R. *The Fight At the Mountain on Both Sides.,* Indian Historian. V111, No. 2. 1975.

Blish, Helen. *A Pictographic History of the Oglala Sioux,* University of Nebraska Press, 1967.

Boller, Henry, *Among The Indians,* Philadelphia, 1868.

Bonner, T. D., *Life of James P. Beckwourth,* Ross and Haines Co., Ltd., 1956.

Bordeaux, William J., *Conquering the Mighty Sioux,* Sioux Falls, South Dakota, 1929.

Bowers, Alfred B., *Hidatsa Ceremonial and Social Organization,* University of Nebraska Press, 1956.

Bradley, James H., (a) *The Crow Indians,* Montana Historical Society Publications, 1879.

(b) *The Bradley Manuscript,* Book Four. Historical Society of Montana, Book *"F."* 1875, (c) *March of the Montana Column,* University of Oklahoma Press, 1961.

Bray, Kingsly, "Lone Horn's Peace", Nebraska History." LXVI, [Spring] 1985.

Bull Plume, "Winter Count", [Piegan Blackfoot]., *In The Blood People,* Adolph Hungry Wolf, 1977 .

Carrington, Margaret, *Apsaroka, Home of the Crows.*

Catlin, Charles, *The North American Indian,* Vols 1 and 2, London, 1841.
Chambers, James,. *Original Journals of James Chambers. Fort Sarpy,* Contributions to the Historical Society of Montana, X, 1940.
Chardon, Francis A., *Chardon's Journal At Fort Clark*, Pierre, South Dakota.
Collins, Casper, "Letters."
Crow Agency. Bilingual Education Program, "A Dictionary of Everyday Crow", 1979.
Curtis, Edward S., (a*) The North American Indian, Vol. 4. Crow and Atsina*. Smithsonian Institution, Washington D.C., 1907 - 1920. (b) *The North American Indian. Vol. V. Sioux,* 1905
Dempsey, Hugh A., *Crowfoot,* University Of Oklahoma Press, 1972.
Denig, Edwin T., (a) *Of the Crow Nation; In Five Indian Tribes of the Upper Missouri,* edited by John C. Ewers, Norman, University of Oklahoma Press, 1961.
Densmore, Frances, *Teton Sioux Music,* University of Nebraska Press, 1992.
DeSmet, Pierre. *Western Missions and Missionaries,* Irish University Press. 1972.
DeVoto, Bernard, *Across The Wide Missouri,* Houghton Mifflin, Boston, 1947.
Eastman, Charles, *Indian Heroes and Great Chieftains,* University of Nebraska Press, 1991.
Ewers, John C, *The Blackfoot. Raiders on the Northwestern Plains,* University of Oklahoma Press, 1958.
Ferris, W. A., *Life in the Rocky Mountains,* Denver, 1940.
Grinnell, George Bird, (a) *The Fighting Cheyennes,* University of Oklahoma Press, 1956.
Hafen, Leroy R., *Broken Hand.* [The Life of Thomas Fitzpatrick], Old West Publishing Company, 1973.
Hamilton, William T., "A Trading Expedition Among The Indians In 1858", Montana Historical Society; Contributions. Vol. 8, 1900.
Hebard, Grace R., *Washakie, Chief of the Shoshoni,* University of Nebraska Press, 1995.
Holmes, Cap; Rueben,. "The Five Scalps. Glimpses of the Past" ,Missouri Historical Society. Vol. 5. 1938.

Howard, James H, (a) "Dakota Winter-counts as sources of History", Smithsonian Institution, Bureau of American Ethnology, Bulletin 173. 1960.(b) "The John K. Bear Winter Count", Plains Anthropologist. Memoir 11.1976.

Hungry Wolf, Adolph, *The Blood People,* Harper and Row Publishers, 1977.

Hyde, George E., (a) *Red Cloud`s Folk,* University of Nebraska Press, 1937. (b) *Life of George Bent,* University of Oklahoma Press, 1967.

Jackson, John C., *The Piikanii Blackfeet,* Mountain Press Publishing Company, 2000.

Kindle, Ben, *Winter Count.* [Sioux], The Portable Indian Reader. Penguin Books, 1994.

Kutz, Rudolph, "The Journal of Rudolph Kutz", Smithsonian Institution, Bureau of American Ethnology, Bulletin.115. Washington. 1937.

Larocque, Francois. "From the Assiniboin to the Yellowstone", Canadian Archives Pub; No.3. 1910.

Leonard, Zenas. *Narrative of Adventures,* Cleveland. 1904

Lewis and Clark. [Edited by Elliot Coues], *History of the Lewis and Clark Expedition,* Dover Publications Inc; New York. [no date]Vols.1 and 3.

Liberty, Margot. [Editor], *Cheyenne Memories,* University of Oklahoma Press, 1968.

Linderman, Frank Bird, (a) *Pretty Shield; Medicine Woman of the Crows,* University of Nebraska Press. 1972. (b) *Plenty Coups; Chief of the Crows,* University of Nebraska Press. 1962.

Llewellyn, Karl N. and Hoebel, E. Adamson, *The Cheyenne Way,* University of Oklahoma Press, 1967.

Lowie, Robert H., (a) *The Crow Indians,* Holt, Rinehart and Winston, 1956, (b) *Material Culture of the Crows.* University of California Press, (c) *Myths and Traditions of the Crow Indians,* University of Nebraska Press, 1993.

Maximilian Zu Wied, *Travels Through the Interior of North America,* Cleveland, 1906.

Medicine Crow, Joe, (a) "From The Heart Of The Crow Country", Library of the American Indian. (b) "Counting Coup", *National Geographic*, 2006.

Milloy, John S., *The Plains Cree.*

Morgan, Lewis Henry, *The Indian Journals,* Dover Publications, 1959.

Nabokov, Peter [Edited by John C. Ewers], *Two Legging,* Thomas Y. Crowell Company, 1967.

Ogden, Peter Skene "The Snake Expedition." *Oregon Historical Society Quarterly*. Vol. 10. No. 4. 1909 -11.

Parkman, Francis, *The Oregon Trail* [various editions], 1897.

Point, Nicholas, [Edited by John C. Ewers]. *Wilderness Kingdom.*

Powers, John K, *An Oglala Winter Count.*

Raczka, Paul M., *Winter Count. A History of the Blackfoot People,* Privately printed 1979, Calgary,

Robinson, Doane, *A History of the Dakota or Sioux Indians,* Ross and Haines, Minneapolis, 1967.

Roe, Frank Gilbert, *The Indian and the Horse.*

Schultz, James Willard, (a) *Rising Wolf. The Story of Hugh Monroe`s First Year on the Plains,* Houghton Miffin and Company, [no date]. (b) *My Life As An Indian,* Houghton Miffin and Company, [no date].

Silliman, Lee. [Editor], *We Seized Our Rifles,* Mountain Press Publishing Company, 1982.

Trenholm, Virginia C., *The Shoshonis,* University of Oklahoma Press, 1964.

Vestal., Stanley, (a) *Sitting Bull,* University of Nebraska Press, 1937. (b) *New Sources of Indian History,* University of Oklahoma Press, 1934. (c) *Warpath,* University of Oklahoma Press, 1932. (d) *Jim Bridger,* University of Nebraska Press, 1970.

Victor,[Mrs] F. Fuller, *The River of The West* [Joe Meek], Toledo, 1870.

Walker, James R., *Lakota Society,* University of Nebraska Press, 1982.

Wildschut, William, *Crow Indian Medicine Bundles,* [Edited by John C. Ewers.] Museum of the American Indian, New York, 1975.

Wilson, Elijah Nicholas, *The White Indian Boy* [edited by Howard R. Driggs], Paragon Press, Salt Lake Utah, 1991.

Wisler, Clark. "Societies and Ceremonial Associations Among The Oglala Sioux*",* American Museum of Natural History. Anthropological Papers. Vol.11. pt.1.

The Author

Brian L. Keefe

Born in 1946, I have been studying and researching the various cultures, history, religions and othe aspects regarding the North American Indian for these past fifty-seven years.

I received a degree in Anthropology from Goldsmith's College, London, although having previously been trained in the plumbing and heating industry, in which I was awarded the "Higher National Certificate," my main employment, necessarily, has been in that field, both as practical engineer and tutor. However, my first love has always been my interest in the field of North American Indian studies, and over the years, I have undertaken extensive research in various museums and archives around Western Europe and the United States, digging out obscure information and manuscripts, and have exchanged a great deal of correspondence with certain eminent scholars, such as the late John C. Ewers and Colin Taylor among others. Occassionally, I have given lectures on intertribal warfare on the North American Continent, and have appeared both on television and radio as an authority on that subject.

I have spent the past eighteen years visiting among a number of Native American tribes, including the Kiowa, Comanche, Sioux, Crow and Northern Cheyenne, during which times, a number of tribal friends and informants have imparted to me many hitherto unpublished details relating to particular episodes in their own people's oral history.

I have a son, Davis, and a daughter, Juliet, along with four grandchildren and one great-grandchild. At present, I live and work in London with my cat and soul-mate "Wilma."

INDEX